The COOK'S
COLOR TREASURY

The COOK'S
COLOR TREASURY

Edited by Norma MacMillan

CONTENTS

Hungarian cabbage soup

Overall timing 2 hours

Freezing Suitable: add flour and sour cream when reheating.

To serve 4

½ lb	Onions
1	Garlic clove
3 tbsp	Oil
¾ lb	Beef for stew
¾ lb	Canned sauerkraut
½ tsp	Fennel seeds
½ tsp	Coarse salt
2 quarts	Beef broth
¼ lb	Slab bacon
2	Frankfurters
1 tbsp	Paprika
2 tbsp	Flour
¼ cup	Water
2 tbsp	Sour Cream

Peel and slice onions; peel and crush garlic. Heat 2 tbsp oil in large saucepan. Add onions and garlic and fry over moderate heat till golden. Cut beef into small cubes, add to pan and brown all over.

Add drained canned sauerkraut, fennel seeds and coarse salt to the pan. Cover with the broth (made with 2 bouillon cubes if necessary) and simmer gently for 1 hour or till meat is tender.

Roughly chop the bacon. Fry bacon in a skillet till crisp, then add the sliced frankfurters and paprika. Cook for 5 minutes, then remove and add to the saucepan.

Blend flour with cold water in a bowl till smooth, then stir into the soup mixture and cook for a further 5 minutes. Stir in the sour cream, adjust the seasoning and serve at once with slices of black bread.

Savory dumpling soup

Overall timing 2½ hours

Freezing Suitable: add dumplings after reheating

To serve 6-8

Dumplings

2 cups	Soft bread crumbs
¼ cup	Chopped bacon
¼ lb	Calf's liver
¼ lb	Ground beef
1	Onion
1	Egg
½ tsp	Dried marjoram
	Salt and pepper

Soup

1 tbsp	Chopped Parsley
1	Onion
¼ lb	Carrots
¼ lb	Parsnips
5	Stalks of celery
6 tbsp	Butter
2 tbsp	Flour
2 quarts	Chicken broth
2 cups	Chopped cooked chicken

First make dumplings. Soak bread crumbs in 1 cup water for 15 minutes. Fry bacon till crisp. Grind liver. Add beef, squeezed out bread crumbs, chopped onion, drained bacon, egg, marjoram, seasoning and parsley. Shape into small dumplings.

Peel and chop onion, carrots and parsnips; chop celery. Melt butter, add onions and cook for 2-3 minutes. Add carrots, celery and parsnips, cover and cook till tender. Purée vegetables and return to pan. Stir in flour then ⅓ broth. Simmer until thickened. Add remaining broth.

Add chicken to soup with dumplings and simmer for 15 minutes.

Scotch broth

Overall timing 2½ hours

Freezing Not suitable

To serve 4

½ cup	Pearl barley
2 lb	Lamb neck for stew
¼ cup	Butter
2	Onions
4	Stalks of celery
1 tbsp	Flour
2½ quarts	Water
1 tsp	Sugar
	Salt and pepper
1 lb	Potatoes
4	Carrots
1	Leek

Wash the barley and drain thoroughly. Wipe and trim the lamb and cut into pieces. Melt the butter in a saucepan or flameproof casserole. Add the lamb and fry over a high heat till browned on all sides.

Peel and chop the onions; trim and slice the celery. Add to the meat and fry till transparent. Add the barley and cook for 2 minutes. Sprinkle in the flour and cook, stirring, till flour begins to brown. Gradually add the water and bring to a boil, stirring constantly. Add the sugar, salt and pepper. Cover and simmer for about 1½ hours.

Peel and quarter the potatoes; scrape and slice the carrots. Add to the soup and simmer for a further 30 minutes. Wash and finely chop the leek and add to the soup. Simmer for 3 minutes more. Taste and adjust the seasoning. Serve immediately with toast or whole-wheat biscuits and butter.

Tregaron broth

Overall timing 1 hour

Freezing Not suitable

To serve 6

1 lb	Slab bacon
1 lb	Beef shank
2 tbsp	Butter
1	Large leek
1 lb	Potatoes
½ lb	Carrots
½ lb	Parsnips
1	Small rutabaga
2 quarts	Water
1	Small head white cabbage
⅓ cup	Fine or medium oatmeal
	Salt and pepper

Cut the bacon into 1 inch pieces. Trim the beef and cut into chunks. Melt the butter in a large saucepan and fry the bacon and beef for 5 minutes.

Meanwhile, trim and slice the leek. Peel the potatoes, carrots, parsnips and rutabaga. Cut into chunks. Add vegetables to pan and fry for 5 minutes. Add the water and bring to a boil.

Shred the cabbage and add to the pan with the oatmeal and seasoning. Cover and simmer for 45 minutes. Adjust the seasoning to taste before serving.

Beef shank soup

Overall timing 4 hours

Freezing Not suitable

To serve 6-8

3 lb	Beef shank, bone-in
	Flour
	Salt and pepper
1	Onion
4	Stalks of celery
1	Leek
3	Carrots
2	Turnips
1 lb	Potatoes
1 lb	White cabbage
	Sprig of parsley
	Sprig of thyme
2 tsp	Powdered mustard
4	Slices of toast

Wipe beef; slash meat through to bone several times. Make a stiff paste of flour and water and use to seal ends of bone to keep in the marrow. Place in large saucepan with 2 quarts water, salt and pepper. Bring to a boil, skim off scum, cover and simmer for 3 hours.

Peel and chop onion; trim and chop celery and leek; scrape and slice carrots; peel turnips and potatoes and cut into chunks; shred cabbage.

Add vegetables to beef with herbs and cook for a further 30 minutes.

Lift out meat and cut into cubes and slices, reserving the bone. Remove vegetables with a slotted spoon and place in serving dish with meat. Keep hot to serve as main course. Pour broth into a warmed soup tureen and keep hot.

Preheat broiler. Scoop out marrow from bone. Mix with salt, pepper and mustard and spread on toast. Broil till bubbling, then cut into fingers and serve with soup.

Turkish soup with meatballs

Overall timing 1¾ hours

Freezing Not suitable

To serve 4-6

1	Veal shank, bone-in
1 lb	Beef shank
1	Large onion
2	Large carrots
1	Stalk of celery
	Parsley stalks
	Salt and pepper
2	Eggs
3 tbsp	Lemon juice
Meatballs	
1 lb	Ground beef
¾ cup	Cooked long grain rice

1	Egg
1 tbsp	Chopped parsley
¼ tsp	Grated nutmeg
	Salt and pepper
2 tbsp	Butter
2 tbsp	Oil

Chop veal shank in half lengthwise. Dice beef. Peel and chop onion and carrots; chop celery. Put meat and vegetables into a saucepan with 2½ quarts water, parsley stalks and seasoning. Cover and simmer for 45 minutes.

Meanwhile, mix ground beef with rice, egg, parsley, nutmeg and seasoning to a stiff paste and shape into small balls.

Heat butter and oil in a skillet. Add meatballs and fry till browned all over.

Strain broth, discarding meat and vegetables. Return to pan and bring back to a boil.

Add meatballs and simmer for 15 minutes.

Put the eggs and lemon juice into a tureen and gradually stir in soup.

New England clam chowder

Overall timing 2 hours

Freezing Suitable

To serve 8

¼ lb	Slab bacon
3	Large Onions
2	Large Tomatoes
2	Leeks
1	Stalk of celery
1	Carrot
2	Potatoes
1 quart	Fish broth
2	Sprigs of parsley
1	Bay leaf
¼ tsp	Grated nutmeg
	Salt and pepper
2 cups	Milk
1 lb	Canned clams
2 tbsp	Butter
2 tbsp	Flour
2 tsp	Worcestershire sauce
¼ tsp	Hot pepper sauce

Dice bacon. Heat a saucepan, add bacon and cook gently. Peel and slice onions and add to pan. Cook till transparent.

Blanch and peel tomatoes. Finely chop leeks and celery. Peel and finely chop carrot and potatoes. Add to pan and cook for 2-3 minutes. Add broth, parsley, bay leaf, nutmeg and seasoning. Cover and simmer for 10 minutes.

Discard parsley and bay leaf. Purée soup in blender, return to rinsed-out pan and add milk and drained clams. Simmer gently for 4 minutes.

Mash butter and flour to a paste. Stir into soup in tiny pieces. Cook for 2-3 minutes until thick. Stir in Worcestershire and pepper sauces and serve.

Fish chowder

Overall timing 1 ½ hours

Freezing Suitable

To serve 4

2 lb	Mixed white fish
¼ cup	Diced bacon
1	Large onion
4	Medium-size potatoes
4	Carrots
4	Stalks of celery
1 tbsp	Chopped parsley
16 oz	Can of tomatoes
1 quart	Fish broth or water
2 tbsp	Tomato ketchup
2 tbsp	Worcestershire sauce
	Dried thyme
	Salt and pepper

Skin and bone fish and cut into bite-size pieces. Heat a saucepan and fry bacon till crisp. Remove from pan. Peel and chop onion and add to pan. Cook gently till transparent.

Peel and chop potatoes and carrots. Finely chop celery. Add to pan with chopped parsley, tomatoes and their juice, fish broth or water, tomato ketchup, Worcestershire sauce, a pinch of thyme and seasoning. Cover and simmer gently for about 45 minutes.

Add the fish pieces and bacon, cover and cook for a further 15 minutes.

Cantonese fish soup

Overall timing 35 minutes plus marination

Freezing Not suitable

To serve 6

¾ lb	White fish fillets
2 tbsp	Soy sauce
2 tsp	Dry sherry
3 tbsp	Oil
2	Medium-size onions
4	Shallots
2	Medium-size carrots
3	Stalks of celery
6 cups	Chicken broth
¼ cup	Long grain rice
	Salt and pepper

Cut across the fillets into thin strips and put into a bowl. Add the soy sauce, sherry and 1 tbsp of the oil. Mix well and leave to marinate in a cool place for 1 hour.

Peel and chop the onions and two of the shallots. Peel and dice the carrots. Trim and chop the celery. Heat remaining oil in a large saucepan, add prepared vegetables, cover and cook gently for 5 minutes. Add the broth and bring to a boil. Stir in rice and salt, bring back to a boil, cover and simmer for 10 minutes.

Add the fish and marinating juices and cook for a further 10 minutes. Taste and adjust seasoning. Pour into soup bowls and garnish with remaining shallots, peeled and finely chopped.

Provençal cod soup

Overall timing 1 hour

Freezing Not suitable

To serve 4

1	Large onion
1	Leek
1	Large tomato
2 tbsp	Oil
2	Garlic cloves
6 cups	Water
	Bouquet garni
	Orange rind
¼ tsp	Saffron
	Salt and pepper
1¾ lb	Potatoes
1 lb	Cod fillets
4	Thick slices of bread
1 tbsp	Chopped parsley

Peel and slice onion. Trim and finely chop leek. Blanch, peel and chop tomato. Heat oil in a large saucepan. Add onion, leek and tomato and cook, stirring, for 5 minutes.

Peel and crush garlic. Add water, bouquet garni, a strip of orange rind, garlic, saffron and pepper. Bring to a boil.

Peel and thickly slice potatoes. Add to pan and cook for 10 minutes. Chop cod fillets into pieces and add with seasoning. Cook for a further 15 minutes.

Remove cod and potatoes with a slotted spoon and place in warmed serving dish. Put the slices of bread in a warmed soup tureen and pour the cooking juices over. Sprinkle with parsley. Serve soup and cod together or as separate courses.

Cock-a-leekie

Overall timing 2¼ hours

Freezing Suitable

To serve 6

2 lb	Leeks
2 tbsp	Butter
3 lb	Stewing chicken
2 quarts	Chicken broth or water
	Bouquet garni
	Salt and pepper
⅔ cup	Prunes (optional)

Wash, trim and slice leeks. Melt butter in a skillet, add leeks and fry quickly for 5 minutes. Put into a saucepan with the chicken, giblets, broth (made with cubes if necessary) or water, bouquet garni, salt and pepper. Bring to a boil, cover and simmer for 1½ hours.

Pit prunes and add to pan, if using. Cook for 30 minutes longer. Discard bouquet garni.

Remove chicken from pan. Cut the meat into strips, discarding skin and bones. Return meat to pan. Taste and adjust seasoning. Serve with oatcakes.

Chicken, lemon and egg drop soup

Overall timing 2¼ hours

Freezing Suitable: add eggs after reheating

To serve 6

1 lb	Veal shank, bone-in
9 cups	Water
3 lb	Stewing chicken with giblets
1	Lemon
2	Onions
2	Cloves
	Salt and pepper
2	Eggs

Place veal shank in saucepan with the water. Bring to a boil, then cover and simmer for 1 hour.

Meanwhile, cut up the chicken and remove skin if liked. Wash giblets. Grate the rind of the lemon and squeeze out the juice. Reserve both. Peel onions and spike each with a clove. Add chicken, giblets, lemon rind, spiked onions and seasoning to pan. Cover and cook gently for 1 hour till chicken is tender.

Strain the broth into a clean pan. Cut meats into small pieces, discarding bones, skin, giblets and onions. Skim broth, add meats and bring to a boil. Stir in lemon juice, then taste and adjust seasoning.

Beat the eggs in a small bowl. Remove saucepan from heat and pour soup into tureen. Drizzle egg in a thin stream into soup, stirring continuously. Serve.

Chicken noodle soup

Overall timing 10 minutes

Freezing Not suitable

To serve 4

6 cups	Chicken broth
3 oz	Fine egg noodles
2 tbsp	Lemon juice
	Salt and pepper
2 tbsp	Chopped parsley

Put the broth into a large saucepan. Bring to a boil and add the noodles. Boil for 3-4 minutes till tender. Add the lemon juice and seasoning and sprinkle with chopped parsley. Serve with a side dish of grated sharp Cheddar cheese.

Bacon dumpling soup

Overall timing 2¾ hours

Freezing Suitable: add dumplings to stock after thawing

To serve 4

¾ lb	Stale white bread
1¼ cups	Milk
2 oz	Lean bacon slices
1	Onion
1	Garlic clove
1 tbsp	Chopped parsley
¼ tsp	Dried marjoram
	Salt and pepper
3	Eggs
1 cup	Flour
5 cups	Broth

Remove crusts from bread, then soak in milk for 2 hours. Chop bacon. Fry till crisp.

Peel and finely chop onion. Peel and crush garlic. Put both into bowl with bread, bacon, parsley and marjoram. Season and add eggs. Mix together well. Sift in flour and stir until absorbed.

Heat the broth in a large saucepan. Shape the bacon mixture into 1 inch balls and roll them in a little flour so they don't fall apart when cooking. Add the dumplings to the broth and simmer for 15 minutes. Serve hot.

Normandy chicken soup

Overall timing 50 minutes

Freezing Suitable: add egg yolk and cream after reheating

To serve 6

½ lb	Chicken breast
1	Bay leaf
1 quart	Milk
6 tbsp	Calvados or brandy
½ lb	Mushrooms
¼ cup	Butter
2 tbsp	Flour
1 tbsp	Lemon juice
¼ tsp	Grated nutmeg
1 tbsp	Chopped parsley
	Salt and pepper
1	Egg yolk
¼ cup	Light cream

Put chicken breast in a saucepan with bay leaf and milk and bring to a boil. Cover and simmer for about 15 minutes till tender. Remove chicken from milk. Discard any bones and skin and cut meat into strips. Put into a shallow bowl and pour Calvados or brandy over. Marinate for 20 minutes.

Meanwhile, thickly slice mushrooms. Melt butter in a large saucepan, add mushrooms and fry gently for 5 minutes without browning. Stir in flour and cook for 1 minute. Gradually add strained milk and bring to a boil, stirring. Add lemon juice and nutmeg and simmer for 5 minutes.

Add chicken and marinade with parsley and seasoning. Simmer for a further 5 minutes.

Lightly beat egg yolk and cream in a bowl. Pour in a little of the soup, stirring constantly. Pour back into the soup and cook, stirring, for 3 minutes; do not boil. Serve hot.

Chicken and corn soup

Overall timing 1 ½ hours

Freezing Not suitable

To serve 6

1	Large onion
2 tbsp	Butter
2 lb	Chicken pieces
¼ tsp	Ground cumin
5 cups	Chicken broth
1 lb	Potatoes
	Salt and pepper
2	Ears of corn
1	Ripe avocado
¾ cup	Plain yogurt or light cream

Peel and chop onion. Heat butter in a large saucepan, add chicken and onion and fry for 5 minutes, turning chicken occasionally. Add cumin and fry for 2 minutes. Add broth and bring to a boil. Cover and simmer for 35 minutes till chicken is tender. Meanwhile, peel and dice potatoes.

Lift chicken out of pan. Add potatoes to broth, season and simmer for 10 minutes till tender. Meanwhile, remove skin and bones from chicken and cut meat into strips. Wash corn, discarding husks. Cut across into 1 inch thick slices.

Mash potatoes in the soup to thicken it. Bring to a boil and add corn slices and chicken meat. Simmer for 10 minutes.

Peel and halve avocado. Remove pit and slice flesh thinly. Place in a tureen with yogurt or cream. Taste soup and adjust seasoning. Pour into tureen and serve.

French pea soup

Overall timing 2 hours plus soaking

Freezing suitable

To serve 4

½ cup	Dried split peas
1	Onion
2	Leeks
1	Stalk of celery
3	Carrots
3	Potatoes
1	Turnip
6 tbsp	Goose fat or butter
1½ quarts	Chicken broth
1	Garlic clove
	Salt and pepper
12	Small slices of bread

Wash and pick over the dried peas, place in a saucepan and cover with plenty of cold water. Bring to a boil and boil for 2 minutes. Remove from heat, cover and leave to soak for 2 hours. Bring peas to a boil again, simmer for 30 minutes and drain thoroughly.

Meanwhile, peel and chop the onion; wash and chop the leeks and celery; peel and chop the carrots, potatoes and turnip. Heat half the goose fat or butter in a saucepan over a low heat and fry the chopped vegetables for 10 minutes, without browning. Add the broth and the peeled garlic clove. Bring to a boil and add the dried peas. Season. Bring back to a boil and simmer for 1 hour. Remove the garlic clove.

Heat the remaining goose fat or butter in a skillet and fry the slices of bread till crisp and golden. Serve hot with the soup.

Pea and ham soup

Overall timing 2¾ hours plus overnight soaking

Freezing Suitable

To serve 6

1½ cups	Dried whole green peas
2½ quarts	Water
2 lb	Ham hock
	Salt and pepper

Put peas in saucepan and cover with the cold water. Leave to soak overnight.

Add the ham hock to the pan and bring to a boil. Skim off any scum. Cover and simmer for 1½-2 hours till the ham and peas are tender.

Remove and drain the ham hock. Discard the skin and bone and cut the meat into small cubes. Reserve one third of the peas. Purée the remaining peas in a blender or by pressing through a sieve. Return the puréed peas and reserved whole peas to the saucepan. Bring to a boil, stirring occasionally.

Add the diced ham, and season to taste. Pour into a warmed tureen and serve with cornbread.

Turkey vegetable soup

Overall timing 1 1/4 hours

Freezing Not suitable

To serve 6

1	Large carrot
1	Large onion
1	Stalk of celery
2	Turkey wings
6 cups	Water
	Salt and pepper
1/2 lb	Waxy potatoes
2	Leeks
4	Thick slices of bread
6 tbsp	Butter

Peel and chop carrot and onion. Trim and chop the celery. Wipe the turkey wings and put into a saucepan with the prepared vegetables, water and seasoning. Bring to a boil, skim off any scum, cover and simmer for 45 minutes.

Peel potatoes and cut into 1/2 inch cubes. trim and slice leeks.

Lift turkey wings out of pan with a slotted spoon and leave to cool slightly. Add potatoes and leeks to the soup and simmer for 5 minutes till vegetables are tender.

Remove the skin and bones from the turkey wings and cut the meat into strips. Add to the soup and reheat gently.

Meanwhile, remove the crusts from bread and cut into cubes. Melt butter in a skillet, add the bread and fry till golden all over. Drain croûtons on paper towels.

Taste soup and adjust seasoning. Pour into a warmed tureen and sprinkle with croûtons. Serve immediately.

Leek and spinach soup

Overall timing 30 minutes

Freezing Not suitable

To serve 4

½ lb	Fresh bulk spinach
4	Leeks
2 tbsp	Butter
	Salt and pepper
3½ cups	Chicken broth
2 tsp	Lemon juice
¼ cup	Long-grain rice
4 tsp	Grated Edam cheese

Wash spinach thoroughly, removing any coarse stalks, and chop finely. Trim and thinly slice the leeks. Melt the butter in a saucepan. Add the spinach and leeks and seasoning. Cover and cook for 5 minutes.

Add broth and lemon juice and bring to a boil. Stir in the rice. Bring back to a boil and cook for 12-15 minutes or until the rice is tender. Taste and adjust seasoning.

Pour soup into four warmed soup bowls. Sprinkle Edam cheese over the top and serve.

Tomato and basil soup

Overall timing 1 hour

Freezing Suitable

To serve 6

2	Carrots
1	Leek
1	Onion
1½ lb	Large ripe tomatoes
1 tbsp	Tomato paste
1	Bouquet garni
	Salt and pepper
1½ quarts	Chicken broth
8	Fresh basil leaves
2	Garlic cloves
2 tbsp	Grated Parmesan cheese
2 tbsp	Olive oil
3	Large potatoes

Peel the carrots; wash and trim the leek; peel the onion. Chop all finely. Blanch, peel and chop the tomatoes. Place in a large saucepan with chopped vegetables, tomato paste, bouquet garni, salt, pepper and broth. Bring to a boil. Cover and simmer for 30 minutes.

Meanwhile, make the pesto. Pound the basil leaves with the peeled and crushed garlic and ¼ tsp salt in a mortar. Gradually add the cheese and oil, pounding between each addition till the mixture is creamy. Alternatively, make the pesto in a blender or food processor.

Peel the potatoes and grate coarsely. Add to the soup and simmer for a further 10 minutes.

Discard the bouquet garni. Stir the pesto into the soup.

Zucchini and rice soup

Overall timing 1 ¼ hours

Freezing Suitable: reheat from frozen, then add cheese

To serve 2

1	Small onion
2	Bacon slices
¼ lb	Zucchini
	Salt and pepper
2 cups	Chicken broth
½ cup	Long-grain rice
2 tbsp	Butter
2 tbsp	Grated cheese

Peel and chop onion; chop bacon. Fry onion and bacon gently in a skillet until bacon is soft.

Trim and dice zucchini. Add zucchini to skillet and cook over a low heat until just tender. Drain off excess fat. Season with salt and pepper.

Put broth in a large saucepan and bring to a boil. Add rice, cover and cook for 10 minutes. Add the zucchini mixture and continue cooking till rice is tender.

Remove pan from heat and add butter and cheese. Stir well and serve at once.

Swiss cream of barley soup

Overall timing 2¾ hours

Freezing Not suitable

To serve 4-6

2	Large onions
3	Cloves
1	Calf's foot
½ cup	Pearl barley
	Bay leaf
2 quarts	Water
	Salt and pepper
¾ lb	Carrots
4	Stalks of celery
2	Small leeks
¼ lb	Bacon slices
1 tbsp	Lard or shortening
2	Egg yolks
½ cup	Light cream
1 tbsp	Chopped chives

Peel one of the onions and spike with cloves. Wash calf's foot, chop in half lengthwise and put into a saucepan with the barley, spiked onion and bay leaf. Add the water and seasoning, then cover and simmer for 2 hours.

Meanwhile, scrape and dice carrots. Peel and chop remaining onion. Trim and slice celery and leeks. Dice bacon. Melt lard or shortening in a large saucepan. Add bacon and vegetables and fry for 10 minutes till golden.

Remove spiked onion and bay leaf from broth and discard. Lift calf's foot out of broth and remove the meat, discarding skin and bones. Add meat to broth with the vegetables. Bring to a boil and simmer for 10 minutes till vegetables are tender.

Put the egg yolks and cream into a tureen and beat together with a fork. Season the soup to taste and gradually stir into tureen. Sprinkle with chives and serve.

Spicy bortsch

Overall timing 2½ hours

Freezing Suitable

To serve 6

1	Carrot
1 lb	Parsnips
4	Tomatoes
1	Onion
9	Cloves
1 lb	Beef bones
1 lb	Beef for stew
½ tsp	Salt
1 tsp	Sugar
6	Peppercorns
1	Bay leaf
6 cups	Cold water
1 lb	Raw beets
¼ lb	Cabbage

Peel and chop carrot and parsnips. Chop tomatoes. Peel onion and spike with cloves. Crack bones; dice beef.

Put vegetables, bones and beef into a large saucepan with salt, sugar, peppercorns, bay leaf and water. Bring to a boil, cover and simmer for 1½ – 2 hours. Remove bones, onion and bay leaf. Peel and coarsely grate beets.

Chop cabbage. Add to pan and simmer, uncovered, for a further 12-15 minutes.

Florentine minestrone

Overall timing 2¾ hours plus soaking

Freezing Suitable: add cabbage and macaroni after reheating

To serve 4

1 cup	Dried navy beans
2	Large carrots
2	Stalks of celery
1	Garlic clove
2	Onions
¼ cup	Oil
1 tsp	Dried mixed herbs
16 oz	Can of tomatoes
½ lb	Cabbage
¼ lb	Elbow macaroni
	Salt and pepper

Place beans in saucepan and cover with cold water. Bring to a boil; boil for 2 minutes. Remove from heat and soak for 2 hours. Drain beans, return to pan, cover with boiling water and simmer for 2 hours.

Peel and chop carrots; chop celery. Peel and crush garlic. Peel and slice onions. In a large saucepan, heat oil and fry vegetables.

Drain beans, reserving cooking liquid. Purée half the beans. Add beans, whole and puréed, to vegetables with cooking liquid, herbs and tomatoes. Bring to a boil. Shred cabbage and add to soup with macaroni and seasoning. Simmer for 20 minutes.

Tuscan vegetable soup

Overall timing 2 hours plus overnight soaking

Freezing Not suitable

To serve 6

1 cup	Dried beans
1¼ lb	Cabbage
1	Onion
1	Large leek
1	Stalk of celery
1	Carrot
1	Garlic clove
3 tbsp	Oil
1	Bay leaf
3	Sprigs of oregano
	Sprig of rosemary
	Salt and pepper
2 tbsp	Tomato paste
2 quarts	Light broth

Soak beans in cold water overnight. The next day, drain beans, put into a large saucepan and cover with fresh cold water. Bring to a boil and simmer for about 1½ hours till tender.

Meanwhile, shred cabbage. Peel and thinly slice onion; trim and slice leek and celery. Scrape and chop carrot. Peel and crush garlic. Heat oil in a large saucepan and fry vegetables, except cabbage, with garlic and herbs till lightly browned. Add cabbage and seasoning and fry for a further 5 minutes.

Remove herbs from pan and add the tomato paste, drained beans and broth. Bring to a boil and simmer for a further 15 minutes. Taste and adjust the seasoning and pour into warmed individual bowls.

Watercress soup

Overall timing 40 minutes

Freezing Suitable: add cream after thawing

To serve 4

1	Large onion
2	Large floury potatoes
2 tbsp	Butter
3	Bunches of watercress
1 quart	Chicken broth
	Salt and pepper
½ cup	Heavy cream

Peel and finely chop onion. Peel and chop or grate potatoes. Melt butter in a saucepan, add onions and potatoes and turn till coated in butter. Cover and cook gently for 10 minutes.

Wash, dry and chop watercress leaves and stalks, reserving some whole leaves. Add to pan with broth and bring to a boil. Cover and simmer for 15 minutes.

Rub soup through sieve or purée in blender. Return to pan, add reserved watercress leaves and reheat. Taste and adjust seasoning. Serve immediately with side dish of whipped cream, or cool, stir in cream and chill well before serving.

Rice and cabbage soup

Overall timing 45 minutes

Freezing Not suitable

To serve 6-8

1	Large onion
½ lb	Slab bacon
1	Garlic clove
1 tbsp	Butter
1 cup	Long grain rice
2 quarts	Light broth
	Salt and pepper
	Bouquet garni
1 lb	Green cabbage
1 cup	Grated cheese

Peel and chop the onion; finely dice the bacon. Peel and crush garlic. Melt the butter in a large saucepan and add the onion, bacon and garlic. Fry gently for 5 minutes without browning.

Add rice and cook, stirring, for 2 minutes till coated with butter. Add the broth, seasoning and bouquet garni. Bring to a boil and simmer for 15 minutes. Meanwhile, coarsely shred the cabbage. Add to the pan, bring to a boil again and simmer for 5 minutes.

Remove pan from the heat and discard the bouquet garni. Stir cheese into soup and adjust seasoning. Pour into a tureen and serve immediately with rye bread.

Pumpkin soup

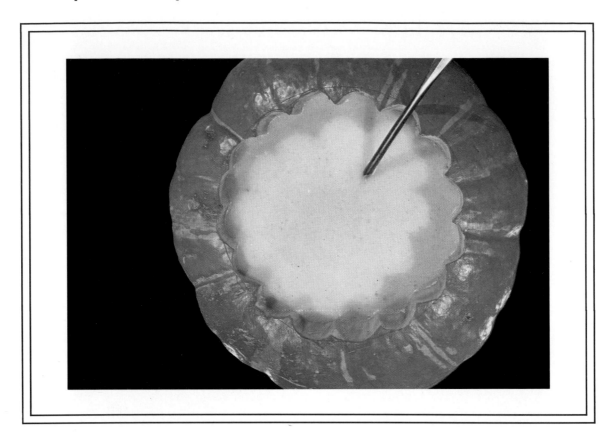

Overall timing 50 minutes

Freezing Not suitable

To serve 6

2 lb	Pumpkin or other squash
1 cup	Water
	Salt and pepper
1 quart	Milk
1 tsp	Sugar
¼ tsp	Grated nutmeg
1	Egg yolk
¼ cup	Light cream

Prepare the squash, discarding fibrous center and seeds. Cut the flesh into chunks, put into a saucepan with the water and salt and bring to a boil. Simmer for about 30 minutes till tender, then purée in a blender or food processor. Place purée in saucepan with milk, sugar and nutmeg. Heat through gently till almost boiling, stirring occasionally.

Beat the egg yolk and cream together in a bowl and pour in a little of the hot soup, stirring constantly. Pour back into the pan and stir over a low heat for 3 minutes — do not boil. Taste and adjust seasoning, then serve immediately with toasted rye bread.

Onion soup with wine

Overall timing 45 minutes

Freezing Suitable: pour soup over bread and add cheese after reheating

To serve 4

3	Large onions
¼ cup	Butter
1 tbsp	Flour
½ tsp	Brown sugar
6 cups	Water
8	Slices of French bread
2 tbsp	Dry white wine
	Salt and pepper
½ cup	Grated Gruyère or Swiss cheese

Peel and slice onions. melt half the butter in a large saucepan and cook onions till transparent. Sprinkle onions with flour. Cook, stirring, until flour colors. Add sugar, then gradually stir in water. Simmer for 20 minutes.

Preheat the oven to 450°F.

Fry bread in remaining butter. Place bread slices in bottom of individual bowls or ovenproof soup tureen. Add wine and seasoning, then pour soup over bread. Sprinkle cheese into the bowls. Bake for 5-10 minutes to melt the cheese.

Mushroom soup

Chicken vermicelli soup

Overall timing 30 minutes

Freezing Not suitable

To serve 4

2	Stalks of celery
½ lb	Mushrooms
2 tsp	Oil
1½ cups	Diced cooked chicken
1 tbsp	Soy sauce
1 tbsp	Dry sherry
8	Water chestnuts
1 quart	Chicken broth
2 cups	Bean sprouts
	Salt and pepper
1	Egg

Finely chop celery. Thinly slice mushrooms. Heat oil in a saucepan and stir-fry vegetables for 5 minutes.

Sprinkle chicken with soy sauce and sherry. Quarter or dice water chestnuts.

Add broth to pan with water chestnuts. Bring to a boil, then add chicken and soaking juices. Simmer for 10 minutes. Add bean sprouts and cook for 2 minutes. Taste and adjust seasoning.

Beat egg. Remove pan from heat and trickle in beaten egg, stirring constantly. Pour soup into soup bowls and serve.

Overall timing 40 minutes

Freezing Not suitable

To serve 6

1 oz	Chinese dried mushrooms
6 cups	Chicken broth
2	Lettuce leaves
4	Eggs
	Salt and pepper
2 tbsp	Butter
2 oz	Chinese vermicelli
1 cup	Cooked chicken meat cut into strips
2 tbsp	Dry sherry

Soak mushrooms in warm water for 30 minutes. Drain, discard woody stems and put into saucepan with broth. Bring to a boil and simmer for 10 minutes.

Meanwhile, shred lettuce. Beat eggs with seasoning. Melt half butter in skillet, add half egg mixture and make a thin omelette. Remove from pan and reserve. Use remaining butter and egg mixture to make another. Roll up both and cut into thin slices.

Add vermicelli and chicken to saucepan and simmer for 2 minutes. Remove from heat and add sherry, omelette strips and lettuce. Serve immediately.

Pumpkin rice soup

Overall timing 1 hour

Freezing Not suitable

To serve 6

1	Large onion
1	Stalk of celery
1	Large carrot
1 tbsp	Butter
¼ cup	Finely chopped bacon
1½ lb	Pumpkin
2 quarts	Chicken broth
1	Garlic clove
	Salt and pepper
¾ cup	Long grain rice
3 tbsp	Grated Parmesan cheese

Peel the onion, trim the celery and scrape the carrot. Finely chop vegetables. Melt the butter, add the vegetables and bacon and fry for 5 minutes, stirring occasionally.

Scrape the seeds and fibrous center out of the pumpkin. Cut into chunks, and add to the pan. Fry, stirring, for a further 5 minutes.

Add the broth (made with cubes if necessary), peeled and crushed garlic and seasoning and bring to a boil. Simmer for 10 minutes.

Rinse the rice and add to the soup. Bring to a boil and simmer for 15-20 minutes till the rice is tender.

Stir in the Parmesan and adjust the seasoning. Pour into warmed serving bowls and serve immediately with bread sticks or fresh crusty rolls and butter.

Minestrone

Overall timing 2¼ hours

Freezing Not suitable

To serve 8

¼ cup	Chopped bacon
1	Onion
1	Small leek
1 tbsp	Olive oil
1	Garlic clove
1 tbsp	Chopped parsley
2	Sage leaves
3	Carrots
1	Zucchini
2	Large potatoes
3	Stalks of celery
1	Large tomato
¾ lb	Savoy cabbage
3	Basil leaves

9 cups	Hot broth
1 tbsp	Tomato paste
	Salt and pepper
16 oz	Can of cannellini beans
¼ lb	Elbow macaroni
	Grated Parmesan cheese

Place bacon in saucepan and fry till fat runs.

Peel and finely chop the onion; trim and chop the leek. Add oil to saucepan and heat, then add onion, leek, peeled and crushed garlic, parsley and chopped sage. Cover and sweat for 10 minutes.

Meanwhile, peel the remaining vegetables, as necessary, and chop them. Add prepared vegetables and chopped basil to pan and cook, stirring, for 5 minutes. Gradually add broth, tomato paste, salt and pepper and bring to a boil. Cover tightly and cook gently for 1¼ hours.

Drain the canned beans and add. Add macaroni and cook for 20 minutes more. Serve with Parmesan cheese.

Majorcan vegetable and bread soup

Overall timing 1 ½ hours

Freezing Not suitable

To serve 6

1 cup	Lentils
2 quarts	Water
¼ lb	Slab bacon
1 lb	Fresh broad or lima beans
1 lb	Fresh peas
1 lb	Cabbage
½ lb	Fresh spinach
	Salt and pepper
18	Thin slices of brown bread

Wash and pick over the lentils and put into a saucepan with the water. Bring to a boil and simmer for 45 minutes.

Meanwhile, dice the bacon. Shell the beans and peas. Shred the cabbage and spinach.

Rub the lentils with their cooking liquid through a sieve or purée in a blender. Return to the saucepan, add seasoning, bacon and vegetables and bring to boil. Simmer for about 25 minutes till the vegetables are tender.

Taste and adjust the seasoning. Arrange three slices of bread in each soup bowl and pour the soup over. Serve immediately.

Irish celery soup

Overall timing 35 minutes

Freezing Suitable: add cream when reheating

To serve 4

1 lb	Celery
2	Potatoes
2	Onions
¼ cup	Butter
	Salt and pepper
1	Bay leaf
1	Garlic clove
	Grated nutmeg
1 quart	Chicken broth
½ cup	Light cream

Cut off base of celery, then wash and chop stalks and leaves. Peel and finely chop potatoes and onions. Melt butter in saucepan over a low heat. Add celery stalks and leaves, potatoes and onions, cover and cook for 5 minutes, stirring to prevent coloring.

Sprinkle with salt and pepper, add the bay leaf, peeled and crushed garlic, pinch of nutmeg and hot broth (made with 2 cubes if necessary). Cover and simmer for 20 minutes.

Remove bay leaf. Push soup through sieve into a bowl, or liquidize, then return to saucepan and add the cream. Heat through without boiling. Adjust seasoning, then serve with croûtons (diced bread fried in oil till brown).

Gazpacho

Overall timing 20 minutes plus chilling

Freezing Suitable

To serve 6

1 ¼ lb	Tomatoes
½	Cucumber
1	Large onion
1	Sweet green or red pepper
2	Garlic cloves
2 cups	Soft white bread crumbs
3 tbsp	Olive oil
1 tbsp	Wine vinegar
1	Sprig of parsley or mint
	Salt and pepper
5 cups	Water

Blanch, peel and chop the tomatoes. Peel, seed and chop the cucumber. Peel and chop the onion. Seed and chop the pepper; peel and chop the garlic.

Place all the vegetables in a blender with bread crumbs, oil, vinegar, parsley or mint, salt and pepper and 2½ cups of the water. Blend to a purée.

Place purée in a large bowl and stir in the remaining water. Cover and chill for 3 hours.

Before serving, add a few ice cubes. Serve with side dishes of chopped onion, hard-cooked eggs, tomatoes, peppers and croûtons.

Creamy cauliflower soup

Overall timing 35 minutes

Freezing Not suitable

To serve 4

1	Large cauliflower
1	Small onion
	Salt and pepper
¼ cup	Butter
¼ cup	Flour
2 cups	Milk
	Lamb seasoning salt
½ tsp	Dried mixed herbs
¼ tsp	Grated nutmeg
1	Egg yolk
¼ cup	Light cream
	Fresh dill

Trim cauliflower, separate into florets and wash. Peel and finely chop onion. Put cauliflower and onion into pan of boiling salted water, cover and cook for 10 minutes. Drain, saving 2 cups cooking liquid. Mash half cauliflower and onion.

Melt butter in a large saucepan. Stir in flour, then milk and reserved cooking liquid. Add a pinch of lamb seasoning salt, the herbs, nutmeg and pulped and whole cauliflower and onion. Simmer for 7 minutes. Taste and adjust seasoning.

Mix egg yolk and cream in warmed tureen. Pour in soup and serve garnished with dill.

Zucchini and egg soup

Overall timing 30 minutes

Freezing Not suitable

To serve 4

1 lb	Zucchini
2 tbsp	Butter
3 tbsp	Olive oil
1	Garlic clove
1 quart	Boiling water
	Salt and pepper
2	Eggs
10	Basil leaves (optional)
2 tbsp	Chopped parsley
½ cup	Grated mild white cheese
Garnish	
¼ cup	Grated mild white cheese
	Croûtons

Wash zucchini, trim off ends, then dice. Heat the butter, oil and peeled garlic clove in a saucepan or flameproof casserole. Cook over a moderate heat till the garlic turns golden, then discard it.

Add diced zucchini to pan and cook for a few minutes. Add the boiling water and a pinch of salt, cover and cook gently for about 15 minutes.

Break eggs into a warmed soup tureen and add chopped basil, parsley and salt and pepper. Add the cheese. Beat well with a fork.

Gradually add about a quarter of the soup and mix well, then pour in the rest. Garnish with cheese and freshly made croûtons.

Endive soup

Overall timing 25 minutes

Freezing Suitable: add vermouth after reheating

To serve 4

4	Heads of Belgian endive
5 tbsp	Butter
2 tsp	Sugar
1 quart	Chicken broth
2 tsp	Flour
6 tbsp	Dry vermouth
	Salt and pepper

Chop endive. Melt ¼ cup of the butter in a saucepan and fry endive over a gentle heat for about 5 minutes. Tilt pan, add sugar and allow to caramelize. Add broth, cover and simmer for 10 minutes.

Mix remaining butter with the flour to a smooth paste. Stir paste a little at a time into the soup. Return to a boil and simmer for 2-3 minutes.

Add vermouth and seasoning and cook, uncovered, for 1-2 minutes more. Pour into serving bowls and garnish with freshly made, hot croûtons.

Cheese soup

Overall timing 30 minutes

Freezing Not suitable

To serve 4-6

1	Onion
6 tbsp	Butter
1 quart	Light broth
½ cup	Dry white wine
4 tsp	Cornstarch
1 cup	Milk
	Salt and white pepper
1 cup	Grated Cheddar cheese
1 cup	Grated Parmesan cheese
	Croûtons

Peel and finely chop the onion. Melt the butter in a saucepan, add onion and fry till transparent. Stir in the broth and wine and bring to a boil slowly.

Blend the cornstarch with a little water and add to the pan, stirring constantly. Bring back to a boil, stirring, and cook for 3 minutes. Add the milk, salt, pepper and grated cheeses. Stir over a very low heat till the cheese has completely melted. Taste and adjust seasoning, then pour into a warmed tureen. Serve immediately garnished with lots of croûtons.

Bean soup

Overall timing 30 minutes

Freezing Suitable: add sour cream after thawing

To serve 4

¼ lb	Slab bacon
1	Sweet red pepper
1	Green pepper
1 quart	Strong beef broth
12 oz	Can of lima beans
	Hot pepper sauce
	Salt
¼ cup	Sour cream

Chop bacon and fry it lightly in a skillet till the fat runs. Place in a deep saucepan.

Seed and finely chop half the red and green peppers and add to the pan with the broth (made up with 3 bouillon cubes if necessary) and drained beans. Bring to a boil and simmer for 20 minutes.

Add pepper sauce and salt to taste. Slice remaining peppers and blanch for 5 minutes in boiling water. Drain well.

Remove soup from the heat and stir in the sour cream. Garnish with pepper slices and serve with a bowl of grated cheese and fresh whole wheat bread.

Barley and mushroom soup

Overall timing 3 hours 50 minutes

Freezing suitable: add butter and cream after reheating

To serve 4

½ cup	Pearl barley
	Salt
2	Carrots
2	Celery stalks
1	Leek
1	Onion
2	Bay leaves
10	Black peppercorns
1	Sprig of parsley
1½ oz	Dried mushrooms
2 tbsp	Vinegar
¼ cup	Butter
½ cup	Light cream

Wash barley, then cook in lightly salted, boiling water for 2½ hours till very soft and gelatinous.

Meanwhile, scrape and chop carrots. Wash and slice celery and leek. Peel and quarter onion. Put all vegetables into a saucepan with bay leaves, salt, peppercorns, parsley, mushrooms and 1 cup water. Cover and simmer gently for 1 hour.

Strain broth into a bowl. Reserve mushrooms and discard remaining vegetables. Slice mushrooms and return to pan with strained broth.

Drain barley and crush with a potato masher, or partly liquidize in a blender. Add barley and vinegar to broth, heat through and season.

Cut butter into small pieces and put in bottom of a warmed soup tureen. Pour in soup, stir in cream and serve.

Brussels sprout soup

Overall timing 1 ¼ hours

Freezing Suitable: add cream and egg yolk mixture when reheating

To serve 4

1 lb	Brussels sprouts
6 tbsp	Butter
1 quart	Hot beef broth
	Salt
2 tbsp	Flour
	Grated nutmeg
6 tbsp	Light cream
1	Egg yolk

Trim sprouts. Cut a cross in base of each. Melt ¼ cup butter in a saucepan, add sprouts and cook for 3 minutes, stirring continuously. Add broth and salt. Cover and cook for 40 minutes.

Sieve sprouts into a bowl, or liquidize.

Melt remaining butter in a pan. Add flour and cook, stirring, for 3 minutes. Remove pan from heat and gradually add sprout purée. Return to heat and cook for 10 minutes over low heat. Season with salt and pinch of nutmeg.

Mix cream with egg yolk. Off heat, stir cream mixture into soup to thicken.

Avocado soup

Overall timing 15 minutes plus chilling if serving cold

Freezing Suitable: add cream after thawing

To serve 4

1 quart	Chicken broth
2	Ripe avocados
1 tbsp	Lemon juice
1	Egg yolk
3 tbsp	Light cream
	Salt and pepper

Heat chicken broth (made up with 4 cubes if necessary) in a saucepan to boiling point.

Cut open avocados and lift out seeds. If intending to serve soup cold, cut eight very thin slices, sprinkle with lemon juice to prevent discoloration and set aside. Scoop out remaining avocado flesh, place in a bowl and mash well with the egg yolk and cream.

Remove broth from heat. Gradually add the avocado mixture, whisking vigorously. Add salt and pepper to taste. Do not reheat.

Serve hot with fried croûtons. If serving cold, chill the soup for at least 1 hour, then serve garnished with reserved avocado slices.

Pipérade

Overall timing 1 hour

Freezing Not suitable

To serve 4

1 lb	Ripe tomatoes
2	Green peppers
2	Onions
1	Garlic clove
5 tbsp	Oil
	Salt and pepper
¼ tsp	Dried marjoram
	Hot pepper sauce
8	Eggs

Blanch, peel and chop tomatoes. Seed and chop peppers. Peel and slice onions. Peel and crush garlic.

Heat oil in skillet. Add onions and garlic and cook till golden. Add peppers and tomatoes and cook over a high heat for 5 minutes. Season with salt, pepper, marjoram and pepper sauce. Reduce heat, cover and simmer for 30 minutes or until the mixture is reduced to a purée.

Lightly beat eggs in a bowl. Season and pour over vegetable purée. Cook over increased heat, stirring, for 2-3 minutes till creamy. Serve with buttered toast and a green salad.

Baked eggs in potatoes

Overall timing 2 hours

Freezing Not suitable

To serve 4

4 x 10 oz	Potatoes
¼ cup	Butter
	Salt and pepper
½ cup	Grated cheese
4	Small eggs
¼ cup	Heavy cream
2 tsp	Chopped chives

Preheat the oven to 400°.

Scrub and dry the potatoes and push a metal skewer lengthwise through each one. Place on a baking sheet and rub a little of the butter over the skins. Bake for 1-1¼ hours.

Remove from the oven. Increase the temperature to 450°F. Cut a slice lengthwise off each potato and scoop out the insides, leaving a shell about ½ inch thick. Mash the scooped-out potato (plus any from the lids) in a bowl with the remaining butter and seasoning. Beat the cheese into potato mixture.

Press the mixture back into the potato shells, leaving a hollow in the center large enough for an egg. Place on baking sheet. Carefully break an egg into each potato. Season and spoon the cream over. Return to the oven and bake for 8-10 minutes till the eggs are lightly set. Sprinkle the chives over and serve hot.

Curried eggs

Overall timing 35 minutes

Freezing Not suitable

To serve 4

6	Eggs
2	Onions
¼ cup	Butter
2 tsp	Curry powder
2½ cups	Chicken broth
1 tsp	Cornstarch
½ cup	Light cream or half-and-half
	Salt and pepper

Place eggs in a saucepan of cold water. Bring to a boil and simmer for 8 minutes, then drain.

Peel and finely chop onions. Melt butter in a skillet, add onions, cover and cook until golden over a low heat (about 15 minutes).

Sprinkle with curry powder and cook for 2 minutes, stirring. Pour in the broth and simmer for 10 minutes. Mix cornstarch and cream or half-and-half together well, then stir into curry mixture with seasoning. Heat gently but do not boil.

Shell eggs and cut in half lengthwise. Remove yolks with a spoon and mash yolks and a little of the curry mixture together with a fork. Spoon back into egg whites. Place eggs in curry sauce and heat through without boiling. Serve with rice or hot buttered toast.

Deep-fried eggs

Overall timing 15 minutes

Freezing Not suitable

To serve 4

	Oil for frying
8	Eggs
	Salt and pepper
2	Tomatoes
	Sprigs of parsley

Half-fill a skillet with oil and heat to 370° or until a cube of bread browns in 1 minute. Swirl fat around with a spoon. Break an egg into a cup and carefully slide into the hot oil. Cook for 1-2 minutes, basting with the hot oil all the time and turning the egg once or twice.

Remove from pan with a slotted spoon and drain on paper towels. Sprinkle with salt and pepper. Keep hot while you fry remaining eggs in the same way. Garnish with tomato wedges and parsley sprigs and serve hot with toast.

Scrambled egg terrine

Overall timing 1 ¼ hours

Freezing Not suitable

To serve 4

1 ½ lb	Frozen spinach
¾ cup	Butter
	Salt and pepper
¼ tsp	Grated nutmeg
9	Eggs
1 cup	Chopped chicken meat
½ cup	Heavy cream
6 tbsp	Chopped parsley
1 tsp	Mustard

Thaw spinach, then squeeze it dry and chop coarsely. Preheat oven to 375°. Grease a 9x5 inch loaf pan.

Melt ¼ cup butter in a skillet. Add spinach and season with salt, pepper and nutmeg. Cook gently, stirring occasionally, until tender and excess water has evaporated. Cool slightly, then mix in one egg. Set aside.

Purée chicken in a food processor or food mill, adding 1-2 tbsp cream or more to achieve a spreadable consistency. Season with pepper and add half the parsley. Set aside.

Beat remaining eggs with salt, pepper and mustard until well mixed. Stir in remaining parsley. Heat remaining butter in a saucepan. When foam subsides, add eggs and cook gently, stirring, till beginning to set. Stir in remaining cream and transfer immediately to a bowl so that mixture does not continue to cook.

Press half spinach mixture onto bottom of loaf pan. Cover with half scrambled eggs, then with all chicken mixture. Finish with remaining scrambled eggs and then spinach. Cover with foil and bake in a roasting pan ⅓-filled with water for 35-40 minutes till set.

Allow to rest for several minutes before unmolding onto a warmed serving dish. Surround with tomato sauce, if liked.

Anchovy-stuffed eggs

Overall timing 35 minutes

Freezing Not suitable

To serve 4

3 tbsp	Soft bread crumbs
1 tbsp	Milk
4	Hard-cooked eggs
1	Small can of anchovy fillets
3 tbsp	Grated cheese
1	Garlic clove
1 tbsp	Chopped fresh basil
2 tbsp	Oil
2 tbsp	Chopped parsley
	Salt and pepper
2 tbsp	Dried bread crumbs
	Fresh basil

Preheat the oven to 350°.

Soak soft bread crumbs in milk. Shell the eggs and cut in half lengthwise. Reserve whites and put yolks into blender or food processor with the soaked bread crumbs, drained anchovies, cheese, peeled and crushed garlic, basil, half the oil and parsley and seasoning. Process till smooth.

Pipe or spoon a little of the mixture into each reserved half of egg white. Pipe or spread remaining mixture in greased ovenproof dish and place stuffed eggs on top. Sprinkle with dried bread crumbs and remaining parsley and pour rest of oil over. Bake for about 15 minutes. Garnish with sprig of fresh basil and serve hot.

Lettuce and egg pipérade

Overall timing 15 minutes

Freezing Not suitable

To serve 4

1	Onion
1	Small head Boston lettuce
¼ cup	Butter
1 tbsp	Chopped parsley
1 cup	Frozen peas
4	Eggs
	Salt and pepper
1 cup	Hot mashed potatoes

Peel and finely chop the onion. Wash, trim and shred lettuce.

Melt the butter in a skillet. Add onion and cook till transparent. Add shredded lettuce, parsley and peas. Cook, stirring, for 5 minutes.

Lightly beat eggs in a bowl and season. Stir into pan, reduce heat and cook, stirring, until egg is lightly scrambled. Remove from heat and arrange on warmed serving dish.

Pipe or spoon mashed potato around the edge of the dish and serve immediately.

Egg and cheese sandwiches

Overall timing 30 minutes

Freezing Not suitable

To serve 4

1	Small onion
½ cup	Butter
2 oz	Mushrooms
¼ cup	Dry white wine
¼ cup	Chicken broth
	Salt and pepper
¼ lb	Cooked ham
6 oz	Cheddar cheese
8	Slices of bread
	Paprika
4	Eggs

Peel and finely chop onion. Melt 2 tbsp of the butter in a pan and cook onion till transparent. Slice mushrooms, add to pan and cook for 3 minutes. Add wine and broth and cook over a high heat until most of the liquid evaporates. Season with salt and pepper.

Preheat the oven to 400°.

Cut the ham and cheese into thin slices. Butter the bread and place four slices in a shallow ovenproof dish, buttered side down. Divide cheese, ham, mushrooms and onion between them and sprinkle with a little paprika. Cover with remaining bread slices, buttered side up. Bake for 10 minutes until crisp and golden.

Meanwhile, melt remaining butter in a skillet. Break eggs one at a time into a cup, then slide into the pan when butter is frothy. Cook for 2-3 minutes. Remove eggs from pan with an egg slice. Place on top of sandwiches, sprinkle with salt and pepper and serve.

Egg and pea scamble

Overall timing 50 minutes

Freezing Not suitable

To serve 2-4

2 lb	Fresh peas
1	Onion
2 oz	Bacon slices
2 tbsp	Butter
	Salt and pepper
4	Eggs
1 cup	Soft bread crumbs
½ cup	Grated cheese

Shell peas. Peel and thinly slice the onion; dice the bacon. Melt the butter in a saucepan and gently fry the onion and bacon till transparent.

Add the peas and salt and enough water to half cover them. Bring to a boil, then cover and simmer for 15-20 minutes till the peas are tender and most of the liquid has evaporated.

Lightly beat the eggs in a bowl with the bread crumbs, cheese and pepper. Pour over the peas and cook, stirring gently, till the eggs are lightly set. Serve immediately.

Eggs florentine

Overall timing 45 minutes

Freezing Not suitable

To serve 4

2 lb	Bulk spinach
¼ cup	Butter
	Salt
¼ tsp	Grated nutmeg
3 tbsp	Flour
2 cups	Milk
¾ cup	Grated cheese
	Cayenne
½ tsp	Prepared mustard
8	Hard-cooked eggs
2 tbsp	Soft white bread crumbs

Preheat the oven to 425°.

Wash spinach well in several changes of water. Remove any coarse stalks. Put into saucepan with only the water that still clings to the spinach after washing. Cook for 5-10 minutes till tender. Stir in 1 tbsp of the butter and season with salt and grated nutmeg, then spread over the bottom of a greased ovenproof dish.

Melt remaining butter in a pan. Stir in the flour and cook for 1 minute. Gradually add the milk, bring to a boil, stirring, and cook for 2 minutes.

Reserve 2 tbsp of cheese for the topping and stir the rest into the sauce with a pinch each of salt and cayenne and the mustard.

Shell eggs and arrange on top of spinach. Pour sauce over eggs. Mix reserved grated cheese and bread crumbs and sprinkle over the top. Bake for 10 minutes till cheese is bubbly and golden. Serve immediately.

Eggs in a nest

Overall timing 50 minutes

Freezing Not suitable

To serve 4

2 lb	Potatoes
	Salt and pepper
1 cup	Milk
6 tbsp	Butter
8	Eggs
2 tbsp	Dried bread crumbs
	Grated nutmeg
	Parsley

Peel the potatoes. Put into a pan of salted water, bring to a boil and cook for 25 minutes. Drain.

Preheat the oven to 425°. Grease ovenproof dish.

Add milk to the potatoes and return to low heat. Mash the potatoes and beat in 4 tbsp of the butter until smooth and creamy. Season to taste.

Spread creamed potatoes in ovenproof dish. Using the back of a spoon, hollow out eight "nests" for the eggs. Break an egg into each of the "nests." Sprinkle with bread crumbs, dot with remaining butter and season with salt, pepper and nutmeg.

Bake for 8-9 minutes or until the eggs are lightly set. Garnish with parsley.

Eggs with sausages

Overall timing 15 minutes

Freezing Not suitable

To serve 2-4

1 tbsp	Oil
12	Link sausages
2 tbsp	Butter
4	Eggs
3 tbsp	Tomato ketchup
	Pepper

Heat the oil in a skillet. Cook the sausages till golden all over, then remove from the pan.

Melt butter in the pan, break in the eggs and place sausages over whites. Fry for 2-3 minutes, then spoon ketchup around the edge of the pan. Sprinkle with pepper and serve with toast and broiled tomatoes.

Variation

Sprinkle grated cheese over the eggs and sausages and broil until the cheese has melted and is golden brown.

Eggs in mushroom sauce

Overall timing 30 minutes

Freezing Not suitable

To serve 6

¾ lb	Mushrooms
6	Large eggs
1 tbsp	Oil
1	Garlic clove
16 oz	Can of tomatoes
2 tsp	Chopped parsley
	Salt and pepper
¼ cup	Butter
1 cup	Grated cheese
1 tbsp	Flour

Wipe, trim and thickly slice the mushrooms. Hard-cook the eggs for 10 minutes.

Meanwhile, heat the oil in a skillet. Add peeled garlic and fry till golden. Discard garlic. Add the mushrooms and fry over a high heat for 3-4 minutes. Sieve canned tomatoes and their juice and add to the pan with the parsley, salt and pepper. Cook for about 10 minutes.

Cool the eggs quickly by running cold water over them. Cut eggs in half lengthwise. Scoop out yolks and place in a bowl.

Soften the butter. Add to the egg yolks with the cheese, flour and seasoning. Mix well with a fork. Shape the mixture into 12 balls about 1 inch in diameter, using floured hands. Place one ball in each egg half.

Add egg halves to pan and spoon a little sauce over them. Cover and cook for a further 5 minutes. Divide between warmed serving dishes. Serve immediately with crusty bread.

Flamenco eggs

Overall timing 45 minutes

Freezing Not suitable

To serve 4-6

1	Onion
¼ lb	Canadian bacon
2 tbsp	Oil
8 oz	Can of tomatoes
2	Potatoes
1	Small sweet red pepper
2 oz	Green beans
2 tbsp	Frozen peas
2 tbsp	Canned asparagus tips
6 oz	Chorizo or other spicy sausage
3 tbsp	Dry sherry
	Salt and pepper
6	Eggs

Peel and finely chop onion. Dice bacon. Heat oil in a saucepan or flameproof casserole. Add onion and bacon and cook till golden. Add tomatoes, mashing them into the onion/bacon mixture till well combined.

Peel potatoes and cut into small dice. Wash, seed and chop pepper. Wash beans. Top and tail them and remove any strings. Cut into short lengths. Add potatoes, pepper, beans and peas to pan and cook for 10 minutes.

Add asparagus tips, sliced sausage and sherry. Season and cook for a further 5 minutes.

Break eggs carefully on top of the mixture. Cover and cook for 5 minutes more or until the eggs are lightly set.

Roe and egg toasts

Overall timing 30 minutes

Freezing Not suitable

To serve 6

¾ lb	Soft herring roes
	Salt and pepper
6 tbsp	Butter
1 tbsp	Flour
1¼ cups	Milk
2	Anchovy fillets
3	Hard-cooked eggs
1 tbsp	Lemon juice
6	Slices of bread
6 oz	Smoked cod roe

Poach soft roes in boiling salted water for 5 minutes. Drain and chop. Melt 4 tbsp of butter in a pan, stir in flour and cook 1 minute. Stir in milk and bring to a boil.

Pound the anchovy fillets in a bowl. Shell the eggs and cut in half. Sieve the yolks and stir into the sauce with the anchovies, soft roes, lemon juice and seasoning. Heat through.

Preheat the broiler. Toast the bread, spread with remaining butter and arrange on the broiler pan. Spread the soft roe mixture over. Finely chop the egg whites and use to decorate the toast. Cut the smoked cod roe into 12 thin slices and place on toast. Broil for 2-3 minutes till golden. Serve hot.

Egg and ham molds

Overall timing 20 minutes

Freezing Not suitable

To serve 4

¼ cup	Softened butter
6 oz	Cooked ham
8	Eggs
	Salt
1	Tomato

Grease 8 dariole molds with the butter. Finely chop the ham and press onto the bottoms and sides of the molds. Carefully break an egg into each mold and sprinkle with salt.

Put molds into heatproof dish containing a little boiling water, cover and cook for 8-10 minutes till eggs are lightly set.

Run a knife blade around the inside of each mold and invert onto a warmed serving plate. Garnish with tomato slices and serve with a green salad.

Tomatoes and eggs American style

Overall timing 20 minutes

Freezing Not suitable

To serve 4-6

½ lb	Bacon slices
6	Large tomatoes
1 cup	Milk
	Salt and pepper
6	Eggs

Preheat the broiler. Cook the bacon till crisp and golden. Remove and keep hot.

Wipe the tomatoes and cut in half. Place the tomatoes cut sides down on the broiler pan and brush with a little fat from the bacon. Broil about 3 inches below heat for 3-4 minutes.

Meanwhile, pour the milk into a skillet, add a pinch of salt and heat till simmering. Break an egg onto a saucer, then slide it into the milk. Repeat with remaining eggs. Cover and poach for 3 minutes.

Turn the tomatoes over, brush with bacon fat and broil for 2 more minutes. Arrange stalk halves cut sides up in a warmed serving dish and season. Lift the eggs out of the milk with a slotted spoon and drain on paper towels. Place one on each tomato half and cover with the remaining halves. Arrange the bacon around the tomatoes and serve immediately with plenty of hot buttered toast.

Spinach quiche

Overall timing 50 minutes

Freezing Not suitable

To serve 6

1½ cups	Whole wheat pie pastry
2 lb	Bulk spinach
	Salt and pepper
½ tsp	Grated nutmeg
	Bunch of marjoram
¼ lb	Bacon
3 tbsp	Butter
1	Onion
3 tbsp	Raisins
¼ cup	Light cream
6 oz	Mozzarella cheese
1 tbsp	Pine nuts

Preheat oven to 400°. Roll out dough to line 9 inch quiche pan. Bake blind for 30 minutes.

Cook spinach with salt and nutmeg for 10 minutes. Drain and chop. Add marjoram.

Chop bacon; fry in a skillet till crisp. Drain and scatter bacon over pastry case.

Add butter to skillet. Peel and finely chop onion and fry till transparent. Add spinach, 2 tbsp raisins, cream and seasoning. Cook for 5 minutes. Spread in pastry case.

Slice cheese and arrange on top. Sprinkle the rest of raisins and pine nuts over and bake for 10 minutes.

Shrimp scrambled eggs

Overall timing 15 minutes

Freezing Not suitable

To serve 4

¼ cup	Butter
½ lb	Shelled shrimp
8	Large eggs
	Salt and pepper

Melt half the butter in a saucepan, add shrimp and fry gently for 3-4 minutes.

Break the eggs into a bowl, add seasoning and beat lightly with a fork. Pour onto the shrimp and stir gently but evenly till the eggs are lightly set.

Remove from the heat, quickly stir in the remaining butter and season to taste. Divide between warmed serving dishes and serve immediately with hot toast.

Italian shredded omelette

Overall timing 35 minutes

Freezing Not suitable

To serve 4

1	Small onion
1	Garlic clove
1	Stalk of celery
1	Carrot
2 oz	Bacon slices
1 tbsp	Oil
16 oz	Can of tomatoes
	Salt and pepper
9	Eggs
1 tsp	Chopped fresh mint
3 tbsp	Chopped parsley
¼ cup	Butter

Peel and finely chop the onion. Peel and crush the garlic. Trim and chop the celery. Scrape and thinly slice the carrot. Finely chop the bacon.

Heat the oil in a saucepan, add the bacon and vegetables and fry gently for 5 minutes. Add the tomatoes and juice, garlic and seasoning, bring to a boil and simmer for 20 minutes, stirring to break up the tomatoes.

Meanwhile, lightly beat the eggs in a bowl with the mint, parsley and seasoning. Melt one-third of the butter in a skillet. Add one-third of the egg mixture and cook over a moderate heat, drawing the liquid into the center as the mixture begins to set. When set, slide the omelette onto a board. Make two more omelettes in the same way.

Roll the omelettes loosely and cut into strips about ½ inch wide. Add to the tomato sauce and heat through for 3 minutes. Season to taste and pour into a warmed serving dish.

Rolled ham omelette

Overall timing 30 minutes plus chilling

Freezing Not suitable

To serve 4

6	Eggs
1 tbsp	Flour
1 tbsp	Grated Parmesan cheese
2 tbsp	Milk
	Salt
¼ cup	Butter
	Radish roses
Stuffing	
¼ cup	Softened butter
1 tbsp	Mustard
2-3	Pickles
4-6	Slices of cooked ham

Beat the eggs with the flour, cheese, milk and salt to taste. Melt the butter in a skillet, pour in the egg mixture and cook until the omelette is set on the bottom. Slide out of the skillet onto a plate, then return to the skillet upside down to cook the other side. Remove the omelette from the pan and allow to cool.

Beat the butter with the mustard and diced pickles. Spread over the omelette and place the ham slices on top. Roll up the omelette tightly like a jelly roll. Leave in the refrigerator for several hours.

To serve, slice the rolled omelette and arrange on a plate garnished with radish roses.

Spanish omelette torte

Overall timing 50 minutes

Freezing Not suitable

To serve 4

6	Eggs
2 tbsp	Flour
3 tbsp	Milk
2 tbsp	Grated Parmesan cheese
	Salt and pepper
2	Carrots
1 cup	Frozen peas
1	Onion
¼ cup	Butter

Lightly beat the eggs with the flour, milk, cheese and seasoning. Set aside.

Peel and dice the carrots. Cook in a little boiling salted water with the peas until almost tender. Drain well.

Peel and chop the onion. Melt half the butter in a small skillet and fry the onion until golden. Add the carrots and peas and mix well, then add the egg mixture.

Melt the remaining butter in a round, flameproof baking dish. Pour in the egg mixture and cook gently for 20 minutes or until the torte is set on the bottom. Meanwhile, preheat the oven to 400°.

Place the pan in the oven and bake until the torte is set and golden on top. Cool in the pan, then unmold and serve cold.

Minted cheese omelette

Overall timing 20 minutes

Freezing Not suitable

To serve 2

10	Fresh mint leaves
6	Eggs
½ cup	Soft bread crumbs
1 cup	Grated cheese
	Salt and pepper
1 tbsp	Chopped parsley
2 tbsp	Butter

Wash, dry and roughly chop the mint leaves. Lightly beat the eggs in a bowl with the bread crumbs, grated cheese and seasoning. Stir in the parsley and mint and leave to stand for 5 minutes.

Melt the butter in a skillet and pour in the egg mixture (or only half if making two omelettes). Tip the pan so that the bottom is coated and cook over a moderate heat until lightly set.

Using a large spatula, carefully turn the omelette over and cook for 2 minutes more. Serve with tomato salad and whole wheat rolls.

Shrimp omelette in béchamel sauce

Overall timing 40 minutes

Freezing Not suitable

To serve 2

1	Small onion
1	Small carrot
1	Stalk of celery
1 cup	Milk
1	Bay leaf
5 tbsp	Butter
2 tbsp	Flour
6 oz	Shelled shrimp
2 tbsp	Light cream
	Salt and pepper
6	Eggs
2 tsp	Chopped parsley

Peel and roughly chop the onion and carrot. Trim and chop the celery. Put the milk into a saucepan with the bay leaf and prepared vegetables, cover and bring to a boil. Remove from heat and leave to infuse for 10 minutes.

Melt ¼ cup of the butter in a saucepan, add the flour and cook for 1 minute. Gradually add the strained milk and bring to a boil, stirring constantly. Cook, stirring, for 2 minutes. Reduce heat, stir in shrimp, cream and seasoning. Heat without boiling.

Lightly beat the eggs in a bowl with a pinch of salt. Melt remaining butter in a skillet, pour in the eggs and cook until set.

Spoon half the shrimp sauce into the centre of the omelette and fold two sides over. Turn out of pan, placing join side down on warmed serving dish. Pour the remaining sauce around. Make a cut along the top of the omelette to expose the filling, sprinkle the parsley over and serve immediately with a tossed green salad.

Liver omelette

Overall timing 15 minutes

Freezing Not suitable

To serve 4

¼ lb	Chicken livers
½ cup	Butter
2	Sage leaves
	Salt and pepper
3 tbsp	Marsala or sherry wine
8	Eggs
	Sprigs of parsley

Trim, wipe and finely chop the livers.

Melt 2 tbsp of the butter in a saucepan and add livers. Chop sage and add to pan with seasoning. Stir-fry for 5 minutes. Pour Marsala or sherry wine over and cook till it has almost evaporated. Remove pan from heat.

Beat eggs in a bowl with a little seasoning. Melt a quarter of the remaining butter in an omelette pan or small skillet. When it begins to foam, pour in a quarter of the egg mixture. Tilt pan so mixture runs evenly over the bottom. As the omelette begins to set underneath, place a quarter of the liver mixture along the center and fold the sides of the omelette over the filling.

Slide omelette onto a warmed serving dish and keep hot. Make three more omelettes in the same way. Garnish with parsley and serve with sauté potatoes.

Chervil omelette

Overall timing 15 minutes

Freezing Not suitable

To serve 4

8	Eggs
	Salt and pepper
3 tbsp	Chopped fresh chervil
1 tbsp	Chopped parsley
¼ cup	Butter

Break the eggs into a bowl. Season with salt and pepper, add herbs and beat together lightly.

Melt one-quarter of the butter in an omelette pan over a high heat. When the butter begins to froth, pour in a quarter of the egg mixture. As the omelette starts to set, run a spatula around the edge to loosen it and tilt pan to let uncooked egg run underneath. When firm at the edges but still runny in the center, fold omelette over and slide onto a warmed serving plate. Keep it hot while you make three more omelettes in the same way. Serve with a tomato salad.

Omelette forestière

Overall timing 25 minutes

Freezing Not suitable

To serve 2

¼ lb	Thick bacon slices
¼ lb	Button mushrooms
2	Small potatoes
2 tbsp	Butter
4-6	Eggs
1 tbsp	Chopped parsley
	Salt and pepper

Cut bacon into thin strips. Thinly slice mushrooms. Peel and thinly slice potatoes. Melt the butter in a skillet, add potatoes and bacon and fry till tender and golden all over. Add mushrooms and cook for 5 minutes more.

Meanwhile, lightly beat the eggs in a bowl with parsley and seasoning. Pour over the ingredients in the skillet. Cook for a few minutes, lifting the edges to ensure the underneath is evenly cooked. Fold over and slide onto warmed serving plate. Serve immediately.

Deviled liver omelette

Overall timing 20 minutes

Freezing Not suitable

To serve 2

2	Bacon slices
¼ lb	Chicken livers
	Salt and pepper
1 tbsp	Flour
2 oz	Mushrooms
1 tsp	Tomato paste
½ tsp	Worcestershire sauce
½ tsp	Dijon-style mustard
2 tbsp	Butter
6	Eggs
1 tsp	Chopped chives

Chop the bacon. Trim and chop the livers and toss in seasoned flour. Slice the mushrooms.

Cook the bacon in a saucepan till light brown. Add the chicken livers and stir-fry till browned. Add the mushrooms, tomato paste, Worcestershire sauce, mustard and seasoning. Mix well, then cover and cook for 3 minutes.

Heat the butter in a skillet. Lightly beat the eggs with seasoning and add to pan. Cook until almost set, then spoon the liver mixture over and sprinkle with the chives. Fold omelette, cut in half and place on two warmed plates. Serve hot with whole wheat bread and a tomato and cucumber salad.

Anchovy brochettes

Overall timing 30 minutes

Freezing Not suitable

To serve 2

4	Large slices of white bread
¼ lb	Mozzarella or Gouda cheese
6 tbsp	Butter
	Salt and pepper
8	Anchovy fillets
¼ cup	Milk

Preheat the oven to 400°.

Cut bread and cheese into small squares. Thread alternately onto four skewers. Arrange in an ovenproof dish so that each end of the skewer is supported by the rim.

Melt half of the butter and brush generously over the brochettes. Season with salt and pepper. Bake for about 15-20 minutes, basting occasionally with butter in dish. The brochettes should be golden brown.

Meanwhile, melt remaining butter in a saucepan. Mash anchovies and add to butter. Gradually add milk and mix well together over gentle heat. Bring to boiling point.

Pour hot anchovy sauce over brochettes and serve immediately.

Welsh rarebit

Overall timing 30 minutes

Freezing Not suitable

To serve 4

8	Slices of bread
6 tbsp	Butter
¾ lb	Cheddar cheese
½ tsp	Ground mace
	Pinch of powdered mustard
5 tbsp	Beer
	Pepper

Preheat the oven to 400°.

Toast the bread, and butter the slices while still hot. Place on baking sheet.

Cut the cheese into small cubes and put in a saucepan with mace, mustard and beer. Cook over a low heat, stirring with a wooden spoon, until cheese melts and is thick and creamy. Spread mixture over toast. Sprinkle generously with pepper and bake for 10 minutes. Serve immediately.

Cheese quiche

Overall timing 1 ½ hours

Freezing Suitable: reheat in 425° oven for 10-15 minutes

To serve 4-6

½ cup+2 tbsp	Butter
¾ cup	Water
	Salt and pepper
2 cups	Self-rising flour
2	Medium-size onions
1 tbsp	Flour
½ cup	Milk
3	Eggs
¼ tsp	Grated nutmeg
	Cayenne
1 cup	Grated Cheddar cheese
1 cup	Grated Gruyère cheese

Melt ½ cup of the butter. Cool slightly, then stir in 3 tbsp of the water and salt. Sift self-rising flour into a bowl. Slowly add butter mixture and mix until smooth. Chill for 30 minutes.

Preheat the oven to 350°.

Peel and chop onions. Melt remaining butter in a saucepan and fry onions for 10 minutes until soft. Cool.

Mix 1 tbsp flour and a little of the milk in a bowl, then add the rest of the milk and the remaining water. Separate the eggs. Mix the yolks into the flour and milk mixture. Season with salt, pepper, nutmeg and a pinch of cayenne. Beat egg whites till stiff, then fold into yolk mixture.

Roll out dough and use to line a greased 9 inch quiche or flan pan. Spread onions over bottom of pastry case then sprinkle both sorts of cheese on top. Cover with egg and milk mixture.

Bake for 15 minutes. Reduce heat to 325° and bake for a further 45 minutes. Serve hot.

Cheeseburgers

Overall timing 30 minutes

Freezing Not suitable

To serve 4

1	Large onion
1 lb	Ground beef
3 tbsp	Soft bread crumbs
¼ cup	Milk
	Salt
	Paprika
1 tsp	Powdered mustard
	Oil
4	Small tomatoes
4	Slices of Cheddar cheese
4	Buns

Preheat the broiler or a charcoal grill.

Peel and finely chop onion. In a large bowl, mix together the onion, ground beef, bread crumbs and milk. Season with salt, a pinch of paprika and mustard. Leave for 10 minutes.

Make 4 hamburgers from the mixture. Brush with oil. Broil for 5 minutes on each side.

Remove from heat. Top the burgers with slices of tomato and strips of cheese. Put back under the broiler till the cheese melts. Serve in warm buns.

Cheese soufflé

Overall timing 45 minutes

Freezing Not suitable

To serve 4-6

6 tbsp	Butter
4	Eggs
½ cup	Cornstarch
2½ cups	Milk
	Salt and pepper
	Paprika
	Grated nutmeg
1 cup	Grated Gruyère, Parmesan or sharp Cheddar cheese

Preheat the oven to 400°.

Grease a 7 inch diameter soufflé dish with 2 tbsp of the butter, and tie with paper collar if liked. Separate the eggs.

Melt the remaining butter in a saucepan, stir in cornstarch and cook for 1 minute. Gradually add the milk, and bring to the boil, stirring all the time until the sauce thickens. Season with salt and pepper and a pinch of both paprika and grated nutmeg. Take pan off heat and allow mixture to cool slightly.

Stir the cheese into sauce. Add egg yolks one at a time to the sauce, beating well.

In a large bowl, beat egg whites till they hold stiff peaks, then carefully fold into the sauce with a metal spoon.

Pour soufflé mixture into prepared dish. Bake for about 25 minutes or until risen and golden. Remove from oven and serve immediately with a crisp green salad, dressed with herb vinaigrette.

Cheesy tapioca fritters

Overall timing 1 hour

Freezing Not suitable

To serve 6

1	Medium-size onion
⅔ cup	Flaked tapioca
4 cups	Milk
1	Bay leaf
	Salt and pepper
3	Eggs
1½ cups	Grated cheese
½ tsp	Powdered mustard
	Oil for deep frying
	Sprigs of parsley

Peel and finely chop the onion. Put into a saucepan with the tapioca, milk and bay leaf. Season and bring to a boil, stirring. Cook for about 30 minutes, stirring occasionally, till thick and creamy. Remove from the heat.

Separate the eggs and beat the yolks one at a time into the mixture. Add the cheese to the mixture with mustard. Mix well and leave to cool.

Heat oil in a deep-fryer to 340°.

Beat the egg whites till stiff but not dry, then fold into the tapioca mixture with a metal spoon. Drop a few large spoonfuls of the mixture into the oil and fry for 3-4 minutes till crisp and golden. Drain on paper towels. Keep hot until all the mixture is cooked. Sprinkle with salt and serve hot, garnished with parsley.

Croque monsieur

Overall timing 20 minutes

Freezing Not suitable

To serve 4

8	Slices of bread
	Butter
8	Slices of Gruyère or Cheddar cheese
4	Slices of cooked ham
	Extra grated cheese (optional)

Preheat the broiler.

Butter four slices of bread. Place a slice of cheese on each of the unbuttered slices of bread. Cover with the ham, then top with the rest of the sliced cheese. Place the buttered bread on top, buttered sides up.

Broil the sandwiches, buttered sides up, until golden brown. Turn and spread the other sides with butter. Continue broiling until golden. Sprinkle with a little extra grated cheese, if liked, and broil until the cheese has melted.

Variation

For a Croque Milady, add sliced tomato to the sandwich and top with fried eggs.

Gnocchi

Overall timing 50 minutes plus cooling

Freezing Suitable: bake from frozen, allowing 1 hour

To serve 4

1 quart	Milk
1 cup	Coarse semolina
	Salt and pepper
	Grated nutmeg
1½ cups	Grated Parmesan cheese
1	Egg yolk
2 tbsp	Milk

Heat milk just to boiling in a saucepan, then sprinkle on semolina. Season with salt, pepper and nutmeg. Cook gently, stirring, for 4-5 minutes till mixture becomes solid. Remove pan from heat and beat in 1 cup of the cheese. Pour into a greased jelly roll pan. Leave in a cool place (not the refrigerator) for 45 minutes to 1 hour till cold.

Preheat the oven to 400°.

Cut the cooled mixture into about 20 rounds, 2½ inches in diameter. Arrange the rounds, overlapping them, in a greased round ovenproof dish. Beat egg yolk and milk and pour over. Sprinkle with the rest of the cheese and bake for 30 minutes till golden brown. Serve immediately.

Gougère

Overall timing 1 ½ hours

Freezing Not suitable

To serve 6

1 cup	Water
½ tsp	Salt
½ cup	Butter
⅔ cup	Flour
4	Eggs
½ lb	Gruyère cheese

Preheat oven to 400°.

Put water and salt into a saucepan with 6 tbsp of the butter, chopped. Bring to a boil, stirring to melt the butter. Remove from heat and quickly add the flour all at once, stirring well. Return pan to heat and beat till the paste is smooth and leaves the sides of the pan cleanly. Remove from heat and allow to cool slightly.

Add three of the eggs, one at a time, beating well between additions. Grate 1¼ cups of the cheese and stir into the paste.

With a large spoon, make a ring of the paste on a greased baking sheet. Beat the remaining egg and brush over paste. Dice remaining cheese and place on top of the paste with tiny pieces of the remaining butter.

Bake for 20 minutes, then lower heat to 375°, and bake for a further 20-25 minutes. Serve hot.

Deep-fried Mozzarella sandwiches

Overall timing 20 minutes

Freezing Not suitable

To serve 4

8	Slices of bread
4	Slices of Mozzarella cheese
	Flour
1	Egg
	Oil for deep frying

Remove the crusts from the bread. Make four sandwiches with the cheese and coat lightly and evenly with flour. Beat the egg in a shallow dish. Dip in the sandwiches so the sides and edges are all coated.

Heat oil in a deep-fryer to 360°. Deep fry the sandwiches until they are golden brown. Drain on paper towels and serve hot, with salad.

Italian deep-fried cheese

Overall timing 1 ¼ hours plus chilling

Freezing Not suitable

To serve 2

½	Onion
2 tbsp	Butter
¼ cup	Long grain rice
½ cup	Chicken broth
1 tsp	Grated Parmesan cheese
	Pinch of grated nutmeg
	Salt and pepper
1 oz	Lean cooked ham
1 ½ oz	Mozzarella cheese
1	Egg
½ cup	Fine soft bread crumbs
	Oil for deep frying

Peel and finely chop onion. Melt butter in a saucepan and fry onion till transparent.

Add rice and stir over a low heat for 2 minutes. Stir in broth, cover and bring to a boil. Simmer gently for 15-20 minutes till rice is tender. Remove from heat and stir in Parmesan, nutmeg and seasoning. Leave to cool completely.

Meanwhile chop ham finely. Cut Mozzarella into four sticks about 1 ½ inches long and ½ inch thick. Break egg onto a plate and beat lightly with a fork. Spread bread crumbs on another plate.

Beat a little egg and the ham into rice. Put 2 tbsp rice mixture in palm of one hand. Place a cheese stick on top and cover with more rice. Pat into a cylinder shape about 2½ inches long and 1 inch thick. Brush beaten egg over croquette, then coat with bread crumbs. Shape and coat three more croquettes. Chill for 1 hour.

Heat oil in a deep fryer to 360°. Fry the croquettes for 5-6 minutes till golden. Drain on paper towels and serve hot.

Sauerkraut cheese rolls

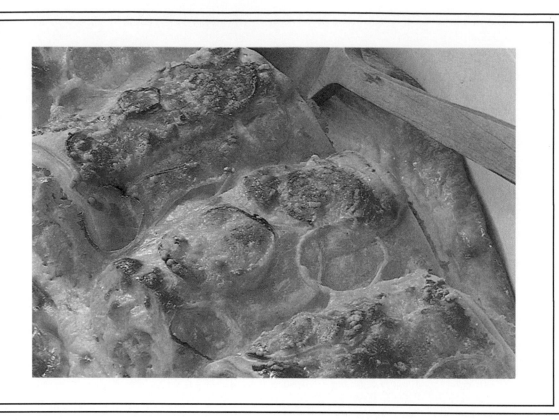

Overall timing 1 ½ hours

Freezing Not suitable

To serve 6

2 cups	Flour
	Salt
½ lb (1 cup)	Cream cheese
½ cup + 2 tbsp	Butter
2	Eggs
¾ cup	Sour cream
	Grated nutmeg
1	Small onion
¾ cup	Grated cheese
Filling	
¼ lb	Slab bacon
1 lb	Can of sauerkraut
1 tbsp	Sugar
	Salt and pepper
1	Bay leaf

Sift flour and salt into bowl and rub in cream cheese and ½ cup butter. Knead till smooth, then chill for 30 minutes.

Meanwhile, for the filling, chop bacon. Place in saucepan and cook till golden, then add sauerkraut, sugar, seasoning and bay leaf. Cover and cook gently for 30 minutes. Remove bay leaf. Cool.

Preheat oven to 400°.

Roll out dough to rectangle 18x10 inches. Spoon filling over dough, leaving border. Beginning at long edge, roll up, then cut roll into six smaller rolls. Arrange rolls in greased ovenproof dish.

Beat eggs with sour cream, salt and nutmeg. Pour over the rolls. Peel and slice onion. Top rolls with onion rings, cheese and remaining butter. Bake for 40 minutes.

Three-cheese savories

Overall timing 10 minutes plus chilling

Freezing Not suitable

To serve 6

¼ lb	Danish blue cheese
3	Petits suisses cheeses
1 cup	Grated Gruyère cheese
2 tbsp	Chopped fresh herbs
1⅓ cups	Dried bread crumbs

Mash Danish blue and Petits suisses cheeses together in a bowl with a fork. Add Gruyère to bowl with herbs. Mix well together.

Shape into flat cakes or cylinders and coat in bread crumbs. Place on a plate and chill for 3 hours before serving with toast, crisp crackers or French bread.

Variation

Use a mixture of cream and cottage cheeses, and flavor with 2 cloves of crushed garlic crushed with salt. Make into shapes (use cookie cutters) and coat in bread crumbs or finely chopped parsley. Or use prepared pepper for steak which is a combination of pepper and mustard. Chill as above before serving.

Individual cauliflower cheeses

Overall timing 35 minutes

Freezing Not suitable

To serve 6

1	Small cauliflower
	Salt and pepper
15 oz	Can of artichoke hearts
2 tbsp	Butter
Cheese sauce	
2 tbsp	Butter
2 tbsp	Flour
1 cup	Milk
1 cup	Grated Gruyère or Cheddar cheese

Preheat the oven to 425°.

Divide cauliflower into small florets. Cut away any large stalks. Cook in boiling salted water for about 10 minutes or till tender. Drain.

Drain the artichoke hearts. Put in another saucepan with the butter and heat through gently.

To make the sauce, melt butter in a saucepan. Stir in the flour and cook for 1 minute. Gradually add the milk. Bring to a boil, stirring. Cook gently for 3-4 minutes. Remove from heat and add pepper and half of the cheese.

Put the artichoke hearts in a greased ovenproof dish. Top each with a cauliflower floret. Pour over the sauce. Sprinkle on remaining cheese. Bake for about 10 minutes until the cheese has melted.

Cheese puffs

Overall timing 1 ½ hours

Freezing Suitable

Makes 15

¾ lb	Frozen puff pastry
1½ cups	Water
6 tbsp	Butter
	Salt
1 cup	Flour
3	Eggs
¾ cup	Grated sharp cheese
6 tbsp	Finely chopped cooked ham
1	Egg yolk
1 tbsp	Milk

Thaw the pastry. Put water, butter and a pinch of salt in a saucepan and heat gently till butter has melted. Bring to a boil, and add sifted flour all at once. Beat vigorously with a wooden spoon until smooth and paste leaves the sides of the pan clean. Remove from heat, cool slightly, then add eggs one at a time. Beat in cheese.

Preheat the oven to 400°.

Roll out puff pastry on a floured surface to about ¼ inch thickness. Cut out 15 rounds with a 3-inch round cookie cutter. Place on a dampened baking sheet. Put a little ham in the center of each pastry round.

Put cheese paste into a pastry bag and pipe a swirl on top of each pastry round. Beat egg yolk and milk in a cup and brush over surface of puffs. Bake for just under 1 hour. Serve hot.

Basque cod casserole

Overall timing 1 hour

Freezing Not suitable

To serve 4-6

1 lb	Cod fillets
	Bouquet garni
	Salt and pepper
4	Large potatoes
2	Hard-cooked eggs
3	Tomatoes
6 tbsp	Butter
3	Garlic cloves
⅓ cup	Ripe olives
2 tbsp	Capers
1 tbsp	Chopped parsley
2 tbsp	Lemon juice

Place cod in a saucepan and cover with water. Add bouquet garni and seasoning and bring slowly to a boil. Remove pan from heat and leave to cool.

Meanwhile, cook unpeeled potatoes in boiling salted water for 30 minutes. Drain well, then peel and slice potatoes. Shell and slice eggs. Blanch, peel and chop tomatoes.

Melt 2 tbsp butter in a pan and fry tomatoes. Season with salt and pepper.

Preheat the oven to 400°.

Arrange egg slices around side of greased soufflé dish and make layers of the potatoes, drained and chopped fish, and the peeled and crushed garlic. Spread tomatoes over top. Dot with remaining butter and bake for 20 minutes.

Garnish with ripe olives, capers and chopped parsley and sprinkle with lemon juice. Serve hot or cold.

Baked cod with rosemary

Overall timing 45 minutes

Freezing Not suitable

To serve 4-6

2½lb	Tail piece of cod
¼ cup	Oil
8	Anchovy fillets
	Fresh rosemary
4	Basil leaves (optional)
2 tbsp	Dried bread crumbs
	Salt and pepper

Ask your fish man to remove bones from cod, leaving two halves attached at one side. Scale fish, using a descaler or the blunt side of a knife.

Preheat the oven to 350°.

Heat half the oil in a flameproof casserole, add the chopped anchovies and heat through. Mash anchovies well, then transfer to a bowl. Put a little of the mashed anchovy mixture inside the fish, together with a few sprigs of fresh rosemary and the basil leaves, if using.

Place fish in the casserole and pour the remaining anchovy mixture and oil over. Add a little more rosemary and sprinkle with bread crumbs, salt and pepper. Bake for about 30 minutes till the fish is cooked and the top is golden. Serve with boiled potatoes and a green vegetable or salad.

Broiled cod with bacon

Overall timing 25 minutes

Freezing Not suitable

To serve 2

2	Large cod fillets
2 tbsp	Oil
	Salt and pepper
2 oz	Thin bacon slices
2 tbsp	Butter
1 tbsp	Lemon juice
	Sprigs of parsley
	Lemon wedges

Preheat the broiler.

Brush the cod fillets with oil and season with salt and pepper. Place under the broiler and cook for about 15 minutes, turning fillets over halfway through cooking time.

Meanwhile, broil or fry bacon. Drain on paper towels. Melt the butter in a small saucepan, taking care not to color it. Arrange the fish and bacon on warmed serving plates. Pour the butter over and sprinkle with lemon juice. Garnish with parsley sprigs and lemon wedges. Serve with boiled potatoes tossed in butter and sprinkled with chopped parsley, and a crisp lettuce salad.

Cod croquettes

Overall timing 45 minutes

Freezing Suitable: bake cooked croquettes from frozen in 375° oven for 30 minutes

To serve 4-6

1 lb	Cooked cod fillets
2 cups	Mashed potatoes
	Salt and pepper
	Grated nutmeg
1	Egg
	Dried bread crumbs
	Oil for deep frying
	Lettuce leaves
1	Lemon

Finely grind cod, or blend in a food processor until coarse-fine then mix with potatoes in a large bowl. Season well with salt, pepper and a pinch of nutmeg. Make small round or oval shapes of the mixture.

Lightly beat egg in a bowl. Dip croquettes in egg, then bread crumbs.

Heat oil in deep-fryer to 360°. Add croquettes and fry for about 5 minutes till golden. Remove croquettes and drain on paper towels. Pile them up on a bed of lettuce with pieces of lemon between. Serve with tomato sauce.

Cod with onions and leeks

Overall timing 35 minutes

Freezing Not suitable

To serve 4-6

1¾ lb	Cod fillets
3 tbsp	Lemon juice
	Salt
2	Large onions
2	Leeks
3 tbsp	Oil
¾ cup	Dry hard cider
2 tbsp	Chopped parsley

Place cod fillets in a bowl with lemon juice and salt.

Peel and chop onions. Trim and chop leeks. Heat oil in a skillet and cook onions and leeks gently till softened.

Add cod fillets, with any juices, and cider to pan, cover and simmer for 15 minutes till fish is cooked through. Sprinkle with parsley before serving with mashed potatoes.

Mustard-topped cod

Overall timing 25 minutes

Freezing Not suitable

To serve 4

1¾ lb	Cod fillets
1	Onion
1 tbsp	Vinegar
1	Bay leaf
6	Peppercorns
6 tbsp	Butter
2 tbsp	Powdered English mustard
1 tsp	Sea-salt
	Sprigs of parsley
	Lemon slices

Cut cod into large pieces. Place in a skillet and cover with water. Peel and halve the onion and add to the pan with the vinegar, bay leaf and peppercorns. Bring to a boil over a high heat, cover, then simmer for 10 minutes.

Melt the butter with the mustard and salt in a small saucepan. Mix well and simmer for 2-3 minutes, being careful not to let mixture stick or burn.

Remove pieces of cod from the saucepan with a slotted spoon and place on a warmed serving plate. Spoon a little of the mustard mixture onto each piece of fish or serve in a separate dish. Garnish with a few sprigs of parsley and lemon slices. Serve with plain boiled rice and peas.

Whiting curls

Overall timing 50 minutes

Freezing Not suitable

To serve 2

2	Small whiting
	Salt and pepper
¼ cup	Flour
	Oil for deep frying
1	Lemon
	Sprigs of parsley

Scale and dry the whiting. Place one on its side on a board and hold it firmly by the tail. Using a sharp knife in a sawing action cut between the flesh and backbone to just behind the head.

Turn the fish over and repeat the action on the other side to expose the backbone. Cut off the backbone just behind the head with kitchen scissors. Repeat with the other whiting.

Curl fish, pushing tail through skin at far side of mouth to hold in place. Lightly coat each fish with seasoned flour. Shake off any excess.

Heat the oil in a deep-fryer to 340°. Fry the whiting for about 10 minutes till tender and golden brown. Drain on paper towels and arrange the fish on a warmed serving dish. Garnish with lemon and parsley and serve immediately, with tartare sauce.

Hake au gratin

Overall timing 30 minutes

Freezing Not suitable

To serve 4

1	Small onion
2 tbsp	Chopped parsley
1¾lb	Hake steaks
	Salt and pepper
	Grated nutmeg
2 tbsp	Lemon juice
2 tbsp	Butter
1 cup	Grated cheese
1 cup	Soft bread crumbs

Preheat oven to 375°.

Peel and chop onion and place in a shallow ovenproof dish with half the parsley and the fish steaks. Season with salt and pepper and a pinch of nutmeg. Sprinkle the lemon juice over the fish and dot with butter. Mix the cheese with the bread crumbs and remaining parsley. Sprinkle over the fish. Bake for about 20 minutes.

Remove from oven and baste with liquid in dish. Bake for another 10 minutes until topping is golden. Serve immediately with baked potatoes.

Halibut with spicy sauce

Overall timing 1 hour

Freezing Not suitable

To serve 4

4	Onions
4-6	Garlic cloves
1 lb	Tomatoes
1	Lemon
¼ cup	Oil
¼ tsp	Cayenne
4	Halibut steaks
	Salt
	Chopped parsley

Peel and slice onions. Peel and crush garlic. Blanch, peel and chop tomatoes. Cut four thin slices from lemon and squeeze juice from remainder.

Heat oil in a saucepan. Add onions, garlic and tomatoes and cook gently for about 25 minutes.

Add cayenne and mix in well. Place fish steaks on top of mixture in pan. Sprinkle with salt and lemon juice, cover with lid and cook for a further 15 minutes, turning the fish steaks once.

Arrange fish steaks on a bed of boiled rice on warmed serving dish. Spoon tomato mixture on top and garnish with lemon slices and chopped parsley.

Baked fish

Overall timing 1 hour

Freezing Not suitable

To serve 4

3 lb	Piece of halibut or other white fish
1	Strip of bacon fat
¼ cup	Butter
	Salt and pepper
4	Bacon slices
1	Large can of imported flageolet beans
¼ tsp	Dried sage
¾ cup	Chicken broth

Preheat the oven to 425°.

Roll up the fish and tie as you would a piece of beef, with the bacon fat wrapped around. Reserve a pat of butter and use half of the rest to grease a roasting pan. Place fish in it. Dot with more butter, season, then bake for 30 minutes.

Chop bacon. Melt reserved pat of butter in saucepan and fry bacon till crisp. Drain can of beans and add to pan with sage and broth. Cook over a low heat for 10 minutes. Put fish on a warmed serving plate. Arrange beans and bacon around fish and serve with parsleyed new potatoes.

Fish and chips

Overall timing 35 minutes plus
30 minutes soaking

Freezing Not suitable

To serve 4

2lb	Waxy potatoes
2	Whole flounder, halved and boned
	Salt and pepper
¼ cup	Flour
	Oil for frying
	Lemon wedges
	Sprigs of parsley
Coating batter	
2 cups	Flour
½ tsp	Salt
2	Eggs
2 tbsp	Oil
6 tbsp	Cold water

Peel the potatoes and cut into chips (french fries). Soak in cold water for 30 minutes.

Wipe the fish. Season the flour and lightly coat the fish.

To make the batter, sift flour and salt into a bowl. Separate eggs. Add yolks, oil and water to flour and beat till smooth.

Heat oil in a deep-fryer to 360°. Drain the chips and dry well. Fry, in batches, for 4-5 minutes till tender but not brown. Remove and drain on paper towels.

Reduce the temperature of the oil to 340°. Beat the egg whites till stiff but not dry and fold into the batter. Coat the fish with batter.

Fry the fish, one at a time if necessary, for 2-3 minutes each side till crisp and golden. Drain on paper towels and keep hot, uncovered.

Increase the temperature of the oil to 360° again, put the chips in the basket and fry till crisp and golden. Drain on paper towels and pile into a warmed serving dish.

Garnish fish with lemon wedges and sprigs of parsley. Serve immediately.

Fried flounder

Overall timing 30 minutes

Freezing Not suitable

To serve 6

6 tbsp	Unsalted butter
2 tbsp	Chopped parsley
1 tbsp	Lemon juice
	Salt and pepper
3 tbsp	Flour
3	Whole flounder, halved and boned
2	Eggs
1 ⅓ cups	Dried bread crumbs
	Oil for frying
	Lemon slices
	Sprigs of parsley

Mash the butter with the chopped parsley and lemon juice. Shape into a roll and chill.

Season the flour and lightly coat the fish. Beat the eggs in a shallow dish. Spread the bread crumbs on a plate. Dip the fish into the egg so that it covers both sides. Dip into the crumbs, pressing them on lightly till evenly coated.

Heat the oil in a large skillet and add two or three of the coated fillets, skin side up. Fry gently for 3-5 minutes, then turn the fish carefully and cook for a further 3-5 minutes till the fish is tender and the coating crisp. Lift out of the pan with a spatula and drain on paper towels. Arrange on a warmed serving platter and keep hot while the rest of the fish is cooked.

Garnish with slices of parsley butter, lemon slices and sprigs of parsley. Serve with sauté potatoes.

Baked fish au gratin

Overall timing 45 minutes

Freezing Not suitable

To serve 4

1 ½ lb	Flounder fillets
1	Small onion
2	Tomatoes
1 tbsp	Olive oil
2	Bay leaves
	Salt and pepper
1 tbsp	Chopped parsley
¾ cup	Dry white wine or milk
¼ cup	Grated cheese
3 tbsp	Dried bread crumbs
2 tbsp	Butter

Preheat the oven to 350°.

Remove the skin from the fish fillets. Peel and finely chop the onion; blanch, peel and slice the tomatoes.

Sprinkle the oil into a shallow baking dish and add the chopped onion. Arrange half the fish fillets on top with the sliced tomatoes and bay leaves. Sprinkle with salt, pepper and the chopped parsley. Cover with the remaining fish. Pour the white wine or milk over. Sprinkle the cheese on top with the bread crumbs. Dot with the butter. Bake for about 25 minutes till golden brown on top. Serve immediately with creamed potatoes and green beans.

Skate with capers

Overall timing 25 minutes

Freezing Not suitable

To serve 2

2x½lb	Pieces of skate
	Salt and pepper
1½ tsp	Vinegar
3 tbsp	Butter
1 tbsp	Capers
1 tbsp	Chopped parsley
1½ tbsp	Lemon juice
2 tbsp	Light cream

Put the skate into a saucepan. Cover with cold water and add a little salt and a few drops of vinegar. Bring to a boil, then remove from the heat, cover and leave to stand for 10 minutes.

Drain and dry the skate; remove the skin. Place on a warmed serving dish and keep hot.

Melt the butter in a small saucepan and stir in remaining vinegar, the capers, parsley, lemon juice, cream and seasoning. Cook for 2-3 minutes, without boiling, till heated through. Pour over the skate. Serve with boiled or steamed potatoes and a tossed green salad.

Broiled herrings with parsley butter

Overall timing 20 minutes

Freezing Not suitable

To serve 4

½ cup	Unsalted butter
2 tbsp	Chopped parsley
1 tbsp	Lemon juice
4	Cleaned whole fresh herrings
1 tbsp	Oil
	Salt and pepper
1	Lemon
	Sprigs of parsley

Mash butter with chopped parsley and lemon juice. Form into a roll, wrap in wax paper and chill till ready to use.

Preheat a charcoal broiler.

Brush herrings with oil and season. Place on broiler and cook for 7 minutes on each side.

Arrange herrings on serving plate. Garnish with lemon, pats of chilled butter and parsley sprigs.

Fishermen's herrings

Overall timing 35 minutes plus chilling

Freezing Not suitable

To serve 6

12	Smoked herring fillets
1	Onion
4	Small gherkins
4 oz	Can of herring roes
1 tbsp	Dijon-style mustard
½ cup	Oil
	Pepper

Put the herring fillets into a bowl, cover with boiling water and leave for 20 minutes.

Drain herring fillets, rinse and dry on paper towels. Peel onion and cut into thin rings. Slice gherkins.

Drain and chop the roes and put into a bowl with the mustard. Beat to a smooth paste with a wooden spoon. Gradually trickle in all but 2 tbsp of the oil, beating well after each addition. Add pepper to taste.

Spread roe sauce over bottom of a serving dish and arrange herring fillets on top. Brush with remaining oil and decorate with onion rings and gherkins. Chill for at least 30 minutes, then serve with potato and beet salads garnished with snipped chives.

Herrings with mustard sauce

Overall timing 20 minutes

Freezing Not suitable

To serve 4

4	Cleaned fresh whole herrings
2 tbsp	Oil
2 tbsp	Flour
	Salt and pepper
Sauce	
2 tbsp	Butter
1 tbsp	Flour
1¼ cups	Fish or chicken broth
½ tsp	Pepper
1 tbsp	Prepared mustard
2 tbsp	Light cream

Preheat a charcoal broiler.

Wash herrings and pat dry on paper towels. Brush with oil and coat lightly with seasoned flour. Broil for 7 minutes on each side.

Meanwhile, make the sauce. Melt the butter in a saucepan. Stir in the flour and cook for 1 minute. Add the broth, bring to a boil and cook, stirring, for 3 minutes. Add pepper. Remove from heat and stir in mustard and cream. Arrange herrings on warmed serving plates and spoon mustard sauce over.

Poached kippers

Overall timing 20 minutes

Freezing Not suitable

To serve 4

8	Kipper fillets
6 tbsp	Butter
2 tsp	Lemon juice
½ tsp	Pepper
	Sprigs of parsley
	Lemon wedges

Place kipper fillets in a large saucepan with the skins facing up. Cover with cold water and slowly bring to a boil.

As soon as the water boils, remove from heat, drain well and place on a warmed serving dish with the skin side down. Garnish with parsley.

Melt the butter and stir in the lemon juice and pepper. Pour over kippers at the table and serve with boiled new potatoes and lemon wedges.

Marinated kipper fillets

Overall timing 15 minutes plus marination

Freezing Not suitable

To serve 6

1	Carrot
2	Onions
1 lb	Kipper fillets
	Sprigs of thyme
4-5	Bay leaves
4-5	Cloves
½ cup	Oil
¼ cup	Wine vinegar or lemon juice

Peel and slice the carrot and onions. Place kipper fillets in a glass or pottery bowl, layered with slices of carrot, onion rings, sprigs of fresh thyme, bay leaves and cloves. Pour oil and wine vinegar or lemon juice over and leave for 24 hours in a cool place.

Serve with potato and onion salad, or bread.

Rollmops

Overall timing 6 days

Freezing Not suitable

To serve 4

4	Filleted fresh herrings
1 quart	Water
1 cup	Salt
2 tbsp	Capers
2	Onions
1	Large gherkin
4 tsp	Prepared mustard
Marinade	
1¼ cups	Cider vinegar
1¼ cups	Water
1	Bay leaf
10	Black peppercorns
2	Cloves
5	Juniper berries
1 tsp	Mustard seed

Soak herrings in half water and salt for 24 hours. Drain and repeat.

Put all marinade ingredients into a pan. Bring to a boil and boil for 5 minutes. Cool.

Chop capers. Peel onions and slice. Quarter gherkin lengthwise. Drain and rinse herrings. Lay skin down, spread with mustard, cover with capers, onion and gherkin. Roll up. Pour over marinade. Eat after 4 days.

Marinated smelts

Overall timing 45 minutes plus overnight marination

Freezing Not suitable

To serve 6

2 lb	Smelts
	Salt and pepper
¾ cup	Flour
	Oil for frying
1	Large onion
8	Sage leaves
6 tbsp	Vinegar
¼ cup	Water

Clean the fish through the gills. Rinse and drain thoroughly. Season the flour and use to coat the fish. Heat 1 inch oil in a deep skillet and fry the floured smelts, a few at a time, for about 4 minutes till crisp and golden. Drain on paper towels, then put into a shallow serving dish.

Peel and slice the onion. Heat 2 tbsp oil in a skillet, add the onion and fry gently till transparent. Add the sage leaves, vinegar and water and bring to a boil. Boil for 3 minutes, then remove from the heat and season.

Pour the hot marinade over the smelts. Cover and leave to marinate in a cool place overnight. Serve cold with crusty bread and butter.

Scrowled smelts

Overall timing 30 minutes plus salting

Freezing Not suitable

To serve 4

1 lb	Fresh smelts
	Salt
2	Sprigs of rosemary
¼ cup	Butter
	Lemon wedges

Cover the smelts with salt and leave overnight.

The next day, rinse off the salt. Cut off the heads and tails, then slit each fish along the belly and remove the insides, including the backbone. Do this under cold running water. Dry the fish with paper towels.

Preheat a charcoal grill.

Strip the rosemary leaves from the sprig. Melt the butter. Arrange the fish on the grill and sprinkle with the butter and rosemary. Grill until cooked, turning once. Serve with lemon wedges.

Garlic baked mackerel

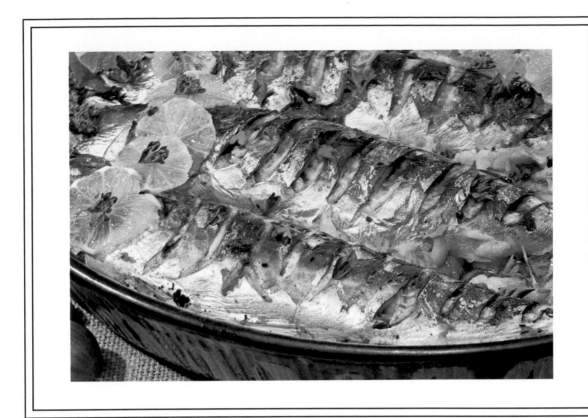

Overall timing 45 minutes

Freezing Not suitable

To serve 4

1	Onion
2	Shallots
4-6	Garlic cloves
2 tbsp	Butter
4	Cleaned mackerel
	Salt and pepper
1	Lemon
	Chopped parsley

Preheat the oven to 350°.

Peel and finely chop the onion, shallots and garlic. Heat the butter in a shallow flameproof casserole and fry the onion, shallots and garlic till golden. Remove from heat.

Slash mackerel with a sharp knife and arrange on top of garlic mixture. Season with salt and pepper. Bake for about 30 minutes, basting from time to time, or until mackerel is done. Garnish with lemon slices and parsley before serving.

Mackerel in mushroom sauce

Overall timing 40 minutes

Freezing Not suitable

To serve 4

½lb	Button mushrooms
2	Onions
1	Garlic clove
¾lb	Tomatoes
5 tbsp	Oil
	Salt and pepper
2 tbsp	White wine vinegar
2lb	Mackerel fillets
2 tbsp	Flour

Slice mushrooms. Peel and finely chop onions. Peel and crush garlic. Wash tomatoes and cut into ½ inch thick slices.

Heat 2 tbsp of the oil in a saucepan. Add onions, mushrooms and garlic and fry for 10 minutes, stirring frequently. Season. Stir in the vinegar and boil rapidly till it evaporates.

Coat fillets with seasoned flour. Heat the remaining oil in a large skillet, add the fillets and fry for 5 minutes on each side. Drain, arrange on a warmed serving dish and keep hot.

Add tomato slices to skillet and fry for 2 minutes. Spoon mushroom mixture over fillets. Season tomatoes and arrange on top. Serve immediately with minted peas.

Porgy with mushrooms

Overall timing 1 hour

Freezing Not suitable

To serve 2

2lb	Porgy or other whole fish
¼lb	Button mushrooms
1	Small onion
	Salt and pepper
½ cup	Water
1 tsp	Chopped parsley
	Pinch of dried thyme
2 tbsp	Butter
1	Lemon

Preheat the oven to 400°.

Clean fish, but don't remove head. Trim tail and fins, and wash well. Dry on paper towels.

Thinly slice button mushrooms. Peel and finely chop onion. Cover bottom of ovenproof dish with most of mushrooms and onion and place the fish on top. Season with salt and pepper, and pour in the water. Sprinkle fish with parsley, thyme and remaining mushrooms and onion.

Melt butter and pour over fish. Cover dish with foil or a lid and bake for 40 minutes, basting frequently with juices in dish. Turn fish over halfway through cooking time and remove foil for last 10 minutes. The fish is cooked when the flesh becomes opaque.

Garnish with lemon and serve with boiled new potatoes.

Haddock creole

Overall timing 1 hour

Freezing Not suitable

To serve 4

1	Onion
1	Garlic clove
1	Sweet red pepper
1	Green pepper
2 tbsp	Butter
2 tbsp	Oil
16oz	Can of tomatoes
	Salt and pepper
2lb	Haddock fillets
3 tbsp	Lemon juice
	Chopped parsley

Preheat the oven to 375°.

Peel and chop onion and garlic. Seed and slice peppers. Heat the butter and oil in a pan. Add onion, garlic and peppers and fry gently for 10 minutes.

Add tomatoes and mash with a wooden spoon to break them up. Season with salt and pepper. Bring to a boil and simmer gently for 10 minutes.

Place half tomato mixture in ovenproof dish, add haddock and season with salt and pepper. Sprinkle with lemon juice and cover with remaining tomato mixture.

Cover with lid or foil and bake for about 25 minutes. Sprinkle with chopped parsley and serve with plain boiled rice.

Haddock with potatoes and onions

Overall timing 45 minutes

Freezing Not suitable

To serve 6

2	Large onions
4	Potatoes
½ cup	Butter
2 lb	Haddock fillets
2 tbsp	Flour
	Salt and pepper
1 tbsp	Chopped parsley
1 tbsp	Vinegar

Peel and thinly slice the onions and potatoes. Melt half the butter in a skillet, add the onions and cook till transparent.

Add remaining butter and potato slices and fry for 15 minutes, turning occasionally.

Meanwhile, wipe the haddock and pat dry with paper towels. Cut into small pieces and coat with seasoned flour. Add to pan and cook for a further 15 minutes, stirring from time to time.

Season with salt and pepper. Add parsley and vinegar and cook over a high heat till vinegar evaporates. Serve immediately with broiled tomatoes.

Barbecued haddock

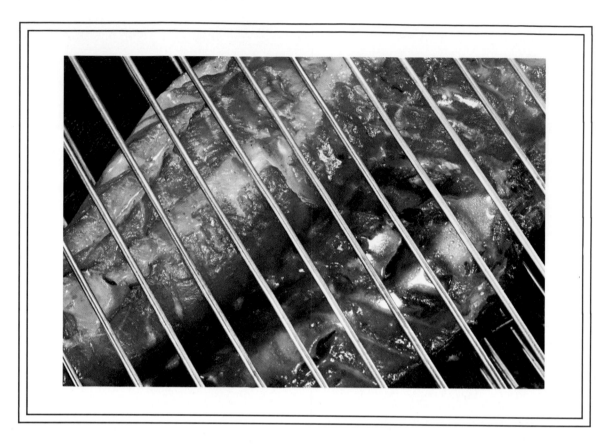

Overall timing 20 minutes plus marination

Freezing Not suitable

To serve 2

1 ½ tbsp	Oil
1 ½ tsp	Lemon juice
1 tbsp	Brown sugar
¼ tsp	Chili powder
½ tsp	Worcestershire sauce
1 tsp	Tomato paste
1 lb	Smoked haddock (finnan haddie)

Mix together oil, lemon juice, sugar, chili powder, Worcestershire sauce and tomato paste in a shallow dish. Add the haddock, cover and marinate in the refrigerator for 1 hour, turning fish once or twice.

Preheat a charcoal broiler.

Remove fish from marinade and place on a large piece of foil on the broiler or in a fish broiling basket. Broil for 5-7 minutes on each side, brushing with marinade from time to time.

Trout with almonds

Overall timing 20 minutes

Freezing Not suitable

To serve 2

2	Trout, cleaned
¼ cup	Flour
¼ cup	Butter
2 tbsp	Chopped parsley
½ cup	Flaked almonds
	Salt and pepper
2	Lemon slices

Dredge trout with flour. Melt butter in skillet. Add trout and cook gently on one side for 5 minutes.

Turn trout over with a spatula. Add half the parsley, the almonds and seasoning. Cook for a further 7-8 minutes till fish is tender and almonds are golden brown (turn them as they cook).

Place fish on warmed serving plates and spoon over almonds. Garnish with lemon slices and remaining chopped parsley. Serve with boiled potatoes and a mixed salad.

Welsh trout

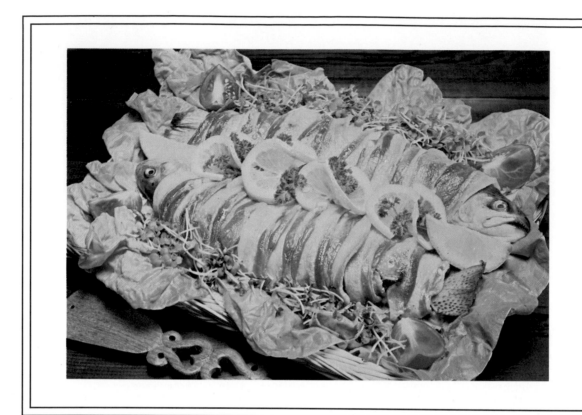

Overall timing 45 minutes

Freezing Not suitable

To serve 2

1 tsp	Chopped fresh sage
1 tsp	Chopped fresh rosemary
1 tsp	Chopped fresh thyme
1 tbsp	Chopped parsley
	Salt and pepper
¼ cup	Butter
2 x 1lb	Trout, cleaned
4	Bacon slices

Preheat the oven to 350°.

Beat the herbs and seasoning into the butter and spread half inside each fish. Stretch the bacon. Wrap two slices around each fish, securing with wooden toothpicks. Place the trout in a greased ovenproof dish, cover with foil and bake for about 25 minutes till tender.

Remove the toothpicks, place the trout on a warmed serving dish and garnish with lemon slices and sprigs of parsley. Surround with lettuce leaves, garden cress and tomato wedges and serve immediately.

Salmon cakes

Overall timing 25 minutes

Freezing Suitable: fry straight from frozen

To serve 4

1 lb	Boiled potatoes
2 tbsp	Milk
2 tbsp	Butter
7½ oz	Can of salmon
2	Lemons
	Salt and pepper
2	Eggs
2 tbsp	Flour
¼ cup	Dried bread crumbs
½ cup	Oil
	Lettuce leaves

Mash the boiled potatoes with the milk and butter. Drain canned salmon and discard skin and bones. Mash flesh and add to potatoes.

Squeeze juice from one of the lemons. Add to salmon with seasoning to taste. Mix well and bind with one of the eggs.

Lightly beat remaining egg. Spread flour and dried bread crumbs on separate plates. Divide salmon mixture into eight and shape into flat patties. Dip first in flour, then egg, then coat lightly with dried bread crumbs.

Heat oil in skillet. Add patties and fry for 5 minutes on each side until crisp and golden. Remove from pan with a slotted spoon and arrange on serving plate. Serve immediately, garnished with lettuce leaves and the remaining lemon, cut into wedges.

Salmon pie

Overall timing 2 hours

Freezing Not suitable

To serve 6-8

1 lb	Frozen puff pastry
¾ lb	Frozen spinach
1 lb	Canned salmon
1	Egg
1 cup	Long grain rice
3 tbsp	Light cream
2 tbsp	Lemon juice
	Salt and pepper
3	Hard-cooked eggs

Thaw pastry and spinach. Drain and flake salmon. Separate egg. Cook rice, then mix with egg yolk, cream, lemon juice and seasoning.

Preheat the oven to 425°. Roll out dough to two rectangles, one 9 x 14 inches, the other 11 x 16 inches. Put smallest one on damp baking sheet.

Spread half rice over dough, leaving a border. Cover with half spinach and the salmon. Arrange hard-cooked eggs along center and cover with remaining spinach and rice. Brush pastry border with lightly beaten egg white.

Place remaining dough over filling, seal edges and glaze with egg white.

Bake for 20 minutes. Reduce temperature to 350° and cook for a further 20 minutes.

Fish kabobs

Overall timing 25 minutes

Freezing Not suitable

To serve 4

1 lb	Thick firm white fish
3 tbsp	Flour
	Salt and pepper
2	Eggs
1 tsp	Curry powder
¼ cup	Dried bread crumbs
8	Tomatoes
1 tbsp	Oil

Preheat the broiler.

Cut the fish into chunks and roll in seasoned flour to coat. Beat the eggs with the curry powder. Dip the floured fish pieces in the egg, then in the bread crumbs, pressing the crumbs onto the fish. Cut the tomatoes into quarters. Thread fish and tomato pieces alternately onto greased skewers. Brush with oil.

Cook under the broiler for 7-10 minutes till the fish is tender. Turn skewers over from time to time. Serve at once.

Fish with orange

Overall timing 35 minutes

Freezing Not suitable

To serve 4

8	White fish fillets
	Salt and pepper
2 tbsp	Flour
2 tbsp	Butter
2	Oranges
1 tbsp	Chopped parsley
	Sprigs of parsley

Skin the fish fillets. Season the flour and use to coat the fish. Melt the butter in skillet, add half the fish fillets and fry for about 3 minutes each side.

Meanwhile, remove the rind and pith from one orange and divide the flesh into segments. Squeeze juice from remaining orange and reserve.

Remove the fish from the skillet and keep hot while you cook the rest. Remove from the skillet and keep hot.

Pour off any fat from the skillet. Add the orange juice and segments and the chopped parsley and mix well.

Return the fish to the pan and simmer for 2-3 minutes till done. Arrange on a warmed serving dish and spoon the orange segments and pan juices over. Garnish with sprigs of parsley.

Indonesian fish curry

Overall timing 40 minutes

Freezing Not suitable

To serve 4

1½lb	Cod fillets
	Salt and pepper
2 tbsp	Flour
1	Onion
1	Large tart apple
1 tbsp	Lemon juice
¼ cup	Butter
2 tbsp	Oil
2 tbsp	Curry powder
2½ cups	Fish broth
2 tbsp	Golden raisins
2 tbsp	Cornstarch
½ cup	Split almonds

Cut fish into pieces, sprinkle with salt and coat with the flour. Peel and slice onion. Peel, core and slice apple and sprinkle with the lemon juice.

Heat the butter and oil in a flameproof casserole. Add curry powder and onion and fry for 5 minutes. Add fish and cook for a few minutes on all sides. Add apple slices and cook for 3 minutes.

Pour broth into casserole and add raisins. Blend cornstarch with a little broth or water and stir in. Bring to a boil and simmer for 10-15 minutes.

Add almonds and cook for a further 2 minutes. Taste and adjust seasoning and serve.

Fish lasagne

Overall timing 1 ¼ hours

Freezing Suitable: reheat from frozen in 350° oven for 1 hour

To serve 4

1 lb	Cleaned mackerel
1	Onion
6 tbsp	Oil
2	Garlic cloves
2 tbsp	Tomato paste
	Salt and pepper
1 lb	Fresh peas
¼ lb	Mushrooms
½ lb	Lasagne
2 tbsp	Grated Parmesan cheese
2 tbsp	Chopped parsley

Cut fish into large pieces. Peel and chop onion. Heat 3 tbsp of oil in saucepan, add onion and fry until golden. Add fish and cook for 5 minutes, turning once.

Peel and crush garlic. Stir tomato paste into ½ cup of water and add to pan with half garlic and seasoning. Cover and cook gently for 10 minutes.

Shell peas. Slice mushrooms. Heat 2 tbsp of oil in another saucepan, add peas, mushrooms and other half of garlic and cook for 5 minutes. Add 6 tbsp of water and seasoning, cover and cook for 10 minutes.

Meanwhile, cook lasagne in boiling salted water for 10-15 minutes or till tender. Drain thoroughly.

Preheat oven to 350°.

Remove fish from pan and cut into pieces, discarding bones. Return to pan with mushroom mixture. Gradually stir in Parmesan and parsley.

Line greased ovenproof dish with one-third of lasagne, cover with one-third of fish mixture and sprinkle with a little oil. Repeat layers, finishing with fish mixture. Sprinkle with oil and bake for 20 minutes.

Cheesy fish croquettes

Overall timing 40 minutes

Freezing Suitable: reheat from frozen in 375° oven for 30 minutes

To serve 2

½lb	White fish fillets
1 cup	Milk
1	Small onion
¼ cup	Butter
¼ cup	Flour
1	Hard-cooked egg
1 tbsp	Grated Parmesan cheese
	Salt and pepper
	Oil for frying

Place the fish fillets in a large skillet with the milk. Cover and cook over a moderate heat for about 10 minutes till fish is tender. Lift fish out of milk. Discard skin and any bones, then mash flesh. Reserve fish and milk.

Peel and finely chop the onion. Melt the butter in clean skillet and fry onion till transparent. Add the flour and cook for 2 minutes, stirring. Gradually stir in the reserved milk and bring to a boil.

Remove pan from the heat and add the reserved fish. Shell and finely chop the hard-cooked egg and add to the sauce with the Parmesan and seasoning. Spread the mixture thickly onto a plate, cover and chill till firm.

Divide the mixture into four and shape on a well floured board into round patties about ½ inch thick.

Heat oil in deep-fryer to 340° and fry the croquettes for 5 minutes till crisp and golden. Drain on paper towels and serve hot.

Baked fish steaks

Overall timing 30 minutes

Freezing Not suitable

To serve 4

4	Cod steaks
	Salt and pepper
¾ cup	Dry white wine or hard cider
¼ cup	Butter
2 tbsp	Chopped fresh coriander (optional)
2 tbsp	Lemon or lime juice

Preheat the oven to 425°.

Wash and dry cod steaks. Place in a greased baking dish and sprinkle well with salt and pepper. Add the wine or cider and dot with butter.

Cover dish with foil and bake for about 25 minutes.

Sprinkle with chopped coriander, if used, and lemon or lime juice. Serve with mashed potatoes.

Fish in piquant sauce

Overall timing 1 hour

Freezing Not suitable

To serve 6

¼ lb	Bacon slices
2 lb	Center cut steak from large firm-fleshed fish
4 tsp	Olive oil
2 tbsp	Butter
	Salt and pepper
1¼ cups	Fish or chicken broth
2 tbsp	Tomato paste
3 tbsp	Lemon juice

Stretch the bacon slices, then wrap them around the fish, securing with toothpicks.

Heat the oil and butter in a flameproof casserole, add the fish and brown all over. Add salt, pepper, broth, tomato paste and lemon juice. Bring to a boil, cover tightly and simmer gently for 40 minutes, turning fish once.

Remove the fish from the casserole and discard bacon. Cut the fish into thick slices, place on a warmed serving dish and keep hot.

Taste the cooking liquid and adjust seasoning. Thicken if liked with 1 tbsp of butter and 1 tbsp flour mashed together, then pour over the fish.

Tuna and pea casserole

Overall timing 40 minutes

Freezing Not suitable

To serve 4

1 lb	Waxy potatoes
	Salt and pepper
½ lb	Frozen peas
7 oz	Can of tuna
¼ cup	Butter
1	Onion
2 tbsp	Flour
1¼ cups	Chicken broth
1¼ cups	Milk
1 cup	Grated Cheddar cheese
2 tbsp	Soft bread crumbs

Peel and dice potatoes. Cook in boiling salted water till tender. Add the peas and cook for a further 3 minutes.

Preheat the oven to 400°. Drain the potatoes and peas; put into an ovenproof dish. Drain and flake tuna and stir into vegetables.

Melt the butter in a saucepan. Peel and finely chop the onion and fry in the butter till pale golden. Add the flour and cook for 1 minute. Stir in the broth and milk and bring to a boil, stirring. Add all but 2 tbsp cheese to the pan, stir and pour over tuna mixture.

Mix cheese with the bread crumbs and sprinkle on top. Bake for 20 minutes.

Tuna stuffed loaf

Overall timing 50 minutes

Freezing Not suitable

To serve 4

2	Small round crusty loaves
1	Onion
¼ lb	Button mushrooms
¼ cup	Butter
2 tbsp	Flour
10½ oz	Can of condensed mushroom soup
2	Egg yolks
2 tbsp	Light cream
2 x 7 oz	Cans of tuna
2 tbsp	Lemon juice
	Salt and pepper
½ tsp	Paprika
2	Lemon slices

Preheat the oven to 400°.

Hollow out each loaf with a sharp knife to leave a thick shell. Place on a baking sheet.

Peel and chop the onion. Wipe and thickly slice the mushrooms. Melt the butter in a saucepan, add the onion and fry till transparent. Add the mushrooms and fry for 2 minutes. Stir in the flour and cook for 1 minute. Gradually add the mushroom soup and bring to a boil, stirring constantly. Simmer for 2 minutes, then remove from the heat and allow to cool slightly.

Beat the egg yolks and cream into the mushroom sauce. Drain and flake the tuna and add to the sauce with the lemon juice. Season to taste.

Divide the hot tuna stuffing between the loaves and sprinkle with the paprika. Bake for about 25 minutes till bubbling and golden.

Arrange the loaves on a warmed serving dish and garnish each with a slice of lemon. Serve immediately.

Shrimp ravigote

Overall timing 20 minutes plus marination

Freezing Not suitable

To serve 2

1 tbsp	Sour cream
¼ cup	Thick mayonnaise
1 tbsp	Lemon juice
1 tbsp	White wine vinegar
½ tsp	Prepared mustard
	Salt and pepper
1	Stalk of celery
½	Sweet red pepper
½	Green pepper
½ lb	Large shelled shrimp
1 tsp	Chopped herbs
½	Head Bibb or Boston lettuce
1	Hard-cooked egg

To make marinade, mix the sour cream and mayonnaise in a bowl. Gradually add the lemon juice and vinegar, a few drops at a time, stirring constantly. Stir in the mustard and season to taste.

Trim the celery and cut into thin strips. Seed and thinly slice the peppers. Place the prepared vegetables in a bowl and add the chopped shrimp and herbs. Pour the marinade over, toss lightly and leave to marinate for 30 minutes.

Wash and dry the lettuce and line serving dish with the leaves. Spoon the shrimp salad into the center.

Shell the egg, cut in half and remove yolk. Slice the white; press yolk through a sieve. Use to garnish the salad.

Chinese-style shrimp with peas

Overall timing 30 minutes

Freezing Not suitable

To serve 4

2 tsp	Cornstarch
1 tbsp	Soy sauce
½ cup	Strong chicken broth
1 tsp	Sugar
	Salt and pepper
¼ tsp	Cayenne pepper
2	Small onions
3 tbsp	Oil
½ inch	Piece of fresh ginger
1	Garlic clove
¾ lb	Shelled shrimp
2 cups	Frozen peas

To make the sauce, blend the cornstarch, soy sauce, chicken broth, sugar, salt and cayenne pepper in a bowl and reserve.

Peel the onions and cut through the root into 8 wedges. Heat the oil in a large skillet and stir-fry the onions over a high heat for 2 minutes. Finely shred or chop the ginger and add to the skillet with peeled and crushed garlic and the shrimp. Stir-fry for 3 minutes.

Mix the sauce and pour into the pan. Bring to a boil, stirring constantly. Add the peas, cover and simmer for 3 minutes.

Adjust the seasoning to taste and pour into a warmed serving dish. Serve immediately with boiled rice.

Shrimp magenta

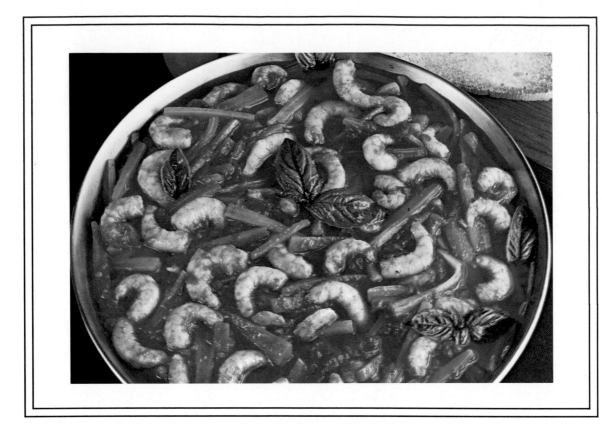

Overall timing 40 minutes

Freezing Not suitable

To serve 2

2	Stalks of celery
1	Large carrot
1	Small leek
2 tbsp	Olive oil
½ lb	Shrimp
¾ cup	Dry white wine
8 oz	Can of tomatoes
	Salt and pepper
3	Fresh basil leaves
2 tbsp	Butter

Trim the celery and cut into thin sticks. Peel the carrot and cut into sticks. Trim and thinly slice the leek.

Heat the oil in a saucepan, add the prepared vegetables, cover and cook over a low heat for 10 minutes to release the flavors without browning vegetables.

Shell the shrimp and add to the pan with the white wine and tomatoes and juice. Season, cover and cook over a low heat for 10 minutes, shaking pan occasionally.

Add the whole basil leaves and butter, adjust the seasoning and serve hot with boiled rice.

Roast pork with stuffing balls

Overall timing 2¼ hours

Freezing Not suitable

To serve 6

2½ lb	Rolled boneless pork loin roast
	Oil
	Salt
Stuffing balls	
1	Onion
¼ cup	Butter
2 cups	Soft bread crumbs
2 tsp	Dried sage
	Salt and pepper
2	Eggs
2 tbsp	Lard

Preheat the oven to 450°.

Score the skin on the roast, then rub it well with oil and sprinkle with salt. Place in a roasting pan and roast for 20 minutes. Reduce the temperature to 375° and continue roasting for 1½ hours.

Meanwhile make the stuffing balls. Peel and chop the onion. Melt the butter in a skillet and fry the onion till golden. Tip the onion into a bowl and add the bread crumbs, sage and seasoning. Bind with the eggs, then shape into small balls.

About 45 minutes before the pork has finished cooking, melt the lard in an ovenproof dish in the oven. Arrange the stuffing balls in the dish and place on a shelf below the pork. Turn once during the cooking.

Transfer the pork to a warm serving platter and surround with the stuffing balls.

Spicy roast pork

Overall timing 3 hours

Freezing Not suitable

To serve 4

⅔ cup	Prunes
1	Large onion
2 tbsp	Butter
2 tbsp	Oil
1 tbsp	Five spice powder
3 lb	Boneless pork roast
	Salt and pepper
1 cup	Chicken broth
⅔ cup	Golden raisins
¾ cup	Sliced almonds

Soak prunes in almost boiling water or strained tea.

Peel and chop onion. Heat butter and oil in a flameproof casserole, add onion and five spice powder and cook till the onion is golden.

Season the pork. Add to casserole and brown on all sides over a high heat. Add broth, bring to a boil, cover and cook gently for 2 hours.

Drain prunes, remove pits and add to casserole with golden raisins and almonds. Simmer for a further 30 minutes.

Place meat on a warmed serving platter and remove string. Surround with plain boiled rice and pour sauce over. Serve with plain yogurt mixed with chopped parsley, and mango chutney.

Roast pork with oranges

Overall timing 2¼ hours

Freezing Not suitable

To serve 6-8

3 lb	Rolled boneless pork blade Boston roast
2 tbsp	Butter
	Salt and pepper
5	Oranges
2 tbsp	Lemon juice
½ cup	Hot water
6	Sugar cubes
1 tbsp	Wine vinegar
2 tsp	Arrowroot

Preheat the oven to 450°.

Place pork in a roasting pan. Spread butter over lean parts and rub salt and pepper into fat. Roast for 20 minutes.

Meanwhile, squeeze juice from two oranges. Peel remaining oranges. Cut two into slices and one into sections.

Remove pork from pan and keep warm. Pour off any fat from pan and add orange and lemon juices and water. Stir well, scraping any sediment from bottom of pan. Reduce oven temperature to 400°.

Replace meat in pan and roast for a further 1½ hours, basting occasionally.

Meanwhile, put sugar cubes into a saucepan with 1 tbsp water. Stir till dissolved, then boil rapidly, without stirring, till golden. Remove from heat and stir in vinegar. Return to heat and stir till caramel dissolves.

Place pork on a warmed serving platter. Stir cooking liquid from pan into caramel. Blend arrowroot with 2 tbsp water and add to caramel. Bring to a boil, stirring. Add the sliced and sectioned oranges. Heat through for 1-2 minutes.

Cut pork into thick slices and arrange the pieces of orange around. Serve the sauce separately in a warmed sauceboat.

Cowboy's pork and beans

Overall timing 50 minutes

Freezing Not suitable

To serve 6

1½ lb	Slab bacon
1	Large onion
2 tbsp	Oil
2	Garlic cloves
¼ tsp	Chili powder
2 tbsp	Molasses
1 tbsp	Vinegar
½ tsp	Powdered mustard
2 tbsp	Tomato ketchup
1 cup	Chicken broth
	Salt and pepper
2x16 oz	Cans of Navy or other
	white beans

Preheat the oven to 425°. Cut the bacon into ½ inch pieces, discarding any bones. Place in roasting pan with no extra fat. Cook in the oven for about 20 minutes till crisp and golden.

Meanwhile, peel and finely chop the onion. Heat the oil in a flameproof casserole and fry the onion till transparent. Peel and crush the garlic and add to the pan with the chili powder. Fry, stirring, for 2 minutes.

Stir in the molasses, vinegar, mustard, ketchup and chicken broth. Bring to a boil, season and simmer for 5 minutes.

Drain and rinse the canned beans and add to the sauce.

Remove the bacon from the oven and reduce the temperature to 350°. Add the bacon pieces to the beans with 1 tbsp of the fat from the pan. Put the casserole in the oven and cook for about 15 minutes, stirring once till liquid is reduced by half. Taste and adjust the seasoning, then serve immediately with a tomato and onion salad and crusty bread.

Country pork with parsnips

Overall timing 2¼ hours

Freezing Not suitable

To serve 4-6

¼ cup	Butter
2½ lb	Boneless pork picnic shoulder roast
2	Onions
2 lb	Parsnips
1 cup	Broth
	Bouquet garni
1 tbsp	Flour
¾ cup	Dry white wine
	Salt and pepper

Preheat the oven to 400°.

Melt the butter in a roasting pan, place the pork in it and roast for 1 hour.

Meanwhile, peel and chop the onions. Peel and slice the parsnips.

Remove the roasting pan from the oven and arrange the onions and parsnips around the pork. Pour in the broth, add the bouquet garni and return to the oven. Roast for a further 45 minutes, basting the parsnips occasionally.

Discard the bouquet garni. Place the pork on a warmed serving platter and arrange the parsnips around it. Keep hot.

Pour all but 2 tbsp of the juices from the roasting pan into a pitcher. Sprinkle the flour into the pan and cook for 1 minute, stirring. Gradually add the reserved cooking juices and the wine and bring to a boil, stirring constantly. Taste and adjust seasoning and spoon over the parsnips.

Meatballs and spinach

Overall timing 45 minutes

Freezing Not suitable

To serve 4

1 lb	Ground pork
1 tbsp	Chopped chives
1	Egg
2 tbsp	Soy sauce
¼ cup	Oil
2 tbsp	Dry sherry
½ cup	Water
2 lb	Bulk spinach
1 tsp	Cornstarch
	Salt and pepper

Pound ground pork with chives, egg and half the soy sauce till mixture binds together. Shape into eight balls.

Heat half the oil in a skillet, add the meatballs and fry over a medium heat for 10 minutes, turning till browned. Add the remaining soy sauce, the sherry and water, bring to a boil, cover and simmer for 15 minutes.

Meanwhile, shred the spinach. Heat the remaining oil in another skillet, add the spinach and stir-fry over a high heat for 3 minutes.

Blend the cornstarch with 1 tbsp cold water and add to the meatballs. Bring to a boil, stirring till thickened. Season to taste.

Arrange the spinach on a warmed serving dish and place the meatballs on top. Spoon the sauce over the meatballs and serve with a side dish of soy sauce.

Braised pork with plum sauce

Overall timing 1¾ hours

Freezing Not suitable

To serve 6

¼ cup	Lard
	Salt and pepper
2 lb	Boned and rolled loin of pork
1¼ cups	Light broth
3	Sage leaves
2 lb	Small potatoes
1½ lb	Red plums
¼ cup	Sugar
1 tbsp	Chopped parsley

Preheat the oven to 400°.

Melt lard in a roasting pan. Season pork and fry quickly over a high heat till browned on all sides. Pour off the fat and reserve. Add the broth and sage leaves, cover the pan with foil and braise in the oven for 45 minutes.

Meanwhile, peel potatoes. Put into a saucepan, cover with cold salted water and bring to a boil. Drain.

Remove meat from oven and strain broth into a saucepan. Add reserved fat to roasting pan with the potatoes, return to the oven and cook uncovered for a further 50 minutes, basting the meat and potatoes occasionally.

Meanwhile, wash plums. Halve 1 lb of them and discard pits. Add to the stock with the sugar. Bring to a boil, then cover and simmer for 10-15 minutes, stirring occasionally. Poach the rest of the plums whole in a little water till tender.

Remove meat from pan, carve into thick slices and arrange on a warmed serving plate. Arrange the potatoes and whole poached plums around the meat. Sprinkle with parsley. Lightly mash remaining plums and pour into a warmed sauceboat.

Iowa skillet chops

Overall timing 1 hour

Freezing Suitable

To serve 4

4	Pork loin chops
	Salt and pepper
3 tbsp	Oil
2 lb	Can of tomatoes
1 tbsp	Tomato paste
1 tbsp	Worcestershire sauce
1	Onion
11½ oz	Can of whole kernel corn
1 tbsp	Arrowroot (optional)
	Sprigs of parsley

Sprinkle chops with salt and pepper. Heat oil in a skillet and cook chops in two batches for 2 minutes on each side. When all chops are cooked, return first batch to pan. Remove from heat.

Purée the tomatoes with juice, tomato paste and Worcestershire sauce in a blender, then pour over chops. Finely chop the onion and add with the drained corn (use some of the corn water if the mixture is too thick). Bring back to a boil and add salt and pepper.

Cover the pan and cook over moderate heat for 25 minutes. Remove lid to reduce sauce a little and cook for a further 10 minutes. Thicken with arrowroot, if you like, blended with a little hot water, and cook till clear. Garnish with parsley and serve straight from the pan.

Barbecued pork chops

Overall timing 20 minutes plus marination

Freezing Not suitable

To serve 4

4	Pork chops
Marinade	
1	Large onion
2 tbsp	Lemon juice or vinegar
2 tbsp	Oil
½ tsp	Powdered mustard
2 tsp	Worcestershire sauce
½ tsp	Salt
½ tsp	Freshly ground black pepper
1 tsp	Sugar
½ tsp	Paprika

Place pork chops in bowl. Peel and grate the onion and place in a pitcher. Add rest of marinade ingredients and mix well, then pour over chops. Leave to marinate for 1 hour in a cool place, turning chops at least twice.

Preheat a charcoal grill or the broiler.

Cook the chops on the grill (or under a broiler), occasionally brushing them with the reserved marinade. Serve with mixed salad, dressed with vinaigrette flavored with fresh dill or other herb of choice.

Chinese spareribs

Overall timing 45 minutes

Freezing Not suitable

To serve 4

1½ lb	Pork country style spareribs
2 tbsp	Oil
1 tbsp	Hoisin sauce
1 tbsp	Soy sauce
Sauce	
½ inch	Piece of ginger root
1	Green pepper
2	Garlic cloves
2 tbsp	Oil
1 tbsp	Soy sauce
2 tbsp	Dry sherry
2 tbsp	Tomato paste
2 tbsp	Vinegar
2 tbsp	Sugar
1 tbsp	Cornstarch
¼ cup	Pineapple juice
3 tbsp	Water

Separate the pork into ribs. Cook in boiling water for 15 minutes, then drain and dry on paper towels.

Heat oil in skillet. Add ribs and stir in hoisin and soy sauces. Cook gently for 20 minutes.

Meanwhile, prepare sauce. Shred ginger. Seed pepper and cut into thin strips. Peel and crush garlic. Heat oil in a saucepan, add garlic, ginger and pepper and stir-fry for 2 minutes. Remove from heat and stir in soy sauce, sherry, tomato paste, vinegar and sugar. Blend cornstarch with fruit juice and water and add to the pan. Bring to a boil and cook for 2 minutes, stirring constantly.

Place ribs in a warmed serving dish. Pour sauce over and serve immediately with boiled rice.

Braised pork chops

Overall timing 55 minutes

Freezing Not suitable

To serve 4

4	Pork chops
	Salt and pepper
2	Tart apples
2	Onions
2 tbsp	Butter
⅓ cup	Broth
2 tsp	Worcestershire sauce
	Fresh parsley

Season chops with salt and pepper. Peel and core apples and cut into wedges. Peel onions and cut into rings.

Melt butter in skillet and brown the chops on all sides.

Add broth and Worcestershire sauce, cover and cook for 10 minutes.

Turn chops over. Add apples and onions. Reduce heat, cover and cook for a further 30 minutes.

Garnish with parsley and serve with creamed potatoes.

Sweetbread bake

Overall timing 50 minutes

Freezing Not suitable

To serve 2

2 oz	Button mushrooms
½ lb	Prepared sweetbreads
	Salt and pepper
2 tbsp	Flour
2 tbsp	Butter
5 tbsp	Chicken broth
1	Small egg
5 tbsp	Plain yogurt
½ cup	Grated cheese
	Chopped parsley

Preheat the oven to 375°.

Slice the mushrooms. Cut the sweetbreads into ¼ inch thick slices. Season the flour and toss the sweetbreads in it till lightly coated.

Melt butter in a skillet, add the sweetbreads and mushrooms and fry for about 10 minutes till golden. Add the broth and seasoning and simmer for 5 minutes.

Meanwhile, beat the egg with yogurt, grated cheese and seasoning.

Arrange the sweetbreads and mushrooms in an ovenproof dish and pour the yogurt mixture over. Bake for 20 minutes till lightly set and golden. Sprinkle with parsley and serve hot.

Orange pork rolls

Overall timing 1 hour

Freezing Not suitable

To serve 6

6x4 oz	Slices of lean pork
1	Onion
6 tbsp	Butter
2 cups	Soft bread crumbs
2 tbsp	Chopped parsley
1 tsp	Dried mixed herbs
	Salt and pepper
1	Large orange
1	Egg
2 tbsp	Flour
½ cup	Hard cider
½ cup	Chicken broth

Preheat the oven to 375°.

Place slices of pork between damp wax paper and beat till very thin. Peel and finely chop onion. Melt 2 tbsp of the butter in a skillet and fry onion till golden. Add bread crumbs, parsley, herbs and seasoning. Cook for 2 minutes, then remove from the heat.

Grate orange rind into stuffing, add egg and mix well. Divide stuffing between pork slices. Roll them up carefully, turning sides in to cover stuffing, and secure with wooden toothpicks.

Arrange rolls in roasting pan and dot with remaining butter. Squeeze orange and pour juice over. Cook in the oven for about 35 minutes, basting occasionally, till pork is tender.

Place pork rolls on a warmed serving dish and keep hot. Sprinkle flour into roasting pan and stir over heat for 1 minute. Gradually add cider and broth and bring to a boil, stirring. Season to taste, pour into a sauceboat and serve with the pork rolls.

Sweet and sour pork

Overall timing 40 minutes plus marination

Freezing Suitable

To serve 4

1 lb	Lean boneless pork
2 tbsp	Dry sherry
	Salt and pepper
1	Egg
3 tbsp	Flour
3 tbsp	Oil
2	Carrots
2	Onions
1	Large cucumber
1	Garlic clove
¼ cup	Tomato ketchup
2 tsp	Soy sauce
2 tbsp	Vinegar
1 tbsp	Brown sugar
1 tbsp	Cornstarch
1¼ cups	Water

Cut meat into ½ inch cubes. Put into a bowl with sherry and seasoning and marinate for 30 minutes.

Lightly beat egg. Dip pork cubes in egg, then coat with flour. Heat oil in a large skillet. Fry pork for 8 minutes till golden brown on all sides. Remove from pan.

Peel and chop carrots, onions and cucumber. Peel and crush garlic. Add all to skillet and stir-fry for 5 minutes over fairly high heat. Reduce heat to moderate. Add ketchup, soy sauce, vinegar, sugar, cornstarch dissolved in water and reserved marinade to the pan. Bring to a boil and cook for 3 minutes, stirring.

Return pork to pan and cook for 3 minutes more till heated through. Serve with plain boiled rice and side dishes of tomato wedges, chunks of cucumber and a little shredded coconut for sprinkling over the finished dish.

Roast pork with turnips

Overall timing 2¼ hours

Freezing Not suitable

To serve 6

2½ lb	Rolled boneless pork loin roast
1	Garlic clove
¼ cup	Butter
	Salt and pepper
2 lb	Small white turnips
2 tsp	Sugar
2 cups	Light broth
1 tbsp	Flour
1 tbsp	Chopped parsley

Preheat the oven to 425°.

Peel the garlic clove, cut in half and rub all over the pork. Place the pork in a roasting pan and spread the butter over. Sprinkle with salt and pepper and roast for 20 minutes. Reduce the temperature to 375° and cook for a further 40 minutes.

Meanwhile, peel and halve or quarter the turnips according to size. Put into a saucepan, cover with cold salted water and bring to a boil. Drain, then dry on paper towels.

Arrange the turnips around the pork. Sprinkle with the sugar and add the broth. Cover with foil and roast for 30 minutes. Remove the foil, turn the turnips over and cook for a further 15 minutes. Test pork for doneness and cook a little longer if necessary.

Place the pork on a warmed serving platter and carve into thick slices. Arrange the turnips on the dish and keep hot.

Pour off liquid from pan and reserve. Sprinkle the flour into the pan and cook, stirring, for 1 minute. Gradually add the reserved liquid and bring to a boil, stirring constantly. Adjust seasoning. Sprinkle the parsley over the turnips and serve.

Polish-style pork with sauerkraut

Overall timing 1 hour

Freezing Not suitable

To serve 6

3 tbsp	Oil
6	Pork loin chops
1	Large onion
1	Garlic clove
	Salt and pepper
2 lb	Sauerkraut
1	Bay leaf
1 cup	Chicken broth
1	Large apple
1 tsp	Cumin seeds

Heat the oil in a flameproof casserole and fry the chops till browned on both sides. Remove from the pan and reserve.

Peel and finely chop the onion; peel and crush the garlic. Add both to the casserole and fry till transparent. Season, and add the drained sauerkraut and bay leaf. Arrange the chops on top. Pour the broth over, bring to a boil and simmer for 15 minutes.

Meanwhile, peel, core and dice the apple. Add to the pan with cumin seeds and stir well, then simmer for a further 15 minutes till the chops are tender.

Taste and adjust the seasoning. Discard the bay leaf. Serve with creamed potatoes, buttered carrots and thin slices of wholewheat bread.

Pork and beans

Overall timing 2¾ hours plus
overnight soaking

Freezing Not suitable

To serve 4

2 cups	Dried navy beans
1	Onion
12	Cloves
2	Garlic cloves
1½ quarts	Boiling water
¼ cup	Oil
	Salt and pepper
1 lb	Slab bacon

Put the beans in a large saucepan of cold
water and soak overnight.

The next day, bring to a boil and cook
beans for 15 minutes. Drain.

Peel onion, spike with cloves and add to
pan with peeled garlic, boiling water, oil,
pepper and bacon, cut into thick slices if
easier to handle. Cover and simmer for
1½ hours. Taste and add salt, then cook for
a further 30 minutes. Remove spiked onion
and garlic. Remove meat and beans from
pan with a slotted spoon and place in
warmed serving dish. Keep hot.

Reduce cooking liquid to about ½ cup
by boiling fast, uncovered. Pour over beans
and serve.

Frankfurter fritter

Overall timing 30 minutes

Freezing Not suitable

To serve 6

1¼ cups	Flour
	Salt and pepper
1	Egg
1 tbsp	Oil
1 cup	Beer
	Oil for frying
16	Frankfurters
2	Egg whites

Sift 1 cup of the flour into a bowl with
1½ tsp salt and make a well in the center.
Add the whole egg and oil and mix with a
wooden spoon. Gradually add the beer and
mix to a smooth batter.

Heat the oil in a deep-fryer to 340°.

Season the remaining flour. Cut the
frankfurters in half and toss in flour. Beat
the egg whites till stiff but not dry and fold
into batter. Dip each frankfurter half into
the batter and fry in the oil for about
3 minutes till crisp and golden. Drain on
paper towels and serve hot.

Pork and sausage stew

Overall timing 1¾ hours

Freezing Not suitable

To serve 6

1½ lb	Onions
¼ cup	Lard
6	Thin cut pork loin chops
1 lb	Coarse pork sausage links
2 tbsp	Flour
2 cups	Chicken broth
3 tbsp	Tomato paste
	Salt and pepper

Peel and thinly slice the onions. Heat the lard in a flameproof casserole, add the onions and fry gently for 10 minutes till pale golden.

Meanwhile, wipe the chops and remove the bones and any excess fat. Twist the sausages in half.

Sprinkle flour over the onions and cook for 1 minute. Gradually add the broth and bring to a boil, stirring. Stir in the tomato paste.

Add the chops and sausages. Bring to a boil, cover and simmer for 1¼ hours, or cook in the oven preheated to 350°, for 1¼ hours.

Adjust the seasoning to taste, then serve immediately with buttered pasta and a green salad.

Belgian pork chops

Overall timing 40 minutes

Freezing Not suitable

To serve 4

4	Pork chops
	Salt and pepper
2 tbsp	Flour
3 tbsp	Oil
2	Onions
½ cup	Beer
½ cup	Chicken broth
1½ lb	Brussels sprouts
2 tbsp	Butter
2 tsp	Cornstarch

Coat the chops with seasoned flour. Heat oil in skillet and cook chops for 3 minutes on each side.

Peel and thinly slice onions. Add to pan and cook for 5 minutes. Pour in beer and broth, season and simmer for 15 minutes.

Meanwhile, trim sprouts and cook in boiling water till just tender. Drain well, toss with butter and keep hot. Remove chops from pan and place on warmed serving plate. Surround with sprouts.

Mix cornstarch with a little cold water and add to pan. Bring to a boil and cook for 2 minutes. Pour sauce over chops.

Porkburgers

Overall timing 25 minutes

Freezing Suitable: cook from frozen

To serve 6

1 lb	Lean boneless pork
	Salt and pepper
1	Onion
1 tsp	Dried thyme
1 tbsp	Oil
	Lemon slices

Grind the pork twice till fine and add plenty of salt and pepper. Peel and finely chop the onion and add to the pork with the dried thyme. Mix well with the fingers.

Divide the meat into six portions and shape into thick burgers about 4 inches in diameter.

Brush a heavy-based skillet or griddle with oil and heat well. Add the burgers and fry for about 10-15 minutes. Turn burgers carefully with a spatula and cook for a further 5-10 minutes according to taste.

Garnish with lemon slices and serve with a chicory and tomato salad or with French fries.

Kidney-stuffed roast pork

Overall timing 3½ hours

Freezing Not suitable

To serve 6-8

1	Veal kidney
4 lb	Boned loin of pork
	Sprig of thyme
	Salt and pepper
¾ cup	Butter
1½ lb	Cooked potatoes
3 tbsp	Oil
1 lb	Button mushrooms
1 tbsp	Chopped parsley

Preheat the oven to 375°.

Prepare kidney. Spread out the pork loin and put kidney in the center with thyme and seasoning. Roll meat tightly around kidney and tie at regular intervals with string. Place meat in roasting pan with ¼ cup of the butter. Roast for 3 hours, basting occasionally.

Meanwhile, slice cooked potatoes. Melt ¼ cup of the butter with the oil in a skillet, add the potatoes and fry until golden.

Halve mushrooms. Melt remaining butter in another skillet and cook the mushrooms for 5 minutes, shaking the pan from time to time.

Place meat on warmed serving platter. Surround with drained potatoes and mushrooms and garnish with chopped parsley. Serve with gravy made from roasting juices.

Pork cassoulet

Overall timing 3 ¼ hours plus soaking

Freezing Not suitable

To serve 6

1 lb	Dried navy beans
1	Pig's foot
¼ lb	Pork rind
2	Garlic cloves
2	Carrots
2	Onions
	Bouquet garni
	Salt and pepper
2 tbsp	Oil
16 oz	Can of tomatoes
½ cup	Soft bread crumbs

Soak beans overnight.

Quarter pig's foot lengthwise. Chop pork rind. Add to beans with peeled garlic, carrots, one onion and bouquet garni. Cover with water, cover and simmer for 1½ hours.

Chop remaining onion. Heat oil in a saucepan and fry onion till transparent. Add 2½ cups water, tomatoes and seasoning. Simmer for 10 minutes.

Preheat the oven to 350°.

Drain beans, reserving pork rind. Add salami and pig's foot to other pan. Line deep ovenproof dish with pork rind. Add layers of beans and meat mixture; top with crumbs. Bake for 30 minutes.

Rib and bean stew

Overall timing 1 hours plus soaking

Freezing Not suitable

To serve 4-6

8 oz	Dried borlotti or other white beans
2	Carrots
2	Stalks of celery
2	Bay leaves
2 lb	Pork spareribs
2	Large onions
¼ cup	Oil
16 oz	Can of tomatoes
¼ cup	Tomato paste
1 tbsp	Sugar
2 cups	Chicken broth
	Salt and pepper

Soak beans overnight, then drain and cover with fresh water. Slice carrots and celery and add to beans with bay leaves. Simmer for 1 hour.

Separate ribs. Peel and finely chop onions. Heat oil in saucepan and fry onions till transparent. Add ribs and brown all over. Add tomatoes, tomato paste, sugar and broth and bring to a boil.

Drain beans and add to meat. Season and simmer for 15 minutes till meat is tender and cooking liquid is thick.

Pork and molasses casserole

Overall timing 1¾ hours

Freezing Not suitable

To serve 6

1 lb	Lean boneless pork
1½ lb	Thick bacon slices
	Salt and pepper
2 tbsp	Flour
3	Large onions
2	Garlic cloves
¼ cup	Lard
3 tbsp	Molasses
2 tbsp	Tomato paste
16 oz	Can of tomatoes
2 cups	Beef broth

Preheat the oven to 350°.

Wipe and trim the pork and cut into cubes. Cut bacon into 1 inch pieces. Toss in seasoned flour. Peel and slice the onions; peel and crush the garlic.

Heat the lard in a flameproof casserole, add the pork and bacon and fry over a high heat till browned all over. Remove with a slotted spoon and reserve.

Add the onions to the pan and fry till transparent. Pour off any excess fat. Stir in the molasses, tomato paste and garlic. Return the pork to the pan and stir till coated. Add the canned tomatoes and juice, broth and seasoning. Bring to a boil, stirring to break up the tomatoes.

Cover and cook for 45 minutes.

Remove the lid and stir the casserole. Cook uncovered for a further 30 minutes till the pork is tender.

Adjust seasoning to taste and serve immediately with buttered noodles.

Pork brochettes

Overall timing 30 minutes

Freezing Not suitable

To serve 4

1 lb	Lean boneless pork
¼ lb	Thick bacon slices
2	Pork kidneys
12	Bay leaves
	Oil
	Salt and pepper

Cut pork into 1 inch cubes. Cut bacon into strips. Wash and dry kidneys. Cut them open, remove the fat and cut each into four.

Preheat charcoal grill or broiler.

Arrange bay leaves, pork cubes, bacon and kidney pieces on skewers. Brush with a little oil and season liberally.

Grill or broil for about 20 minutes, turning skewers occasionally. Serve with boiled rice and peas or a mixed salad with vinaigrette dressing.

Baked pork chops

Overall timing 40 minutes

Freezing Not suitable

To serve 4

4	Pork chops
	Salt and pepper
2 tbsp	Oil
1 lb	Tart apples
2 tbsp	Butter
1 tbsp	Chopped fresh rosemary
½ cup	Broth

Preheat the oven to 400°.

Season chops with salt and pepper. Heat oil in a flameproof casserole and brown the chops for 2 minutes on each side.

Peel, core and slice apples. Arrange in casserole around the chops and dot with the butter.

Sprinkle with rosemary, add broth and cover casserole. Bake in the oven for about 30 minutes, removing lid for last 10 minutes of cooking time. Serve with creamed potatoes and salad.

Pork chops with bananas

Overall timing 30 minutes

Freezing Not suitable

To serve 4

2 tbsp	Butter
4	Pork chops
3	Small, firm bananas
	Salt and pepper
	Pinch of cayenne
1	Lemon
	Sprigs of parsley
1 tsp	Flour
½ cup	Broth

Melt the butter in a skillet over medium heat. Add the chops and cook for 10-12 minutes on each side depending on thickness.

Five minutes before the chops are cooked, peel bananas and cut in half lengthwise. Add to the skillet and sprinkle with salt, pepper and cayenne.

Lift out the pork chops and bananas and arrange on a warmed serving dish. Garnish with lemon and parsley. Stir the flour into the pan juices and add the broth gradually. Simmer for 2-3 minutes, then pour this gravy into a small serving pitcher.

Serve with plain boiled rice which will provide a contrast to the sweeter meat and bananas.

Pot roast pork with apples

Overall timing 1½ hours

Freezing Not suitable

To serve 4-6

¼ cup	Butter
2¼ lb	Boned pork roast
	Salt and pepper
2 tbsp	Cinnamon
8	Granny Smith apples

Preheat oven to 400°.

Melt 2 tbsp butter in a flameproof casserole. Roll pork roast in a mixture of salt, pepper and half the cinnamon, then brown on all sides. Cover casserole and cook in the oven for about 1 hour, turning roast over halfway through. Peel and core apples and cut into quarters.

Put into a saucepan with remaining butter and cinnamon. Cover and cook for about 10 minutes over a low heat, shaking the pan to prevent sticking.

Arrange the apples around the roast and cook, uncovered, for a further 15 minutes.

Remove pork from casserole; slice and place on warmed serving plate. Surround with apples. Make gravy from cooking juices and serve separately.

Russian pork chop casserole

Overall timing 30 minutes

Freezing Not suitable

To serve 4

1 lb	Potatoes
2 tbsp	Oil
4	Pork rib chops
	Salt and pepper
3 tbsp	Water
¼ lb	Button mushrooms
1 tsp	Garlic salt
½ cup	Sour cream
2 tbsp	Chopped parsley

Peel potatoes and cut them into very small, thin pieces. Melt the oil in a flameproof casserole and fry the potatoes for 5 minutes. Remove from pan with slotted spoon.

Season chops with salt and pepper. Add to casserole and cook for 1 minute on each side.

Drain off excess fat. Add water, cover and cook for 10 minutes.

Slice mushrooms. Add to casserole with fried potatoes and garlic salt and cook for a further 10 minutes. Stir in sour cream and 1 tbsp of the chopped parsley. Heat through. Sprinkle with remaining parsley just before serving.

Scandinavian pork

Overall timing 2 ½ hours plus soaking

Freezing Not suitable

To serve 6-8

½ lb	Plump prunes
1	Large tart apple
2 tbsp	Lemon juice
3 lb	Boneless pork blade
	Boston roast
	Salt and pepper
1 tbsp	Oil
1 cup	Broth
1 tbsp	Flour
	Sprig of parsley

Soak prunes in 1 cup hot water for 1 hour.

Preheat oven to 375°.

Drain prunes, reserving soaking water, and remove pits. Peel, core and slice apple. Toss in lemon juice to prevent browning and add to prunes.

Season pork. Place apple and prunes along the center, then roll up lengthwise and tie into a neat shape with fine string. Place in a roasting pan and rub oil into skin. Sprinkle with salt and roast for 45 minutes.

Pour prune soaking water and broth over pork. Reduce the temperature to 350° and roast for a further 1¼ hours.

Place meat on a warmed serving dish discard the string and keep hot. Drain pan juices into a small saucepan and skim off any fat. Blend flour to a smooth paste with ¼ cup cold water. Add to meat juices and bring to a boil, stirring constantly. Simmer for 4-5 minutes. Carve pork into thick slices and garnish with sprigs of parsley. Serve with gravy.

Pork with bananas and peanuts

Overall timing 1¾ hours

Freezing Not suitable

To serve 4

¾ lb	Onions
2	Garlic cloves
¼ cup	Oil
2 lb	Boneless pork
½ cup	Rice
16 oz	Can of tomatoes
1	Chicken bouillon cube
¼ tsp	Paprika
¼ tsp	Ground cinnamon
½ lb	Potatoes
2	Bananas
½ cup	Salted peanuts
	Salt

Peel and chop onions. Peel and crush garlic. Heat 2 tbsp of the oil in saucepan.

Add onions and garlic and fry until browned.

Cut pork into cubes and add to pan with rice. Cook till rice has absorbed oil, stirring frequently to prevent sticking. Add a little water if necessary to prevent burning. Remove from heat.

Pour juice from canned tomatoes into measuring cup.

Crumble in bouillon cube and add enough boiling water to give 2 cups. Chop tomatoes and add to pan with bouillon mixture, paprika and cinnamon. Cover and simmer gently for 20 minutes.

Meanwhile, peel and cube potatoes. Heat remaining oil in a skillet and fry potatoes over a low heat for about 10 minutes. Add them to the pan. Peel and slice bananas and stir into the stew with the peanuts. Cook for 10 minutes. Taste and add salt if necessary.

Pork chops with wine sauce

Overall timing 30 minutes

Freezing Not suitable

To serve 2

2 tbsp	Butter
2	Pork chops
	Salt and pepper
1	Small onion
3 tbsp	Dry white wine
3 tbsp	Water
1 tsp	Tomato paste
4	Gherkins
1 tsp	Chopped parsley
½ tsp	Prepared mustard

Melt the butter in the skillet and cook the pork chops gently for 10-12 minutes on each side. Season. Place on warmed serving dish and keep warm.

Peel and finely chop onion. Add to pan and fry till transparent. Stir in wine, water, tomato paste and seasoning and bring to a boil, stirring. Simmer for 3 minutes.

Remove pan from heat. Thinly slice two of the gherkins and stir into the sauce with parsley and mustard. Pour sauce over chops.

Garnish with remaining gherkins, cut into fan shapes, and serve with macaroni or noodles.

Pork with apples

Overall timing 1 ¼ hours

Freezing Suitable

To serve 6

2 lb	Slices of boneless pork loin
	Oil or oil and butter for frying
1 lb	Onions
¼ lb	Mushrooms
	Salt and pepper
1 cup	Hard cider
2 tsp	Dried sage
2	Cooking apples
1 cup	Grated cheese
2 cups	Soft bread crumbs
¼ cup	Butter

Preheat oven to 375°.

Brown pork slices in oil or oil and butter in a skillet. Remove from pan and set aside.

Peel and chop onions. Add to skillet and fry till lightly browned. Slice mushrooms, add to onions and cook for 1-2 minutes. Season with salt and pepper.

Pour hard cider into a small pan and boil until reduced by half.

Put layer of half onions and mushrooms on bottom of greased shallow casserole. Cover with half the pork and add a little sage. Repeat layers. Peel, core and slice apples and arrange on top with remaining sage. Add hard cider and salt and pepper to taste. Cover and bake for 1½ hours till meat is tender and apples soft.

Preheat broiler. Mix cheese and bread crumbs. Sprinkle in thick layer on top of apples. Dot with butter. Brown topping under the broiler. Serve hot, with baked potatoes and a green vegetable.

Beef pot roast

Overall timing 3 hours plus marination

Freezing Suitable: reheat in sauce in 400° oven for 1 hour

To serve 8-10

4 lb	Beef pot roast
	Salt and pepper
6 oz	Pork fat with rind
1	Large onion
3	Carrots
3	Stalks of celery
1	Garlic clove
	Sprigs of parsley
2	Bay leaves
	Sprigs of thyme
1 cup	Red or white wine
2 tbsp	Butter
2 tbsp	Oil
1	Pig's foot
½ cup	Water
1 tbsp	Tomato paste

Season the beef. Slice the pork fat. Wrap the fat around the beef and secure with string.

Peel and chop the onion and carrots. Trim and chop the celery. Peel and crush the garlic. Tie the parsley, bay leaves and thyme together with string (or use a bouquet garni).

Put the beef in a bowl and add the prepared vegetables, herbs, wine and seasoning. Marinate overnight.

The next day, drain the beef, reserving the marinade. Pat the beef dry with paper towels.

Melt the butter with the oil in a flameproof casserole and brown the beef on all sides.

Split the pig's foot and add to the casserole with the marinade, water and tomato paste.

Bring to a boil, then cover and simmer for 2½ hours.

Transfer the beef to a warmed serving platter and keep hot. Strain the cooking liquid discarding the foot and vegetables, and return to the casserole. Boil the liquid till reduced, then pour into sauceboat. Serve beef with sauce, and carrots and button onions.

Corned beef

Overall timing 3½ hours plus 2 weeks salting

Freezing Not suitable

To serve 8-10

2 lb	Coarse salt
½ cup	Sugar
1 tbsp	Saltpeter
1 oz	Pickling spice
4	Bay leaves
1	Sprig of thyme
5 lb	Brisket of beef
3	Large onions
5	Cloves
1	Stalk of celery
1 tsp	Black peppercorns
1 lb	Medium-size carrots
2	Medium-size white turnips
1 lb	Leeks

Put salt, sugar and saltpeter into a large saucepan with pickling spices tied in cheesecloth. Add bay leaves, thyme and 4½ quarts water and heat gently, stirring, till sugar and salt have dissolved. Bring to a boil, then pour into bowl and cool.

Add meat to bowl, making sure that salt solution covers it. Cover with clean dish-towel and leave to soak in cold place for up to 2 weeks. Turn meat occasionally.

To cook, remove from brine and wash under cold running water. Put into a large saucepan with one onion, peeled and spiked with cloves. Chop celery and add to pan with peppercorns. Cover with cold water and bring to a boil slowly. Skim, reduce heat, cover and simmer for 2½ hours.

Meanwhile, peel and chop carrots and turnips. Peel remaining onions and slice thickly. Chop leeks. Add vegetables to pan, bring back to a boil and simmer for 30 minutes. Use strained cooking liquid to make a sauce.

Steak and onions

Overall timing 30 minutes

Freezing Not suitable

To serve 2

¾ lb	Medium-size onions
6 tbsp	Butter
1 tbsp	Oil
2	Porterhouse or sirloin steaks
5 tbsp	White wine
	Pinch of sugar
	Salt and pepper

Peel and slice the onions into rings. Melt 2 tbsp of the butter with the oil in a skillet and fry the onions, stirring frequently, till brown and tender.

Meanwhile, melt the remaining butter in another skillet and fry the steaks for about 4 minutes on each side, according to taste. Place the steaks on a warmed serving plate and keep hot.

Add the steak cooking juices to the onions with the wine, sugar and seasoning. Stir well, then cook over high heat till the liquid reduces by about half. Pour over the steaks and serve with boiled new potatoes.

Beef and bean casserole

Overall timing 3 hours plus soaking

Freezing Suitable: reheat from frozen in 325° oven.

To serve 4-6

1 cup	Dried navy beans
2	Onions
2 tbsp	Oil
1 lb	Beef for stew
¼ tsp	Chili powder
1 tsp	Curry powder
2 tbsp	Flour
1 cup	Beef broth
16 oz	Can of tomatoes
2 tbsp	Tomato paste
2 tsp	Sugar
	Salt and pepper
1	Large tart apple
⅓ cup	Golden raisins

Put beans in a large saucepan and cover with cold water. Bring to a boil. Boil for 2 minutes, them remove from the heat, cover and leave to soak for 2 hours.

Preheat the oven to 325°.

Peel and chop onions. Heat oil in a flameproof casserole and fry onions for 3 minutes. Cut beef into chunks. Add to pan and fry quickly till brown. Stir in the chili and curry powder and flour. Fry for 2 minutes.

Gradually add broth and bring to a boil, stirring. Add the tomatoes with their juice and tomato paste. Drain beans and add to casserole with the sugar and seasoning. Cover and cook in the oven for 2 hours.

Peel, core and chop apple. Stir into casserole with raisins and cook for a further 30 minutes. Taste and adjust seasoning. Serve with crusty bread.

Beef and mushroom stuffed tomatoes

Overall timing 1 ¼ hours

Freezing Not suitable

To serve 3-6

6	Large tomatoes
1	Onion
2 tbsp	Butter
1 lb	Lean ground beef
¼ lb	Mushrooms
1 tbsp	Chopped parsley
6 tbsp	Dry white wine
	Salt and pepper
½ cup	Soft bread crumbs
	Lemon wedges

Preheat the oven to 350°.

Halve the tomatoes and scoop out the flesh. Chop the flesh. Peel and chop the onion.

Melt the butter in a skillet and fry the onion till transparent. Add the beef and fry for 5 minutes.

Chop the mushrooms and add to the pan with the parsley, chopped tomato flesh, wine and seasoning. Cover and cook for 10 minutes.

Stir in the bread crumbs. Spoon the mixture into the tomato halves. Arrange in an ovenproof dish and bake for 25-30 minutes till the tops are brown and crisp. Garnish with lemon wedges and serve with mashed potatoes.

Beef and split pea stew

Overall timing 2 hours plus soaking

Freezing Not suitable

To serve 6

1 ½ cups	Split peas
1	Onion
1 ½ lb	Beef for stew
2 tbsp	Butter
2 tbsp	Oil
2	Large carrots
	Bouquet garni
¼ tsp	Grated nutmeg
3 ½ cups	Beef broth
	Salt and pepper
½ lb	Potatoes
½ lb	Fresh bulk spinach

Wash and pick over the split peas and put into a saucepan of cold water. Bring to a boil and boil for 2 minutes. Remove from the heat, cover and leave to soak for 2 hours.

Peel and chop the onion. Cut the meat into bite-sized pieces. Heat the butter and oil in a flameproof casserole and fry the onion and meat till lightly browned.

Drain the split peas and add to the meat.

Scrape the carrots, slice thinly and add to the pan with the bouquet garni, grated nutmeg and broth. Add seasoning and bring to a boil. Reduce the heat, cover and simmer for 1 hour.

Peel and dice the potatoes. Chop the spinach and add both to the meat. Cook for a further 30 minutes. Taste and adjust the seasoning. Serve with creamed potatoes and a green vegetable, or boiled rice, or with crusty bread for a lighter meal.

Beef and vegetable stew

Overall timing 2 hours

Freezing Suitable: simmer for 30 minutes only; add vegetables after reheating in 350° oven for 45 minutes.

To serve 6-8

2 lb	Beef for stew
	Salt and pepper
¼ cup	Flour
1 lb	Onions
3 tbsp	Oil
3 cups	Beef broth
2 tbsp	Tomato paste
	Bay leaf
1 lb	Carrots
1 lb	Potatoes
1 lb	Parsnips
½ lb (2 cups)	Frozen peas

Wipe and trim the meat and cut into 1½ inch cubes. Season the flour and toss pieces of meat in it till evenly coated. Peel and slice the onions.

Heat the oil in a heavy-based saucepan and fry the onions till transparent. Add the meat and fry till browned all over, then add any remaining flour. Gradually add the broth and bring to a boil, stirring constantly. Add the tomato paste, bay leaf and seasoning, cover and simmer for 1 hour.

Scrape the carrots and peel the potatoes and parsnips. Cut all into chunks and add to the meat. Cover and simmer for a further 30 minutes. Taste and adjust seasoning.

Stir in the peas and simmer for 10 minutes, then serve.

Beef carbonnade

Overall timing 2-2½ hours

Freezing Suitable

To serve 4

2¼ lb	Beef for stew
6 tbsp	Butter
½ lb	Onions
1 tbsp	Flour
1 tbsp	Brown sugar
1 tbsp	Wine vinegar
2¼ cups	Dark beer
	Salt and pepper
1	Bouquet garni

Trim off any fat, then cut meat into large thin slices. Melt ¼ cup of the butter in a flameproof casserole. Add the meat and brown over a high heat. Remove beef from pan and put aside.

Peel and finely chop onions. Add onions to pan with remaining butter. Reduce heat, cover and cook for 10 minutes without burning.

Sprinkle flour into pan with the brown sugar and stir with a wooden spoon. Add vinegar, then the beer and stir till thick.

Replace beef in pan, season with salt and pepper and add bouquet garni. Cover and simmer for about 1½-2 hours over a low heat or cook in the oven at 350°. Discard bouquet garni before serving with mashed potatoes and chicory salad.

Pot au feu

Overall timing 4 hours

Freezing Not suitable

To serve 6

1	Onion
2	Cloves
2	Stalks of celery
1 tbsp	Chopped parsley
10 cups	Water
	Salt and pepper
1 lb	Beef shank
½	Stewing chicken
2	Leeks
1	Carrot
2	Potatoes

Peel onion and spike with cloves. Chop celery. Put into a flameproof casserole with the parsley, water and seasoning. Bring to a boil, then add beef and chicken. Reduce heat and simmer for 3 hours, skimming occasionally.

Remove beef and chicken from pan.

Cut meat off bones in small chunks. Trim and thinly slice leeks. Peel and slice carrot. Peel and chop potatoes. Strain broth and return to pan. Add meat and vegetables. Bring back to a boil, then reduce heat and simmer for 30 minutes. Serve hot with toasted bread.

Boeuf en croûte

Overall timing 1 ½ hours plus cooling and chilling

Freezing Not suitable

To serve 6

1 lb	Frozen puff pastry
3 lb	Fillet of beef
1	Garlic clove
2 tbsp	Softened butter
	Salt and pepper
1 tsp	Dried thyme
½ cup	Smooth liver pâté
1	Egg

Thaw pastry. Preheat the oven to 425°.

Trim meat of all fat, then tie into a neat shape with fine string. Make tiny slits in meat with tip of a sharp knife and insert slivers of peeled garlic. Spread butter over beef, season and sprinkle with half the thyme. Place in roasting pan and roast for 10 minutes. Take meat out of pan, place on a wire rack and leave to cool completely.

Remove string from meat. Roll out dough to a large rectangle just over twice the size of the meat. Place meat on one half of dough rectangle and brush dough edges with water.

Spread pâté over top of meat and sprinkle with remaining thyme. Fold dough over to enclose meat and seal edges. Trim around three sides and, if liked, make a hole in the top. Make a funnel from foil and place in hole if liked.

Place on dampened baking sheet.

Cut decorative shapes out of dough trimmings, dip them into beaten egg and arrange on dough. Glaze all over with egg and chill for 1 hour.

Preheat oven to 425°. Bake for 35 minutes till pastry is well risen and golden. Place on a warmed serving platter, garnish with watercress and serve, cut into thick slices.

Bohemian goulash

Overall timing 2¼ hours

Freezing Suitable: add cream after reheating

To serve 4

½ lb	Boneless shoulder of lamb
½ lb	Boneless pork
½ lb	Chuck steak
¼ cup	Butter
2	Onions
3	Garlic cloves
2 tsp	Paprika
	Bouquet garni
1 tbsp	Tomato paste
	Salt and pepper
½ cup	Sour cream

Cut meats into chunks. Melt the butter in a flameproof casserole and brown the meats on all sides.

Peel and slice the onions. Peel and crush the garlic. Add both to the casserole and cook gently till golden brown. Stir in the paprika and cook for 2 minutes.

Add bouquet garni, tomato paste and seasoning. Cover with water and bring to a boil. Cover and simmer for 1½ − 2 hours. Discard bouquet garni; adjust seasoning.

Stir in sour cream and serve with boiled new potatoes and a crisp green salad.

Chile con carne

Overall timing 3¼ hours plus overnight soaking

Freezing Suitable

To serve 4-6

1 cup	Dried brown or red beans
1 quart	Water
2 lb	Beef for stew
1	Onion
1 tbsp	Pork drippings or olive oil
2 tbsp	Butter
	Salt and pepper
1 tsp	Chili powder
1 tbsp	Sweet paprika
8 oz	Canned tomatoes
2 tsp	Cornstarch (optional)

Soak beans in water overnight. The next day, place water and beans in saucepan, cover and cook gently for 1½ hours.

Cut the beef into 1 inch cubes.

Peel and chop onion. Heat the drippings or oil and butter in a skillet. Add the beef. Cook till brown, then add the onion and cook till transparent.

Mix the meat and onion in with the cooked beans and season with salt, pepper, chili powder and paprika. Cover and cook gently for 1 hour.

Add the drained tomatoes, cover and cook for 30 minutes more. Adjust seasoning. If you wish to thicken the sauce, blend the cornstarch with a little water and add it to the mixture.

Cook for a few minutes, then serve from the cooking pot with plain boiled rice or wholewheat bread and a crisp green salad.

Corned beef hash

Overall timing 1 hour

Freezing Not suitable

To serve 4

2	Medium-size onions
6 tbsp	Oil or drippings
1	Stalk of celery
1	Large carrot
1 lb	Corned beef
	Salt and pepper
½ tsp	Powdered mustard
1 lb	Potatoes
2½ cups	Beef broth

Peel and thinly slice onions. Heat oil or drippings in saucepan. Add the onions and cook gently till transparent.

Finely chop celery. Peel and grate or dice carrot. Cut corned beef into 1 inch cubes. Add all of these to onions and cook for a few minutes, then season with salt, pepper and mustard (add more if a stronger taste is preferred). Cook gently for 5 minutes.

Meanwhile, peel potatoes and cut into chunks. Add to pan with boiling broth and cook for 20 minutes. Serve in warm bowls topped with fried or poached eggs, and with lots of fresh bread to mop up the juices.

Corned beef patties

Overall timing 30 minutes

Freezing Suitable: Cook from frozen

To serve 4

1 cup	Soft bread crumbs
3 tbsp	Warm milk
1 lb	Corned beef
2	Eggs
2 tbsp	Grated Parmesan cheese
	Grated rind of ½ lemon
	Flour
¼ cup	Butter
1 tbsp	Oil
	Lemon wedges
	Sprigs of parsley

Soak ¼ cup bread crumbs in the milk. Cut off any excess fat from the edge of the corned beef and discard. Mash beef in a bowl with a fork, then add squeezed-out bread crumbs, 1 egg, the cheese and lemon rind. Mix well.

With well floured hands, make patties from the mixture, then coat with flour. Lightly beat remaining egg. Using two forks, dip the patties first into beaten egg, then into remaining bread crumbs.

Heat butter and oil in a large skillet.

Add the patties and cook over a moderate heat till brown on both sides. Remove from pan and drain on paper towels. Garnish with lemon wedges and parsley.

Danish Meatballs

Overall timing 40 minutes

Freezing Suitable: fry meatballs after thawing, or fry from frozen, allowing 25 minutes

To serve 4

2 cups	Soft bread crumbs
½ cup	Milk
1	Small onion
½ lb	Ground beef
½ lb	Ground pork
	Salt and pepper
½ tsp	Ground allspice
1	Egg
2 tbsp	Flour
¼ cup	Butter
3 tbsp	Oil
8	Lettuce leaves
2	Pickled beets
¼ cup	Pickled red cabbage

Put bread crumbs into a bowl with the milk and soak for 10 minutes.

Peel onion and grate into a large bowl. Add the beef and pork, squeezed out bread crumbs, salt, pepper and allspice. Mix well and bind together with the beaten egg. Shape mixture into eight balls and coat lightly with flour. Heat butter and oil in a skillet. Add meatballs and fry gently for 15 minutes till brown all over and cooked through.

Meanwhile, wash and dry lettuce leaves and arrange in a shallow basket or serving dish.

Drain and dice pickled beets.

Remove meatballs from pan with a slotted spoon and drain on paper towels. Put one meatball on each lettuce leaf and spoon a little drained pickled cabbage and beet around. Serve with a lettuce, tomato and olive salad.

Flemish hotpot

Overall timing 3¾ hours

Freezing Not suitable

To serve 6

2	Pig's feet
1 lb	Piece of fresh pork sides
1 lb	Beef flank steak
3 quarts	Water
1 tbsp	Salt
2	Bay leaves
12	Peppercorns
3	Onions
4	Cloves
1½ lb	Potatoes
1 lb	Carrots
1 lb	Cabbage
	or
¾ lb	Bulk spinach

Split feet lengthwise, then halve each half.

Cut pork into 3 x 2 inch strips. Roll up beef and tie with string. Put water into a large kettle and add meats with salt, bay leaves and peppercorns. Peel onions and spike one with cloves. Add it to pan and bring to a boil. Skim and simmer for 2 hours.

Remove meats from pan. Strain stock and return to pan with meats.

Peel and chop potatoes. Scrape and thickly slice carrots. Chop cabbage or spinach.

Quarter remaining onions. Bring stock to a boil and add vegetables. Simmer for 20-25 minutes till vegetables are tender.

Lift meats out of stock. Remove string from beef and carve into thick slices. Strain off 2½ cups of the stock and reserve.

Taste the remaining stock and adjust the seasoning. Pour into a warmed tureen and serve immediately. Serve the meats after the soup with the reserved stock thickened and made into gravy.

Beef with onions

Overall timing 1 ½ hours

Freezing Suitable

To serve 4

1 ½ lb	Chuck steak
¾ lb	Onions
2 tbsp	Butter
1 tbsp	Oil
1 tbsp	Flour
1 ¼ cups	Beef broth
1	Garlic clove
½ tsp	Ground cumin
	Pinch of dried marjoram
2 tbsp	Wine vinegar
	Salt and pepper

Cut meat across the grain into thin finger-length strips. Peel onions, slice crosswise and separate rings. Heat the butter and oil in skillet. Add the onion rings and cook, covered, over a low heat till transparent. Turn them over frequently so that they cook evenly but do not brown. Remove from pan.

Increase heat, put strips of meat into pan and brown them. Return onion rings. Sprinkle with flour and stir. When flour begins to color, stir in broth, peeled and crushed garlic, cumin, marjoram, wine vinegar and seasoning. Cover and simmer for 1 hour. Serve with potatoes or rice and a crisp mixed salad.

Beef paprika

Overall timing 2¼ hours
Freezing Suitable

To serve 6

2 lb	Beef for stew
¼ cup	Pork drippings
½ lb	Onions
2	Garlic cloves
1 tbsp	Flour
2½ cups	Beef broth
½ tsp	Dried marjoram
½ tsp	Caraway seeds
	Brown sugar
2 tsp	Paprika
	Salt and pepper

Cube beef. Heat drippings in a large kettle or flameproof casserole. Add beef and fry till brown on all sides. Peel and chop onions and garlic. Add to pan and cook till transparent.

Sprinkle in flour and stir into mixture. Add broth, marjoram, caraway seeds, a pinch of sugar, paprika and seasoning. Cover tightly and cook gently for 1¾ − 2 hours.

Beef with oranges

Overall timing 1 ½ hours

Freezing Not suitable

To serve 6

2¼ lb	Sirloin tip or boneless rump roast
	Salt and pepper
	Pinch of dried thyme
3	Oranges
3 tbsp	Oil
½ cup	Hot beef broth
2 tbsp	Cornstarch
½ cup	Light cream
1 tbsp	Grand Marnier
1 tbsp	Brandy

Preheat the oven to 425°.

Score fat on beef with a sharp knife, then rub all over with salt, pepper and thyme. Grate rind of one orange, then squeeze juice from it and from a second orange. Thinly slice third orange.

Heat oil in roasting pan. Add beef and brown on all sides. Add orange juice. Roast for 50-55 minutes, basting at intervals. Place beef on serving platter with orange slices. Leave to stand for 10 minutes.

Meanwhile, make the sauce. Add broth to cooking liquid and cook for a few minutes, then strain into a saucepan. Cool a little and skim off any fat. Mix cornstarch with a little water, then stir in half of cream. Add to pan over gentle heat, stirring. Gradually stir in rest of cream, grated orange rind and seasoning. Cook gently for 3 minutes.

Warm Grand Marnier and brandy in a ladle, pour over beef and set alight. Serve with sauce.

Beef casserole

Overall timing 1 ½-2 hours

Freezing Suitable

To serve 4

2 lb	Chuck steak
¼ cup	Butter
2 tbsp	Oil
1	Large onion
1	Sweet red pepper
1	Sweet green pepper
1 tsp	Sugar
	Salt and pepper
1 tsp	Paprika
2 cups	Beef broth
6	Tomatoes

Wipe meat and dry well. Cut into large cubes. Heat butter and oil in a flameproof casserole, add meat and brown quickly on all sides over a high heat. Remove from pan.

Peel and finely chop onion. Seed and slice peppers. Add to the casserole and sprinkle with sugar. Stir well and add salt, pepper and paprika. Cover and cook for 10 minutes. Add beef and broth, cover again and simmer gently for 1-1½ hours till beef is tender.

Blanch tomatoes and remove skins. Quarter and add to casserole. Cover and cook for 5 minutes more.

Goulash

Overall timing 2¼ hours

Freezing Suitable

To serve 6

2 lb	Beef for stew
¼ cup	Pork drippings
½ lb	Onions
2	Garlic cloves
1 tbsp	Flour
1	Beef bouillon cube
2½ cups	Boiling water
	Salt and pepper
½ tsp	Dried marjoram
½ tsp	Caraway seeds
	Brown sugar
½ tsp	Paprika
½ lb	Potatoes
2	Green peppers
5	Tomatoes
½ cup	Red wine
½ cup	Sour cream (optional)

Cube beef. Heat drippings in a large kettle.

Add beef and fry till meat is brown on all sides. Peel and chop onions and garlic. Add to meat and cook till transparent.

Sprinkle in flour and stir into mixture.

Mix bouillon cube into boiling water and pour over meat. Season with salt, pepper, marjoram, caraway seeds, a pinch of sugar and paprika. Cover tightly and cook gently for 1¼ hours.

Peel and roughly chop the potatoes. Seed and slice peppers. Blanch, peel and chop tomatoes. Add all to pan, cover and cook for a further 25 minutes.

Add wine and check seasoning. Bring to simmering point and stir in sour cream, if using, or serve it separately.

Spicy meatballs

Overall timing 30 minutes

Freezing Not suitable

To serve 4-6

1	Small onion
1	Garlic clove
1½ lb	Lean ground beef
1	Egg
½ cup	Soft white bread crumbs
	Salt and pepper
½ tsp	Ground allspice
	Oil for frying

Peel and finely chop the onion; peel and crush the garlic. Put with rest of ingredients (except for the oil) into a bowl and mix well together.

Shape mixture into walnut-sized balls.

Fry the meatballs in shallow oil for about 15 minutes, turning once. Arrange on a warmed serving plate and serve with rice or pasta, and a tomato sauce or gravy.

Beef and carrot fry-up

Overall timing 45 minutes

Freezing Suitable

To serve 4

1 lb	Carrots
2	Leeks
¼ cup	Butter
1 cup	White wine or beef broth
	Salt and pepper
1 lb	Ground beef
½ tsp	Worcestershire sauce

Scrape carrots and chop into 1 inch pieces. Trim, wash and cut leeks into ½ inch slices. Melt half the butter in a skillet or saucepan and fry chopped carrots for 3 minutes. Pour in white wine or broth, cover and cook over a low heat for 20 minutes.

Add the leeks, season with salt and pepper and cook for a further 15 minutes, or until tender.

Meanwhile, put beef in bowl and mix in salt and pepper with a fork. Roughly shape mince into 1 inch pieces. Melt remaining butter in another skillet and fry meat for about 15 minutes until lightly browned and no longer pink in the middle. Stir from time to time.

Reduce any excess liquid in vegetable pan by boiling rapidly for a minute or two. Add meat and sprinkle with Worcestershire sauce.

Serve from the pan, with creamy mashed potatoes and a green vegetable.

Mustardy beef balls

Overall timing 25 minutes

Freezing Suitable: fry from frozen for 15 minutes

To serve 4

2	Large onions
1	Carrot
1 lb	Ground beef
1 tbsp	Chopped parsley
1	Egg
2 tsp	Mustard seeds
	Salt and pepper
3 tbsp	Flour
¼ cup	Oil
	Sprigs of parsley

Peel and finely chop the onions. Peel and finely grate the carrot. Put into a bowl with the beef, parsley and egg.

Roughly grind the mustard seed in a mortar or pepper mill and add to the beef with plenty of salt and pepper. Mix with a fork till the ingredients are well blended. Shape into 12 balls and coat with seasoned flour.

Heat the oil in a skillet and fry the meatballs for about 10 minutes till crisp and golden on all sides. Drain on paper towels and arrange on a warmed serving plate. Garnish with sprigs of parsley.

Hamburgers

Overall timing 20 minutes

Freezing Suitable: cook after thawing

To serve 4

1 lb	Finely ground beef
2	Onions
	Salt and pepper
3 tbsp	Oil
4	Hamburger buns
¼ cup	Butter
1 tbsp	Dijon-style mustard

Put the beef into a large bowl. Peel and finely chop one of the onions and add to the beef with plenty of seasoning. Mix. Divide into four portions and shape each into a thick burger.

Preheat a skillet or griddle and brush lightly with 1 tbsp oil. Fry the burgers for about 5 minutes, then turn carefully cook for a further 3-5 minutes.

While the hamburgers are cooking, peel and slice the second onion into rings. Heat the remaining oil in another skillet and cook the onion till golden.

Meanwhile, halve and lightly toast the rolls, then spread cut sides with the butter mixed with the mustard.

Place a hamburger in each roll and top with fried onions. Serve immediately.

Hamburgers with eggs

Overall timing 20 minutes

Freezing Not suitable

To serve 2

2	Onions
½ lb	Finely ground beef
	Salt and pepper
2 tsp	Oil
2	Tomatoes
¼ cup	Butter
2	Eggs
	Cayenne
	Watercress

Peel the onions. Finely chop half of one and cut the other half and the second onion into rings. Mix the chopped onion with the beef and season. Divide in half and shape into burgers.

Heat the oil in a skillet and fry the burgers for about 5 minutes on each side. Add the tomatoes halfway through the cooking.

Meanwhile, melt 2 tbsp butter in another skillet and fry the onion rings till crisp. Remove from the pan and keep hot. Add the eggs to the pan with the remaining butter and fry till set.

Top each burger with an egg and arrange on warmed plates with the onions and tomatoes. Sprinkle a little cayenne over the eggs. Keep hot.

Put the watercress into the pan with the butter and fry quickly. Use to garnish the burgers.

Neapolitan beef

Overall timing 2½ hours

Freezing Not suitable

To serve 4

2 oz	Canadian bacon
2 oz	Pork fatback
1 tbsp	Chopped parsley
1 tbsp	Raisins
	Salt and pepper
1 lb	Boneless beef rump roast
1	Onion
1	Garlic clove
2 tbsp	Oil
16 oz	Can of tomatoes
1¼ cups	Beef broth
¾ lb	Rigatoni
2 tbsp	Grated Parmesan cheese

Chop or finely grind bacon and pork fat and mix with parsley to form a smooth paste.

Work in raisins and seasoning. With a larding needle, make several deep holes in meat and firmly stuff paste into them. Tie meat into a neat roll with string.

Peel and finely chop onion. Peel and crush garlic. Heat oil in flameproof casserole, add onion and garlic and fry till transparent. Add the meat roll and fry, turning frequently, to seal. Press tomatoes and their juice through a sieve and add to casserole with the broth and seasoning. Mix well, cover and simmer for 1½ hours or till tender. Meanwhile, cook rigatoni in boiling salted water till tender.

Drain and keep hot.

Lift meat out of casserole, remove string and slice.

Pile on a warmed serving dish and arrange rigatoni around meat. Taste sauce and adjust seasoning. Spoon sauce over meat and rigatoni. Sprinkle with Parmesan. Serve immediately.

Pot roast beef with milk

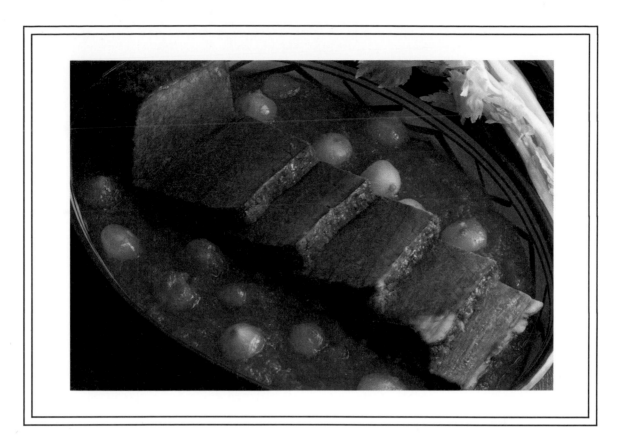

Overall timing 3 hours plus overnight marination

Freezing Not suitable

To serve 6-8

3 lb	Beef pot roast
1	Large onion
1	Large carrot
4	Stalks of celery
4	Fresh basil leaves
	Salt and pepper
2 cups	Milk
2 tbsp	Brandy (optional)
16 oz	Can of tomatoes
2 tbsp	Tomato paste
½ lb	Pearl onions
2 tbsp	Butter

Tie the meat into a neat shape. Put into a flameproof casserole. Peel and chop the onion and carrot. Wash, trim and chop the celery. Add to the meat with the basil leaves, salt, pepper, milk and brandy (if used), cover and marinate in a cool place overnight.

The next day, preheat the oven to 325°. Stir the tomatoes with juice and tomato paste into the casserole. Cover and cook in oven for 2 hours.

Meanwhile, peel the small onions and blanch in boiling water for 5 minutes. Melt butter in a skillet and fry onions till golden. Add to casserole and cook for further 30 minutes. Remove the meat from the casserole and discard the string. Place the meat on a warmed serving dish and keep hot.

Purée the cooking liquid in a blender or rub through a sieve, setting aside the pearl onions. Put purée and onions into saucepan and reheat. Meanwhile, cut the meat into slices. Taste and adjust the seasoning of the sauce and pour around the meat.

Hungarian beef

Overall timing 2½ hours

Freezing Suitable: reheat in 325° oven for 20 minutes, then add vegetables

To serve 4

1½ lb	Chuck steak
¼ cup	Lard
2	Onions
1 tbsp	Paprika
½ tsp	Caraway seeds
2 cups	Beef broth
	Salt and pepper
2	Green peppers
½ lb	Tomatoes
1 lb	Potatoes

Preheat the oven to 325°.

Cut steak into four equal-size pieces. Melt half the lard in a flameproof casserole, add the steaks and brown quickly on both sides. Remove from casserole and reserve. Peel and chop the onions. Add remaining lard to casserole and fry onions gently for about 10 minutes till golden, stirring frequently. Remove casserole from the heat and stir in the paprika, mixing well. Add the caraway seeds, one-third of the broth, the steak and seasoning. Cover and cook in the oven for 1½ hours.

Meanwhile, seed and slice peppers. Blanch, peel and chop tomatoes. Peel and thinly slice potatoes. Remove casserole from oven and stir in remaining broth, peppers, tomatoes and potatoes. Cover and cook for a further 30 minutes till potatoes are tender.

Taste and adjust seasoning.

Lift out meat and place in individual deep serving plates. Spoon vegetables and sauce over.

Steak and eggs

Overall timing 10 minutes

Freezing Not suitable

To serve 4

6 tbsp	Butter
4	Thick sirloin steaks
4	Eggs
	Salt and pepper
	Sprigs of parsley

Melt ¼ cup of the butter in a skillet.

Add the steaks and fry for about 3 minutes on each side or until browned and cooked to your taste.

Meanwhile, melt the remaining butter in another skillet and fry the eggs until just set. Use buttered poaching rings to make the eggs the same shape as the steaks, if possible. Place the steaks on a warmed serving plate and top with the eggs. Pour the steak cooking juices over and season. Garnish with parsley.

Yugoslav kabobs

Overall timing 25 minutes plus marination

Freezing Suitable: reheat in 400° oven for 25 minutes

To serve 6

1	Onion
1½ lb	Finely ground beef
¼ cup	Red wine
	Salt and pepper
1	Egg
2 tbsp	Oil
Garnish	
	Lemons
	Tomato slices
	Onion rings

Peel and finely chop the onion and add to the beef with the red wine and plenty of seasoning. Mix well and leave to marinate for 1 hour.

Preheat the broiler. Add the egg to the beef and mix together. Divide into 18 portions and shape each into a croquette.

Thread three onto each of six skewers. Broil the kabobs for 10-15 minutes, turning and basting with oil.

Arrange the kabobs on a warmed serving dish and serve with lemons cut into halves or wedges, tomato slices, onion rings and baked potatoes.

Steamed steak and kidney pudding

Overall timing 5¾ hours

Freezing Suitable: steam from frozen for 2½-3 hours

To serve 6

1½ lb	Chuck steak
½ lb	Beef kidney
1	Large onion
	Salt and pepper
3 tbsp	Flour
3 cups	Self-rising flour
¾ cup	Shredded suet
1¼ cups	Cold beef broth

Cut the meat into 1½ inch cubes. Trim the kidney, removing any core, and cut into 1 inch cubes. Peel and thinly slice the onion. Season flour and use to coat the steak, kidney and onion.

Sift the self-rising flour and 1½ tsp salt into a bowl and stir in the suet and enough cold water to mix to a soft but not sticky dough. Knead lightly till smooth.

Roll out on a floured surface to a round, big enough to line a 2 quart pudding basin or steaming mold (about 14 inches in diameter).

Cut out one-quarter of the dough round and reserve. Lift the large piece and place it in the basin, curving it so it fits neatly, and sealing the edges together. Place the meat mixture in the basin and add the cold broth to come half-way up the meat.

Roll out the reserved dough to a round slightly larger than the top of the basin. Brush the top edge of the dough lining with water and cover with the dough lid. Seal the edges well.

Cover with greased, pleated parchment paper and pleated foil, or a pudding cloth and secure with string. Steam for 5 hours, replenishing with boiling water as required.

Texan stew

Overall timing 2¼ hours

Freezing Suitable

To serve 4

1½ lb	Chuck steak
2 tbsp	Butter
1 tbsp	Oil
2½ cups	Beef broth
2	Green peppers
4	Tomatoes
11½ oz	Can of whole kernel corn
10 oz	Can of peas and carrots
	Salt and pepper
2 tsp	Cornstarch

Chop meat into 1 inch cubes. Heat butter and oil in saucepan, add meat and cook for 10 minutes till brown all over. Pour in broth and cook, covered, for 1½ hours over a gentle heat.

Wash, seed and cut green peppers into strips. Blanch, peel and chop tomatoes. Drain corn and peas and carrots. Add vegetables to meat and season well with salt and pepper.

Cook, covered, for 15 minutes over a moderate heat.

Blend cornstarch with a little water in a cup.

Stir into saucepan, then bring to a boil again, stirring until thickened. Serve stew in warmed bowls.

Beef and horseradish loaf

Overall timing 1 hour

Freezing Suitable: Reheat in 375° oven for 30 minutes.

To serve 4

½ cup	Strong beef broth
2 cups	Soft bread crumbs
1 lb	Ground beef
1	Large onion
1 tbsp	Grated horseradish
3	Eggs
2 tbsp	Cream sherry
	Salt and pepper

Preheat the oven to 350°.

Put the broth in a saucepan and bring to a boil. Sprinkle in the bread crumbs and stir till the crumbs have absorbed all the broth.

Put ground beef into a bowl with the bread crumb mixture. Peel and finely chop onion and add to meat with the grated horseradish, eggs, sherry and seasoning. Mix well with a wooden spoon until all ingredients are well blended.

Grease ovenproof dish and press in the mixture. Smooth the top and bake for 45 minutes. Serve hot with boiled potatoes and buttered carrots.

Tripe and onions french style

Overall timing 1 hour 50 minutes

Freezing Not suitable

To serve 4

1	Large carrot
1½ lb	Onions
2	Stalks of celery
2 quarts	Cold water
	Bay leaf
6	Peppercorns
1 tbsp	Lemon juice
1½ lb	Dressed tripe
6 tbsp	Butter
	Salt and pepper
2 tbsp	Chopped parsley
2 tbsp	White wine vinegar

Peel and chop carrot and one of the onions.

Trim and chop celery. Put into a saucepan with water, bay leaf, peppercorns and lemon juice. Bring to a boil and simmer for 30 minutes.

Strain and return to pan.

Cut tripe into pieces. Place in pan with broth and bring to a boil. Skim off any scum, cover and simmer for 1½ hours till tender.

Peel and slice remaining onions. Melt butter in a skillet, add the onions and fry gently till golden.

Drain the tripe thoroughly, discarding the broth, and cut into thin strips. Add to the onions with plenty of seasoning and fry over a moderate heat for 10 minutes, stirring frequently. Add the parsley and vinegar and mix lightly. Season to taste and pour into a warmed serving dish. Serve immediately with crusty bread.

Italian-style tripe

Overall timing 2½ hours plus soaking

Freezing Not suitable

To serve 6

½ cup	Dried navy beans
1½ lb	Blanket tripe
½ lb	Honeycomb tripe
2 oz	Slab bacon
1	Sprig of sage
1 lb	Ripe tomatoes
1	Onion
1	Carrot
1	Stalk of celery
¼ cup	Butter
	Salt and pepper
2 cups	Broth
¼ cup	Grated Parmesan cheese

Soak beans in cold water overnight.

The next day, wash and drain both types of tripe, shred the blanket tripe and cut the honeycomb tripe into squares. Finely chop the bacon. Wash the sage. Blanch, peel and seed the tomatoes and cut into small pieces. Peel and finely chop the onion and carrot. Wash and slice the celery.

Melt the butter in a saucepan and fry bacon and onion till just golden. Add the celery, carrot and sage and fry for 5 minutes longer.

Add the two types of tripe and the tomatoes. Season. Add the broth and bring to a boil. Cover the saucepan and simmer over a low heat for about 1 hour, stirring frequently to prevent the sauce from sticking to the saucepan.

Drain beans, rinse and add to the pan.

Cover and simmer for 1 hour more.

Taste and adjust seasoning and sprinkle with the grated Parmesan.

Roast lamb with garlic

Overall timing 2 hours

Freezing Not suitable

To serve 6

2-3	Garlic cloves
3½ lb	Leg of lamb
2 tbsp	Butter or drippings
	Salt and pepper

Preheat the oven to 350°.

Peel the garlic cloves and cut each into thin slivers. Place lamb in roasting pan with the thickest fat uppermost. Using a sharp, thin bladed knife, make incisions about 1 inch deep in the meat. Insert a sliver of garlic into each incision, pressing it down so it is level with the surface of the meat.

Spread the softened butter or drippings over the lamb and season well. Roast for 1¾ hours or until the juices run clear when a skewer is inserted into the thickest part of the meat.

Transfer meat to warmed serving plate and make the gravy in the usual way. Serve with green beans and tomatoes.

New Zealand roast lamb

Overall timing 3-3½ hours

Freezing Not suitable

To serve 4-6

4 lb	French-style leg of lamb
2 tbsp	Oil
	Fresh rosemary or dried rosemary
	Salt and pepper
¾ cup	Water
2 lb	Potatoes

Preheat oven to 350°.

Place lamb in roasting pan, then rub the oil into the skin. Either make small slits in the meat and insert fresh rosemary leaves, or sprinkle surface with dried rosemary leaves, then season well. Add water to the pan and roast for 3-3½ hours — the meat should almost be falling off the bone.

Meanwhile, peel, halve, parboil and dry the potatoes. Add them to the roasting pan 1½ hours before end of cooking time and turn them till coated in fat. Turn again once during roasting.

Cold roast lamb

Overall timing 2 hours

Freezing Not suitable

To serve 6

3½ lb	Shoulder of lamb
2 tbsp	Butter
2 tbsp	Oil
	Salt and pepper
6 tbsp	Broth or white wine
	Parsley sprigs

Preheat oven to 350°.

Place meat in roasting pan. Rub with butter and sprinkle with oil, salt and pepper. Pour broth or wine into pan. Bake for about 1¾ hours, basting frequently.

Remove lamb from pan and place on serving dish. Using a sharp knife, cut lamb through to the bone into squares, but do not remove meat. Leave to cool completely. Garnish with parsley.

Marinated lamb kabobs

Overall timing 1 hour

Freezing Not suitable

To serve 6-8

1½ lb	Boned leg of lamb
1 lb	Lean boneless veal
1	Large garlic clove
¼ cup	Oil
¼ cup	Lemon juice
	Cayenne pepper
	Salt and pepper
12-16	Pearl onions
4	Tomatoes
1	Eggplant
12-16	Cubes of bread
6-8	Small bay leaves
6-8	Mushrooms

Cut lamb and veal into bite-size pieces. Peel and crush the garlic and mix with the oil, lemon juice, a pinch of cayenne pepper and seasoning. Add the meat and marinate for 30 minutes, stirring frequently.

Peel onions. Quarter tomatoes and cut eggplant into pieces. Preheat the broiler and line broiling pan with foil.

Drain meat, reserving marinade, and thread onto 6-8 skewers with bread, onions, bay leaves, tomatoes, eggplant and mushrooms (flute them if liked). Broil kabobs for 15 minutes, turning and basting with marinade freqently. Serve hot.

Lamb and scallions

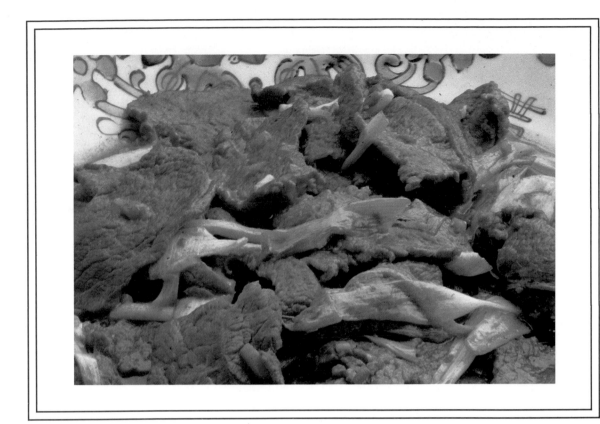

Overall timing 15 minutes plus marination

Freezing Not suitable

To serve 6

2 lb	Boned leg of lamb
2	Garlic cloves
2	Slices of fresh ginger
2 tbsp	Soy sauce
1 tbsp	Sherry
½ tsp	Salt
4	Scallions
3 tbsp	Oil

Slice lamb into thin, bite-size pieces. Peel and crush the garlic; cut ginger into tiny strips. Place lamb, ginger and garlic in a bowl and add soy sauce, sherry and salt. Mix well and marinate for 30 minutes.

Slice the scallions in half lengthwise, then across into 1 inch pieces.

Heat oil in skillet or wok. Add lamb and marinade, increase heat and stir-fry for 2 minutes. Add scallions and stir-fry for another minute. Serve immediately.

Lamb and eggplant mold

Overall timing 1 ¼ hours

Freezing Not suitable

To serve 6

2 lb	Eggplants
	Flour for dusting
¾ cup	Oil
2	Onions
3	Garlic cloves
1 lb	Ground lamb
16 oz	Can of tomatoes
	Chopped fresh thyme
	Salt and pepper
2	Eggs
1 tbsp	Tomato paste

Preheat the oven to 350°.

Cut eggplants into ¼ inch slices. Flour lightly. Heat most of the oil in a skillet and brown slices on both sides. Remove.

Peel and chop 1 onion and 2 garlic cloves. Heat another tablespoon oil in skillet. Fry onion and garlic until soft. Add lamb. Stir well and cook for 5 minutes.

Drain tomatoes, reserving juice. Chop tomatoes and add to lamb, mixing well. Simmer till fairly thick. Add 1 tsp thyme, salt and pepper. Remove from heat and cool slightly. Beat eggs. Stir eggs into lamb mixture.

Line bottom of a 1½ quart charlotte mold or soufflé dish with oiled waxed paper, then with slices of eggplant, overlapping edges. Line sides of mold, overlapping slices again. Press lamb into mold, overlapping slices again. Press lamb into mold. Cover with remaining eggplant slices. Bake for 45 minutes.

Meanwhile, peel and chop remaining onion and garlic finely. Cook gently in 1 tbsp oil in skillet until soft and transparent. Add juice from tomatoes, salt, pepper, a little thyme and tomato paste. Simmer for 10 minutes. Add a little water if necessary.

Unmold lamb and eggplant onto a plate and serve surrounded by sauce.

Beanpot with lamb

Overall timing 2 hours 50 minutes plus overnight soaking

Freezing Not suitable

To serve 4

1 cup	Dried navy beans
½ tsp	Salt
2 tbsp	Drippings
1 lb	Lamb blade chops
1	Onion
¼ cup	Tomato paste
½ tsp	Ground cumin
1	Bay leaf
½ tsp	Dried rosemary
½ tsp	Garlic salt
	Brown sugar
½ tsp	Vinegar
1 tbsp	Chopped chives

Soak beans in 1½ quarts water overnight. Next day, transfer beans and water to a saucepan and cook for 1 hour. Add salt.

Melt drippings in a flameproof casserole and brown chops well on all sides. Peel and chop onion and add to casserole. Cook till transparent. Add beans and water, tomato paste, cumin, bay leaf, rosemary and garlic salt. Cover and cook for 1 hour.

Uncover and cook for a further 20 minutes till meat is tender.

Just before serving, stir in a pinch of sugar and the vinegar and sprinkle with chopped chives.

Minted lamb meatballs

Overall timing 30 minutes

Freezing Suitable: fry after thawing

To serve 4

1¼ lb	Ground lamb
4	Garlic cloves
2 tbsp	Chopped fresh mint
1	Egg
	Salt and pepper
1 tsp	Ground coriander
	Flour
2 tbsp	Oil
	Mint or coriander
	leaves

Place the lamb in a bowl with the peeled and finely chopped garlic, chopped mint, egg, salt, pepper and coriander and mix with a wooden spoon till well combined. Make little balls of the mixture, flouring your hands so it doesn't stick, and roll the balls in the flour to coat.

Heat oil in a skillet, add meatballs and cook over a moderate heat for 8-10 minutes on each side till well browned. Drain on paper towels, then garnish with mint or coriander leaves and serve with rice.

Lamb curry

Overall timing 1 ½ hours

Freezing Suitable

To serve 2

1 lb	Boneless lamb
1	Onion
2 tbsp	Butter
1 tbsp	Oil
1 tsp	Curry powder
	Salt and pepper
1 ½ tbsp	Flour
1 cup	Broth
½ tsp	Tomato paste
	Bouquet garni
1	Tomato
½	Green pepper
2 oz	Button mushrooms
6 oz	New potatoes

Cut meat into cubes. Peel and chop onion.

Heat butter and oil in a skillet and fry onion till transparent.

Add curry powder and cook, stirring, for 2 minutes. Add meat and cook till golden on all sides. Season with salt and pepper, sprinkle with flour and stir over a high heat for a few minutes.

Reduce heat and stir in broth and tomato paste. Add bouquet garni and bring to a boil, stirring. Cover and cook gently for 40 minutes, stirring occasionally.

Chop tomato; seed and slice pepper; halve or slice larger mushrooms. Scrub potatoes but don't peel; cut into chunks.

Add prepared vegetables to pan and cook for a further 20 minutes. Discard bouquet garni before serving with plain boiled rice.

Casseroled lamb

Overall timing 2 hours

Freezing Not suitable

To serve 6

1	Carrot
1	Onion
1	Stalk of celery
4	Scallions
3 oz	Bacon
1	Garlic clove
2 tbsp	Oil
3 tbsp	Chopped parsley
2½ lb	Boneless shoulder of lamb
2 oz	Mushrooms
1 cup	Dry hard cider
½ cup	Broth
	Salt and pepper
1 lb	Potatoes

Peel and chop carrot and onion. Trim and chop celery and scallions. Chop bacon. Peel and crush garlic. Heat oil in flameproof casserole, add bacon, onion, scallions, celery, carrot, garlic and parsley and fry till lightly browned.

Tie meat into shape, if necessary, add to casserole and brown on all sides over high heat. Pour off excess fat from casserole. Chop mushrooms. Add to casserole with cider, broth and seasoning. Cover and cook for 1 hour over low heat.

Meanwhile, peel and quarter potatoes. Add to casserole and cook, covered, for a further 30 minutes. Taste and adjust seasoning then serve with broccoli.

Stuffed shoulder of lamb

Overall timing 2 hours

Freezing Not suitable

To serve 6

2	Onions
6 tbsp	Butter
¾ lb	Bulk sausage meat
2 tbsp	Chopped parsley
	Salt and pepper
2½ lb	Boneless shoulder of lamb
1 cup	Dry white wine
1 cup	Broth
	Bouquet garni
2½ lb	New potatoes
2	Tomatoes

Peel and chop onions. Melt 2 tbsp of butter in a skillet, add onions and fry until golden.

Add to the sausage meat with the parsley and seasoning.

Spread the lamb out, skin side down, on a board and season. Shape stuffing mixture into a large ball and place on lamb. Fold meat around stuffing to make a ball and tie firmly with string.

Melt 2 tbsp of butter in a flameproof casserole and brown meat all over. Add wine, broth, bouquet garni, salt and pepper. Cover and cook slowly for 1 hour.

Meanwhile, scrape potatoes. Melt remaining butter in a skillet, add potatoes and fry until golden brown. Arrange around the meat and cook uncovered for 20 minutes.

Blanch and peel tomatoes. Add to casserole and cook for 10 minutes more.

Remove bouquet garni. Place meat on warmed serving platter and remove string. Arrange potatoes and tomatoes around. Keep hot.

Transfer cooking liquid to a saucepan.

Thicken with 1 tbsp each of butter and flour mashed together. Serve this gravy separately.

Moussaka

Overall timing 2¼ hours

Freezing Suitable: bake from frozen in 375° oven for 1½ hours; add cheese sauce and bake 30 minutes more

To serve 6

1 lb	Onions
4	Garlic cloves
½ cup	Oil
1 tbsp	Chopped parsley
2 lb	Ground lamb
4	Tomatoes
2 tbsp	Tomato paste
	Salt and pepper
½ cup	Broth
1 cup	Soft bread crumbs
2 lb	Eggplants
¼ cup	Flour
2	Egg yolks
2 cups	Thick white sauce
1 cup	Grated sharp cheese

Peel and chop onions; peel and crush garlic.

Heat 1 tbsp oil in saucepan and fry onions, parsley, garlic and lamb till browned.

Peel and quarter tomatoes and add to pan with tomato paste, seasoning and broth.

Cover and simmer for 45 minutes. Remove from heat and stir in bread crumbs.

Preheat oven to 350°.

Thinly slice eggplants. Dust lightly with flour. Heat remaining oil in skillet and brown eggplants. Drain on paper towels.

Arrange two-thirds of eggplants to cover bottom and sides of greased casserole. Add meat mixture, then top with remaining eggplants. Stir beaten egg yolks into sauce with half cheese. Pour sauce over eggplants. Cover with rest of grated cheese.

Put casserole in a roasting pan containing a little water. Bake for 1 hour.

Lamb kabobs with prunes

Overall timing 50 minutes

Freezing Not suitable

To serve 4

12	Prunes
¾ cup	Red wine
1 lb	Boneless lamb cut from the leg
3 tbsp	Oil
	Salt and pepper
½ tsp	Dried thyme
2	Firm tomatoes
1	Medium-size onion
3	Thick slices of bacon

Put the prunes into a saucepan, add the red wine and bring to a boil. Remove from the heat and leave to soak for 30 minutes.

Cut lamb into 12 large cubes. Place in bowl with oil, seasoning and thyme. Cover and leave for 30 minutes.

Meanwhile, quarter the tomatoes. Peel the onion and cut through the root into eight wedges. Cut each bacon slice into four. Preheat a charcoal grill or the broiler.

Drain the prunes, reserving the wine. Make a slit in each prune and remove the pit.

Thread the lamb, prunes, tomatoes, bacon and onion onto four skewers. Brush the kabobs with the lamb marinade and the wine from the prunes, then sprinkle with salt and pepper.

Cook for about 15 minutes, turning occasionally, till the lamb is tender. Arrange on a warmed serving dish and serve with boiled rice.

Lamb steaks with beans

Overall timing 45 minutes

Freezing Not suitable

To serve 4

1½ lb	Green beans
¼ cup	Butter
	Salt and pepper
½ cup	Meat broth
5 tbsp	Oil
2	Slices of white bread
¼ tsp	Garlic salt
4	Lamb steaks (slices from top leg)
1 tsp	Mustard seed
2 tbsp	Chopped parsley
2	Tomatoes
	Sprigs of parsley

Trim beans and remove strings, if necessary. Break or cut into short lengths. Melt the butter in a saucepan. Add the beans and cook for a few minutes. Season with salt and pour in the broth. Cook for 10-15 minutes till tender. Meanwhile, heat half the oil in a skillet.

Halve the slices of bread and lightly brown them on both sides in the oil. Remove from pan and keep warm. Add rest of oil to pan and heat. Sprinkle garlic salt over the lamb steaks. Cook the steaks for 5 minutes on each side. Sprinkle with salt, then with pepper mixed with ground mustard seed.

Mix chopped parsley into beans and spread over bottom of warmed serving dish. Put lamb steaks on the bread and place on top of beans. Garnish with tomatoes, cut into eighths, and a few parsley sprigs.

Lamb casserole

Overall timing 2 hours

Freezing Not suitable

To serve 4

2 lb	Lean boneless lamb
1	Onion
2 tbsp	Butter
2 tbsp	Oil
5 tbsp	Dry white wine or sherry wine
	Salt and pepper
¼ lb	Slab bacon
1	Garlic clove
3 tbsp	Chopped parsley
½ cup	Light broth

Wipe and trim the meat and cut into neat pieces. Peel and finely chop the onion. Heat the butter and oil in a flameproof casserole, add the onion and fry for 5 minutes, stirring.

Add the meat and fry till browned on all sides. Add the white wine or sherry, salt and pepper. Finely chop the bacon. Add to the casserole with the peeled and crushed garlic, 2 tbsp of parsley and the broth. Stir, then cover and simmer for about 1½ hours till the meat is tender.

Taste and adjust the seasoning. Sprinkle with the remaining parsley and serve immediately with boiled potatoes and buttered carrots.

Braised lamb with green beans

Overall timing 1¾ hours

Freezing Suitable: cook for only 1 hour;
reheat from frozen in 400° oven for
1½ hours.

To serve 4

1½ lb	Green beans
2 tbsp	Oil
2 lb	Lamb arm chops
2	Large onions
16 oz	Can of tomatoes
	Salt and pepper
¼ tsp	Allspice
¼ tsp	Grated nutmeg
2	Sweet red peppers

Preheat oven to 350°.

Wash, trim beans and, if necessary, remove strings. Cut into 2 inch lengths.

Spread over the bottom of large ovenproof dish.

Heat oil in a large skillet. Trim lamb, removing excess fat. Fry in oil until brown on all sides. Drain and arrange on top of beans in casserole.

Peel onions and cut into wedges. Fry in oil until golden. With a spoon, break up tomatoes in their juice. Add to onions with salt, pepper, allspice and nutmeg, stir well and cook for 5 minutes.

Seed and slice peppers and add to casserole with tomato mixture. Cover tightly and cook in oven for 1½ hours. Serve with boiled rice.

Navarin

Overall timing 1¾ hours

Freezing Not suitable

To serve 6

¼ cup	Butter
2½ lb	Lamb neck slices
4	Small onions
1 tbsp	Flour
2 cups	Broth
3 tbsp	Tomato paste
	Bouquet garni
	Salt and pepper
1 lb	Carrots
1 lb	White turnips
1 lb	Potatoes
2 cups	Frozen peas
1 tbsp	Chopped parsley

Melt butter in flameproof casserole, add lamb and brown on all sides. Peel and quarter the onions. Add to casserole and fry gently for 5 minutes.

Sprinkle flour over and cook, stirring, for 2 minutes. Gradually stir in the broth, then add tomato paste, bouquet garni and seasoning and bring to a boil. Cover and simmer gently for 45 minutes.

Scrape and chop carrots. Peel turnips and cut into cubes. Add to casserole and cook for 15 minutes.

Meanwhile, peel potatoes and cut into chunks. Add to casserole and cook, covered, for 20 minutes. Add peas and cook for a further 10 minutes. Remove bouquet garni and adjust seasoning. Garnish with parsley and serve hot.

Summer casserole of lamb

Overall timing 1 hour

Freezing Suitable: add potatoes, beans and peas after reheating

To serve 6

½ lb	Pearl onions
2 tbsp	Butter
1 tbsp	Oil
2½ lb	Lamb blade chops
6	New carrots
2	Garlic cloves
1 tbsp	Flour
4	Tomatoes
2 tbsp	Tomato paste
2 cups	Broth
	Bouquet garni
	Salt and pepper
1 lb	New potatoes
¾ cup	Green beans
½ cup	Peas

Peel pearl onions. Heat butter and oil in flameproof casserole and fry onions for 5 minutes. Remove from pan and reserve. Add chops and brown on all sides over a high heat.

Scrape carrots and halve if liked. Add to pan with peeled and crushed garlic and cook for 5 minutes. Sprinkle flour over and cook, stirring, for 3 minutes. Blanch, peel and chop tomatoes. Add to the pan with tomato paste, broth, bouquet garni and seasoning. Cover and simmer for 30 minutes.

Scrape potatoes and add to the casserole.

Cook for a further 10 minutes. Top and tail the beans and cut into short lengths. Add to pan with peas and reserved onions. Cover and cook for a further 10 minutes. Taste and adjust seasoning if necessary. Discard bouquet garni and serve.

Dolma kara

Overall timing 1¾ hours

Freezing Not suitable

To serve 6

2 tbsp	Oil
2	Onions
1 lb	Boneless lamb
½ cup	Canned chickpeas
1¼ cups	Broth
	Salt and pepper
2 tbsp	Tomato paste
½ lb	Ground cooked lamb
⅓ cup	Cooked rice
1	Egg
1 tsp	Lemon juice
2 tbsp	Chopped parsley
	Ground cinnamon
1 lb	Zucchini

Heat oil in a saucepan. Peel and chop one of the onions and fry till tender. Cut the raw lamb into small pieces and add to the pan. Cook for 5-10 minutes.

Add the drained chickpeas, broth, salt, pepper and tomato paste. Cover and simmer for 30 minutes.

Preheat the oven to 375°.

Mix the cooked lamb with the cooked rice, remaining onion, peeled and finely chopped, egg, lemon juice, half the parsley, seasoning and a pinch of cinnamon.

Trim zucchini, then cut them in half lengthwise. Scoop out the seeds with a teaspoon. Blanch zucchini in boiling salted water for 5 minutes. Drain, then stuff the zucchini with the rice and lamb mixture.

Put the lamb and chickpea stew in an ovenproof dish and place stuffed zucchini on top. Cover with foil and bake for 40 minutes.

Serve hot sprinkled with remaining parsley.

Brittany roast lamb

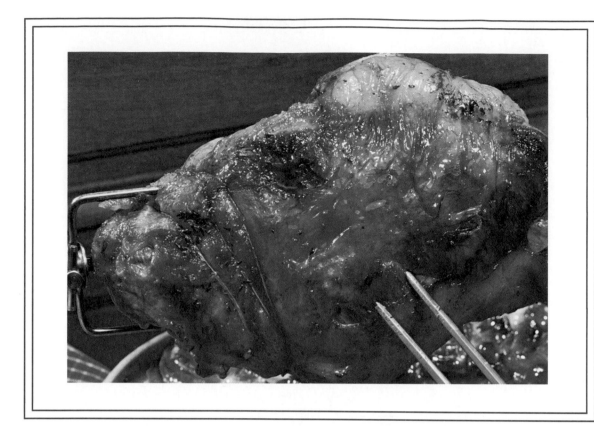

Overall timing 2½ hours

Freezing Not suitable

To serve 6

3	Garlic cloves
4 lb	Leg of lamb
¼ cup	Butter
	Salt and pepper
3 lb	Waxy potatoes
1 tsp	Dried thyme

Preheat the oven to 375°.

Peel the garlic cloves and slice very thinly.

Make incisions through the skin of the lamb and push the garlic into them. Rub half the butter over the lamb and season well.

Grease ovenproof dish with 2 tbsp butter. Peel potatoes and cut into slices about ⅛ inch thick. Arrange half over bottom of dish. Sprinkle with half the thyme and seasoning and dot with half the remaining butter. Repeat layer.

Place dish centrally on shelf below center of the oven. Place the lamb directly onto the oven shelf above the potatoes so the juices will run onto the potatoes. Roast for 1¾-2 hours till the juices are only slightly pink when thickest part of meat is pierced with a fine skewer.

Place the lamb on a warmed serving dish and carve. Serve the potatoes from the ovenproof dish with a separate dish of cauliflower and whole green beans.

Lamb with lima beans and potatoes

Overall timing 1½ hours

Freezing Not suitable

To serve 6

4	Tomatoes
¼ lb	Bacon slices
2	Onions
2	Garlic cloves
2 tbsp	Oil
6	Lamb blade chops
1¼ cups	Broth
1 tbsp	Lemon juice
½ tsp	Dried thyme
	Salt and pepper
1½ lb	Shelled fresh lima beans
1½ lb	Potatoes

Blanch, peel and chop tomatoes. Chop bacon. Peel and slice onions. Peel and crush garlic. Heat oil in a flameproof casserole and fry onion and garlic till transparent. Add the chops and bacon and brown on all sides. Pour off excess fat from pan.

Add tomatoes, broth, lemon juice, thyme and seasoning. Cover and simmer for 30 minutes.

Blanch beans in boiling water for 5 minutes, then drain. Peel and slice the potatoes. Add potatoes to casserole and cook for 10 minutes. Add beans and cook for a further 15 minutes. Serve immediately.

Italian-style roast lamb

Overall timing 1 ½ hours

Freezing Not suitable

To serve 4

2 lb	Lamb sirloin roast
	Sprigs of rosemary
2 lb	Potatoes
2 tbsp	Oil
6 tbsp	Butter
1	Garlic clove
	Salt and pepper

Preheat the oven to 350°.

Slash through the chops, leaving the loin joined at the bottom. Place sprigs of rosemary in the slashes. Peel potatoes and cut into chunks.

Heat oil and butter in roasting pan. Add the meat and arrange potatoes around it. Peel and crush garlic and add to the lamb and potatoes with salt and pepper. Roast for 45 minutes – 1 hour, basting occasionally and turning potatoes halfway through cooking. Serve with a mixed salad or a seasonal green vegetable and gravy.

Sweet sour lamb riblets

Overall timing 1 ¼ hours plus
overnight marination

Freezing Not suitable

To serve 4

1	Onion
2	Garlic cloves
2 tbsp	Honey
1 tbsp	Oil
¼ cup	Soy sauce
½ cup	Dry sherry
1 tsp	Ground ginger
¼ cup	Sugar
1 tsp	Ground allspice
2½ lb	Breast of lamb riblets

Peel and slice onion. Peel and crush garlic. Put into a bowl with honey, oil, soy sauce, sherry, ginger, sugar and allspice. Add the breast riblets, cover and marinate overnight in the refrigerator, turning occasionally.

The next day, preheat the oven to 375°.

Put the meat into a roasting pan and spoon the marinade over. Bake for 1 hour, basting frequently with the marinade. Serve with plain boiled rice.

Turkish lamb stew

Overall timing 2¾ hours plus overnight soaking

Freezing Not suitable

To serve 6

1½ cups	Dried chickpeas
	Bouquet garni
2 lb	Boneless shoulder of lamb
1	Onion
1	Garlic clove
¼ cup	Butter
3 tbsp	Oil
1 tsp	Ground cumin
1 tsp	Ground cinnamon
	Sprig of rosemary
1	Bay leaf
	Salt and pepper
16 oz	Can of tomatoes
2 tbsp	Lemon juice
1 tbsp	Chopped parsley

Soak chickpeas in water to cover overnight. The next day, drain chickpeas and put into saucepan. Cover with boiling water and add bouquet garni. Cover and simmer for 1 hour.

Cut the lamb into large pieces. Peel and chop the onion. Peel and crush garlic. Heat the butter and oil in flameproof casserole and fry the onion, garlic, cumin and cinnamon for 5 minutes. Add meat pieces to pan and brown on all sides.

Drain chickpeas and add to casserole with the rosemary, bay leaf, seasoning and tomatoes. Cover and cook gently for 1½ hours. Adjust seasoning and sprinkle with lemon juice and parsley just before serving.

Lamb with cauliflower

Overall timing 1 ½ hours

Freezing Not suitable

To serve 6

1	Small cauliflower
1 ¼ cups	Water
	Salt and pepper
½ lb	Tomatoes
1	Large onion
2	Garlic cloves
2 tbsp	Oil
2 lb	Breast of lamb riblets
½ cup	Tomato juice

Trim cauliflower and divide into florets. Bring water and ½ tsp salt to a boil in a saucepan, add cauliflower and cook for 5 minutes. Drain, reserving cooking liquid.

Blanch, peel and chop tomatoes. Peel and chop onion. Peel and crush garlic. Heat the oil and garlic in a saucepan, add onion and cook till transparent. Season meat, add to pan and brown quickly on all sides over a high heat, turning frequently to prevent the riblets burning.

Add tomatoes to pan with reserved cooking liquid and tomato juice. Bring to a boil. Add pepper and cook, covered, for 1 hour.

Add cauliflower and cook for a further 15 minutes. Adjust seasoning, then serve with boiled potatoes.

French lamb hot-pot

Overall timing 1¾ hours

Freezing Not suitable

To serve 4

¼ lb	Slab bacon
2	Onions
2 tbsp	Butter
2½ lb	Lamb neck slices
1 tbsp	Flour
2 cups	Light broth
1 lb	White turnips
1 lb	Potatoes
2	Garlic cloves
1 tsp	Sugar
	Bouquet garni
	Salt and pepper
4	Large tomatoes

Cut the bacon into strips. Peel onions and slice into thin rings. Heat the butter in a saucepan and fry the bacon and onions. Add lamb and fry over a high heat till browned on both sides. Sprinkle in the flour and cook, stirring, till it browns. Gradually add the broth and bring to a boil.

Peel the turnips and potatoes and cut into quarters. Add to the pan with the peeled and crushed garlic, sugar, bouquet garni and seasoning. Cover and simmer for 1¼ hours.

Remove bouquet garni. Add the tomatoes and cook for a further 15 minutes. Taste and adjust the seasoning. Arrange the meat and vegetables on a warmed serving dish and spoon the cooking liquid over. Serve immediately.

Shepherd's pie

Overall timing 1 hour

Freezing Not suitable

To serve 4

2 lb	Potatoes
	Salt and pepper
1	Large onion
3 tbsp	Oil
1	Garlic clove
1 lb	Ground cooked
	lamb
¼ cup	Butter
½ cup	Milk
¾ cup	Grated cheese

Peel and halve potatoes. Cook in boiling salted water for 25-30 minutes.

Peel and finely chop onion. Heat oil in a skillet, add onion and cook for about 10 minutes. Peel and crush garlic. Add garlic and meat to pan and cook for about 5 minutes, stirring.

Preheat the oven to 425°.

Drain potatoes and mash with half the butter and the milk. Season to taste. Cover bottom of overproof dish with half of the mashed potato, cover with the meat, then spread or pipe the remaining potato on top.

Sprinkle cheese over potato, dot with remaining butter and bake for about 15 minutes till the top is browned. Serve with green salad.

Lamb stew

Overall timing 2 hours

Freezing Suitable; add potatoes after reheating

To serve 4

¼ cup	Butter
1 tbsp	Oil
2½ lb	Lamb arm chops
2 tbsp	Flour
1¼ cups	Broth or water
½ lb	White turnips
2	Onions
½ lb	Carrots
1	Stalk of celery
	Bouquet garni
	Salt and pepper
1 lb	Potatoes

Heat the butter and oil in a flameproof casserole, add the chops and brown well on all sides. Sprinkle flour over and cook, stirring, for 3 minutes. Gradually stir in broth or water.

Peel and chop turnips and onions. Peel carrots and cut into pieces lengthwise. Add to casserole with celery stalk, bouquet garni and seasoning. Cover and cook for 1½ hours over low heat.

Peel potatoes and cut into large chunks. Add to casserole and cook, covered, for a further 20 minutes. Discard bouquet garni before serving.

Russian lamb burgers

Overall timing 30 minutes

Freezing Suitable; coat with flour and fry after thawing.

To serve 2

½ cup	Soft bread crumbs
2 tbsp	Milk
½ lb	Ground lamb
¼ cup	Grated Gruyère cheese
1	Small egg
	Salt and pepper
1 tbsp	Flour
2 tbsp	Butter
8 oz	Can of tomatoes

Put bread crumbs in a large bowl with the milk and soak for a few minutes. Add the lamb, grated cheese, egg and seasoning and mix well. Divide the mixture into four and shape into patties. Coat lightly with flour.

Melt butter in a skillet and fry for 5 minutes on each side. Remove from pan with a spatula and place on a warmed serving dish. Keep hot.

Heat tomatoes in a saucepan. Drain and arrange on serving dish with the burgers. Serve a hot tomato sauce separately, if liked, and mashed potatoes topped with crisp fried bread crumbs and bacon bits.

Shoulder of lamb with turnips

Overall timing 2 hours

Freezing Not suitable

To serve 6

3 lb	Boneless shoulder of lamb
	Salt and pepper
1	Carrot
1	Onion
6 tbsp	Butter
	Bouquet garni
¾ cup	Broth
2 lb	White turnips
½ lb	Pearl onions

Preheat the oven to 350°.

Season the lamb inside and out. Roll up and tie firmly with string into a neat shape. Peel and thinly slice carrot and onion.

Melt the butter in flameproof casserole, add onion and carrot and fry till golden. Add lamb and brown on all sides. Season and add bouquet garni and broth. Cover and cook in the oven for 1 hour.

Peel turnips and pearl onions. Place in a saucepan of cold salted water and bring to a boil. Drain and dry on paper towels. Arrange turnips and onions around the meat and baste with juices. Return to oven and cook for a further 45 minutes.

Remove bouquet garni and string. Transfer lamb to warmed serving plate and surround with turnips and onions.

Greek lamb stew with spinach

Overall timing 1½ hours

Freezing Not suitable

To serve 6

2 lb	Boneless shoulder of lamb
1	Large onion
2 tbsp	Oil
2 tbsp	Butter
1 lb	Ripe tomatoes
2 tbsp	Tomato paste
	Dried oregano
	Salt and pepper
2½ cups	Hot water or broth
1¼ lb	Fresh bulk spinach

Cut the lamb into bite-size pieces. Peel and thinly slice the onion. Heat the oil and butter in a flameproof casserole, add the lamb and onion and fry over a moderate heat for about 10 minutes till browned, stirring occasionally.

Blanch, peel and chop the tomatoes. Add to the pan with the tomato paste, a pinch of oregano, seasoning and water or broth. Mix well and bring to a boil. Cover and simmer for 1½ hours till the lamb is tender.

Wash spinach and shred finely. Add to the pan, stir, cover and cook for a further 10 minutes. Taste and adjust the seasoning. Pour into a warmed dish and serve.

Lamb with potatoes and onions

Overall timing 2½ hours

Freezing Not suitable

To serve 8

4½ lb	Leg of lamb, french-style
½ cup	Butter
	Salt and pepper
1 lb	Onions
2 lb	Potatoes
2 cups	Broth
	Sprigs of rosemary
	Bouquet garni

Preheat the oven to 350°.

Place the meat in roasting pan, spread with half the butter and season. Roast for 1¼ hours.

Peel and slice the onions. Peel and quarter potatoes. Melt remaining butter in skillet, add onions and potatoes and fry till golden brown. Add broth, rosemary, bouquet garni and seasoning and cook for 5 minutes, stirring occasionally.

Arrange potato mixture around meat and roast for a further 45 minutes till meat is tender.

Remove bouquet garni. Place lamb on warmed serving dish and surround with potato mixture. Serve with green vegetables.

Stuffed breast of lamb

Overall timing 2½ hours

Freezing Not suitable

To serve 8

Stuffing

3	Lamb kidneys
½ lb	Slab bacon
½ lb	Bulk sausage meat
½ tsp	Ground allspice
3 tbsp	Chopped parsley
1 tsp	Dried marjoram
1	Egg
	Salt and pepper
1 or 2	Boneless breasts of lamb
2 lb	Potatoes
1½ lb	Small carrots
4	White turnips
2	Stalks of celery
4	Leeks
1	Onion
4	Cloves
¼ cup	Butter
2½ cups	Broth
	Bouquet garni

Preheat the oven to 325°.

Prepare and finely chop kidneys. chop bacon. Mix all stuffing ingredients.

Cut a deep pocket in lamb and fill with stuffing. Sew up opening. If using two breasts, place together with skin side out and sew around sides.

Peel potatoes and carrots. Peel and halve turnips. Chop celery and leeks. Peel onion and spike with cloves. Melt butter in flameproof casserole, add meat and brown all over. Remove. Add vegetables and fry for 2 minutes. Return meat and add broth, bouquet garni and salt. Cover and cook in oven for 2 hours.

Slice meat. Arrange vegetables around meat, discarding onion. Boil broth till reduced by half. Strain over vegetables.

Lamb with vegetables

Overall timing 2 hours

Freezing Not suitable

To serve 6

3 lb	Shank half of leg of lamb
5 cups	Water
1 lb	Small rutabaga
½ lb	Carrots
2	Large leeks
	Salt and pepper
1 lb	Waxy potatoes
1 tbsp	Chopped parsley
2 tbsp	Flour

Wipe and trim the lamb, removing any skin. Put into a large saucepan with the water and bring slowly to a boil. Meanwhile, peel the rutabaga thickly and cut into quarters. Scrape and thickly slice the carrots. Wash and trim the leeks; slice the white parts and reserve the green.

Add the prepared vegetables to the pan with salt and pepper and bring back to a boil. Cover and simmer for 1 hour.

Peel the potatoes and cut into quarters. Add to the pan and simmer for 20 minutes.

Shred the green part of the leeks and add to the pan with the parsley. Simmer for 5 minutes.

Remove the meat from the pan and keep hot. Blend the flour to a smooth paste with 5 tbsp water. Add to the cooking liquid and bring to a boil, stirring constantly. Simmer for 3 minutes. Taste and adjust the seasoning, then pour into a warmed serving dish. Arrange the meat on top and serve.

Lamb fricassee

Overall timing 1 ¼ hours

Freezing Not suitable

To serve 4

1 ½ lb	Boneless shoulder of lamb
1	Onion
1	Stalk of celery
¼ cup	Butter
1 tbsp	Flour
½ cup	Milk
½ cup	Broth
1	Carrot
2	Sprigs of parsley
2	Sprigs of basil
2	Sprigs of sage
	Salt and pepper
2	Egg yolks
1 tbsp	Lemon juice

Cut the lamb into neat pieces. Peel and chop the onion. Trim and chop the celery. Melt half the butter in a flameproof casserole. Add onion and celery and fry over low heat for 5 minutes without browning.

Stir in the flour and fry until golden. Gradually add milk and broth, stirring constantly. Bring to a boil, then remove from heat.

Scrape and chop carrot. Tie in a piece of cheesecloth with parsley, basil and sage. Add to casserole with remaining butter, the lamb and seasoning. Stir well. Cover and cook gently for 1 hour, stirring occasionally. Remove cheesecloth bag.

Beat the egg yolks in a bowl and blend with the lemon juice. Stir gently into the fricassee until blended; do not boil. Taste and adjust seasoning, then serve with creamed potatoes and minted peas.

Tarragon chops

Overall timing 25 minutes plus chilling

Freezing Not suitable

To serve 4

½ cup	Softened butter
1 tbsp	Chopped fresh tarragon
1 tbsp	Dry white wine
	Salt and pepper
4	Double loin lamb chops
	Tarragon leaves

Mash the butter in a bowl with the tarragon, wine and seasoning till evenly mixed. Put half into a small serving dish and chill for 1 hour till firm.

Preheat the broiler. Curl the thin tail pieces of the chops in next to the eye to make a neat shape and secure with skewers. Arrange on the broiling pan. Spread half the soft tarragon butter over the chops and broil for 6-7 minutes.

Turn the chops with tongs and spread with the remaining soft tarragon butter. Broil for a further 5-7 minutes according to taste.

Arrange the chops on a warmed serving dish and pour the juices from the broiling pan over. Top each chop with a curl of the chilled tarragon butter and a tarragon leaf. Serve immediately with remaining tarragon butter.

Paprika lamb stew

Overall timing 2 hours

Freezing Suitable

To serve 6

2	Green peppers
2	Onions
1	Garlic clove
4	Slices bacon
2 lb	Boneless shoulder of lamb
16 oz	Can of tomatoes
2 tbsp	Tomato paste
1 tsp	Paprika
1 tsp	Sugar
2½ cups	Broth
	Salt and pepper
½ cup	Sour cream

Seed the peppers and cut into strips. Peel and finely chop the onions. Peel and crush the garlic. Dice the bacon. Heat a flameproof casserole, add the onions, garlic and bacon and fry over a high heat till golden.

Cut the meat into cubes and add to casserole. Brown on all sides. Stir in peppers, tomatoes and their juice, tomato paste, paprika, sugar, broth and seasoning. Cover and cook gently for 1½ hours till meat is tender.

Taste and adjust seasoning and serve with boiled potatoes and sour cream for everyone to spoon on top of the stew.

Piquant kidneys

Overall timing 30 minutes

Freezing Not suitable

To serve 2

½ lb	Lamb kidneys
2	Bacon slices
1	Onion
½ lb	Long macaroni
	Salt and pepper
2 tbsp	Butter
1½ tsp	Flour
1¼ cups	Beef broth
1½ tsp	Tomato paste
¼ tsp	Dried sage

Prepare and thinly slice kidneys. Dice bacon. Peel and chop onion. Cook macaroni in boiling salted water for 15 minutes till tender.

Meanwhile, melt butter in skillet and fry kidneys for 3 minutes, stirring from time to time. Remove from pan.

Add bacon and onion to pan and fry gently till golden. Sprinkle flour over and cook, stirring, for 2 minutes. Add broth, tomato paste, sage and seasoning. Bring to a boil, stirring, then return kidneys to pan, reduce heat and simmer for 15 minutes.

Drain macaroni and arrange in warmed serving dish. Spoon kidneys and sauce over and serve hot with crisp lettuce and cucumber salad.

Hot lamb mold with mint

Overall timing 40 minutes

Freezing Suitable

To serve 4

10	Blanched almonds
1	Small onion
1	Garlic clove
2 tbsp	Oil
1 lb	Ground lamb
⅓ cup	Raisins
½ cup	Chopped almonds
3 tbsp	Dried bread crumbs
2 tbsp	Chopped fresh mint
1	Egg
	Salt and pepper

Preheat oven to 350°. Lightly oil a ring mold and arrange blanched almonds around the bottom.

Peel and finely chop onion and garlic. Heat oil in a skillet and fry onion and garlic till soft. Add lamb and cook until browned. Tip onion, garlic and lamb into a bowl and add raisins, chopped almonds, bread crumbs, mint, egg, salt and pepper. Mix well.

Press lamb mixture into ring mold. Cover with foil and bake 30 minutes.

Unmold onto a warmed serving dish, and fill center with mixed cooked vegetables.

Kidneys in their jackets

Overall timing 45 minutes

Freezing Not suitable

To serve 4

8	Lamb kidneys in their suet
4	Slices of bread
	Salt and pepper
1	Tomato
	Sprigs of parsley

Preheat the oven to 400°.

Place kidneys in their suet in a roasting pan.

Bake for about 35 minutes till the fat is crisp and golden. Pour a little of the melted fat from the roasting pan into a skillet and fry the bread till golden on both sides.

Arrange slices in warmed individual dishes.

Cut a deep cross in the top of the kidneys and open out like petals. Season inside and place on top of fried bread. Wash tomatoes and cut into wedges. Arrange with parsley sprigs on top of kidneys. Serve with sauté or mashed potatoes.

Kidney brochettes

Swiss liver kabobs

Overall timing 25 minutes

Freezing Not suitable

To serve 4

½ cup	Unsalted butter
2 tbsp	Chopped parsley
1 tbsp	Lemon juice
1 lb	Lamb kidneys
3	Tomatoes
1 tsp	Dried rosemary
2 tbsp	Oil
	Salt and pepper

Mash the butter with the parsley and lemon juice until well combined. Form into a roll, wrap in wax paper and chill until firm.

Preheat the broiler.

Prepare kidneys and cut in half. Cut tomatoes into thin wedges. Thread kidneys and tomato wedges alternately on skewers. Sprinkle with rosemary and brush with oil.

Broil for 10-15 minutes, turning once. Season and garnish with slices of parsley butter. Serve immediately with matchstick potatoes and sprigs of watercress.

Overall timing 35 minutes

Freezing Not suitable

To serve 4

1 lb	Calf's or lamb's liver
	Salt and pepper
10	Sage leaves
10	Bacon slices
¼ cup	Butter

Preheat the broiler.

Cut the liver into 20 bite-size lengths. Season. Wash and dry sage leaves. Stretch the bacon slices then cut in half. Wrap bacon slices around liver pieces, including a sage leaf in alternate rolls. Thread onto four oiled skewers.

Melt the butter in the bottom of the broiler pan. Balance the skewers across the pan and brush butter over. Broil for 10-15 minutes till cooked and crisp, turning frequently and brushing with butter. Serve immediately with boiled new potatoes.

Liver and bacon

Overall timing 20 minutes

Freezing Not suitable

To serve 4

4	Slices of lamb's or calf's liver
	Salt and pepper
2 tbsp	Flour
8	Bacon slices
2 tbsp	Butter
1 tbsp	Chopped parsley
1 tbsp	Lemon juice

Trim and wipe the liver. Dust with seasoned flour.

Heat a large skillet, add the bacon and fry till crisp and golden. Remove from pan and keep hot.

Melt the butter in skillet, add the liver and fry over a moderate heat for 3-4 minutes on each side.

Arrange liver on serving plate and put bacon on top. Add the parsley and lemon juice to the pan and bring to a boil. Season and spoon over liver. Serve immediately with watercress, matchstick potatoes and broiled whole tomatoes.

Liver with sultanas

Overall timing 20 minutes

Freezing Not suitable

To serve 4

1 lb	Calves' or lamb's liver
2 tbsp	Oil
2 tbsp	Butter
⅓ cup	Golden raisins
1 tbsp	Flour
1 tbsp	Red wine vinegar
	Water
	Salt and pepper

Cut the liver into 8 slices. Heat the oil and butter in a frying skillet, add liver and fry for 3-4 minutes each side till tender. Remove from skillet with slotted spatula and arrange on warmed serving dish. Keep hot.

Toss the raisins in the flour and add to the skillet. Fry, stirring, for 3 minutes. Add vinegar, water and seasoning to taste. Cook for a further 3 minutes, stirring continuously. Pour the sauce over the liver and serve with boiled potatoes.

Liver and onions

Overall timing 20 minutes

Freezing Not suitable

To serve 6

1½ lb	Onions
6	Slices of calf's or lambs' liver
	Salt and pepper
3 tbsp	Flour
6 tbsp	Butter
2 tbsp	Chopped parsley (optional)

Peel and slice onions. Trim and wipe liver. Season the flour and use to coat the liver.

Melt the butter in a large skillet. Add the onions and fry till golden. Add liver slices and fry for 3-4 minutes on each side. Stir in parsley if using.

Transfer to a warmed serving dish and top with fried onions. Spoon pan juices over. Serve with boiled potatoes and parsleyed baby carrots.

Liver and bacon kabobs

Overall timing 25 minutes

Freezing Not suitable

To serve 4

¾ lb	Piece of lamb's liver
6 oz	Slab bacon
¼ lb	Button mushrooms
¼ cup	Melted butter
⅔ cup	Fine bread crumbs
½ tsp	Paprika
	Salt
	Lemon slices

Wipe and trim the liver and cut into 1 inch cubes. Cut the bacon into thick slices then into squares. Wipe and trim the mushrooms.

Preheat the broiler. Thread the bacon, liver and mushrooms onto four skewers. Brush with melted butter. Mix the bread crumbs, paprika and salt together on a plate. Turn the kabobs in the crumbs till evenly coated. Arrange on the broiler pan and broil for about 15 minutes, turning the kabobs frequently and brushing them with the fat that runs from the bacon.

Arrange the kabobs on a warmed serving dish and serve immediately with lemon slices for squeezing, and saffron rice.

Brains Milan-style

Overall timing 15 minutes plus soaking and cooling

Freezing Not suitable

To serve 4

4	Lambs' brains
2 tsp	Vinegar
	Salt and pepper
	Bouquet garni
¼ cup	Flour
1	Egg
¼ cup	Soft bread crumbs
¼ cup	Butter
	Sage leaves
	Lemon wedges

Put the brains in a bowl of cold water with 1 tsp of the vinegar. Soak for 15 minutes.

Drain the brains. Holding them under running water, carefully pull away membranes and blood vessels. Put the brains into a saucepan and cover with cold water. Add the remaining vinegar, salt and bouquet garni. Bring to a boil, then remove from the heat. Leave to cool in the liquid.

Drain the brains and dry on paper towels. Break into small pieces and coat with the flour. Beat the egg. Dip the brains into the egg, then coat with the bread crumbs.

Melt the butter in a skillet till foaming. Add the brains and cook for 5 minutes till brown on all sides. Garnish with sage leaves and serve with lemon wedges.

Braised stuffed hearts

Overall timing 2 hours

Freezing Not suitable

To serve 6-8

1	Onion
¼ cup	Butter
½ cup	Long-grain rice
2 cups	Broth
2	Calves' hearts
	or
4	Lambs' hearts
1	Lemon
2 tbsp	Chopped parsley
1 tbsp	Chopped fresh sage
1	Egg
	Salt and pepper
½ lb	Bacon slices
2 tbsp	Dry sherry wine

Preheat the oven to 350°.

Peel and chop onion. Melt half the butter in a pan and fry onion till golden. Add rice and 1¼ cups of the broth. Bring to a boil, cover and
simmer for 20 minutes till tender. Remove from the heat.

Prepare hearts, using kitchen scissors to cut through pockets inside. Wash well and dry with paper towels. Grate rind and squeeze juice from lemon. Add both to pan with parsley, sage, egg and seasoning. Mix well and spoon into hearts.

Stretch bacon with the back of a knife. Wrap around the hearts, tying them on with fine string.

Melt remaining butter in flameproof casserole and brown hearts all over. Pour over remaining broth, add sherry wine, cover and cook in the oven for 1 hour.

Remove string and slice hearts. Arrange on serving dish, garnish with sage and serve.

Hearts with potatoes and onions

Overall timing 1¾ hours

Freezing Not suitable

To serve 4

2	Calves' hearts
	or
4	Lambs' hearts
½ cup	Butter
2½ cups	Beef broth
	Bouquet garni
6 oz	Bacon slices
½ lb	Pearl onions
2 lb	Potatoes
	Salt and pepper
2 tbsp	Red currant jelly
1 tbsp	Chopped parsley

Prepare hearts. Melt ¼ cup butter in saucepan, add hearts and brown on all sides. Pour in broth, add bouquet garni, cover and simmer for 1½ hours until tender.

Meanwhile, cut bacon into strips. Peel onions. Peel and chop potatoes. Cook onions in boiling salted water for 5 minutes, then add potatoes and cook for a further 5 minutes. Drain well.

Melt remaining butter in skillet. Add bacon and fry till golden. Add potatoes, onions and seasoning and cook till golden brown, turning occasionally. Pour off excess fat from pan.

Remove hearts from pan and place on warmed serving dish. Keep hot. Reduce liquid in pan to about ½ cup, then stir in red currant jelly. Pour over vegetables in skillet and cook for 2 minutes. Arrange vegetables around hearts. Spoon over cooking juices and serve sprinkled with parsley.

Sweetbread kabobs

Overall timing 35 minutes plus marination

Freezing Not suitable

To serve 4

1 lb	Prepared lambs' sweetbreads
4	Thick bacon slices
6 tbsp	Oil
1 tbsp	Lemon juice
	Salt and pepper
½	Lemon
	Sprigs of parsley

Cut the sweetbreads in half. Cut the bacon into 1 inch pieces. Thread the sweetbreads and bacon alternately onto four greased skewers.

Mix the oil, lemon juice and seasoning in a shallow dish. Add the kabobs, turning them to coat with the marinade. Leave in a cool place for 1 hour.

Preheat the broiler. Place each kabob on a piece of foil, shaping the foil into a dish so it will hold the marinade, and pour the marinade over. Arrange the kabobs on the broiler pan and broil for 15-20 minutes, turning frequently in the marinade, till the sweetbreads are tender.

Arrange the kabobs on a warmed serving dish and pour the marinade over. Garnish with the lemon and parsley and serve immediately with crusty bread.

Honey-glazed smoked pork

Overall timing 1 ½ hours

Freezing Not suitable

To serve 6-8

4 lb	Smoked pork shoulder roll
	Whole cloves
2 tbsp	Clear honey
3 tbsp	Brown sugar
2	Granny Smith apples
¼ cup	Butter

Place the pork in a large kettle and cover with cold water. Bring to a boil. Remove any scum. Reduce heat, cover and simmer gently for 1 hour. Preheat the oven to 350°. Remove pork from pan, allow to cool slightly, then cut off any rind. Score fat in a lattice pattern and put a clove in the center of each "diamond." Put in a roasting pan.

Gently heat honey and sugar in a small saucepan until melted. Brush over the surface of the pork. Cook in the oven for 20 minutes, basting from time to time. Take care not to let the glaze burn.

Five minutes before the pork is cooked, peel, core and slice apples into ¼ inch thick rings. Melt butter in a skillet and fry the apple rings on both sides until lightly golden and tender.

Serve pork on a dish surrounded by apple rings.

Ham roasted in stout

Overall timing 2½ hours plus cooling

Freezing Suitable; slice meat and cover with sauce; reheat from frozen in moderate oven.

To serve 6

3 lb	Ham
2	Onions
1¼ cups	Stout or other dark beer
2 tbsp	Butter
2 tbsp	Flour
¼ tsp	Crushed caraway seed
	Pepper

Preheat the oven to 400°.

Place ham in an ovenproof dish. Peel and chop onions. Cover ham with onion. Pour stout over. Roast for 2 hours, turning meat once during cooking.

Remove meat from dish and place on warmed serving dish. Keep hot. Skim fat from surface of cooking liquid. Place liquid in measuring cup and make up to 1¼ cups with water if necessary.

Melt butter in saucepan. Stir in flour and allow to brown lightly. Gradually add cooking liquid and simmer, stirring, till thickened. Season with crushed caraway seed and black pepper. Cook for 5 minutes, then pour over the roast and serve.

Bacon and cabbage casserole

Overall timing 1 ¼ hours

Freezing Not suitable

To serve 4

1	Medium-size head white cabbage
2	Onions
2 tbsp	Lard
½ lb	Canadian bacon
1 lb	Ground beef
1 tsp	Caraway seeds
½ cup	Beef broth
	Salt and pepper
¼ cup	Butter
½ lb	Bacon slices

Preheat the oven to 375°.

Discard any marked outer leaves of the cabbage. Save two or three good ones. Cut the remaining cabbage in half. Remove the core, then shred the cabbage. Put with reserved leaves into a saucepan of cold water. Bring to a boil and drain. Set aside.

Peel and chop the onions. Melt the lard in a large saucepan, add the onions and cook gently for 3-4 minutes. Chop Canadian bacon. Add to the saucepan. Cook for 2-3 minutes. Add the ground beef and cook, stirring, until brown. Add the caraway seeds, broth and seasoning. Simmer for 10 minutes.

Melt the butter in a small saucepan. Put half of the shredded cabbage in the bottom of an ovenproof dish and pour the melted butter over. Spread the beef mixture evenly over the cabbage. Cover with remaining shredded cabbage and top with whole leaves. Arrange the bacon slices over the top of the cabbage. Bake for 45 minutes.

Frankfurters with apple purée

Overall timing 20 minutes

Freezing Suitable; add frankfurters when reheating

To serve 4

8	Apples
1¼ cups	Sweet white wine or hard cider
	Salt and pepper
½ cup	Butter
8	Frankfurters

Peel, core and chop apples. Place in a saucepan with the wine or cider. Cover and cook over a low heat till the apples are soft, then beat until pulpy with a wooden spoon. Season to taste.

Melt butter in a skillet, add the frankfurters, cover and cook gently over low heat till heated through.

Put apple purée on a warmed serving dish, place the frankfurters on top and serve immediately with crusty bread or baked potatoes.

Smoked pork with lentils

Overall timing 2½ hours

Freezing Not suitable

To serve 6

2¼ lb	Smoked pork arm picnic roast	
1	Carrot	
2	Onions	
1	Garlic clove	
	Bouquet garni	
8	Peppercorns	
2 cups	Brown lentils	
	Salt and pepper	

Put roast in a large saucepan and cover with cold water. Peel and slice the carrot; peel and quarter the onions; peel and halve the garlic. Add to the pan with the bouquet garni and peppercorns. Bring to a boil, cover and simmer for 45 minutes.

Remove bouquet garni. Wash and pick over the lentils. Add to pan, cover and cook for a further hour till lentils are tender. Adjust seasoning, then arrange on warmed dish and serve with mustard.

Sausage surprise

Overall timing 35 minutes

Freezing Not suitable

To serve 4-6

2 lb	Potatoes
	Salt and pepper
1 lb	Pork link sausages
1 ¼ cups	Milk
¼ cup	Butter
1 ½ cups	Grated cheese
½ tsp	Grated nutmeg

Preheat the broiler. Peel the potatoes and cut into quarters. Cook in boiling salted water for about 10 minutes till tender.

Meanwhile, broil the sausages for about 15 minutes, turning occasionally till well browned.

Drain the potatoes in a colander. Add the milk to the pan and bring just to a boil. Return the potatoes to the pan with the butter and mash till smooth.

Beat 1 cup of the cheese into the potatoes with nutmeg and seasoning. Spread the mixture in a flameproof dish and push the sausages diagonally into the potato so that the tops are just showing.

Sprinkle the remaining cheese over and broil for about 5 minutes till golden.

Savory smoked pork mold

Overall timing 2½ hours plus setting

Freezing Not suitable

To serve 8-10

2 lb	Smoked pork shoulder or arm picnic
1	Onion
1	Clove
1	Stalk of celery
2	Garlic cloves
	Bouquet garni
	Salt and pepper
5 tbsp	Chopped parsley
1 tbsp	White wine vinegar
2 tsp	Unflavored gelatin
1 tsp	Dried tarragon
1 tsp	Dried chervil
2	Egg whites
	Cucumber peel
1	Sweet red pepper
¼ cup	Pitted ripe olives

Put pork in a pan, cover with water and bring to a boil. Drain off water. Peel onion and spike with clove. Chop celery. Peel garlic. Add vegetables to pan with 2 quarts water, the bouquet garni and seasoning. Bring to a boil and simmer for 1 hour.

Soak parsley in vinegar.

Lift pork out of pan. Remove meat from bone and chop. Reduce cooking liquid to 1¼ cups by boiling fast. Strain cooking liquid and return to pan. Add gelatin and herbs. Lightly beat egg whites and add. Leave for 30 minutes, then bring nearly to a boil, beating. Remove from heat and pour through a scalded jelly bag or several layers of cheesecloth.

Spoon a little gelatin into dampened mold. Chill till set.

Chop cucumber peel. Seed and slice pepper. Arrange decoratively in mold with olives. Add a little more gelatin and chill again till set. Arrange pork pieces and parsley in layers in mold. Pour remaining gelatin over, cover and chill overnight.

Frankfurter crescents

Overall timing 45 minutes

Freezing Suitable (dough only)

To serve 4-6

2 cups	Flour
½ tsp	Salt
6 tbsp	Butter
¼ cup	Cottage or cream cheese
2	Eggs
4	Frankfurters

Preheat the oven to 400°.

Sift the flour and salt into a bowl. Rub in the butter, then mix in the cheese and 1 of the eggs. Roll out the dough and cut into 4 inch squares.

Cut the frankfurters into small pieces and place one on a corner of each dough square. Roll up in the dough, to the opposite corner, then curve the ends of the roll slightly inwards to make a crescent shape. Place the crescents on a baking sheet.

Beat the remaining egg and brush over the crescents. Bake for 20 minutes or until golden and crisp. Cool on a wire rack.

Sautéed sausage and peppers

Overall timing 30 minutes

Freezing Suitable

To serve 6

2	Large onions
3-4	Sweet, red, yellow or green peppers
1	Large tomato
2 tbsp	Olive oil
12	Large, spicy fresh Italian sausages or similar
2	Garlic cloves
1¼ cups	Chicken broth
1 tsp	Tomato paste
	Salt and pepper
5	Sprigs of fresh thyme or
½ tsp	Dried thyme
	Sprig of parsley

Peel and slice onions. Halve and seed peppers, and cut into ½ inch strips. Peel and chop tomato.

Heat oil in a large skillet and quickly sauté peppers until lightly colored. Remove and set aside. Add sausages and allow them to brown over a high heat, turning several times. Remove and set aside.

Lower heat and add onions. Cook for 5 minutes till golden, stirring occasionally. Peel and chop garlic and add to pan. Stir in broth, tomato paste, chopped tomato, salt, pepper and thyme. Add sausages. Cover and simmer for about 10 minutes till sausages are cooked and sauce has thickened slightly.

Add peppers to pan. Stir and simmer for a further 5 minutes. Garnish with parsley sprig and serve hot with rice or noodles.

Sausage and vegetable stew

Overall timing 3¼ hours

Freezing Not suitable

To serve 6

1	Head white cabbage
3	Carrots
1	Leek
1	Smoked pig's knuckle
1	Fresh pig's knuckle
2 quarts	Water
	Salt and pepper
2	Large potatoes
½ lb	Pork link sausages

Shred cabbage. Peel and chop carrots. Trim and slice leek. Put vegetables into a pan with the knuckles, water and seasoning. Bring to a boil, then cover and cook for 2½ hours.

Remove knuckles from pan and cut meat from bones. Peel potatoes and cut into large chunks. Cut sausages in half. Add meat, potatoes and sausages to pan and cook for a further 30 minutes. Taste and adjust seasoning before serving.

Sausages in cider sauce

Overall timing 50 minutes

Freezing Not suitable

To serve 4

1 lb	Boneless pork chops
8	Pork link sausages
2 tbsp	Lard
1	Large onion
1	Carrot
1	Stalk of celery
4	Large tomatoes
1	Garlic clove
½ cup	Dry hard cider
	Salt and pepper
2 tbsp	Butter
1½ cups	Long grain rice
1 quart	Chicken broth
3 tbsp	Grated Parmesan cheese

Cut the pork chops into bite-size pieces. Twist each sausage in half to make 16 small sausages. Melt the lard in a skillet and fry the pork and sausages gently, turning frequently, for 10 minutes.

Meanwhile, peel and chop the onion and carrot. Trim and chop the celery. Quarter the tomatoes. Peel and crush the garlic. Add the vegetables to the skillet with the cider and seasoning. Cover and simmer for 20 minutes.

Melt the butter in a saucepan, add the rice and fry, stirring, for 2 minutes. Add the broth and bring to a boil, stirring. Cover and simmer for about 15 minutes till rice is tender and liquid is absorbed.

Remove the rice from the heat and stir in the cheese. Taste and adjust the seasoning and fluff with a fork. Pile into a warmed serving dish and arrange sausages and pork on top. Spoon cider sauce over and serve immediately with a mixed salad.

Roast ginger chicken

Overall timing 1 ¼ hours

Freezing Not suitable

To serve 4

1	Tart apple
1 inch	Piece of ginger root
⅔ cup	Cooked long grain rice
¾ cup	Plain yogurt
6 tbsp	Softened butter
	Salt and pepper
3 lb	Roaster chicken

Preheat the oven to 400°.

Peel, core and grate apple. Grate or finely chop ginger and add to apple with rice, yogurt, ¼ cup of the butter and seasoning. Mix well together. Use to stuff chicken.

Place chicken on its side in a roasting pan and dot with remaining butter. Roast for 15 minutes, then turn chicken onto its other side and roast for 15 minutes. Turn chicken onto its back and continue roasting for a further 30 minutes or until tender. Baste frequently.

Remove chicken from roasting pan and place on warmed serving dish. Serve with gravy made from pan juices, green or mixed salad and sauté or creamed potatoes.

Alsatian chicken

Overall timing 1 ½ hours

Freezing Not suitable

To serve 4-6

8	Chicken pieces
1	Garlic clove
2 oz	Slab bacon
¼ cup	Oil
2	Onions
1 cup	Dry white wine
¼ lb	Mushrooms
2	Bay leaves
2 tbsp	Chopped parsley
2 tbsp	Chopped chives
	Salt and pepper
1 tbsp	Arrowroot
½ cup	Light cream
	Sprigs of fresh parsley

Rub the chicken all over with halved garlic clove. Dice bacon. Fry in flameproof casserole till brown. Add oil and when hot brown chicken pieces on all sides.

Peel and finely chop onions. Add to casserole and brown. Pour in half the wine, cover and cook for 35 minutes.

Slice mushrooms and add to casserole with bay leaves, half the chopped parsley and chives, and seasoning. Cover and cook for 10 minutes.

Discard bay leaves. Take out chicken pieces with a slotted spoon and place on warmed serving dish. Keep hot. If there's a lot of liquid in casserole, boil till reduced by half. Mix arrowroot with remaining wine and stir into pan juices. Cook, stirring, till sauce thickens, then gradually stir in cream. When hot (it must not boil) pour sauce over chicken. Garnish with remaining chopped parsley and chives and parsley sprigs.

Cheesy chicken rolls

Overall timing 45 minutes

Freezing Not suitable

To serve 6

6	Boneless chicken breast halves
	Salt and pepper
2 tsp	Prepared mustard
6	Thin slices of sharp cheese
6	Thin bacon slices
	Flour
¼ cup	Butter
2 tbsp	Oil
1¼ cups	Light beer
12	Pitted green olives

Remove skin from chicken breasts. Season underside and spread with mustard. Place a slice of cheese on each. Roll up and wrap a bacon slice around. Tie firmly and coat in flour.

Heat butter and oil in flameproof casserole. Lightly brown chicken rolls all over. Add beer. Cover and simmer for 10 minutes.

Drain olives and add to casserole. Cover and simmer for 10 minutes more. Carefully remove string from chicken rolls and serve with rice or potatoes.

Chicken with turnips

Overall timing 1 hour

Freezing Not suitable

To serve 6

½ lb	Pearl onions
6	Saffron strands
3 lb	Roaster chicken
1 lb	Small white turnips
½ lb	Zucchini
¼ cup	Butter
2 tbsp	Oil
1 cup	Chicken broth
4	Bay leaves
	Salt and pepper

Blanch and peel onions. Soak saffron in 2 tbsp warm water. Cut chicken into 12 portions. Peel and quarter turnips. Slice zucchini.

Heat butter and oil in skillet and brown chicken pieces all over. Remove from pan with a slotted spoon. Add onions and turnips and fry for 3 minutes, then add zucchini and fry for a further 2 minutes till browned.

Return chicken to pan with saffron and soaking water, broth, bay leaves and seasoning. Cover and simmer for 20 minutes till chicken is tender.

Lombardy chicken

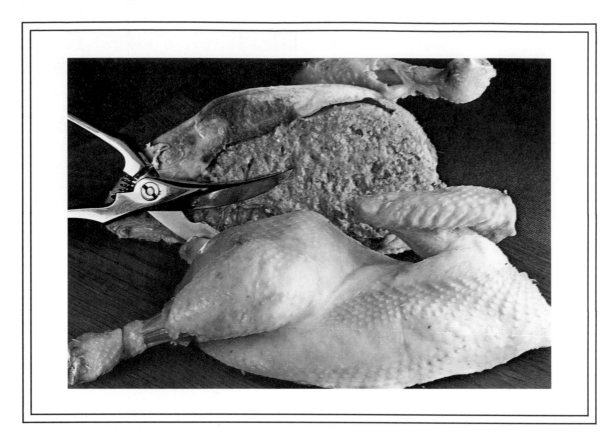

Overall timing 2¼ hours

Freezing Not suitable

To serve 4

1 cup	Bread crumbs
½ cup	Milk
¼ lb	Cooked ham
3 lb	Chicken with giblets
¼ lb	Bulk sausage meat
2 tbsp	Chopped parsley
1	Egg
½ cup	Grated Parmesan cheese
2 tbsp	Dry vermouth
	Salt and pepper
1	Stalk of celery
1	Carrot
1	Onion
2 tsp	Arrowroot

Soak bread crumbs in milk. Grind or finely chop ham, and liver and heart from giblets. Place in a bowl with the sausage meat, parsley, egg, Parmesan, vermouth, salt and pepper. Squeeze liquid out of the bread crumbs and add them to the mixture. Mix well together.

Wipe chicken and stuff with the mixture, leaving a little space for expansion. Close opening with a small skewer or by sewing with thick thread.

Half fill a large saucepan with lightly salted water and bring to a boil. Chop celery and carrot. Peel and quarter onion. Add them all to the pan and bring back to a boil.

Add the chicken and the rest of the giblets. Cover and simmer for 1¾ hours or until chicken is tender.

Lift chicken out and keep warm on serving dish. Dissolve the arrowroot in a little of the strained broth, then add a further 1 cup strained broth. Cook, stirring, until thick and clear.

Chicken à la king

Overall timing 35 minutes

Freezing Suitable

To serve 4

1 lb	Cooked boneless chicken
1	Onion
1	Large green pepper
¼ cup	Butter
¼ cup	Flour
2 tbsp	Cold milk
1¼ cups	Warm milk
	Salt and pepper
	Grated nutmeg
2 tbsp	Sherry

Cut the chicken into small pieces. Peel and finely chop onion. Seed pepper and finely chop half of it.

Melt the butter in a saucepan and gently fry onion and pepper till onion is transparent.

Stir in the flour with a wooden spoon, then the cold milk. Remove from heat and gradually add the warm milk. Bring to a boil. Season with salt, pepper and a pinch of nutmeg. Reduce heat and simmer gently for 15 minutes.

Add chicken and sherry and cook for 5 minutes more. Stir frequently during this time to prevent mixture sticking.

Meanwhile, slice the remaining pepper and blanch in boiling water for 5 minutes.

Place chicken and sauce on a warmed serving plate and surround with the pepper slices. Serve with boiled rice or noodles.

Mustard chicken casserole

Overall timing 1 hour

Freezing Not suitable

To serve 4

3½ lb	Roaster chicken
1	Onion
¼ cup	Oil
	Salt and pepper
1 lb	Potatoes
2 oz	Canadian bacon
1 tbsp	Vinegar
2	Cloves
1	Bay leaf
¼ tsp	Grated nutmeg
1 tsp	Powdered mustard
¾ cup	Chicken broth
8 oz	Can of tomatoes

Wipe the chicken and cut into 8 portions. Peel and finely slice the onion. Heat the oil in a flameproof casserole and fry the onion till transparent.

Add the chicken portions and fry for about 10 minutes, turning frequently. Season.

Meanwhile, peel and dice the potatoes. Add to the pan with the bacon, vinegar, cloves, bay leaf, nutmeg and seasoning. Stir the mustard into the broth and pour into pan with the canned tomatoes and juice. Mix well, pressing tomatoes to break them up, and bring to a boil. Reduce the heat and simmer for about 30 minutes till the chicken and potatoes are tender.

Adjust the seasoning and discard bay leaf before serving.

Chicken baked in salt

Overall timing 1¾ hours

Freezing Not suitable

To serve 4-6

3½ lb	Roaster chicken
1	Sprig of fresh tarragon
	Black pepper
8 cups	Coarse sea-salt

Preheat the oven to 450°.

Wipe the chicken, put the tarragon inside and sprinkle inside and out with pepper. Truss with string.

Line a casserole with a large sheet of foil and spread with one-third of the salt. Place chicken breast bone down on salt. Cover completely with remaining salt. Fold the foil over the top of the chicken and join together at top, sealing well. Bake, covered, for 1½ hours.

Take the chicken out of the oven, unwrap and remove the crust of salt. Brush off any salt that clings, then carve the chicken in the usual way.

Pastry-wrapped stuffed chicken

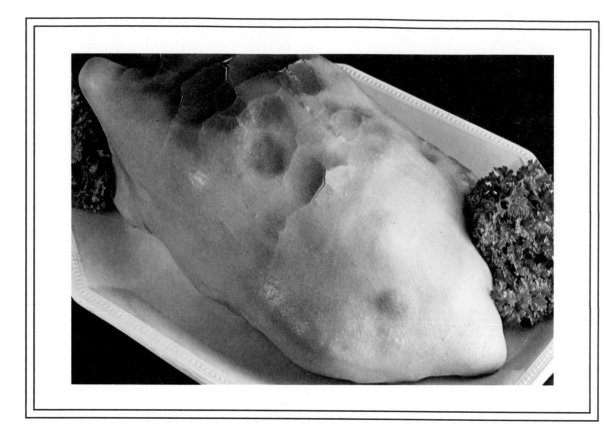

Overall timing 2¼ hours

Freezing Not suitable

To serve 4

3 lb	Roaster chicken
	Salt
2 tbsp	Butter
¾ lb	Pie pastry
1	Egg
Stuffing	
½ lb	Mushrooms
2 tbsp	Butter
2 tbsp	Sherry wine
	Salt and pepper
6 oz	Chicken livers
1	Small onion
⅔ cup	Soft bread crumbs

First make the stuffing. Slice mushrooms. Melt butter in a pan and fry mushrooms for 3 minutes. Add sherry wine and cook for 3 minutes. Season with salt and pepper.

Finely chop chicken livers. Peel and finely chop onion. Add both to pan with bread crumbs and mix well. Cook gently for 5 minutes. Cool.

Season chicken inside and out with salt. Stuff with liver mixture and close the opening. Melt butter in a roasting pan and brown chicken on all sides. Cool slightly.

Preheat the oven to 400°.

Roll out dough on a lightly floured surface till about ¼ inch thick and large enough to wrap around chicken. Remove chicken from roasting pan. Drain, then place, breast side down, on dough. Moisten edges and wrap dough around chicken. Press edges together well.

Place chicken on greased baking sheet with seam underneath. Use dough trimmings to decorate top. Brush with beaten egg and bake for 1½-1¾ hours. If pastry shows signs of overbrowning, cover with foil.

Chicken in sour cream

Overall timing 1 hour

Freezing Not suitable

To serve 4

3 lb	Chicken pieces
2 tbsp	Flour
¼ lb	Button mushrooms
1	Onion
¼ cup	Butter
2 tbsp	Oil
	Salt and pepper
2 tbsp	Brandy
½ cup	Sour cream

Wash chicken pieces and dry on paper towels. Coat lightly with the flour. Wipe and slice mushrooms. Peel and slice onion.

Heat butter and oil in a skillet and fry onion till golden. Add floured chicken pieces and brown on all sides. Season with salt and pepper. Cover and cook for 40 minutes.

Pour brandy over the chicken and heat for a few minutes, then set alight. When the flames have died down, add the sliced mushrooms and cook over a gentle heat for 5 minutes.

Add sour cream to pan. Heat through, stirring, for 2 minutes. Do not allow to boil. Serve at once with noodles and a mixed salad.

Poached chicken

Overall timing 1 hour

Freezing Not suitable

To serve 4

4	Chicken quarters
¾ lb	Carrots
½ lb	Pearl onions
2	Stalks of celery
	Salt
1 lb	Potatoes

Put chicken pieces in a large saucepan and cover with cold water. Peel and chop carrots; peel onions; chop celery. Add a few pieces of carrot, four onions, all the celery and salt to chicken. Bring slowly to a boil, then reduce the heat until just simmering, cover and cook for about 30 minutes.

Meanwhile, cook remaining carrots and onions in boiling salted water for 5 minutes. Peel and chop potatoes and add to pan. Simmer for a further 20 minutes. Drain and keep hot.

Drain chicken (keep the cooking liquid and vegetables for soup) and serve on a warmed plate with the separately cooked carrots, onions and potatoes.

Chicken Kiev

Overall timing 1 ½ hours

Freezing Suitable: fry after thawing.

To serve 4

½ cup	Softened butter
2 tbsp	Lemon juice
1	Garlic clove
1 tbsp	Chopped parsley
	Salt and pepper
4	Boneless chicken
	breasts
	Oil for frying
3 tbsp	Flour
1	Egg
2 cups	Soft white bread crumbs

Work together the butter and lemon juice until smooth. Peel and crush the garlic and add to the butter with the parsley and seasoning. Mix well. Shape into a cylinder, wrap in foil and place in freezer for 1 hour to firm.

Place the chicken breasts between two sheets of dampened wax paper on a flat surface and beat flat with a heavy knife or wooden mallet until thin.

Heat the oil in a deep-fryer to 350°.

Place a piece of butter on each chicken breast. Roll chicken around butter and secure with a toothpick. Coat each piece of chicken all over with the flour, then dip in the beaten egg to cover and finally in the bread crumbs, pressing them on well. Fry for 12-15 minutes until golden brown. Drain on paper towels, remove toothpicks and serve immediately with lemon wedges and a green salad.

Soufflé-topped chicken

Overall timing 1 ¼ hours

Freezing Not suitable

To serve 4-6

2 tbsp	Oil
3 lb	Chicken pieces
	Salt and pepper
1 lb	Can of whole kernel corn
2 tbsp	Soft bread crumbs
Sauce	
6 tbsp	Butter
¼ cup	Flour
¾ cup	Milk
2	Eggs
¾ cup	Light cream
	Salt and pepper
	Grated nutmeg

Preheat the oven to 400°.

Heat oil in flameproof casserole. Add chicken and cook for about 10 minutes until pieces are browned on all sides. Season with salt and pepper.

Drain corn and add to the casserole with ¼ cup of the liquid.

To make the sauce, melt ¼ cup of the butter in a saucepan, sprinkle with the flour and cook till browned, stirring all the time. Gradually add milk and cook, stirring, for 5 minutes. Remove from heat.

Separate eggs. Mix cream, egg yolks, salt, pepper and a pinch of nutmeg in a bowl. Stir into the sauce and heat through but do not boil. Remove from heat and set aside.

Beat egg whites in a bowl until they hold stiff peaks. Fold into sauce with a metal spoon and pour over corn and chicken mixture, sprinkle with bread crumbs, dot with remaining butter and bake for 45 minutes. Serve with broccoli garnished with chopped hard-cooked eggs.

Crisp lemon chicken

Overall timing 30 minutes plus marination

Freezing Not suitable

To serve 4

8	Chicken pieces
3 tbsp	Lemon juice
2 tbsp	Oil
½ cup	Flour
	Salt and pepper
½ tsp	Paprika
	Lemon wedges

Wash and dry chicken pieces. Mix together lemon juice and oil and rub into the chicken. Cover and leave to marinate for 2-3 hours.

Preheat the broiler. Mix together the flour, seasoning and paprika.

Arrange chicken pieces skin-side down on broiler rack. Sift half the seasoned flour over the chicken and broil for 7-10 minutes.

Turn chicken pieces over. Sprinkle with remaining sifted flour and broil for a further 7-10 minutes until crisp and golden, and juices run clear when a skewer is inserted. Arrange on a warmed serving dish and garnish with lemon wedges. Serve with a bean, cucumber and tomato salad.

Chicken Maryland

Overall timing 1¾ hours

Freezing Not suitable

To serve 8

Corn fritters

1 cup	Flour
1	Egg
1 cup	Milk
11½ oz	Whole kernel corn
1	Egg white

8	Boneless chicken breasts
	Salt
	Cayenne
½ cup	Flour
2	Eggs
2 cups	Soft bread crumbs
	Oil for frying
4	Bananas

12	Bacon slices

To make the fritter batter, sift flour and pinch of salt into a bowl and make a well in the center. Add the whole egg and gradually beat in the milk. Drain corn and add. Leave batter to stand.

Cut each chicken breast in half. Season with salt and cayenne. Dip into the flour, then into beaten eggs, then into bread crumbs.

Heat the oil in a deep-fryer until hot enough to brown a cube of bread in 30 seconds. Fry the chicken pieces a few at a time for about 10-15 minutes, depending on thickness. Remove from pan, drain on paper towels and keep hot. Skim surface of oil.

Peel bananas and cut into three, then halve each piece lengthwise. Stretch bacon slices and cut in half. Wrap a piece of bacon around each piece of banana and secure with a wooden toothpick. Fry in hot oil, then drain and keep hot.

Beat egg white till stiff and fold into fritter batter. Drop in spoonfuls into hot oil and fry till puffed and golden brown. Drain. Arrange fritters, chicken and bacon-wrapped bananas on plate and serve.

Tunisian chicken

Overall timing 2¼ hours

Freezing Not suitable

To serve 4

3 lb	Roaster chicken with giblets
	Salt and pepper
1½ cups	Whole kernel corn
3	Carrots
3	Medium-size potatoes
4	Tomatoes
¼ lb	Cheddar cheese
1	Egg
2 tbsp	Bread crumbs
1	Hard-cooked egg
1	Stalk of celery
1	Sprig of parsley
¼ cup	Butter
¼ cup	Oil

Season chicken inside and out. Chop heart, liver and gizzard. Drain corn. Peel carrots and potatoes. Blanch, peel and quarter tomatoes.

Dice the cheese and mix with the corn, giblets, egg and bread crumbs. Mash the hard-cooked egg with a fork and add to the mixture with seasoning. Mix well. Stuff the chicken with the mixture, then close opening.

Put carrots, potatoes and tomatoes into a flameproof casserole with celery and parsley. Cover with 1½ quarts water and bring to a boil. Lower heat and add chicken with half the butter. Cover and simmer for 1½ hours.

Remove chicken and drain on paper towels. Strain cooking liquid and return to casserole. Purée vegetables and add to casserole. Heat soup through.

Heat remaining butter and oil in a skillet. Put in whole chicken and brown evenly, turning it over with two spoons. Bring the chicken and soup to table in separate dishes.

Sweet and sour chicken

Overall timing 1 1/4 hours

Freezing Not suitable

To serve 4-6

8	Chicken pieces
	Salt and pepper
3 tbsp	Oil
1 1/4 cups	Hot chicken broth
8 oz	Can of pineapple chunks
1/4 cup	Butter
1 cup	Sliced almonds
2	Bananas
1	Orange
1/2 cup	Maraschino cherries
2 tbsp	Mild curry powder
2 tbsp	Cornstarch
1/2 cup	Plain yogurt

Preheat oven to 375°. Wash and dry chicken pieces. Rub with salt and pepper. Heat the oil in flameproof casserole and brown chicken on all sides. Put the chicken in the oven and cook, uncovered, for 40 minutes. Baste with broth frequently.

Meanwhile, drain the pineapple and save the juice. Melt butter in a saucepan, add almonds and cook till golden brown. Peel and slice bananas and orange and add to almonds with drained cherries and pineapple chunks. Turn mixture over, heat through then remove from heat.

Remove casserole from the oven. Place the chicken pieces on a warm serving dish. Cover with the fruit and almond mixture and keep warm. Combine any remaining chicken broth with chicken juices and pineapple juice. Make up to 2 cups with water.

In saucepan, mix curry powder and cornstarch together. Gradually stir in measured liquid. Bring to a boil, stirring, and cook for 1-2 minutes. Remove from heat and stir in yogurt. Pour some sauce over chicken; put remainder in a gravy boat.

Maharajah's chicken

Overall timing 20 minutes

Freezing Not suitable

To serve 2

1-2	Large garlic cloves
1	Large onion
1-inch	Piece of fresh ginger
1	Lemon
¼ cup	Butter
¾ lb	Boneless chicken breasts
	Salt
1 tsp	Turmeric
2 tbsp	Chopped fresh coriander

Peel garlic, onion and ginger. Squeeze juice from lemon. Using a food processor or blender, process garlic, ginger and one-quarter of the onion to a fine pulp with half the lemon juice. Set aside.

Slice remaining onion thinly. Melt butter in a skillet and fry sliced onion till soft and beginning to brown.

Meanwhile, cut chicken into ½ inch cubes, discarding all skin. Add chicken cubes to onion and cook, stirring, till chicken changes color. Add salt, turmeric and garlic pulp and stir well. Cook, stirring frequently, about 5 minutes.

Add remaining lemon juice, and serve sprinkled with chopped coriander.

Indian-style chicken

Overall timing 1 ¼ hours

Freezing Suitable: add cream after thawing

To serve 4

1	Onion
2 tbsp	Butter
1 tbsp	Oil
3 lb	Chicken pieces
2 tbsp	Mild curry powder
1 ¼ cups	Chicken broth
1	Garlic clove
2 tbsp	Lemon juice
	Salt
	Cayenne pepper
2 tbsp	Light cream

Peel and chop onion. Heat butter and oil in a flameproof casserole and cook onion till transparent. Add chicken pieces, a few at a time, and brown on all sides. Sprinkle chicken with curry powder and pour in broth. Add peeled and crushed garlic, lemon juice and a pinch each salt and cayenne pepper. Cover and simmer for 35 minutes over a low heat.

Add cream and cook gently for 10 minutes. Do not boil. Serve with plain boiled rice and side dishes of apple slices, cucumber sprinkled with salt and grated fresh coconut, if liked.

Hawaiian chicken

Overall timing 1 hour

Freezing Not suitable

To serve 4

3 lb	Chicken pieces
1	Bay leaf
1	Onion
	Salt and pepper
3	Black peppercorns
½	Small head of white cabbage
2 tbsp	Oil
½ cup	Finely diced celery
2 tbsp	Soy sauce
½ cup	Shelled Brazil nuts
½	Fresh pineapple *or*
8 oz	Can of unsweetened pineapple chunks

Put chicken portions in pan with bay leaf, peeled and halved onion, ½ tsp salt and peppercorns and cover with water. Bring to a boil, then simmer for 30 minutes.

Remove chicken from pan with a slotted spoon. Take meat off the bones. Strain cooking liquid and reserve.

Shred cabbage. Heat the oil in the saucepan, add cabbage, celery and chicken meat and cook, stirring, for 5 minutes over a medium heat. Pour off oil from pan.

Add soy sauce, seasoning and nuts. Pour in 1 cup of reserved liquid. Mix well and cook on a high heat for 5 minutes.

Peel and chop fresh pineapple or drain canned chunks. Stir into pan and cook for a further 3 minutes.

Garlic chicken

Overall timing 1¾ hours

Freezing Not suitable

To serve 4

¼ cup	Butter
1 tbsp	Oil
8	Chicken legs and wings
	Salt and pepper
1	Whole garlic bulb
½ cup	Dry white wine
2 cups	Hot milk
1 tsp	Cornstarch
2 tbsp	Light cream
¼ tsp	Cayenne pepper

Heat half the butter and the oil in a flameproof casserole. Add the chicken and brown on all sides. Season and cook for 10-15 minutes over a low heat. Remove chicken from pan and keep warm.

Peel and crush all the garlic cloves. Add remaining butter to casserole with garlic and cook over a low heat, stirring with a wooden spoon, till soft.

Add the wine, bring to a boil and simmer for 3 minutes. Replace chicken in casserole and pour in hot milk. Cover and simmer for 20-30 minutes.

Blend the cornstarch and cream in a bowl. Stir in 3 tbsp cooking liquid from the casserole and add cayenne. Stir cream mixture into casserole and simmer for 2-3 minutes.

Put chicken pieces into a warmed serving dish and spoon sauce over. Serve with green beans and mashed potatoes.

Chicken with rosemary

Overall timing 1 hour

Freezing Suitable

To serve 8

¾ cup	Butter
2 tbsp	Oil
8	Chicken pieces
2½ cups	Chicken broth
10	Sprigs of rosemary
¼ tsp	Dried thyme
	Salt and pepper
¼ cup	Flour
1 cup	Heavy cream
½ lb	Carrots
½ lb	Mushrooms

Heat ¼ cup butter with the oil in a flameproof casserole. Add chicken pieces and brown on all sides. Remove from the pot and set aside.

Add broth to casserole and stir well to mix in sediments from bottom. Add 8 sprigs of rosemary, the thyme and seasoning. Simmer for 20 minutes. Strain and set aside.

Melt ¼ cup butter in a clean casserole, stir in flour and cook for 1 minute. Gradually stir in broth mixture and simmer till thickened. Stir in cream.

Add chicken pieces to sauce, with their juices. Simmer for about 20 minutes, stirring occasionally, till chicken is tender. Add more broth if sauce becomes too thick.

Meanwhile, peel and slice the carrots. Cook in boiling salted water till just tender. Drain. Fry mushrooms in remaining butter.

About 5 minutes before chicken is ready, add carrots and mushrooms to casserole.

Break up remaining 2 sprigs of rosemary and add to casserole. Serve with rice.

Chicken with pimientos

Overall timing 45 minutes

Freezing Suitable

To serve 4

2 tbsp	Butter
4	Chicken legs
	Salt and pepper
1 tsp	Dried thyme
1 tsp	Paprika
½ cup	Red wine
14 oz	Jar of pimientos
	Black olives (optional)
	Chopped parsley

Melt butter in a large skillet. Add chicken pieces and brown on all sides, about 10 minutes. Season with salt, pepper, thyme and paprika. Add wine and bring to a boil. Let simmer for 2-3 minutes.

Meanwhile, drain pimientos and cut into 1 inch wide strips. Add pimiento strips to chicken, cover and simmer gently for about 20 minutes till chicken is tender.

Transfer chicken mixture to a warmed serving dish. Add olives, if desired, and sprinkle with parsley.

Chicken, leek and rice casserole

Overall timing 1¾ hours

Freezing Suitable

To serve 4

4	Large leeks
¼ cup	Butter
2½ cups	Milk
4	Chicken pieces
¾ cup	Long-grain rice
	Salt

Preheat oven to 300°.

Trim leeks and cut into 1 inch pieces. Wash well. Melt 2 tbsp butter in a skillet and cook leeks till soft. Set aside.

Heat milk almost to the boiling point.

Grease a large casserole with remaining butter. Arrange leeks, chicken and rice in layers in casserole and season with salt. Pour in hot milk. Cover tightly and cook in the oven for 1½ hours till chicken is tender and rice has absorbed milk.

Chicken pineapple salad

Overall timing 30 minutes plus chilling

Freezing Not suitable

To serve 4-6

½ cup	Long grain rice
	Salt and pepper
1 cup	Frozen whole kernel corn
1	Celery heart
1	Cold roast chicken
8 oz	Can of pineapple rings
4	Small firm tomatoes
½ cup	Ripe olives
3 tbsp	Salad oil
1 tbsp	Lemon juice
1 tbsp	Chopped chives
1	Bibb lettuce
1	Hard-cooked egg

Cook the rice in boiling salted water till tender, adding the corn for the last 5 minutes of cooking. Drain and rinse under cold water, then drain thoroughly.

Trim celery heart and cut into 2 inch lengths. Put into a large bowl with the celery leaves. Cut the chicken into bite-size pieces, discarding the skin and bones. Add to the bowl.

Drain the pineapple; chop three of the rings. Quarter the tomatoes and add to the bowl with the chopped pineapple, olives, rice and corn.

Mix together the oil, lemon juice, chives and seasoning. Pour over the salad and toss lightly. Chill for 30 minutes.

Wash and dry the lettuce and use to line a salad bowl. Pile the salad into the center and garnish with the remaining pineapple rings and the hard-cooked egg quartered lengthwise. Serve with crusty bread.

Chicken croquettes

Overall timing 30 minutes

Freezing Suitable: reheat in 375° oven for 20 minutes.

To serve 4-6

¾ lb (1½ cups)	Cooked chicken
6 tbsp	Butter
¾ cup + 2 tbsp	Flour
1¼ cups	Milk
	Salt and pepper
	Grated nutmeg
2	Egg yolks
1 tbsp	Grated cheese
1 tbsp	Chopped parsley
	Oil for frying
1	Egg
1⅓ cups	Dried bread crumbs
	Sprigs of parsley
	Lemon wedges

Finely chop or grind chicken.

To make sauce, melt the butter in a saucepan over a low heat and stir in 2 tbsp of the flour. When the mixture begins to froth, add the cold milk, salt, pepper and a pinch of grated nutmeg. Whisk until the sauce thickens.

Remove from heat and stir in egg yolks and cheese. Turn into a bowl and mix in chicken and chopped parsley. Cool.

Heat oil for frying to 340° or till a bread cube browns in 1 minute.

Using your hands, shape chicken mixture into small cylindrical croquettes. Roll them in the remaining flour, then in the lightly beaten egg to coat them completely and finally in the bread crumbs, pressing them on well with a palette knife.

Fry the croquettes, four or five at a time, in the hot oil until golden brown. Drain on paper towels and serve hot, garnished with parsley and lemon.

Welsh chicken and mace pie

Overall timing 1 hour

Freezing Not suitable

To serve 6

1 lb (3 cups)	Cooked chicken meat
¼ lb	Cooked tongue
1	Onion
4	Leeks
3	Stalks of celery
¼ cup	Butter
1 tsp	Ground mace
1 tbsp	Chopped parsley
1¼ cups	Chicken broth
	Salt and pepper
¾ lb	Pie pastry
1	Egg

Preheat the oven to 400°.

Chop chicken into medium-size pieces. Cut the tongue into strips. Peel and thinly slice onion. Trim leeks, then cut into thin slices. Trim and finely chop the celery. Melt butter.

Mix chicken, tongue and prepared vegetables with mace, parsley and butter in a large deep dish. Add broth and seasoning.

Roll out dough and place on dish. Press edge to dish to seal. Lightly beat the egg and brush over the dough. Bake for 40 minutes, or until the pastry is golden. Serve immediately with mashed potatoes.

Chicken pieces with nutty sauce

Overall timing 1 hour plus marination

Freezing Not suitable

To serve 4

5	Onions
1	Garlic clove
½ cup	Walnuts
	Salt
3 tbsp	Lemon juice
4	Boneless chicken breasts
2 tbsp	Groundnut oil
	Pinch of chili powder
½ cup	Roasted peanuts
2 tsp	Soy sauce
1¼ cups	Water

Peel and finely chop two onions. Peel and crush garlic. Place both in a mortar or blender with walnuts and salt. Crush or blend to a paste, gradually adding 2 tbsp lemon juice to give a creamy mixture. Cut chicken into bite-size pieces. Place in a shallow dish and pour walnut mixture over. Leave to marinate for 1 hour, turning occasionally.

Meanwhile, peel and finely chop two onions. Heat half oil in a skillet and fry onions till crisp and golden. Remove from pan and drain. Preheat the broiler.

Peel and finely chop remaining onion and purée in mortar or blender with chili powder, salt and peanuts till smooth. Heat remaining oil in skillet and fry peanut mixture for 3 minutes, stirring constantly. Stir in soy sauce, water and remaining lemon juice. Cook over low heat for 5 minutes.

Thread chicken pieces onto four oiled skewers. Broil for 10 minutes, turning frequently and brushing with walnut mixture. Add any remaining walnut mixture and fried onions to peanut sauce and heat through.

Poule-au-pot

Overall timing 4 hours

Freezing Not suitable

To serve 6

4	Bacon slices
¼ lb	Bulk pork sausage meat
1 cup	Soft bread crumbs
2 tbsp	Chopped parsley
	Salt and pepper
2	Eggs
3½ lb	Stewing chicken
4	Medium-size onions
4	Small white turnips
6	Large carrots
2	Leeks
4	Stalks of celery
¼ cup	Drippings
	Bouquet garni
1½ cups	Long grain rice

Chop bacon finely. Mix sausage meat, bacon, bread crumbs, parsley and seasoning and bind with eggs. Spoon into chicken and truss.

Peel onions, turnips and carrots. Trim leeks and celery. Heat drippings in a large pan and brown chicken all over. Add one each of the onions, turnips, leeks and celery stalks and two carrots and fry for 3 minutes. Pour off excess fat.

Add bouquet garni, giblets and cold water to cover the chicken and bring to a boil. Skim off any scum. Cover and simmer for about 2¼ hours.

Discard vegetables and bouquet garni. Add remaining vegetables and seasoning. Cover and simmer for a further 45 minutes. Remove from heat. Strain 5½ cups of broth into another saucepan. Keep chicken hot.

Add rice to stock with salt and cover tightly. Bring to a boil and simmer for 15-20 minutes till rice is tender.

Fluff rice and arrange on a serving dish. Place chicken on rice and discard trussing strings. Arrange vegetables around chicken and serve.

Chicken supreme

Overall timing 2 hours

Freezing Not suitable

To serve 4

2	Carrots
2	Onions
2	Leeks
1	Stalk of celery
	Salt
1½ quarts	Water or broth
3 lb	Roaster chicken
½	Lemon
1 cup	Rice
Sauce	
¼ cup	Butter
1 tbsp	Flour
2	Egg yolks
2 tbsp	Light cream
	Salt and pepper

Peel carrots and onions. Chop leeks and celery. Bring salted water or broth to a boil in a flameproof casserole, add prepared vegetables and cook for 15 minutes.

Rub chicken with the lemon. Add to casserole, cover and simmer gently for 1 hour. (If you prefer, chicken joints can be used instead of a whole chicken – they need only to be cooked for 45 minutes.)

Measure out 2½ cups broth from casserole and place in a saucepan. Continue cooking chicken for a further 15 minutes. Bring stock in saucepan to a boil, add rice and cook for 15 minutes.

Meanwhile, prepare sauce. Melt butter in a saucepan and stir in flour. Measure out another 2½ cups broth from casserole and gradually stir into pan. Cook, stirring till thickened. Remove from heat and stir in egg yolks and then cream. Season.

Drain rice and place on warmed serving dish. Remove chicken from casserole, cut into portions and arrange on top of rice. Pour sauce over and serve.

Chicken with eggplant and tomatoes

Overall timing 50 minutes

Freezing Not suitable

To serve 4

1	Eggplant
	Salt and pepper
1	Green pepper
2	Large onions
6 tbsp	Oil
4	Chicken pieces
2 cups	Tomato juice
¾ lb	Ripe tomatoes

Slice the eggplant. Sprinkle with salt and leave for 15 minutes. Meanwhile, seed and slice the pepper. Peel and slice the onions.

Heat the oil in a flameproof casserole, add the chicken and fry over a moderate heat, turning frequently, till browned all over. Remove from the pan and reserve.

Add the onions and pepper and fry for 5 minutes. Return the chicken to the casserole, add the tomato juice and seasoning and bring to a boil.

Rinse the eggplant and pat dry on paper towels. Add to the chicken, cover and simmer for 25 minutes.

Blanch, peel and quarter the tomatoes. Add to the chicken and cook for a further 5 minutes. Serve with plain boiled rice and a green salad.

Chicken parcels

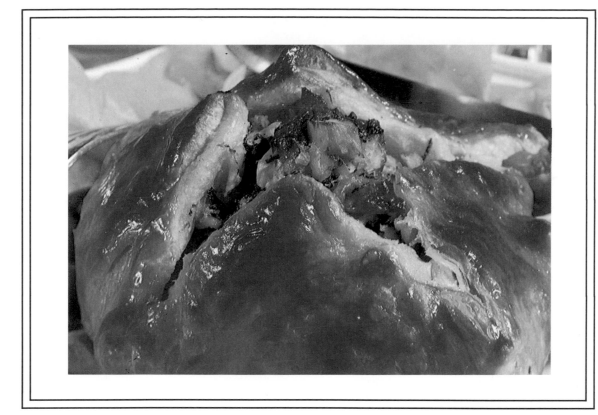

Overall timing 45 minutes

Freezing Suitable: bake from frozen, allowing 35-45 minutes

To serve 6

¾ lb	Frozen puff pastry
1	Medium-size onion
2 tbsp	Butter
1¼ cups	Cooked chicken meat
3 tbsp	Chopped parsley
¼ cup	Heavy cream
	Salt and pepper
3	Slices of cooked ham
1	Egg yolk
6	Lettuce leaves

Thaw pastry. Preheat oven to 400°.

Peel and chop onion and fry in the butter till transparent.

Set aside six fairly large pieces of chicken and finely chop the rest. Put chopped chicken into a bowl with the parsley and fried onion. Lightly beat the cream, then stir into the chicken with seasoning.

Roll out the dough on a lightly floured surface. Cut out six 5 inch squares. Cut ham slices in half and place one piece in center of each dough square. Top with a piece of chicken, then cover with chopped chicken mixture. Dampen dough edges with cold water. Fold corners to center to cover the filling, pinching the edges together, but leaving a small hole in the top. Place parcels on a greased baking sheet.

Beat the egg yolk with a pinch of salt and brush over the parcels. Bake for 25 minutes or until well risen and golden brown. Serve the parcels on lettuce leaves.

Chicken in a basket

Overall timing 40 minutes

Freezing Not suitable

To serve 2

2x1 lb	Squab chickens
2 tbsp	Oil
	Salt and pepper
1 lb	Potatoes
	Oil for frying
	Fresh parsley
1	Small onion

Preheat the oven to 400°.

Place the chickens in roasting pan. Brush with oil and season well. Roast for 30 minutes, or until juices from the legs run clear when pierced with skewer.

Meanwhile, peel potatoes and cut into thin, matchstick fries. Heat oil in a deep-fryer to 340°. Fry potatoes for 3-5 minutes till golden. Drain well.

Arrange napkins in two small baskets. Place fries in folds of cloth. Place chickens in baskets. Garnish with parsley sprigs and onion rings. Eat with your fingers or a knife and fork if preferred.

Variation

To make barbecue-style chickens, mix together 2 tbsp tomato paste, 1 tbsp Worcestershire sauce, 1 tbsp oil, 1 peeled and crushed garlic clove and seasoning. Spread over chickens, cover with foil and roast for 40 minutes. Serve as above.

Chicken with lentils

Overall timing 1 ¼ hours

Freezing Not suitable

To serve 6

1 ½ cups	Brown lentils
1	Onion
1	Carrot
	Bouquet garni
	Salt and pepper
1 lb	Boneless chicken
1 tbsp	Oil
6 tbsp	Butter
1 tbsp	Chopped parsley

Wash and pick over lentils. Place in a saucepan and add enough cold water just to cover. Peel and finely chop onion. Peel and halve carrot. Add to lentils with bouquet garni and seasoning. Bring to a boil, cover and simmer for 35 minutes.

Meanwhile, cut chicken into neat pieces. Heat oil and half the butter in a skillet, add chicken pieces and fry for 5 minutes, turning once. Add chicken to lentils, cover and simmer for a further 30 minutes.

Discard bouquet garni and carrot. Stir the remaining butter into lentils. Taste and adjust seasoning. Arrange chicken and lentils on a warmed serving dish and sprinkle with parsley. Serve immediately with a mixed salad.

Chicken with pineapple

Overall timing 45 minutes

Freezing Not suitable

To serve 2

1½ lb	Chicken pieces
2 tsp	Potato flour or cornstarch
3 tbsp	Oil
1 tbsp	Soy sauce
1½ tsp	Dry sherry wine
	Salt and pepper
4 oz	Canned pineapple rings or chunks

Remove meat from chicken pieces and cut it into chunks.

Mix together potato flour or cornstarch, half the oil, the soy sauce, sherry and seasoning in a bowl. Add the chicken pieces and coat well. Leave to marinate for 15 minutes.

Heat the rest of the oil in a heavy-based saucepan. Drain the chicken, saving the marinade, and add to the pan. Cook over a fairly high heat for 5 minutes, stirring constantly.

Drain the pineapple, reserving ¼ cup of the syrup. Cut the rings into sections or halve the chunks. Add the reserved marinade from the chicken and the pineapple pieces to the pan and cook for a further 12 minutes, continually turning the chicken over.

When the chicken is golden brown, add the reserved pineapple syrup, adjust seasoning and cook for a further 5 minutes. Serve with saffron rice.

Chicken in foil

Overall timing 1 hour

Freezing Not suitable

To serve 2

2	Boneless chicken or turkey breasts
	Salt and pepper
1 tbsp	Flour
¼ cup	Butter
2	Sage leaves
1 tbsp	Brandy
½ cup	Chicken broth
¼ lb	Chicken livers
2 oz	Mushrooms
1 oz	Cooked ham

Coat chicken or turkey breasts with seasoned flour. Melt half butter in a skillet and fry chicken or turkey breasts on each side till golden. Add sage, brandy and broth and bring to a boil. Cover and simmer for 15 minutes. Preheat the oven to 400°.

Finely chop chicken livers, mushrooms and ham. Melt remaining butter in another skillet and stir-fry liver, mushrooms and ham for 5 minutes. Remove from heat.

Cut two large foil rectangles and put a chicken or turkey breast in center of each. Spread liver mixture on top and spoon over pan juices. Wrap securely then place in roasting pan. Bake for 20 minutes.

Stuffed turkey rolls

Overall timing 1 ¼ hours

Freezing Not suitable

To serve 2

1	Small onion
1	Garlic clove
¼ cup	Butter
1	Large tomato
	Salt and pepper
½ cup	Soft bread crumbs
1 ½ tsp	Chopped parsley
½	Egg
2 x 6 oz	Turkey scaloppine
2	Bacon slices
5 tbsp	Dry white wine
1 tsp	Lemon juice

Peel and chop onion and garlic. Melt half butter in a pan and fry onion till golden.

Blanch, peel and chop tomato and add to pan with garlic and seasoning. Simmer till thick. Remove from heat; add crumbs, parsley and egg.

Season scaloppine. Divide stuffing between them and roll up. Wrap a bacon slice around each roll and secure with wooden toothpick.

Melt remaining butter in skillet and fry rolls till browned all over. Add wine and lemon juice, cover and simmer for 20 minutes.

Turkey fries

Overall timing 40 minutes plus marination

Freezing Not suitable

To serve 8

¼ cup	Oil
3 tbsp	Lemon juice
	Salt
8 x ¼ lb	Slices of turkey breast (scaloppine)
4 tsp	Dijon-style mustard
2	Eggs
3 cups	Soft bread crumbs
¼ cup	Butter
	Chopped parsley
	Lemon wedges

Mix 2 tbsp of the oil with the lemon juice and a pinch of salt in a shallow dish. Add the turkey, mix well and leave to marinate for 1 hour.

Drain the turkey and pat dry on paper towels. Spread thinly with the mustard. Beat the eggs lightly on a plate and use to coat turkey. Dip turkey slices into the bread crumbs, pressing them on gently.

Melt the butter and remaining oil in a skillet and gently fry the turkey for about 10 minutes on each side, till tender and golden.

Drain on paper towels and arrange on a warmed dish. Garnish with chopped parsley and lemon wedges and serve immediately with a tomato and onion salad dressed with vinaigrette.

Turkey with lemon sauce

Overall timing 30 minutes

Freezing Not suitable

To serve 6

6	Slices of turkey breast (scaloppine)
	Salt and pepper
2 tbsp	Flour
2	Thick slices of Canadian bacon
6 tbsp	Butter
½ cup	Chicken broth
2 tbsp	Lemon juice
2 tbsp	Chopped parsley
	Lemon slices
	Sprigs of parsley

Place each slice of turkey between two sheets of damp wax paper and flatten with a rolling pin. Season the flour and use to coat the turkey. Cut bacon into strips.

Melt the butter in a skillet and cook the bacon for 5 minutes. Add turkey pieces and fry for 3-5 minutes on each side. Remove turkey and bacon from pan and arrange on a warmed serving plate. Keep hot.

Add any remaining seasoned flour to skillet and stir well with a wooden spoon, scraping the sediment from the bottom of the pan. Gradually add the broth and bring to a boil. Simmer gently for 5 minutes.

Remove pan from heat and stir in the lemon juice and chopped parsley. Taste and adjust seasoning. Pour over the turkey breasts and garnish with lemon slices and parsley sprigs. Serve immediately with a mixed salad.

Oven-fried rabbit

Overall timing 1 ¼ hours

Freezing Not suitable

To serve 4-6

2 lb	Young rabbit
	Salt and pepper
3 tbsp	Flour
½ tsp	Paprika
2	Eggs
2 tbsp	Milk
⅔ cup	Dried bread crumbs
2 tbsp	Butter
¼ cup	Oil
¼ cup	Thick mayonnaise
2 tbsp	Horseradish sauce
2 tbsp	Light cream
1 tsp	Lemon juice

Preheat the oven to 350°.

Cut rabbit into neat pieces, removing small bones. Season flour, add paprika and coat rabbit pieces.

Beat eggs with milk. Dip rabbit into egg mixture then into bread crumbs.

Heat butter and oil in a skillet and brown rabbit pieces on both sides. Place on baking sheet and bake for about 40 minutes till tender.

Meanwhile, mix mayonnaise, horseradish sauce, cream, lemon juice and seasoning. Serve with rabbit.

Stuffed drumsticks

Overall timing 2 hours

Freezing Not suitable

To serve 4

2 x 1 lb	Turkey drumsticks
	Salt and pepper
¼ lb	Canadian bacon
	Rosemary leaves
¼ cup	Butter
2 tsp	Flour
¾ cup	Chicken broth
¼ cup	Dry vermouth

Preheat the oven to 375°.

Remove bone from drumsticks. Return drumsticks to their original shape, then season. Chop bacon and stuff into cavities in the drumsticks. Close openings with skewers. Pierce the skin in several places and insert the rosemary leaves. Rub butter over drumsticks and place in a flameproof casserole. Cover and bake for about 1¼ hours.

Lift out the drumsticks and remove the skewers. Cut into thick slices, arrange on a serving dish and keep hot.

Add the flour to the casserole and stir over a low heat for 1 minute. Gradually add the broth and vermouth and bring to a boil, stirring. Simmer for 2 minutes then adjust the seasoning to taste.

Pour sauce over the turkey.

Rabbit carbonnade

Overall timing 2½ hours

Freezing Not suitable

To serve 4-6

2½ lb	Rabbit
3 tbsp	Flour
2	Carrots
1	Onion
¼ lb	Bacon slices
¼ cup	Butter
	Bouquet garni
1	Garlic clove
	Salt and pepper
2½ cups	Beer

Preheat the over to 350°.

Put the rabbit into neat pieces. Toss in the flour till lightly coated.

Peel and thinly slice the carrots. Peel and chop the onion. Cut the bacon into strips. Melt the butter in a flameproof casserole and fry the carrots, onion and bacon for 5 minutes. Add the rabbit pieces and fry till browned.

Add the bouquet garni, peeled and crushed garlic seasoning. Pour the beer over, cover tightly and cook in the oven for 1¾ − 2 hours till the rabbit is tender. Serve with boiled potatoes.

Roast squab with mushrooms

Overall timing 50 minutes

Freezing Not suitable

To serve 2

¼ lb	Small onions
2	Squab
2	Sprigs of rosemary
4	Sage leaves
6	Bacon slices
2 tbsp	Butter
¼ lb	Mushrooms
5 tbsp	Dry white wine
	Salt and pepper

Preheat the over to 450°.

Blanch the onions in boiling water for 5 minutes, then peel. Wipe the squab and put a sprig of rosemary, two sage leaves and a slice of bacon into each. Put into a roasting pan and spread half the butter over each. Roast for about 15 minutes till browned.

Meanwhile, chop the remaining bacon. Heat a flameproof casserole and fry the onions and bacon till just golden. Thickly slice the mushrooms. Add to onions and bacon and fry for 2 minutes.

Remove the squab from the oven and reduce the temperature to 400°. Put the squab into the casserole on top of the vegetables, pour the wine over and season.

Cover the casserole, place in the oven and cook for a further 15-20 minutes till the squab are tender. Adjust the seasoning before serving.

Pigeons with saffron

Overall timing 1 hour

Freezing Not suitable

To serve 6

3	Wild or wood pigeons
	Salt and pepper
1 tbsp	Flour
1 tbsp	Oil
¼ cup	Butter
6	Saffron strands
3 tbsp	Lemon juice
1	Small onion
2 tbsp	Chopped parsley

Quarter the pigeons. Lightly coat with seasoned flour. Heat the oil and butter in a saucepan, add the pigeon pieces and fry for about 10 minutes till lightly browned on all sides.

Meanwhile, pound the saffron in a small bowl. Add 2 tbsp warm water and leave to soak for 10 minutes.

Add saffron, soaking liquid and lemon juice to the pan. Cover and cook over a low heat for 20 minutes till meat is tender. Remove pigeons pieces from the pan, place on a warmed serving dish and keep hot.

Peel and finely chop the onion. Add to the liquid in the pan with parsley and seasoning. Cook for 3 minutes, then spoon over the pigeon quarters and serve immediately with boiled rice.

Duck with oranges

Overall timing 2 hours

Freezing Not suitable

To serve 4

4 lb	Duck
	Salt and pepper
1¼ cups	Hot chicken broth
2 tsp	Sugar
2 tbsp	White wine vinegar
4	Oranges

Preheat the oven to 400°.

Prick duck all over with a fork. Season well and place on rack in roasting pan. Roast for 45 minutes till brown and crisp.

Remove all but 1 tbsp of the fat from the pan. Pour hot broth over duck. Cover and roast for a further 30 minutes till cooked.

Heat sugar gently in a pan until it caramelizes, then remove from heat and add vinegar. Remove duck and strain juices from roasting pan into sugar mixture. Replace duck in pan and keep warm.

Cut the ring from one orange into thin matchsticks. Squeeze the juice from two oranges and add to the pan with the rind. Cook gently for 5 minutes till the rind has softened.

Remove duck from oven and cut into portions. Arrange on warmed serving dish and spoon over a little of the orange sauce. Peel and section remaining oranges and use to garnish duck. Serve with sautéed potatoes and peas, and with the rest of the sauce served in a sauce or gravy boat.

Duck with apples and cream

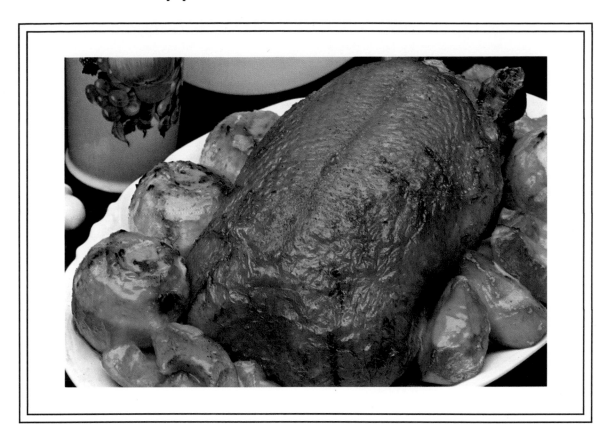

Overall timing 1 hour 20 minutes

Freezing Not suitable

To serve 4

4 lb	Duck
	Salt and pepper
6	Granny Smith apples
2 tbsp	Butter
1¼ cups	Light cream

Preheat the oven to 400°.

Sprinkle duck inside and out with salt and pepper. Prick all over with a fork and place on wire rack in roasting pan. Roast for 20 minutes, then reduce heat to 350°.

Peel and core the apples. Cut two of them into quarters and leave the rest whole. Arrange around the duck, dot with butter and continue roasting for 1 hour or till tender.

Remove duck and apples from the pan. Place duck on serving plate. Keep hot. Pour off excess fat from pan juices, then stir in the cream. Replace apples in pan and baste thoroughly with the sauce. Cook for a further 5 minutes.

Arrange apples around duck. Spoon some sauce over. Serve rest separately.

Chicken liver brochettes

Overall timing 25 minutes

Freezing Not suitable

To serve 4

½ lb	Chicken livers
2 oz	Slab bacon
¼ lb	Mushrooms
	Salt and pepper
¼ cup	Butter

Wash the chicken livers and dry on paper towels. Chop bacon into bite-size pieces. Wipe mushrooms.

Thread livers, bacon and mushrooms alternately onto skewers. Season with salt and pepper.

Melt the butter in a skillet and cook brochettes for about 8 minutes, turning them from time to time. Alternatively, brush brochettes with oil and cook under a hot broiler. Serve hot with tomato sauce, rice and a mixed salad for lunch, or with crusty bread and butter for supper.

Chicken liver crêpes

Overall timing 45 minutes

Freezing Suitable: add cream and chesse and bake from frozen, covered, allowing 30-40 minutes

To serve 4

¼ lb	Chicken livers
½ lb	Button mushrooms
1	Small onion
¼ cup	Butter
	Salt and pepper
6	Slices of cooked ham
3 tbsp	Light cream
	Grated nutmeg
½ cup	Grated Cheddar cheese
Crêpes	
1¼ cups	Flour
¼ tsp	Salt
2	Eggs
1¾ cups	Beer
	Oil for frying
	Chopped parsley

Chop chicken livers. Chop mushrooms. Peel and finely chop onion. Melt butter in a saucepan and gently fry mushrooms and onion for 5 minutes. Add chopped livers and fry for 3-4 minutes. Season with salt and pepper.

To make crêpes, sift flour and salt into a bowl and make a well in the center. Add eggs and beer and beat to a smooth batter. Heat a little oil in an 8 inch crêpe pan and make 12 crêpes.

Preheat oven to 400°.

Cut slices of ham in half. Place one half on each crêpe. Divide liver mixture between crêpes, then roll them up. Place side by side in greased baking dish. Pour cream over and sprinkle with nutmeg and grated cheese.

Bake for 15-20 minutes, or broil for 5 minutes. Sprinkle parsley over. Serve hot.

Giblet fricassee

Overall timing 1 ½ hours

Freezing Not suitable

To serve 4

1 ¼ lb	Poultry giblets
1	Onion
3 tbsp	Oil
2 cups	Chicken broth
1 tsp	Ground cumin
	Salt and pepper
1 tbsp	Flour
2	Egg yolks
2 tbsp	Lemon juice

Chop giblets. Peel and chop onion. Heat the oil in a saucepan and fry onion till transparent. Add giblets and brown on all sides. Pour in the broth and add cumin and seasoning. Bring to a boil, cover and simmer for about 1 hour or until giblets are tender.

Blend the flour with the egg yolks and mix in the lemon juice. Stir into fricassee and cook for a further 5 minutes, stirring. Serve with creamed potatoes and a mixed salad.

Rich leek quiche

Overall timing 1 hour

Freezing Suitable: reheat from frozen, covered, in 375° oven for 35 minutes.

To serve 6-8

¾ lb	Frozen puff pastry
2 lb	Leeks
¼ cup	Butter
1 tbsp	Flour
1¼ cups	Light broth
	Salt and pepper
1	Egg
1	Egg yolk
1 cup	Light cream

Thaw pastry. Preheat the oven to 425°.

Trim leeks. cut into 1 inch lengths. Blanch in boiling water for 5 minutes, then drain thoroughly.

Melt butter in a skillet and fry the leeks for 5 minutes. Sprinkle with flour and cook until lightly browned. Gradually stir in the broth and bring to a boil. Season and cook gently for 10 minutes.

Meanwhile, roll out dough and use to line a 9 inch quiche pan. Prick bottom several times with a fork.

Beat the whole egg, yolk and cream together in a bowl. Remove leeks from heat and add cream mixture. Pour into pastry case and spread evenly. Bake for 30 minutes till lightly set and golden. Serve hot.

Quiche lorraine

Overall timing 1 ½ hours

Freezing Suitable: reheat in hot oven

To serve 4-6

2 cups	Flour
	Salt and pepper
½ cup	Butter
	Water
2	Thick bacon slices
¾ cup	Grated Cheddar cheese
2	Eggs
1 cup	Milk or light cream

Sift the flour, salt and pepper into a bowl. Rub in the butter till mixture resembles bread crumbs. Gradually add the water to bind and knead to a dough. Roll out and use to line a greased 8 inch pie or quiche pan. Leave to stand for 30 minutes.

Preheat the oven to 400°.

Dice the bacon, fry lightly. Sprinkle bacon and cheese over the bottom of the pastry case. Beat together the eggs, milk or cream and seasoning in a bowl. Pour mixture into pastry case. Do not overfill.

Bake for 15 minutes, then reduce heat to 325° and bake for further 25-30 minutes. Serve hot or cold with salad and potatoes.

Onion quiche

Overall timing 1 ½ hours

Freezing Suitable: reheat from frozen, covered, in 350° oven for 20 minutes.

To serve 4

1 lb	Medium-size onions
¼ cup	Lard
¼ lb	Slab bacon
6 oz	Rich pie pastry
3	Eggs
½ cup	Milk
½ cup	Light cream
	Salt and pepper

Preheat the oven to 400°.

Peel, halve and thinly slice the onions. Melt the lard in a skillet and fry the onions over a moderate heat till pale golden.

Dice the bacon and add to the pan. Fry for a further 4-5 minutes till the onions and bacon are golden brown.

Roll out the dough and use to line an 8½ inch quiche pan. Prick the bottom and bake blind for 15 minutes.

Spread the onion and bacon mixture over the pastry base. Mix the eggs with the milk and cream and seasoning. Pour over the onions.

Bake for a further 25 minutes till lightly set and golden. Serve hot with mixed salads.

Bacon and corn quiche

Overall timing 1 hour

Freezing Suitable: reheat in 425° oven for 10-15 minutes.

To serve 6-8

¼ lb	Slab bacon
½ lb	Pie pastry
2	Eggs
½ cup	Milk
	Salt and pepper
¼ tsp	Grated nutmeg
	Cayenne
16 oz	Can of cream-style corn
1 cup	Grated sharp Cheddar cheese

Preheat the oven to 450°.

Finely chop bacon. Put into a small ovenproof dish in the oven to draw off the fat.

Roll out the dough and use to line a 9 inch quiche or pie pan. Beat the eggs and milk together in a bowl and add salt, pepper, nutmeg and a pinch of cayenne. Blend in the corn. Mix three quarters of the cheese into the egg and corn mixture.

Remove bacon from oven and brush a little fat on the inside of the pastry case. Drain the bacon pieces and add half of them to the egg and corn mixture. Pour mixture into the pastry case. Sprinkle the rest of the cheese and remaining bacon on the top and bake for 20 minutes. Reduce the temperature to 350° and bake for a further 25 minutes. Serve hot or cold.

Cream cheese and broccoli quiche

Overall timing 50 minutes

Freezing Suitable: thaw for 4 hours then reheat in a hot oven for 10-15 minutes

To serve 4-6

10-inch	Frozen or freshly made unbaked pie crust
½ lb	Broccoli
1 cup	Cream cheese
1 cup	Light cream
3	Eggs
2	Egg yolks
	Salt and pepper
¼ tsp	Grated nutmeg
¼ cup	Chopped parsley

Thaw the pie crust if frozen. Preheat the oven to 425°.

Prick the bottom of the pie crust. Bake for 10 minutes. Remove the pie crust from the oven and reduce heat to 400°.

Cook the broccoli in boiling salted water for 5 minutes; it should remain firm. Refresh in cold water and drain well.

In a mixing bowl mash the cream cheese with the cream. Beat well to make smooth. Beat in the eggg and egg yolks. Season well with salt, pepper and nutmeg. Stir in the chopped parsley.

Arrange the broccoli in the pie crust. Pour the cheese and egg mixture over it. Bake the quiche 25-30 minutes, or until the filling is firm. Serve immediately with whole wheat bread and a green salad.

Onion tarts

Overall timing 40 minutes

Freezing Suitable: reheat from frozen in 425° oven for 10 minutes

Makes 8

½ lb	Frozen puff pastry
¾ lb	Onions
¼ lb	Bacon or salt pork
3	Eggs
1 ¼ cups	Milk
	Salt and pepper

Thaw the pastry. Preheat the oven to 425°.

Peel and thinly slice the onions. Dice the bacon. Fry the bacon and onions in a skillet till lightly browned. Cover and sweat for 15 minutes. Drain off excess fat.

Roll out the dough on a lightly floured board. Cut out eight rounds with a cookie cutter and use to line eight greased 2½-inch tart pans. Prick the bottom of each several times with a fork.

Mix the eggs, milk, onions and bacon. Season and divide between the tart pans. Bake for 10-15 minutes till lightly set and golden.

Garnish with fried onion rings if desired, arrange on a plate with lettuce leaves and serve hot.

Welsh parsley quiche

Overall timing 1 hour

Freezing Suitable: reheat from frozen in 350° oven for 25 minutes.

To serve 4-6

½ lb	Pie pastry
¼ lb	Slab bacon
3	Eggs
1 cup	Milk
3 tbsp	Chopped parsley
	Salt and pepper

Preheat the oven to 400°.

Roll out the dough and use to line a 9 inch quiche pan. Prick the bottom with a fork and bake blind for 15 minutes. Meanwhile, chop the bacon. Heat a skillet and fry the bacon till golden. Arrange the bacon in the pastry case. Reduce oven temperature to 350°.

Beat the eggs, milk and parsley together, season to taste and pour over the bacon. Bake for a further 20-25 minutes till set. Serve hot or cold.

Tomato quiche

Overall timing 1 hour plus chilling

Freezing Suitable: reheat in 350° oven for 25-30 minutes.

To serve 6

2¼ cups	Flour
	Salt
¼ cup	Sour cream
10 tbsp	Butter
Filling	
5	Tomatoes
6 oz	Cheese
8	Thin slices of French bread
½ cup	Heavy cream
½ cup	Sour cream
4	Eggs
	Salt
	Grated nutmeg
½ tsp	Paprika
2 tbsp	Butter

Sift flour and salt into bowl. Add sour cream, dot with butter pieces and knead lightly until smooth. Chill for 30 minutes.

Thinly slice tomatoes. Slice cheese and cut crusts off bread.

Preheat oven to 400°.

Roll out dough and use to line 12 inch quiche pan. Cover with layer of sliced tomatoes, then cheese and bread.

Beat heavy cream with sour cream, eggs, a pinch each of salt and nutmeg, and paprika. Pour into pastry case and dot top with butter. Bake for 30-40 minutes until firm and golden. Serve hot.

Onion quiche

Overall timing 2¼ hours

Freezing Suitable: reheat from frozen in 350° oven for 20 minutes.

To serve 4-6

1 tsp	Active dry yeast
	Pinch of sugar
¾ cup	Lukewarm water
2 cups	Flour
1 tsp	Salt
1	Egg
Filling	
5 oz	Bacon slices
6 oz	Onions
2 tbsp	Butter
5 oz	Cheddar cheese

Mix yeast and sugar with most of the water and leave in a warm place for 15 minutes till frothy.

Sift flour and salt into bowl, make a well in the center and add yeast mixture, any remaining water and egg. Mix well to a dough, then turn onto floured surface and knead for 5 minutes until smooth and elastic. Place dough in a clean bowl, cover with a damp cloth and leave to rise in a warm place for 45 minutes – 1 hour, until doubled in size.

Preheat oven to 400°.

Roll out dough on a floured surface and use to line a greased 10 inch loose-bottomed French flan pan. Prove for 15 minutes.

Chop bacon. Peel onions and cut into rings. Melt butter in a pan and fry onions and bacon for 5 minutes till golden. Slice the cheese.

Cover quiche base with onions and bacon and arrange cheese slices on top. Bake for 30-35 minutes. Remove from pan and serve hot.

Asparagus quiche

Overall timing 1¼ hours

Freezing Suitable: thaw and refresh in hot oven for 10 minutes.

To serve 4

½ lb	Pie pastry
2 tbsp	Butter
2 tbsp	Flour
2 cups	Milk
	Salt and pepper
	Pinch of grated nutmeg
2	Eggs
1 cup	Grated sharp cheese
12 oz	Can of asparagus

Preheat the oven to 425°.

Roll out the dough to ¼ inch thick and use to line a greased 10 inch quiche or pie pan. Prick with fork. Bake blind for 5 minutes.

Melt the butter in a small saucepan. Stir in flour. Gradually stir in 1¼ cups of the milk. Season with salt, pepper and nutmeg. Bring to a boil, stirring constantly. Cook for 2 minutes. Remove pan from heat. Separate the eggs and stir one yolk into sauce. Add cheese to the sauce. Pour the sauce into pastry case. Return to the oven and bake for 15 minutes.

Remove quiche from oven. Reduce heat to 375°. Drain asparagus, cut into small lengths and arrange evenly over surface. Mix together the rest of the milk, the remaining egg yolk and 2 egg whites and pour this over top. Bake for 30 minutes more.

Tomato marjoram pizza

Overall timing 1 ½ hours

Freezing Suitable: cook in 450° oven for 35 minutes.

To serve 4

1 ½ lb	Ripe tomatoes
1	Large onion
2	Garlic cloves
¼ cup	Oil
2 tsp	Dried marjoram
6	Basil leaves
1 tsp	Sugar
	Salt and pepper
Base	
10 oz	Package of bread mix
1 cup	Grated Cheddar cheese
¼ tsp	Powdered mustard

Blanch, peel and roughly chop the tomatoes. Peel and finely chop the onion. Peel and crush the garlic. Heat 3 tbsp of the oil in a saucepan and fry the onion till transparent. Add the tomatoes, garlic, 1 tsp of the marjoram, the basil leaves, sugar and seasoning. Bring to a boil, stirring. Cover and simmer for 15 minutes.

Empty the bread mix into a large bowl. Stir the cheese into mix with powdered mustard. Add hot water (according to package instructions) and mix to a soft, but not sticky dough. Knead for 5 minutes, then roll out on a floured surface to a round 10 inches in diameter. Place on a greased 10 inch pizza pan or baking sheet. Pinch up the edges to make a slight lip.

Spread the tomato mixture over the pizza base and sprinkle with the remaining marjoram. Put pizza in a warm place to rise for about 30 minutes till base has almost doubled in size.

Preheat the oven to 425°.

Sprinkle the remaining oil over the pizza and bake for 25 minutes.

Pantry pizza

Overall timing 1 hour 10 minutes

Freezing Suitable: reheat from frozen in 400° oven for 40 minutes.

To serve 4-6

16 oz	Can of tomatoes
2	Garlic cloves
1	Small onion
½ tsp	Dried basil
	Salt and pepper
4 oz	Can of sardines
6 oz	Cheddar cheese
1	Can of anchovy fillets
12	Small ripe olives
2 tbsp	Grated Parmesan cheese
Base	
2 cups	Self-rising flour
	Pinch of salt
3 tbsp	Oil

Preheat oven to 450°.

Mix together mashed tomatoes and juice, crushed garlic, chopped onion, herbs, seasoning and drained and chopped sardines. Leave for 15 minutes.

Meanwhile, for the base, sift flour and salt into
a bowl. Stir in oil and sufficient water to mix to a soft dough. Roll out dough to a large round and place on a greased baking sheet. Pinch up edge to make a rim. Brush with oil.

Spread tomato mixture over base. Cover with grated or sliced cheddar and arrange anchovy fillets in a lattice shape on top. Garnish with olives and sprinkle with Parmesan.

Bake for 15 minutes. Reduce heat to 375° and bake for a further 20-25 minutes.

Olive and caper pizza

Overall timing 1¾ hours

Freezing Not suitable

To serve 2

6 oz	Potatoes
	Salt and pepper
2 cups	Self-rising flour
¼ cup	Butter
¾ lb	Tomatoes
4	Anchovy fillets
1 tbsp	Capers
1 cup	Ripe olives
¾ cup	Milk
2 tsp	Dried oregano
1 tbsp	Olive oil

Preheat the oven to 425°.

Peel potatoes and cut into small chunks. Cook in boiling salted water till tender.

Meanwhile, sift the flour into a bowl and rub in the butter till the mixture resembles fine bread crumbs. Blanch, peel and chop tomatoes. Chop anchovy fillets. Drain capers. Pit olives.

Drain potatoes and mash well. Stir into rubbed-in mixture. Add milk and mix to form a soft dough. Knead lightly till smooth. Roll out dough and use to line a greased 9 inch pizza pan.

Arrange tomatoes, anchovies, capers and olives on top. Sprinkle with salt, pepper and oregano. Sprinkle olive oil over and bake for about 35 minutes till well riscn and golden. Cut into wedges to serve.

Spring vegetable pie

Overall timing 2 hours

Freezing Not suitable

To serve 6

1 lb	Collard greens
2	Small globe artichokes
1 lb	Fresh peas
	Salt and pepper
1	Large onion
6 tbsp	Butter
½ lb	Pie pastry
4	Eggs
¼ cup	Grated Parmesan cheese
1 tbsp	Chopped parsley

Pick over the greens, discarding any damaged parts, and chop coarsely. Remove stems and tough outer leaves from artichokes and cut artichokes into quarters, discarding the hairy chokes. Shell peas. Bring a pan of lightly salted water to a boil, add the artichokes and peas and simmer for 10 minutes.

Peel and chop onion. Melt butter in large saucepan, add onion and fry till golden.

Drain artichokes and peas and add to the onion with the greens and seasoning. Mix well, cover tightly and simmer for 10 minutes, shaking the pan occasionally. Cool.

Preheat oven to 400°.

Roll out two-thirds of dough and use to line an 8 inch springform pan. Spread vegetables in pan. Beat three of the eggs lightly with cheese and parsley, then pour over vegetables. Roll out remaining dough and cover filling. Beat remaining egg and brush over pie. Place pan on a baking sheet and bake for 30 minutes.

Remove sides of pan. Brush sides of pie with egg and bake for a further 10-15 minutes till golden.

Vegetable quiche

Overall timing 1 hour

Freezing Suitable

To serve 4-6

10-inch	Frozen or freshly made unbaked pie crust
2	Tomatoes
1	Onion
½ cup	Butter
¼ lb	Mushrooms
¼ lb	Zucchini
¼ lb	Green beans
¼ lb	Broccoli
1 cup	Light cream
3	Eggs
	Salt and pepper
1 tsp	Dried thyme
1 tsp	Powdered mustard
¼ cup	Chopped parsley
½ cup	Grated cheese

Thaw pie crust if frozen. Preheat oven to 425°.

Prick crust with a fork and bake for 15 minutes. Remove from oven and lower heat to 400°.

Peel, seed and chop tomatoes. Place in a sieve over a bowl to drain. Peel and chop onion. Heat ¼ cup butter in a skillet and fry onion till golden. Drain and set aside.

Trim mushrooms. Slice zucchini. Heat remaining butter in a skillet and add mushrooms and zucchini. Cook over high heat, stirring, for 4-5 minutes till evenly browned. Set aside.

Trim beans. Cook beans and broccoli in boiling water for 3-4 minutes. Drain, refresh in cold water and set aside.

Beat together cream, eggs, salt, pepper, thyme, mustard and parsley.

Spread onion over bottom of crust and put all vegetables, except tomatoes, on top. Pour over cream mixture. Spread chopped tomatoes over surface and sprinkle with cheese. Bake for 30 minutes till set. Serve hot.

Sicilian fish pie

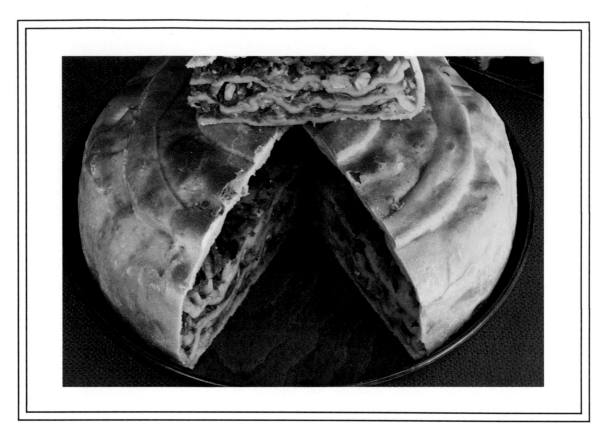

Overall timing 2 hours

Freezing Not suitable

To serve 8

3 cups	Flour
12 tbsp	Butter
2 tbsp	Sugar
½ tsp	Grated lemon rind
3	Egg yolks
¾ lb	White fish steaks
1	Large stalk of celery
¾ cup	Pitted green olives
1	Large onion
3 tbsp	Olive oil
1 tbsp	Drained capers
2 tbsp	Tomato paste
3	Zucchini
1	Egg
3 tbsp	Flour
	Oil for deep frying
1	Egg yolk

Make pastry, put flour in bowl, rub in butter. Add sugar and lemon rind, mix to a dough with egg yolks. Cube fish; chop celery; slice olives. Peel and thinly slice onion. Heat oil in a saucepan, add onion and fry till golden. Add celery, olives, capers, tomato paste, fish, ½ cup water and seasoning. Simmer for 15 minutes. preheat oven to 350°.

Cut zucchini into thin fingers. Beat egg, season flour. Dip zucchini into egg, then into flour. Deep fry till golden.

Drain.

Divide dough into thirds. Roll out one and use to line a greased and floured 8 inch springform pan. Roll out remaining dough to two 8 inch rounds.

Layer fish mixture, and zucchini with a dough round between them in pan. Top with remaining pastry. Brush with beaten egg yolk and bake for 50 minutes. Remove from tin and serve hot.

Pork and apple pie

Overall timing 1 ½ hours

Freezing Not suitable

To serve 6

Pastry	
2½ cups	Flour
2 tsp	Salt
¼ tsp	Powdered mustard
10 tbsp	Lard
Filling	
¼ lb	Slab bacon
2	Medium-size onions
1½ lb	Lean ground pork
¼ tsp	Dried sage
½ cup	Chicken broth
	Salt and pepper
3	Apples
¼ cup	Light brown sugar
¼ tsp	Grated nutmeg

Preheat the oven to 400°.

Sift the flour, salt and mustard into a bowl and rub in the lard. Add enough cold water to mix to a soft but not sticky dough and knead till smooth. Roll out two-thirds of the dough and use to line an 8½ inch round deep pie dish.

Dice the bacon. Peel and finely chop the onions. Mix the pork with the bacon, onions, sage, broth and plenty of seasoning.

Peel, quarter, core and slice the apples. Put into a bowl with the sugar and nutmeg and toss gently till mixed.

Spread one-third of the pork in the pie dish and arrange half the apple mixture on top. Repeat the layers, finishing with the pork mixture.

Roll out the remaining dough to a round and use to cover the pie. Crimp the edges to seal. Place the pie on a baking sheet. Bake for 1 hour, covering the top of the pie lightly with foil after the first 30 minutes.

Ham, veal and pork pie

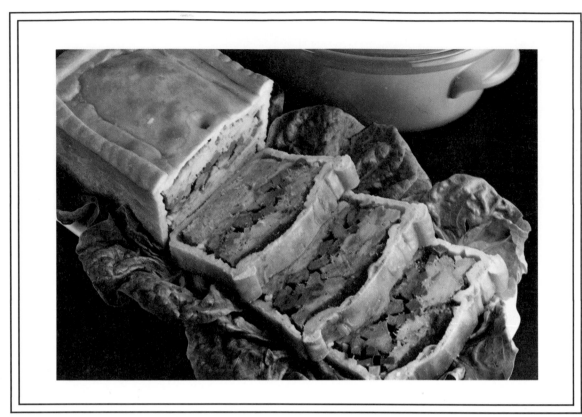

Overall timing 2½ hours plus
overnight marination and chilling
Freezing Suitable

To serve 6-8

¾ lb	Veal for stew
2	Bay leaves
1 tbsp	Brandy
	Salt and pepper
½ lb	Cooked ham
¾ lb	Fresh pork sides
¼ lb	Slab bacon
4 cups	Flour
10 tbsp	Butter
1¼ cups	Water
2	Egg yolks

Cut veal into thin strips and place in a bowl
with bay leaves, brandy and a pinch of salt.
Leave to marinate overnight. Cut ham into
thin strips, add to veal and leave to marinate
for another 2 hours.

Preheat the oven to 375°.
Pass pork and bacon through a grinder twice,
or process finely in a food processor. Mix with
a little of the marinade and seasoning.

Sift flour and 1 tsp salt into a large bowl and
make a well in the center. Melt butter in water
and bring to a boil. Pour quickly into the flour
and mix well. Add one egg yolk and knead to a
smooth dough.

Working quickly, roll out two-thirds of
dough and use to line a greased 9 x 5 x 3 inch
loaf pan. Spread half the pork mixture on
bottom, cover with ham and veal mixture and
spread remaining pork mixture on top. Roll
out remaining dough to fit pie. Seal edges.

Lightly beat remaining egg yolk with a
pinch of salt and brush over dough. Bake for
1 hour, then reduce heat to 325°, cover with
foil to prevent over-browning and bake for
another hour.

Australian-style lamb pie

Overall timing 1 1/4 hours

Freezing Suitable: thaw, then bake as recipe

To serve 4

1 1/2 lb	Boneless shoulder of lamb
	Salt and pepper
2 tbsp	Flour
1	Onion
1/2 lb	Carrots
1/4 lb	Mushrooms
2 tbsp	Butter
2 tbsp	Oil
2 cups	Broth
2 tbsp	Chopped parsley
6 oz	Pie pastry
1	Egg

Wipe meat and cut into thin slices. Coat in seasoned flour. Peel and chop onion. Scrape and grate carrots. Wipe and slice mushrooms.

Heat butter and oil in skillet and brown meat on all sides. Add onion, carrots and mushrooms and cook for 5 minutes. Stir in broth and add seasoning. Cover and simmer gently for 10 minutes.

Preheat oven to 400°.

Transfer meat mixture to pie dish and sprinkle with parsley. Roll out pastry and cover pie dish. Brush surface with lightly beaten egg and bake for 40-45 minutes until golden brown. Serve hot with baked potatoes and minted peas.

Suet and bacon tart

Overall timing 45 minutes plus resting

Freezing Not suitable

To serve 4

½ lb	Bacon slices
1 cup	Cracklings from rendered suet
3 cups	Self-rising flour
¼ cup	Chopped suet
2	Eggs
1 tbsp	Tomato paste
¼ tsp	Chili sauce
	Salt and pepper

Cook the bacon, till crisp. Allow to cool, then break into pieces and mix with the suet cracklings.

Grease an 8 inch loose-bottomed cake pan. Sift flour into bowl and add half the crackling mixture, the suet, eggs, tomato paste, chili sauce, salt and pepper. Mix to a soft but not sticky dough. Knead lightly, then press into cake pan. Leave to rest for 20 minutes.

Preheat oven to 400°.

Sprinkle rest of crackling mixture over dough and press in lightly. Bake for about 30 minutes till well risen and golden.

Cottage pie

Overall timing 1 ¼ hours

Freezing Suitable: reheat in 425° oven for 1 hour.

To serve 6

2 lb	Floury potatoes
	Salt and pepper
2	Large onions
2 tbsp	Beef drippings
2 lb	Ground beef
2 tbsp	Flour
1 ¼ cups	Strong beef broth
16 oz	Can of tomatoes
½ lb	Frozen vegetables
½ cup	Milk
¼ cup	Butter

Peel and quarter the potatoes; cook in boiling salted water till tender.

Preheat the oven to 375°. Peel and thinly slice onions. Heat drippings in a flameproof casserole and fry onions till transparent. Add beef and fry till browned.

Sprinkle in the flour and cook, stirring for 1 minute. Gradually add broth and bring to a boil, stirring. Add tomatoes and juice, seasoning and frozen vegetables and simmer for 5 minutes.

Drain potatoes. Add milk and butter and mash well. Spread potato over beef mixture. Bake for 30 minutes.

Savory strudel

Overall timing 1½ hours

Freezing Suitable: bake from frozen, allowing extra 10-15 minutes.

To serve 4-6

¾ lb	Frozen puff pastry
1	Onion
2	Tomatoes
1	Green pepper
3 tbsp	Oil
1 lb	Ground beef
3 tbsp	Tomato ketchup
½ tsp	Worcestershire sauce
	Salt and pepper
1 cup	Grated sharp Cheddar cheese
1	Egg yolk

Thaw pastry. Preheat oven to 425°. Grease baking sheet.

Peel and finely chop onion and tomatoes. Seed and finely chop pepper. Heat oil in a skillet. Cook onion till golden, then add beef and pepper. Cook for 5 minutes, then add tomatoes. Cook for 5 more minutes. Cool, then stir in tomato ketchup, Worcestershire sauce and seasoning.

Roll out dough thinly to a rectangle about 12 x 8 inches. Spread beef mixture over dough, leaving border clear. Scatter cheese over beef mixture, then fold borders on short sides over filling. Roll up from a long side and seal join.

Place strudel on baking sheet. Decorate with trimmings, then brush with beaten egg yolk. Bake for 20 minutes. Reduce heat to 350° and cook for a further 20 minutes. Cut into slices to serve.

Cottage spinach roll

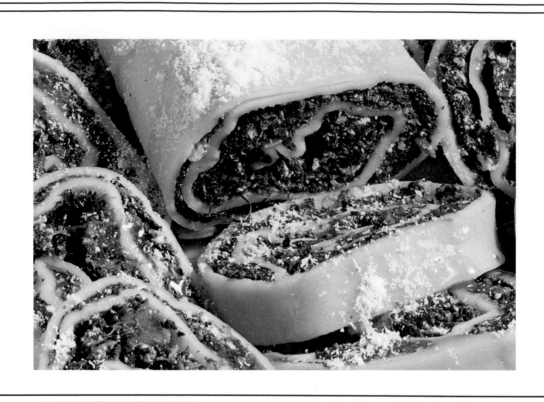

Overall timing 1¾ hours

Freezing Not suitable

To serve 4-6

2 cups	Flour
	Salt and pepper
2	Eggs
2 lb	Bulk spinach
6 tbsp	Butter
1 cup	Cottage cheese
¼ tsp	Grated nutmeg
6 tbsp	Grated Parmesan cheese

Sift the flour and ½ tsp salt into a bowl. Beat the eggs lightly in a bowl, pour half into the flour and mix with a palette knife. Add enough of the remaining egg to make a stiff dough. Knead till smooth, then chill for 30 minutes.

Meanwhile, wash and pick over the spinach. Put into a saucepan with only the water that clings to it. Cover and cook gently for 5 minutes. Drain thoroughly, then shred.

Melt 2 tbsp of the butter in a skillet, add the spinach and cook for 5 minutes, stirring occasionally. Pour into a bowl and add the cottage cheese, nutmeg, half the Parmesan and seasoning. Mix well. Leave to cool.

Roll out the dough on a floured surface to a rectangle about 15 x 12 inches. With a long side nearest you, spread the filling over the dough, leaving a 1 inch border. Fold the bottom border over the filling and roll up. Pinch the ends together to seal.

Wrap the roll in a double thickness of cheesecloth, tying the ends with string. Place in a large pan of boiling salted water, cover and simmer for 25 minutes.

Drain and unwrap the roll and place on a warmed serving dish. Melt the remaining butter. Cut the roll into thick slices, pour the butter over and sprinkle with the remaining Parmesan. Serve immediately.

Brazilian meat turnovers

Overall timing 50 minutes

Freezing Suitable: omit hard-cooked eggs and bake from frozen in 425° oven for 30 minutes.

To serve 4

¾ lb	Frozen puff pastry
1	Onion
¼ lb	Thick bacon slices
2 tbsp	Butter
½ lb	Ground beef
3 tbsp	Raisins
	Pinch of ground cloves
	Salt and pepper
¼ tsp	Paprika
2	Hard-cooked eggs
8	Pitted green olives
1	Egg

Thaw the pastry. Roll out to a rectangle 8 x 16 inches. Cut into eight 4 inch squares.

Preheat oven to 400°.

Peel and finely chop the onion. Grind or coarsely process the bacon. Melt the butter in a skillet and fry the onion and bacon till golden. Add the beef and fry briskly, stirring frequently, till brown.

Remove from heat and add the raisins, cloves, salt, pepper and paprika. Mix well. Shell and coarsely chop the hard-cooked eggs. Chop the olives, add to the pan with the eggs and mix well.

Place one eighth of the meat mixture on half of each dough square. Brush the edges with a little of the beaten egg and fold dough over. Crimp edges to seal.

Arrange on a dampened baking sheet and brush tops with beaten egg. Bake for about 25 minutes till well risen and golden.

Deep chicken and ham pie

Overall timing 2¾ hours plus cooling

Freezing Suitable

To serve 6

1 lb	Pie pastry
1½ lb	Boneless chicken
	Salt and pepper
1 tsp	Grated lemon rind
¼ tsp	Dried sage
¼ lb	Sliced cooked ham
1 tsp	Unflavored gelatin
6 tbsp	Chicken broth

Roll out two-thirds of pastry and use to line a greased 6 inch loose-bottomed cake pan. Reserve remaining pastry for lid. Preheat oven to 375°.

Finely dice chicken, keeping breast and dark meat separate. Season both well and add lemon rind and sage. Dice ham. Cover pastry case with half breast meat, then with half dark meat. Spread all ham on top, then repeat layering of dark and breast meats.

Roll reserved pastry to make lid. Moisten dough edges and place lid in position. Press down firmly to seal. Make a hole in center and decorate top. Glaze with lightly beaten egg.

Bake for 1 hour, then reduce oven temperature to 350° and bake for a further 1 – 1¼ hours. Remove pie from oven, cool for 30 minutes then remove from pan and leave until cold.

Meanwhile, dissolve gelatin in chicken broth. When the gelatin mixture begins to set, put a funnel or cone of foil or wax paper into the center hole in the pie. Pour in gelatin and chill in refrigerator till set. Serve cold with salad.

Sausage in brioche

Overall timing 2½ hours plus rising

Freezing Not suitable

To serve 6-8

1 lb	Piece of fresh continental sausage
	Bouquet garni
1	Onion
2 cups	Flour
¼ tsp	Salt
1½ tsp	Active dry yeast
2 tbsp	Lukewarm water
1 tbsp	Sugar
2	Eggs
¼ cup	Butter
1	Egg yolk

Put sausage into a saucepan with bouquet garni and peeled onion and cover with cold water. Bring to a boil and simmer very gently for 1¾ hours.

Meanwhile, sift flour and salt into a bowl. Sprinkle yeast onto the water, add a pinch of the sugar and mix well. Leave in a warm place till frothy, then add to flour with remaining sugar. Add eggs and melted butter to flour and mix to a soft dough. Knead till glossy, cover with oiled plastic wrap and leave in a warm place to rise.

Drain sausage, discarding flavorings, and allow to cool slightly. Remove the skin.

Preheat the oven to 425°.

Roll out dough to a rectangle large enough to enclose the sausage. Place sausage in center and fold dough around it, pinching edges to seal. Place, join down, on a baking sheet. Leave to rise for 15 minutes.

Brush with beaten egg yolk and bake for about 25 minutes till crisp and golden. Serve hot, cut into thick slices.

Leek pie

Overall timing 1 hour

Freezing Suitable: reheat in 350° oven for 30 minutes.

To serve 4

1½ lb	Leeks
2	Onions
¼ cup	Butter
	Salt and pepper
½ lb	Bacon slices
¾ lb	Pie pastry
1 tbsp	Cornstarch
½ cup	Light cream
1	Egg

Preheat the oven to 400°.

Wash, trim and slice leeks. Peel and slice onions. Melt butter in a skillet and fry onions till golden. Add sliced leeks, salt and pepper and cook gently for 5 minutes.

Meanwhile, fry bacon slices in another skillet.

Roll out two-thirds of the dough and use to line a shallow pie dish. Cover with leek mixture and arrange bacon slices on top. Mix cornstarch with the cream and pour over.

Roll out remaining dough and cover filling. Seal and crimp edges, using any trimmings to decorate top. Glaze with beaten egg. Bake for 45 minutes until golden brown.

Ham pie

Overall timing 1 hour

Freezing Not suitable

To serve 4

½ lb	Pie pastry
1 lb	Can of ham
1	Egg

Preheat the oven to 425°.

Roll out the dough to ¼ inch thickness. Place ham in center. Dampen the dough edges and fold around the ham. Seal well. Place in an ovenproof dish and decorate with trimmings, if liked.

Lightly beat the egg and brush all over the dough. Bake for 40 minutes till golden.

Ham and vegetable bake

Overall timing 1 hour 10 minutes

Freezing Suitable: top with egg after reheating in 350° oven for 1¼ hours

To serve 4

½ lb	Frozen spinach
1 lb	Celeriac
2 lb	Potatoes
	Salt and pepper
5 tbsp	Butter
3 tbsp	Light cream
6 tbsp	Hot milk
1	Small head of celery
½ lb	Sliced cooked ham
1 cup	Grated Cheddar cheese
2	Eggs

Place spinach in a strainer to thaw. Peel celeriac and potatoes and cut into small chunks. Put prepared vegetable chunks into saucepan of cold salted water and bring to a boil. Cook for 20 minutes till tender. Drain well and mash or purée with ¼ cup of the butter, the cream and enough milk to give a creamy purée. Season to taste.

Preheat over to 400°.

Wash and trim celery. Blanch in boiling water for 5 minutes. Drain well and cut into pieces.

Grease ovenproof dish with remaining butter. Spread the well-drained spinach over, arrange the chopped celery on top and cover with ham slices. Sprinkle over half the cheese and cover with the celeriac and potato purée. Bake for 15 minutes.

In a bowl, lightly beat the eggs with salt and pepper. Pour over the purée, top with remaining cheese and return to oven. Bake for another 15 minutes till golden. Serve immediately.

Club sandwiches

Overall timing 30 minutes

Freezing Not suitable

To serve 4

4-8	Bacon slices
12	Slices of bread
	Mayonnaise
4	Slices of cooked chicken or turkey
4	Lettuce leaves
5	Tomatoes

Preheat the broiler.

Broil the bacon until crisp. Toast four slices of bread on both sides, but toast the remaining slices of bread on one side only. Slice the tomatoes.

To assemble the sandwiches, spread the untoasted sides of bread with mayonnaise. Place four pieces, toasted side down, on a board and top with the chicken or turkey slices. Cover with the completely toasted bread. Add the lettuce, bacon, tomato slices (reserving some for the garnish) and remaining bread, mayonnaise side down. Press lightly together, then halve diagonally. Garnish with the reserved tomato slices.

Ham and potatoes au gratin

Overall timing 55 minutes

Freezing Not suitable

To serve 4

1	Onion
2 tbs	Oil
¼ cup	Butter
1	Garlic clove
¼ lb	Sliced cooked ham
2	Eggs
1 cup	Milk
¾ cup	Grated Cheddar cheese
	Salt and pepper
¼ tsp	Grated nutmeg
1 lb	Potatoes

Preheat the oven to 375°.

Peel and chop the onion. Heat the oil with half the butter in a skillet, add the onion and when it softens, add the garlic, peeled and chopped. Cut the ham into matchsticks or chop. Add it to the onion, heat through and keep warm.

Meanwhile, beat the eggs and add the milk, cheese, salt, pepper and nutmeg. Peel and grate the potatoes. Squeeze excess water from them. Blanch them for 4 minutes in boiling, salted water. Drain well and add the grated potato to the egg mixture. Stir well. Add the ham and onions.

Lightly butter a shallow ovenproof dish and fill with the mixture. Dot the top with the remaining butter. Bake for 30-35 minutes, browning the top for the last 5 minutes under the broiler.

Ham and horseradish rolls

Overall timing 15 minutes

Freezing Not suitable

To serve 8

½ cup	Heavy cream
½ cup	Thick mayonnaise
1 tbsp	Grated horseradish
1 tbsp	Lemon juice
	Salt
8	Slices of cooked ham

Whip the heavy cream until soft peaks form. Beat in the mayonnaise to give a smooth piping consistency. Fold in grated horseradish and lemon juice, season, then spoon mixture into a pastry bag fitted with a large star nozzle. Roll up ham slices to form tubes 1 inch in diameter. Pipe horseradish mixture into rolls.

Arrange rolls, seamed side down, on a large serving dish. Garnish with pickle fans, sliced stuffed olives, fine slices of cucumber, wedges of tomato and matchsticks of green pepper.

Mixed meat satay

Overall timing 45 minutes plus marination

Freezing Not suitable

To serve 4

½ lb	Lean boneless lamb
½ lb	Sirloin or flank steak
½ lb	Boneless chicken breast
3	Onions
2	Garlic cloves
1 tsp	Ground coriander
1 tsp	Ground cumin
1 tsp	Ground ginger
1 tsp	Sugar
½ tsp	Salt
7 tbsp	Soy sauce
	Pinch of chili powder
½ cup	Shelled roasted peanuts
1 tbsp	Oil
1 cup	Water
1 tbsp	Lemon juice

Wipe meats and cut into small cubes. Peel and chop 2 onions and place in a large bowl. Add peeled and crushed garlic, spices, sugar and salt. Pound well to form a paste and add 6 tbsp soy sauce. Add meat, mix, then leave to marinate for 1 hour, turning occasionally.

Meanwhile, prepare sauce. Peel and finely chop remaining onion. Purée in blender with chili powder, salt and peanuts until smooth. Heat oil in a pan and fry peanut mixture for 3 minutes, stirring. Stir in remaining soy sauce, water and lemon juice. Cook gently for 5 minutes.

Thread 4 or 5 pieces of meat onto each skewer. Brush with extra oil and broil or barbecue for about 5 minutes, turning and brushing with oil at frequent intervals.

Pour sauce into individual shallow dishes. Serve with the meat, accompanied by cucumber, onion and potato cubes or rice.

Meatballs with dill and sour cream

Overall timing 1 hour
Freezing Suitable

To serve 4-6

3 cups	Soft bread crumbs
½ cup	Milk or sour cream
1	Large onion
½ cup	Butter
1 lb	Ground beef
½ lb	Ground pork
½ lb	Ground lamb
2	Eggs
	Salt and pepper
5 tbsp	Chopped fresh dill or
2 tbsp	Dried dill
½ cup	Beef broth
½ cup	Sour cream
	Sprig of fresh dill

Soak bread crumbs in milk or sour cream. Peel and finely chop onion. Heat 2 tbsp butter in a skillet and fry onion till soft. Tip onion into a mixing bowl and add bread crumb mixture, beef, pork, lamb, eggs, salt, pepper and half the dill. Mix well. Shape mixture into balls about 2 inches in diameter.

Heat 2 tbsp butter in skillet and gently cook meatballs in several batches, adding more butter as necessary. As meatballs brown on all sides, remove from the skillet and keep warm.

When all meatballs have been browned, add broth to skillet. Stir, scraping up any brown bits from bottom of skillet, and bring to a boil. Boil until reduced by half, then add sour cream. Cook gently, stirring, for 1 minute. Stir in remaining dill, and season well.

Return meatballs to skillet, cover and heat through for 2-3 minutes. Serve garnished with a sprig of dill.

Liver soufflé

Overall timing 45 minutes

Freezing Not suitable

To serve 4

¾ lb	Calf's or lamb's liver
¼ cup	Butter
3 tbsp	Brandy
2 cups	Thick white sauce
	Salt and pepper
2	Eggs

Preheat the oven to 400°.

Cut liver into thin slices. Melt butter in a skillet, add liver and fry for 2-3 minutes on each side. Heat the brandy in a ladle, set it alight and pour over the liver. Put liver into blender or food processor and process till smooth.

Mix liver with white sauce and seasoning. Separate the eggs and beat the egg yolks into the liver mixture, one at a time. Beat the egg whites till stiff but not dry and fold into the liver mixture with a metal spoon.

Pour mixture into a greased 8-inch soufflé dish, smooth the top and bake for about 25 minutes till well risen and golden. Serve immediately with a crisp green salad.

Country-style liver pâté

Overall timing 3 hours plus maturing

Freezing Suitable

To serve 12

1½ lb	Pork liver
1 lb	Canadian bacon
½ lb (1 cup)	Lard
1	Egg
1 tbsp	Flour
	Salt and pepper
½ tsp	Ground allspice
	Caul fat
	(optional)

Preheat the oven to 350°.

Chop the liver. Dice bacon. Put liver and bacon through a fine grinder or chop finely in a food processor. Melt the lard in a saucepan and gradually beat into ground liver and bacon in bowl. Beat egg and add with flour, seasoning and allspice. Mix well.

Line greased ovenproof dish with caul fat, if using, leaving edges hanging over sides. Add liver mixture and smooth top. Wrap caul edges over. Cover dish with lid or foil and place in a roasting pan containing 1 inch water. Bake for 1¾ hours.

Allow to cool, then leave in the refrigerator for 2-3 days to mature. Serve with crusty bread.

Bacon and apple rings

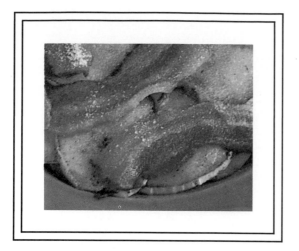

Overall timing 40 minutes

Freezing Not suitable

To serve 4

½ lb	Bacon slices
2	Yellow Golden Delicious apples
2 tbsp	Sugar

Fry the bacon in a skillet until crisp. Drain on paper towels, place on a warmed serving plate and keep hot.

Wash, dry and core apples, but don't peel them. Cut into thin rings and cook in the skillet till tender, turning them over with a spatula. Drain on paper towels, then arrange on the serving plate with the bacon.

Sprinkle with sugar and serve immediately with hot toast and butter.

Spanish kabobs

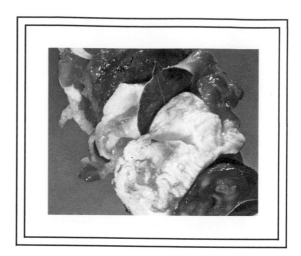

Overall timing 25 minutes plus marination

Freezing Not suitable

To serve 4

1 lb	Thick white fish fillets
2 tbsp	Oil
2 tbsp	Lemon juice
	Salt and pepper
½ lb	Garlic sausage
8	Bacon slices
16	Bay leaves
6 tbsp	Butter

Cut the fish into 16 neat cubes and put into a bowl with the oil, half the lemon juice and salt and pepper. Marinate for 1 hour, turning occasionally.

Preheat the broiler. Cut the sausage into ½ inch slices. Stretch the bacon slices and cut each in half. Thread the fish cubes, sausage, bay leaves and folded bacon onto greased skewers.

Place on the broiler pan and brush the marinade over. Broil for about 10 minutes, turning and basting frequently, till the fish is tender.

Melt the butter in a saucepan and add the remaining lemon juice and seasoning. Serve with the kabobs.

Blood sausage with apples

Overall timing 25 minutes

Freezing Not suitable

To serve 2

½ lb	Blood sausage
¼ cup	Butter
1	Onion
2	Apples
	Fresh parsley

Thickly slice the sausage. Melt the butter in a skillet and add the sausage. Cook till crispy — if you cook them gently the slices will stay intact, instead of breaking away from the skin. Lift out with slotted spoon and keep hot.

Peel onion and slice into rings. Fry gently in the butter till brown and just tender.

Core and slice the apples. Add to pan and cook for 5 minutes, turning slices over halfway through. Add the sausage and cook the mixture for 2 minutes more.

Place sausage, onion and apples on two warmed plates. Garnish with parsley sprigs and serve hot.

Crusty mushroom bread

Overall timing 1 hour

Freezing Suitable: cook after thawing

To serve 6-8

1	Round loaf of bread
½ cup	Butter
1 lb	Mushrooms
	Salt and pepper
3 tbsp	Lemon juice
1 cup	White sauce
2	Eggs

Preheat the oven to 350°.

Slice the top off the bread and scoop out most of the crumbs, leaving a ½ inch thick shell. Spread the inside with half the butter, place on a baking sheet and bake for 10 minutes.

Meanwhile, finely chop the mushrooms. Melt the remaining butter in a saucepan and fry the mushrooms for 5 minutes, stirring frequently. Add salt, pepper and lemon juice. Stir the mushrooms into the white sauce. Separate the eggs and beat the egg yolks, one at a time, into the sauce. Return to the heat and heat through gently. Beat the egg whites till stiff but not dry. Gently fold into the mushroom mixture.

Pour the mixture into the bread shell and sprinkle the top with a few of the scooped out bread crumbs, grated finely. Bake for 30 minutes till well risen and crisp. Serve hot.

Broccoli toasts

Overall timing 40 minutes

Freezing Not suitable

To serve 4

1 lb	Broccoli
1 cup	Beef broth
8	Slices of bread
1 cup	Thick white sauce
	Salt and pepper
	Grated nutmeg
½ tsp	Mixed herbs
2	Hard-cooked eggs
1	Tomato
	Sprigs of parsley
½	Sweet red pepper

Trim broccoli and chop into large pieces. Bring broth to a boil, add broccoli and cook for 7-10 minutes.

Toast bread and place on baking sheet. Drain broccoli well, then arrange on the toast.

Preheat oven to 375°.

Heat sauce, then add seasoning, pinch of nutmeg and herbs. Finely chop one of the hard-cooked eggs and add to the sauce. Pour sauce over broccoli. Bake for 15 minutes.

Serve hot, garnished with remaining egg, sliced tomato, parsley and strips of pepper.

Pirozski

Overall timing 1 hour

Freezing Suitable: refresh in 350° oven for 10 minutes

To serve 6

½ lb	Frozen puff pastry
½ lb	Liver pâté
1	Egg

Thaw pastry. Preheat the oven to 400°.

Roll out dough very thinly on a floured surface and cut into 3 inch squares. Cut in half diagonally to make triangles. Put about 1 tsp liver pâté on half of the triangles. Moisten dough edges and cover with remaining triangles. Press edges together to seal.

Arrange triangles on greased baking sheet and brush with beaten egg. Bake for 10-15 minutes till well risen and golden. Serve hot.

Provençal sandwiches

Overall timing 15 minutes

Freezing Not suitable

To serve 4

4	Crusty rolls
1	Garlic clove
4	Large lettuce leaves
2	Large tomatoes
2	Hard-cooked eggs
	Pickled vegetables or gherkins
	Ripe olives
	Cooked green beans
	Anchovy fillets
	Sweet green or red pepper
	Olive oil
	Vinegar

Halve the rolls and the garlic clove. Rub the cut surfaces of the rolls with the garlic. Place the lettuce leaves on the bottom halves of the rolls.

Slice the tomatoes. Shell and slice the eggs. Place the tomatoes and eggs on the lettuce, then add pickled vegetables or gherkins, olives, beans, anchovies and pepper strips, according to taste. Sprinkle with oil and vinegar, then place the tops of the rolls on the filling. Press gently together and serve.

Hot frankfurter salad

Overall timing 45 minutes

Freezing Not suitable

To serve 4

1 lb	Waxy potatoes	
	Salt and pepper	
4	Frankfurters	
2	Onions	
4	Anchovy fillets	
2 tbsp	Oil	
2 tbsp	White wine vinegar	
¼ cup	Chopped gherkins	

Peel and slice potatoes, then cook in boiling salted water for about 7 minutes till tender.

Heat frankfurters in boiling water for 5 minutes, then drain and slice. Peel and slice onions into rings. Finely chop anchovies. Drain potatoes and mix with frankfurters and onions.

Beat together oil and vinegar, season and pour over the warm salad. Mix well and leave for 10 minutes. Add anchovies and gherkins and serve.

Tuna buns

Overall timing 15 minutes

Freezing Not suitable

To serve 4

4	Hot dog buns	
	Butter	
	Mayonnaise	
7 oz	Can of tuna fish	
	Chopped parsley	
2	Hard-cooked eggs	
	Radish roses	

Halve the buns, not cutting all the way through, and butter the cut surfaces. Spread a thick layer of mayonnaise over the bottom cut surface.

Drain the tuna and flake it. Divide between the buns and sprinkle with parsley. Arrange on a serving plate.

Shell and slice the eggs and use, with radish roses, to garnish.

Beefy tomatoes

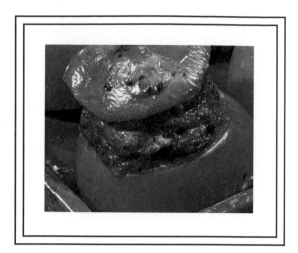

Overall timing 45 minutes

Freezing Not suitable

To serve 6

6	Large tomatoes
1	Large onion
½ lb	Corn beef
½ lb	Bulk sausage meat
2 tbsp	Chopped parsley
1	Egg
¼ tsp	Ground allspice
	Salt and pepper
	Oil

Preheat the oven to 425°.

Cut tops off tomatoes and reserve. Scoop out most of the flesh and place it in a bowl. Peel and finely chop onion. Add to bowl with the corn beef, sausage meat and chopped parsley. Mash well. Beat in the egg, allspice and seasoning and mix well.

Stuff tomatoes with beef mixture and put the reserved "lids" on top. Place on a baking sheet and brush with oil. Bake for 20 minutes. Serve with crusty bread.

Nutty hamburgers

Overall timing 45 minutes

Freezing Not suitable

To serve 4

1 cup	Hazelnuts
2 tbsp	Butter
1	Large onion
1 lb	Lean ground beef
2 tbsp	Capers
1 tbsp	Grated lemon rind
¼ tsp	Paprika
½ tsp	Powdered mustard
	Salt and pepper
4	Egg yolks

Preheat the oven to 375°.

Chop nuts. Melt butter in a skillet and cook nuts till golden. Peel onion. Cut four equal rings and reserve. Finely chop remainder and mix with nuts, beef, half the capers, the lemon rind, paprika, mustard and seasoning.

Divide mixture into four portions. Shape into balls, place on a baking sheet and flatten slightly making a well in center of each. Bake for 25 minutes.

Place each burger on a lettuce leaf on serving plate. Press an onion ring into each well, then carefully place a raw egg yolk in each ring and garnish with remaining capers. If liked, bake for 10 minutes to cook eggs.

Ham and potato cake

Overall timing 1 ¼ hours

Freezing Not suitable

To serve 4

1 ½ lb	Medium-size potatoes
	Salt and pepper
½ lb	Sliced cooked ham
6 tbsp	Butter
3 tbsp	Soft bread crumbs
2 cups	Grated cheese
½ cup	Milk

Cook potatoes in boiling salted water for 20 minutes. Meanwhile, chop the ham. Grease a 7 inch springform pan with a little of the butter and sprinkle breadcrumbs over the bottom and sides, shaking off any excess. Preheat oven to 350°.

Drain and peel the potatoes, then cut into ¼ inch thick slices. Arrange a few of the slices, slightly overlapping, in the bottom of the pan. Melt the remaining butter and brush a little over the potatoes. Scatter some of the ham, then some of the cheese over and season. Continue layering, reserving a little of the butter, and finishing with a layer of potato topped with cheese. Pour the milk over and brush with remaining butter.

Bake for about 30 minutes till potatoes are tender and cheese has melted. Unmold cake from pan to serve.

Roast veal salad

Frankfurter kabobs

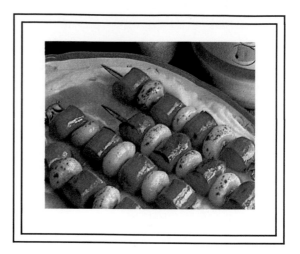

Overall timing 20 minutes

Freezing Not suitable

Overall timing 20 minutes

Freezing Suitable: cook from frozen

To serve 2

½	Head Bibb lettuce
¼	Cucumber
2	Large firm tomatoes
4	Radishes
2	Hard-cooked eggs
6 oz	Cold roast veal
2 tbsp	Oil
2 tsp	White wine vinegar
½ tsp	Powdered mustard
	Salt and pepper
	Sprigs of parsley

To serve 2

4	Frankfurters
12	Pearl onions
3 tbsp	Oil
2 tsp	Coarse-grain mustard

Preheat the broiler.

Cut each frankfurter into three pieces. Blanch onions in boiling water for 5 minutes, then drain and peel. Thread onions and frankfurters alternately onto greased skewers.

Mix oil and mustard together. Brush over kabobs and broil for about 10 minutes, turning and brushing with mustard mixture frequently. Serve with mashed potatoes and pour any cooking juices over.

Wash and dry lettuce. Use outside leaves to line a serving dish. Shred rest and put in bowl. Cut cucumber into matchsticks and add to shredded lettuce.

Cut tomatoes into wedges. Slice radishes. Add half of each to lettuce and cucumber.

Shell and halve hard-cooked eggs. Cut veal into neat cubes.

Put oil, vinegar, mustard and seasoning into a screw-top jar, cover and shake to mix. Add to shredded lettuce mixture and toss lightly. Place in lettuce-lined dish. Arrange eggs, veal and remaining tomatoes and radishes on top. Garnish with parsley.

Welsh sausages

Overall timing 25 minutes

Freezing Suitable: reheat in 350° oven
for 20-25 minutes.

Makes 18-20

1	Small onion
1¼ cups	Grated hard cheese
4½ cups	Soft white bread crumbs
1 tbsp	Chopped parsley or fresh mixed herbs
1 tsp	Powdered mustard
	Salt and pepper
2	Eggs
	Flour for coating
⅔ cup	Dried bread crumbs
	Oil for frying

Peel and finely chop onion. Place in bowl
with cheese, soft bread crumbs, herbs,
mustard and generous seasoning. Add 1
whole egg and 1 yolk and mix into ingredients
with wooden spoon till well combined. Form
mixture into small sausage shapes.

Lightly coat shapes with flour, then lightly
beaten egg white, then dried bread crumbs.

Heat ½ inch oil in a skillet and when hot
cook a few sausages at a time till crisp and
golden all over. Drain on paper towels and
serve hot or cold.

Peasant omelette

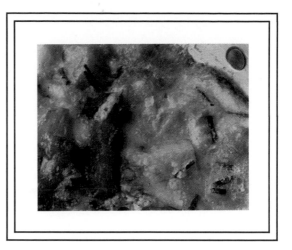

Overall timing 25 minutes

Freezing Not suitable

To serve 4

2	Waxy potatoes
1	Carrot
	Salt and pepper
6	Bacon slices
1 tbsp	Butter
6	Eggs
1 tbsp	Chopped chives
4	Thin slices of cheese

Peel and dice the potatoes; scrape and dice
the carrot. Put into a pan, cover with cold
salted water and bring to a boil. Simmer for
4 minutes, then drain.

Cut bacon into strips. Preheat the broiler.

Melt the butter in a skillet and fry the
bacon till transparent. Add the potatoes
and carrots and fry over a moderate heat
for 5 minutes, stirring frequently, till
golden and tender.

Lightly beat the eggs in a bowl with salt,
pepper and chives. Pour over the bacon and
vegetables and cook till lightly set. Top
with the slices of cheese and broil till
melted. Serve immediately, cut into wedges.

Poached scallops

Overall timing 55 minutes

Freezing Not suitable

To serve 4

2	Small onions
2	Carrots
3½ cups	Water
1 cup	Dry white wine
1	Bouquet garni
	Salt and pepper
	Cayenne pepper
16	Sea scallops
1 tbsp	Chopped parsley
1 cup	Lemony mayonnaise

Peel and slice the onions; peel and slice the carrots. Put in pan with water, wine, bouquet, salt, pepper and a pinch of cayenne. Bring to a boil, then boil uncovered for 20 minutes. Leave to cool.

Put the scallops into the cold court-bouillon and bring slowly to a boil. Simmer for 5 minutes till tender. Remove bouquet garni.

Lift out the scallops and vegetables with a slotted spoon and arrange them in a warmed serving dish. Cover and keep hot.

Boil the bouillon rapidly till reduced by half. Adjust seasoning to taste, then pour liquid over scallops and sprinkle with parsley. Serve with lemony mayonnaise, boiled rice and French bread and butter.

Pilau rice

Overall timing 45 minutes plus soaking

Freezing Not suitable

To serve 4-6

1 lb	Patna rice
1	Large onion
1	Garlic clove
6	Whole allspice
8	Cardamom pods
½ cup	Butter or ghee
2 inch	Cinnamon stick
8	Cloves
1 tsp	Ground turmeric
	Salt
½ cup	Flaked almonds
⅔ cup	Golden raisins

Soak rice in cold water for 1 hour, then drain thoroughly.

Peel and finely chop the onion. Peel and crush garlic. Lightly crush allspice and cardamom pods. Melt 6 tbsp of the fat in a saucepan. Add onion, garlic and spices and fry till onion is transparent but not browned.

Add rice and cook over a low heat, stirring for 3-4 minutes. Add salt to taste and enough boiling water to come 1 inch above the rice. Cover pan tightly and simmer over a very low heat for about 20 minutes till water is absorbed and rice is tender.

Melt remaining fat in skillet and fry almonds and raisins for 3-5 minutes. Mix lightly into rice and serve immediately.

Shrimp pilaf

Overall timing 1 hour

Freezing Not suitable

To serve 4

2	Large onions
2	Fresh green chilies
2	Garlic cloves
½ lb	Bacon slices
1 cup	Long-grain rice
16 oz	Can of tomatoes
	Salt
2 cups	Chicken broth
1 lb	Shelled shrimp
2 tbsp	Chopped parsley
2 tbsp	Grated Parmesan cheese

Peel and slice onions. Seed and slice chilies. Peel and crush garlic. Chop bacon.

Heat a flameproof casserole. Add bacon and fry until well browned. Add the onions, chilies and garlic to the casserole. Cook until onions are soft and transparent but not brown, stirring occasionally.

Add the rice and stir for 2-3 minutes until grains are coated with fat. Add the tomatoes with their juice, salt and chicken broth. Bring rapidly to a boil, then reduce heat, cover and simmer for 15 minutes on a very low heat.

Stir and add the shrimp. Cover and cook for a further 5 minutes.

Turn mixture into warmed serving dish. Sprinkle with parsley and cheese and serve immediately.

Fish paella

Overall timing 45 minutes

Freezing Not suitable

To serve 6

1	Large onion
2	Garlic cloves
¼ cup	Oil
2 cups	Long-grain rice
16 oz	Can of tomatoes
4	Saffron strands
2 quarts	Chicken broth or water
	Salt and pepper
1½ lb	White fish fillets
1	Sweet red pepper
16 oz	Can of artichoke hearts
16 oz	Can of kidney beans
2 cups	Frozen peas

Peel and chop the onion. Peel and crush the garlic. Heat the oil in a flameproof casserole, add the onion and fry till transparent. Add the rice and garlic and fry, stirring, for 2 minutes.

Add the tomatoes and juice, the saffron, broth or water and seasoning and bring to a boil. Reduce the heat and simmer for 10 minutes.

Meanwhile, cut the fish into chunks. Halve and seed the pepper and cut into 1 inch pieces. Drain the artichoke hearts and cut in half lengthwise. Drain the beans.

Add all these ingredients to the pan with the peas and mix lightly. Cover and cook for a further 10 minutes till the rice is tender and the liquid is absorbed. Fluff the mixture with a fork. Taste and adjust seasoning. Serve immediately.

Lentil risotto

Overall timing 1 hour

Freezing Not suitable

To serve 6

1 cup	Brown lentils
1	Onion
½ cup	Butter
	Salt and pepper
1½ cups	Long-grain rice
5 cups	Broth
½ cup	Grated Parmesan cheese

Wash and pick over lentils. Peel and finely chop the onion. Melt the butter in a large saucepan, add the onion and cook till transparent. Add the lentils and enough water to cover. Season and bring to a boil. Reduce heat, cover and simmer for 1 hour.

Add the rice and broth. Bring back to a boil, reduce heat. Cover and simmer for a further 15-18 minutes or until rice is just tender.

Stir in the Parmesan and taste and adjust seasoning. Serve hot.

Arabian pilaf

Overall timing 30 minutes

Freezing Not suitable

To serve 4

2 tbsp	Butter
2 oz	Capelli d'angelo (angels' hair pasta)
3 cups	Chicken broth
1 cup	Long-grain rice
2 tbsp	Grated Parmesan cheese
	Salt and pepper

Melt the butter in a saucepan. Break up the pasta, add to the pan and fry, stirring, over a moderate heat till golden. Remove from pan and reserve.

Add the broth to the pan and bring to a boil. Stir in the rice, bring back to a boil and simmer gently for 15 minutes till the rice is just tender.

Stir in the fried pasta and cook for 2-3 minutes till pasta and rice are tender and all the liquid has been absorbed. Stir in Parmesan and seasoning with a fork. Transfer to a warmed serving dish and serve immediately.

Cannelloni with tuna fish

Overall timing 1 1/2 hours

Freezing Suitable: reheat in 350° oven for 1 hour

To serve 4

12	Sheets of lasagne
	Salt and pepper
2	Onions
2	Garlic cloves
2 oz	Capers
7 oz	Can of tuna fish
1 cup	Soft bread crumbs
1 tbsp	Lemon juice
1	Egg
2 tbsp	Chopped parsley
16 oz	Can of tomatoes
2 tbsp	Grated Parmesan cheese

Place lasagne in saucepan of boiling, salted water and cook for 10-15 minutes or until tender. Drain in a colander, rinse with boiling water and spread out on a damp dishtowel to cool for a few minutes.

Peel and chop onions. Peel and crush garlic. Drain capers. Drain tuna fish oil into a skillet, heat, add onions and fry until golden. Add garlic, tuna fish and capers and cook over low heat for 5 minutes, stirring. Remove from heat.

Preheat oven to 400°. Grease ovenproof dish.

Add bread crumbs (reserving 2 tbsp) to fish mixture with lemon juice, egg, parsley and seasoning. Mix well. Place some of the fish mixture in center of each lasagne sheet and roll around filling. Arrange rolls, joins down, in ovenproof dish.

Press tomatoes in their juice through a sieve, season and spread over cannelloni. Sprinkle with reserved bread crumbs and then with Parmesan. Bake for 30 minutes.

Eggplant and pasta casserole

Overall timing 1 hour

Freezing Not suitable

To serve 4-6

1	Large eggplant
	Salt and pepper
1	Onion
1	Garlic clove
6 tbsp	Butter
1 lb	Tomatoes
2 tsp	Chopped fresh basil
6 tbsp	Oil
¾ lb	Rigatoni pasta
3 oz	Mozzarella cheese

Preheat oven to 400°.

Cut eggplant into thin slices lengthwise. Arrange slices on a plate, sprinkle with salt and leave for 30 minutes.

Meanwhile, peel and chop onion. Peel and crush garlic. Melt ¼ cup of the butter in a saucepan, add onion and garlic and fry till transparent.

Blanch, peel and finely chop tomatoes. Add to onion with seasoning. Simmer gently for 15 minutes. Remove from heat and stir in basil.

Rinse eggplant slices under running cold water and pat dry with paper towels. Heat oil in skillet, add slices and cook for 4-5 minutes each side. Drain on paper towels.

Cook rigatoni in boiling salted water till tender. Drain and mix with tomato sauce. Season to taste. Put half the rigatoni mixture into greased ovenproof dish and arrange eggplant slices on top. Add remaining rigatoni mixture. Thinly slice cheese and arrange on top. Dot with remaining butter and bake for 15 minutes. Serve hot.

Seafood spaghetti

Overall timing 20 minutes

Freezing Not suitable

To serve 4

¾ lb	Spaghetti
	Salt and pepper
1	Garlic clove
3 tbsp	Oil
½ lb	Large shelled shrimp
10 oz	Can of baby clams or mussels
8 oz	Can of tomatoes
1 tbsp	Chopped parsley

Cook spaghetti in boiling salted water till tender.

Meanwhile, peel and crush garlic. Heat oil in a large saucepan, add garlic and fry for 1 minute. Add shrimp and fry, stirring, for 2-3 minutes.

Drain clams or mussels and add to pan with tomatoes and their juice and seasoning. Cook for about 3 minutes, stirring to break up tomatoes.

Drain spaghetti thoroughly. Add to seafood sauce with parsley and toss lightly over a low heat till well coated. Serve immediately.

Spaghetti with goat's cheese

Overall timing 35 minutes

Freezing Not suitable

To serve 2

1	Garlic clove
2	Anchovy fillets
2 tbsp	Olive oil
1 tbsp	Chopped parsley
	Salt and pepper
½ lb	Spaghetti
¼ lb	Firm goat's cheese
2 tbsp	Butter

Peel and crush the garlic into a bowl. Add the anchovy fillets and pound to a paste with a wooden spoon. Beat in the oil, parsley and seasoning. Leave to stand for 15 minutes.

Meanwhile, cook the spaghetti in boiling salted water till tender. Derind the cheese and cut into small cubes.

Drain the spaghetti in a colander. Melt the butter in the spaghetti pan and add the cheese. Cook, stirring, over a low heat for 2 minutes.

Return spaghetti to the pan and toss lightly till coated with butter. Arrange in a warmed serving dish, pour the anchovy dressing over and toss lightly before serving with crusty bread.

Crisp-topped macaroni with tuna

Overall timing 35 minutes

Freezing Not suitable

To serve 4

1	Onion
6 tbsp	Butter
½ cup	Chicken broth
	Salt and pepper
1	Medium-size cauliflower
½ lb	Short-cut macaroni
6	Anchovy fillets
½ cup	Soft bread crumbs
7 oz	Can of tuna
¼ cup	Grated Parmesan cheese

Peel and chop the onion. Melt 2 tbsp of the butter in a large saucepan and fry the onion till golden. Add the chicken broth and seasoning. Bring to a boil and simmer for 5 minutes.

Divide cauliflower into florets and cook in boiling salted water for 4 minutes. Remove with a slotted spoon and reserve. Add macaroni to boiling water and cook till tender.

Meanwhile, melt remaining butter in a skillet and fry cauliflower till golden. Roughly chop anchovies and add to pan with bread crumbs. Fry till crisp. Remove from heat.

Preheat the broiler.

Drain the macaroni and add to the broth mixture. Drain and flake tuna and stir carefully into the macaroni with half the Parmesan. Taste and adjust seasoning and heat through gently.

Pour the macaroni mixture into a flameproof dish and scatter cauliflower and bread crumb mixture over it. Sprinkle with remaining cheese, then broil for 5 minutes till golden.

Lasagne alla bolognese

Overall timing 2 hours

Freezing Suitable: reheat in 350° oven for 1 hour.

To serve 6

1	Onion
1	Carrot
1	Stalk of celery
¼ lb	Slab bacon
¼ lb	Chuck steak
¼ lb	Fresh pork sides
6 tbsp	Butter
1 tbsp	Tomato paste
½ cup	Hot broth
3 tbsp	Dry white wine
½ cup	Milk
1 lb	Fresh bulk spinach
	Salt and pepper
¾ lb	Green lasagne
2½ cups	White sauce
¾ cup	Grated Parmesan cheese

Peel and chop onion and carrot. Chop celery. Chop bacon. Grind meats. Melt 2 tbsp of butter in a saucepan, add bacon and meats and brown. Add vegetables, tomato paste, broth, wine and milk. Simmer gently for 45 minutes, stirring occasionally.

Meanwhile, wash spinach and remove coarse stalks. Place in a saucepan with 2 tbsp of the butter and seasoning. Cook gently for 5-10 minutes. Chop finely and add to meat mixture.

Preheat oven to 375°.
Cook lasagne in boiling, salted water till tender. Drain on damp dish-towel.

Cover bottom of greased ovenproof dish with a quarter of the lasagne. Spread half the meat mixture on top, then another quarter of the lasagne, half the white sauce and Parmesan. Repeat layers, finishing with white sauce and Parmesan. Dot with remaining butter. Bake for 20 minutes.

Spaghetti alla carbonara

Overall timing 20 minutes

Freezing Not suitable

To serve 4

¾ lb	Spaghetti
	Salt and pepper
2	Eggs
2 tbsp	Half-and-half
¼ lb	Bacon slices
1 tbsp	Oil
½ cup	Grated Parmesan cheese

Cook the spaghetti in boiling water till tender.

Meanwhile, beat eggs, half-and-half and pepper in a bowl. Dice the bacon. Heat the oil in a large skillet, add the bacon and fry till crisp.

Drain the spaghetti and add to the bacon. Pour in the egg mixture, stirring, and toss over a gentle heat till the eggs just begin to set. Serve immediately, sprinkled with grated Parmesan.

Spaghetti with chicken sauce

Overall timing 1 hour

Freezing Suitable: cook spaghetti and almonds after reheating sauce

To serve 4

2	Thick bacon slices
¾ lb	Boneless chicken breasts
¼ cup	Butter
1 lb	Ripe tomatoes
1	Garlic clove
2 tbsp	Tomato paste
½ tsp	Sugar
	Salt and pepper
½ cup	Dry white wine
¾ lb	Spaghetti
¼ cup	Chopped almonds

Dice the bacon. Wipe and trim the chicken, discarding skin. Cut the meat into strips. Heat half the butter in a flameproof casserole, add the bacon and chicken and fry for 5 minutes till browned all over.

Blanch, peel and chop the tomatoes. Add to the pan with the peeled and crushed garlic, tomato paste, sugar and salt and pepper. Add the wine and bring to a boil, stirring. Reduce the heat, cover the pan tightly and simmer for 20 minutes.

Meanwhile, cook the spaghetti in boiling salted water till just tender. Drain in a colander.

Melt remaining butter in the saucepan, add the almonds and fry over a high heat till golden. Return the spaghetti to the pan with half the tomato chicken sauce, toss lightly and adjust seasoning to taste. Place in a warmed serving dish.

Season remaining sauce, pour into a warmed sauceboat and serve separately.

Turkey noodle bake

Overall timing 1 ½ hours

Freezing Not suitable

To serve 4

¼ lb	Button mushrooms
½ lb	Noodles
	Salt and pepper
3 tbsp	Flour
1	Chicken bouillon cube
¼ tsp	Paprika
5 tbsp	Light cream
1 cup	Diced cooked turkey meat
½ cup	Grated Cheddar cheese
½ cup	Soft bread crumbs
1 tbsp	Butter

Wipe and slice the mushrooms. Cook the noodles in boiling salted water for about 5 minutes, till tender. Drain the noodles thoroughly, reserving 2½ cups of the cooking water.

Blend the flour in a small bowl with a little of the measured cooking water. Put rest of the measured cooking water into a saucepan, stir in blended flour, crumbled bouillon cube, salt, pepper and paprika. Bring to a boil, stirring. Reduce the heat and add the mushrooms. Simmer for 10 minutes.

Preheat the oven to 350°. Grease an 8 inch soufflé dish.

Remove pan from heat and stir in cream.

Spread half the drained noodles over the bottom of the souffle dish. Arrange half the turkey over the noodles. Cover with half the sauce. Repeat the layers, finishing with sauce. Scatter cheese over top. Sprinkle with bread crumbs and dot with butter. Bake for 30 minutes.

Noodles with tomato sauce

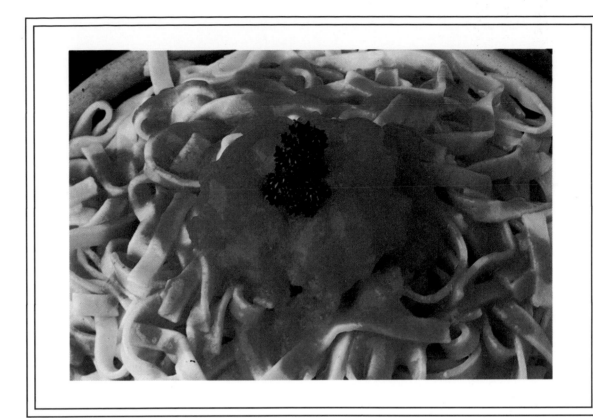

Overall timing 30 minutes

Freezing Not suitable

To serve 4

1½ lb	Tomatoes
1	Onion
¼ cup	Butter
	Salt and pepper
	Pinch of sugar
¼ tsp	Grated nutmeg
¾ lb	Noodles
¼ cup	Grated Parmesan cheese
	Parsley

Blanch, peel and chop tomatoes. Peel and chop the onion. Heat half the butter in a saucepan. Add onion and fry till transparent. Add the tomatoes, cover and simmer for 10 minutes. Add salt, pepper, sugar and nutmeg and simmer for a further 5 minutes.

Meanwhile, cook the noodles in boiling salted water for about 10 minutes till tender. Drain the noodles thoroughly and pile into a warmed serving dish. Stir in the remaining butter and the grated cheese and keep hot.

Put the tomato sauce through a blender or food processor and pour over the noodles. Garnish with parsley and serve immediately with a green salad.

Variation

Add 1 chopped carrot and 1 chopped stalk of celery to the onion. Fry till the onion is transparent, then add ½ cup diced cooked ham to the pan. Complete the recipe as above.

Macaroni casserole

Overall timing 2 hours

Freezing Suitable

To serve 4-6

1	Small onion
½ cup	Butter
½ lb	Ground beef
1 cup	Canned tomatoes
2	Bay leaves
	Salt and pepper
¾ lb	Macaroni
¼ cup	Grated Parmesan cheese
1 tbsp	Flour
1 cup	Milk
1	Egg

Peel and chop the onion. Heat ¼ cup of the butter in a saucepan and fry the onion until softened. Add the beef and fry until browned and crumbly, then stir in the undrained tomatoes, bay leaves and seasoning. Cover and cook gently for 30 minutes.

Preheat the oven to 400°.

Cook the macaroni in boiling salted water until tender. Drain well. Add to the beef sauce with half the Parmesan and pour into a baking dish. Set aside.

Melt 2 tbsp of the remaining butter in another pan and stir in the flour. Cook for 1 minute, then gradually stir in the milk. Bring to a boil, stirring, and simmer until thickened. Remove from the heat and beat in the egg, remaining Parmesan and seasoning. Pour over the macaroni mixture. Dot with the remaining butter and bake for 30 minutes or until golden brown. Serve hot.

Macaroni bake

Overall timing 1¾ hours

Freezing Not suitable

To serve 6

¼ lb	Chicken livers
¼ cup	Butter
1 cup	Diced cooked chicken meat
¼ cup	Diced smoked ham
½ cup	White sauce
1	Egg
	Salt and pepper
1 lb	Ripe tomatoes
1	Onion
2	Garlic cloves
1 tsp	Sugar
1 tbsp	Chopped fresh basil
¾ lb	Long macaroni
½ cup	Grated Parmesan cheese

Wash and chop livers. Heat 2 tbsp butter in a skillet and fry livers for 5 minutes, turning frequently. Place chicken and ham in a blender or food processor and add livers and their cooking juices, sauce, egg and seasoning. Process till smooth. Chill.

Blanch, peel and chop tomatoes. Peel and chop onion. Heat remaining butter in a saucepan and fry onion with peeled and crushed garlic for 5 minutes. Add tomatoes, sugar, basil and seasoning and bring to a boil. Cover and simmer gently for 15 minutes.

Meanwhile, break macaroni into 4 inch lengths and cook in boiling salted water for 5 minutes. Drain. Fill with liver stuffing, using a pastry bag.

Preheat oven to 350°. Process tomato sauce in blender or food processor. Spread one-third over bottom of ovenproof dish, then layer macaroni and remaining sauce on top.

Sprinkle Parmesan over and bake for 20 minutes till golden.

Corsican spaghetti

Overall timing 1 hour

Freezing Suitable (sauce only): add olives after reheating

To serve 2

1	Onion
¼ cup	Butter
½ lb	Ripe tomatoes
1	Garlic clove
½ lb	Ground beef
	Small dried chili pepper
	Salt and pepper
½ lb	Spaghetti
6	Pitted green olives
¼ cup	Grated cheese

Peel and finely chop onion. Melt half the butter in a saucepan and fry the onion till lightly browned.

Blanch, peel and chop the tomatoes. Peel and crush the garlic and add to onions with the beef, tomatoes, the chili pepper and salt. Simmer for 45 minutes.

Cook the spaghetti in boiling salted water till tender. Drain thoroughly in a colander, then add remaining butter and toss well.

Remove chili from sauce. Slice the green olives and add to the sauce. Taste and adjust seasoning.

Pile spaghetti in a warmed serving dish and pour meat sauce over. Serve the grated cheese separately.

Cheesy macaroni

Overall timing 30 minutes

Freezing Not suitable

To serve 4

½ lb	Long macaroni
	Salt and pepper
2	Eggs
¼ lb	Cooked ham
1½ cups	Grated Cheddar cheese
6 tbsp	Butter
	Cayenne

Preheat the oven to 425°. Grease an 8 inch soufflé dish.

Place macaroni in saucepan of boiling salted water and cook till tender.

Meanwhile, lightly beat the eggs. Coarsely chop the ham. Drain macaroni and place in soufflé dish. Add ¼ cup of the butter, 1¼ cups of the cheese, the eggs and ham to the dish. Add a pinch of cayenne and season to taste. Mix well. Sprinkle with remaining cheese and dot with the rest of the butter.

Bake for 10 minutes or till golden and lightly set. Serve immediately with a tomato salad.

Cheesy noodles with ham

Overall timing 1 hour

Freezing Not suitable

To serve 4

½ lb	Tagliatelle
	Salt and pepper
1 cup	Grated cheese
3	Eggs
2 cups	White sauce
¼ lb	Sliced cooked ham

Preheat the oven to 400°.

Cook the noodles in boiling salted water for about 10 minutes till tender.

Separate eggs. Stir yolks, ¾ cup of the cheese and seasoning into sauce.

Cut ham into strips and stir into the sauce. Drain noodles thoroughly and fold into sauce. Season to taste. Beat the egg whites in a bowl till stiff but not dry and fold into the mixture with metal spoon.

Pour the mixture into a greased ovenproof dish. Sprinkle remaining grated cheese over and bake for about 30 minutes till set and golden. Serve immediately with whole green beans mixed with flaked almonds and butter.

Veal ravioli

Overall timing 1 hour 35 minutes

Freezing Suitable: cook after thawing

To serve 2

2 cups	Flour
	Salt and pepper
2	Eggs
½ lb	Bulk spinach
6 oz	Boneless veal
1 oz	Lean cooked ham
2 tbsp	Butter
2 tbsp	Soft bread crumbs
1 tbsp	Milk
1	Egg
½ cup	Grated Parmesan cheese
¼ tsp	Dried marjoram
	Pinch of grated nutmeg
¾ cup	Tomato sauce

Sift flour and ½ tsp salt into a bowl. Add eggs and mix to a smooth glossy dough. Add a little water if necessary.

Wash spinach. Cook, covered, for 5 minutes. Drain.

Chop the veal and ham. Melt butter in skillet and fry veal and ham till brown. Drain and cool. Soak bread crumbs in milk.

Put meats and spinach through a grinder or food processor, then mix to a paste. Add egg, soaked bread crumbs, 2 tbsp of the Parmesan, the marjoram, nutmeg and seasoning. Mix together well.

Roll out half dough to large rectangle. Arrange spoonfuls of filling at intervals. Brush between them with water. Roll out remaining dough, place on top sealing well between filling. Cut into ravioli. Cook ravioli in boiling, salted water for about 10 minutes. Drain, place in warmed serving dishes and cover with hot tomato sauce. Sprinkle with remaining Parmesan. Serve with a crisp green salad.

Spaghetti omelette

Overall timing 30 minutes

Freezing Not suitable

To serve 4-6

¾ lb	Spaghetti
	Salt and pepper
1	Garlic clove
¼ cup	Grated Parmesan cheese
¼ cup	Grated Cheddar cheese
4	Eggs
1 tbsp	Chopped parsley
6	Basil leaves
¼ cup	Butter

Cook the spaghetti in boiling salted water till tender.

Meanwhile peel and crush the garlic. Mix together the garlic, cheeses, eggs, parsley, chopped basil and seasoning.

Drain the spaghetti and put into a large bowl. Pour the egg and cheese mixture over and mix well. Melt 2 tbsp butter in skillet. Add spaghetti mixture and press down well with the back of a spoon to form a cake. Fry over a low heat for about 5 minutes, pressing down to keep the cake flat.

Run a knife around the edge of the omelette to loosen it, then turn it out onto a board. Add remaining butter to the pan and, when melted, slide the omelette back into the pan. Fry for 3-5 minutes till firmly set. Place on a warmed serving dish and serve immediately, cut into wedges.

Lasagne col pesto

Overall timing 1 hour

Freezing Suitable: reheat, covered with foil in 350° oven for 1 hour

To serve 4

¾ lb	Lasagne
	Salt
¼ cup	Grated Parmesan cheese
¼ cup	Butter
Pesto	
2	Garlic cloves
¼ cup	Chopped fresh basil
¼ cup	Olive oil
¼ cup	Grated Parmesan cheese
	Pinch of salt

Cook the lasagne in boiling salted water for 15-20 minutes till tender. Drain thoroughly and spread out on a damp cloth to cool.

Preheat oven to 350°.

To make the pesto, peel and chop garlic and put in mortar with basil. Pound with pestle, gradually adding oil, Parmesan and salt.

Spread one-third of the lasagne over the bottom of a greased ovenproof dish. Spread with one-third of the pesto and sprinkle over 1 tbsp Parmesan. Repeat layers twice, adding extra Parmesan to the top. Dot with butter, cover, and bake for 20 minutes till heated through.

Spaghetti with eggplant

Overall timing 45 minutes plus draining

Freezing Not suitable

To serve 4

1	Large eggplant
	Salt and pepper
1 lb	Ripe tomatoes
1	Garlic clove
	Oil
2 tsp	Chopped fresh basil
¾ lb	Spaghetti
½ cup	Grated Parmesan cheese
	Sprig of basil

Wash and thinly slice the eggplant. Put into a colander and sprinkle with salt. Leave to drain for 1 hour.

Blanch, peel and chop the tomatoes. Peel and crush garlic. Heat 3 tbsp oil in a saucepan, add garlic and fry for 1 minute. Add tomatoes, basil and seasoning, stir well and cook over a low heat for 15 minutes.

Cook spaghetti in boiling salted water till tender.

Meanwhile, rinse eggplant slices under running water and gently squeeze dry. Heat ½ inch oil in a skillet and fry eggplant slices, a few at a time, till crisp on both sides. Drain on paper towels and keep hot.

Drain spaghetti thoroughly. Put into a warmed serving dish and pour tomato sauce over. Add eggplant slices, sprinkle with cheese, garnish with sprig of basil and serve.

Macaroni niçoise

Overall timing 30 minutes

Freezing Not suitable

To serve 4

3	Anchovy fillets
¾ lb	Tomatoes
1	Garlic clove
¾ lb	Rigatoni pasta
	Salt
¼ cup	Butter
½ cup	Grated Parmesan cheese
1 tbsp	Chopped fresh basil

Chop the anchovies. Blanch, peel and cut tomatoes into thin slices. Place in a serving bowl with the anchovies and peeled and crushed garlic.

Cook the rigatoni in a large saucepan of boiling salted water till just tender. When cooked, drain in colander.

Melt butter in the saucepan and when frothy, add rigatoni and toss well. Add to the tomatoes and garlic, toss, then sprinkle with Parmesan and basil and serve immediately.

Spaghetti with bacon sauce

Overall timing 45 minutes

Freezing Not suitable

To serve 4

¾ lb	Slab bacon
1	Small sweet red pepper
16 oz	Can of tomatoes
	Salt and pepper
¾ lb	Spaghetti
6 tbsp	Grated Parmesan cheese

Cut the bacon into ¼ inch thick slices, then cut across into strips. Heat a saucepan, add the bacon and fry till golden all over.

Seed and finely chop the pepper. Add to the pan and fry for 1 minute. Press the tomatoes and juice through a sieve into the pan and bring to a boil, stirring. Add seasoning, cover and simmer for 15 minutes.

Meanwhile, cook the spaghetti in boiling salted water till tender. Drain thoroughly and return to the pan. Add the sauce and all but 1 tbsp of the cheese. Toss lightly over a low heat for 2 minutes. Adjust the seasoning to taste.

Place spaghetti in a warmed serving dish and sprinkle with the remaining cheese. Serve immediately with fresh crusty bread.

Boer-style noodle supper

Overall timing 20 minutes

Freezing Not suitable

To serve 2

2½ cups	Milk
	Blade of mace
6 oz	Noodles
2 tbsp	Butter
2	Eggs
¼ tsp	Ground cinnamon
	Salt and pepper

Put the milk in a saucepan with the mace and bring to a boil. Add the noodles and cook for about 5 minutes till tender. Drain, reserving the milk. Divide the noodles between individual soup bowls and add half the butter to each. Keep hot.

Separate the eggs. Beat the egg yolks in a bowl with the cinnamon and seasoning. Gradually strain the reserved milk onto the yolks, stirring constantly. Return to the pan.

Beat the egg whites till stiff and fold into the yolk mixture. Cook over a low heat for 2-5 minutes without stirring till mixture begins to thicken. Do not allow to boil.

Pour egg mixture over the noodles and serve immediately with bread and a mixed salad.

Spaghetti with piquant sauce

Overall timing 50 minutes

Freezing Not suitable

To serve 4

1	Can of anchovy fillets
¼ cup	Milk
1 lb	Ripe tomatoes
1	Garlic clove
1	Dried red chili pepper
6 tbsp	Olive oil
1 tbsp	Tomato paste
2 tbsp	Capers
¾ lb	Spaghetti
	Salt and pepper
1 cup	Pitted ripe olives

Drain the anchovies and put into a small bowl with the milk. Soak for 10 minutes. Blanch, peel and chop tomatoes. Peel and crush the garlic; seed and finely chop the chili.

Heat the oil in a saucepan, add the garlic and cook for 2 minutes. Drain the anchovies, discarding the milk. Chop and add to the pan with the chili. Fry for 3 minutes, pressing the anchovies with the back of a wooden spoon to break them up.

Add the tomatoes, tomato paste and capers. Bring to a boil, then cover and simmer for 15 minutes.

Meanwhile, cook the spaghetti in boiling salted water till tender. Drain thoroughly. Return to the pan and add the tomato and anchovy sauce and the olives. Stir over a low heat for 3 minutes. Adjust seasoning to taste and serve hot.

Mushroom ravioli

Overall timing 45 minutes

Freezing Suitable: Cook from frozen

To serve 4

3 cups	Flour
	Salt and pepper
3	Eggs
1 lb	Mushrooms
1	Onion
¼ cup	Butter

Sift flour and 1 tsp salt into a bowl. Add eggs and mix to a smooth, glossy dough. Add a little water if necessary.

Chop the mushrooms. Peel and finely chop onion. Melt half the butter in a skillet and fry the onion for 5 minutes till transparent. Add mushrooms and seasoning and stir-fry over a high heat for about 5 minutes to evaporate any liquid. Reduce heat and cook gently for a further 5 minutes. Remove from heat and leave to cool.

Roll out the dough on a lightly floured surface and cut into 3 inch squares with a pastry wheel. Divide the mushroom mixture between the squares, then fold them over, pressing the edges together well to seal.

Put plenty of lightly salted water in a large saucepan and bring to a boil. Add the ravioli and cook for 10-15 minutes, then drain and place in a warmed serving dish. Melt the remaining butter, pour over the ravioli and toss well.

Neapolitan cannelloni

Overall timing 1 ½ hours

Freezing Suitable: reheat from frozen in 350° oven for 1 hour

To serve 4

12	Sheets of lasagne
½ lb	Mozzarella cheese
2 oz	Cooked ham
½ lb	Cream cheese
2	Eggs
	Salt and pepper
6 tbsp	Grated Parmesan cheese
Tomato sauce	
1	Onion
1	Garlic clove
1 tbsp	Oil
16 oz	Can of tomatoes
1 tbsp	Chopped fresh basil

Cook lasagne in boiling salted water for 10-15 minutes till tender. Drain and spread on a damp cloth to cool.

Thinly slice the Mozzarella. Dice ham. Place in a bowl with the cream cheese, eggs and seasoning. Mix well.

For the sauce, peel and finely chop onion. Peel and crush garlic and fry until golden. Add tomatoes in their juice, basil, salt and pepper. Cook for 10 minutes, stirring occasionally.

Preheat oven to 425°.

Divide cheese mixture between lasagne sheets. Roll lasagne around filling and arrange, joins down, in greased ovenproof dish. Pour the tomato sauce over. Sprinkle half the Parmesan on top and bake for 15 minutes or until golden. Sprinkle with the rest of the Parmesan and serve immediately.

Spaghetti with sardine dressing

Overall timing 20 minutes

Freezing Not suitable

To serve 4

¾ lb	Spaghetti
	Salt and pepper
11½ oz	Can of sardines
2	Garlic cloves
6 tbsp	Butter

Cook the spaghetti in boiling salted water till tender.

Drain the sardines and put into a mortar. Peel and crush garlic and add to sardines. Pound to a paste with a pestle. Add the butter and mix well. Season to taste.

Drain the spaghetti and return to the pan. Add the sardine paste and toss lightly over a low heat till the spaghetti is coated. Place in a warmed serving dish and serve immediately with wedges of lemon.

Spaghetti with tomato sauce

Overall timing 30 minutes

Freezing Not suitable

To serve 4

1	Onion
2 lb	Cherry or plum tomatoes
	Bouquet garni
	Pinch of sugar
	Cayenne or hot pepper sauce
	Salt and pepper
1 tbsp	Chopped fresh basil or parsley
¾ lb	Spaghetti

Peel and chop the onion. Halve the tomatoes. Put the onion and tomatoes in a saucepan with the bouquet garni and simmer gently until mushy.

Discard the bouquet garni, then rub the tomato sauce through a sieve, or purée in a blender. Return to the pan and add the sugar, a little cayenne or pepper sauce and seasoning. Stir in the herbs and reheat gently.

Meanwhile, cook the spaghetti in boiling salted water till just tender. Drain well and turn into a warmed serving dish. Pile the tomato sauce on top and serve.

Neapolitan rigatoni

Overall timing 50 minutes

Freezing Not suitable

To serve 2

2	Bacon slices
1	Onion
1	Garlic clove
2 tbsp	Lard
6 oz	Ground beef
5 tbsp	Beef broth
5 tbsp	Red wine
1 tbsp	Tomato paste
1 tsp	Chopped fresh basil
	Salt and pepper
½ lb	Rigatoni

Finely chop bacon. Peel and chop onion. Peel and crush garlic. Melt the lard in a saucepan, add bacon, onion and garlic and fry for 10 minutes till golden.

Add the ground beef and fry, stirring, till brown. Gradually stir in the broth, wine, tomato paste, basil and seasoning. Cover and simmer for 30 minutes.

Meanwhile, cook rigatoni in boiling salted water till tender. Drain thoroughly and pile in warmed serving dish. Keep hot.

Taste the sauce and adjust seasoning. Purée in a blender then reheat and spoon over rigatoni. Serve immediately with a mixed salad and grated Parmesan cheese.

Macaroni with mushrooms

Overall timing 30 minutes

Freezing Not suitable

To serve 4

¼ lb	Button mushrooms
½ cup	Butter
1 cup	Light cream
¾ lb	Short-cut macaroni
	Salt and pepper
¼ lb	Cooked ham
½ cup	Grated Parmesan cheese
1 cup	White sauce

Finely chop the mushrooms. Place in a small saucepan with ¼ cup of the butter and cook gently for 5 minutes. Remove from heat and stir in cream.

Cook macaroni in boiling salted water till tender. Drain. Cut the ham into pieces and add to the macaroni with ¼ cup of cheese, 2 tbsp of butter and seasoning. Place macaroni in a flameproof dish with mushroom mixture and stir well. Cook gently for 10 minutes.

Preheat broiler.

Pour hot white sauce over macaroni, sprinkle with remaining cheese and dot with remaining butter. Broil for 5 minutes.

Noodle tortilla

Overall timing 45 minutes

Freezing Not suitable

To serve 4

¾ lb	Noodles
	Salt
6 tbsp	Butter
½ cup	Cottage cheese
3	Eggs
¼ tsp	Ground allspice
2 tbsp	Chopped parsley

Cook the noodles in boiling salted water for about 5 minutes till tender. Drain thoroughly and put into a warm bowl. Stir in ¼ cup of the butter and the sieved cottage cheese. Lightly beat the eggs and stir into the noodles with salt, allspice and chopped parsley.

Preheat the broiler. Melt the remaining butter in a skillet. Add the noodle mixture and smooth the top. Cook over a moderate heat for 5 minutes till lightly set. Put the pan under the broiler to brown the top.

Unmold tortilla onto a warmed serving plate and serve immediately.

Pasta with lamb and tomato sauce

Overall timing 1¼ hours

Freezing Not suitable

To serve 2

2	Bacon slices
½ lb	Tomatoes
1	Onion
1	Garlic clove
6 oz	Ground lamb
½ cup	Red wine
	Salt and pepper
½ lb	Pasta shapes

Chop bacon. Blanch, peel and chop tomatoes. Peel and chop onion and garlic. Heat a saucepan, add the bacon and fry for 5 minutes. Add onion and garlic and fry gently till transparent. Add the ground lamb and fry for about 15 minutes till browned.

Stir in the red wine, tomatoes and seasoning. Cover and simmer for 40 minutes.

Meanwhile, cook pasta in boiling salted water till tender. Drain and place in a warmed serving dish.

Spoon meat sauce over pasta and serve hot with a green salad.

Spaghetti with tuna

Overall timing 30 minutes

Freezing Not suitable

To serve 4

1	Onion
2	Garlic cloves
7 oz	Can of tuna
1 tbsp	Olive oil
¾ lb	Spaghetti
	Salt and pepper
4	Anchovy fillets
2 tbsp	Tomato paste
½ tsp	Sugar
6 tbsp	Water
1 tbsp	Chopped parsley
2 tsp	Chopped fresh basil

Peel and finely chop the onion; peel and crush the garlic. Drain the oil from the tuna into a saucepan. Add the olive oil and heat. Add the onion and garlic and fry till just golden.

Put the spaghetti into a saucepan of boiling salted water and cook gently till just tender.

Meanwhile, chop the anchovies and add to the onion with the tomato paste, sugar and water. Bring to a boil.

Flake the tuna fish and add to the pan with seasoning. Cover and simmer for 5 minutes.

Drain the spaghetti and add to the pan with herbs. Toss lightly over a low heat for 2-3 minutes. Adjust seasoning to taste and serve immediately.

Striped vermicelli

Overall timing 45 minutes

Freezing Not suitable

To serve 4

1	Can of anchovies
6 tbsp	Milk
1	Large onion
1	Garlic clove
2 tbsp	Oil
16 oz	Can of tomatoes
	Salt and pepper
	Chili powder
1 tbsp	Chopped parsley
¾ lb	Vermicelli
½ cup	Heavy cream

Drain the anchovies and soak in the milk for 10 minutes.

Meanwhile, peel and finely chop the onion; peel and crush the garlic. Heat the oil in a small saucepan, add onion and garlic and fry till transparent. Add tomatoes and juice, salt, a pinch of chili powder and parsley. Simmer for 20 minutes, stirring frequently.

Drain the anchovies and add to the tomato mixture. Purée in a blender or food processor. Season and reheat gently.

Cook the vermicelli in boiling salted water for 3 minutes till tender. Drain thoroughly and arrange on a warmed flat serving dish. Smooth the top and keep hot.

Warm the cream, then spread it in a wide band across the center of the vermicelli. Spread the tomato sauce in a wide band on either side of the cream. Serve with hot garlic bread.

Tagliatelli with ham

Overall timing 25 minutes

Freezing Not suitable

To serve 4

¾ lb	Tagliatelli
	Salt and pepper
1	Large onion
¼ cup	Butter
2 tbsp	Oil
1	Garlic clove
¼ lb	Lean cooked ham
2 tsp	Dried marjoram
16 oz	Can of tomatoes
6 tbsp	Grated Parmesan cheese

Cook the tagliatelli in boiling salted water till tender.

Meanwhile, peel and finely chop the onion. Heat the butter and oil in a large saucepan and fry the onion till transparent. Peel and crush the garlic and add to the pan. Chop the ham very finely and add to the pan with the marjoram and tomatoes in their juice. Season and cook for 10 minutes, stirring to break up the tomatoes.

Drain the tagliatelli and place in a warmed bowl. Add the sauce and Parmesan and toss well, adding seasoning to taste. Serve immediately with a watercress, cucumber and lettuce salad.

Crusty noodle shapes

Overall timing 55 minutes

Freezing Not suitable

To serve 4

¾ lb	Egg noodles
	Salt
¼ cup	Grated cheese
2 cups	White sauce
¼ tsp	Grated nutmeg
2	Eggs
⅓ cup	Dried bread crumbs
6 tbsp	Oil
¼ lb	Sliced cooked ham
¼ lb	Mozzarella cheese
	Sprigs of parsley
	Lemon

Cook the noodles in boiling salted water for about 5 minutes till tender. Drain the noodles thoroughly and put into a bowl.

Mix the cheese into the white sauce with nutmeg. Pour the sauce over the noodles and mix well. Press into a roasting pan to 1 inch thickness and leave to cool.

Preheat the oven to 450°.

Beat the eggs in a bowl with salt. Spread the bread crumbs on a sheet of wax paper.

Cut the noodle mixture into diamond shapes or rounds with a cookie cutter. Dip the shapes into the egg, then the bread crumbs, pressing the crumbs onto the shapes to make them stick. Heat the oil in a skillet and fry the shapes until golden on both sides. Drain on paper towels. Using a sharp knife, slice each one through the center.

Halve each slice of ham and put a piece on the bottom half of each shape; top with a thin slice of Mozzarella. Replace the top half of each shape and arrange on a baking sheet. Bake for about 10 minutes. Serve hot, garnished with parsley sprigs and lemon.

Ratatouille

Overall timing 1 1/2 hours

Freezing Suitable

To serve 8

2	Large eggplants
1 lb	Zucchini
	Salt and pepper
3	Large onions
2-3	Garlic cloves
2	Green peppers
1 lb	Ripe tomatoes
5 tbsp	Olive oil
1 tsp	Sugar

Cut the eggplants into 1 inch chunks. Cut zucchini into quarters lengthwise, then into 1 inch lengths. Put the vegetables into a colander, sprinkle with salt and leave to drain for 30 minutes.

Meanwhile, peel and slice the onions. Peel and crush the garlic. Seed and thinly slice the peppers. Blanch, peel and halve the tomatoes.

Heat the oil in a flameproof casserole, add the onions and garlic and fry gently till transparent. Dry the eggplants and zucchini on paper towels and add to the pan with the peppers, tomatoes, sugar and plenty of pepper. Cook for about 45 minutes till the vegetables are tender but not mushy. Adjust the seasoning and serve hot, or cool and chill before serving.

Tomato, eggplant and cheese casserole

Overall timing 1 ½ hours

Freezing Suitable

To serve 4-6

1	Small onion
1	Garlic clove
	Oil
1 ½ lb	Ripe tomatoes
1 tbsp	Dried basil
	Salt and pepper
4	Eggplants
¼ cup	Grated Parmesan cheese
6 oz	Mozzarella cheese
2 tbsp	Dried bread crumbs

Peel and finely chop onion and garlic. Heat 2 tbsp oil in a saucepan and fry onion and garlic till soft. Peel, seed and chop tomatoes. Add to pan with ½ tsp basil and salt and pepper to taste. Cover and cook for 30-35 minutes, stirring occasionally.

Meanwhile, peel and thinly slice eggplants. Sprinkle with salt and drain for 20 minutes. Rinse and pat dry. Brown in hot oil, a few slices at a time. Drain well.

Preheat oven to 400°.

Make a layer of half the eggplant slices in a greased ovenproof dish. Sprinkle with half the Parmesan and half the remaining basil. Slice the Mozzarella cheese and arrange half the slices on the Parmesan. Cover with half the tomato sauce. Repeat these layers, then sprinkle top with bread crumbs.

Bake for 30 minutes. Serve hot or cold.

Red cabbage with smoked sausage

Overall timing 3½-4½ hours

Freezing Not suitable

To serve 8

3 lb	Head of red cabbage
1 lb	Cooking apples
¾ lb	Onions
3	Garlic cloves
1	Bouquet garni
½ cup	Water
½ cup	Red wine vinegar
⅓ cup	Brown sugar
3	Strips of orange peel
½ tsp	Grated nutmeg
½ tsp	Ground cinnamon
	Salt and pepper
1 lb	Smoked ham
2½ lb	Smoked sausage or smoked meat or poultry

Preheat oven to 300°.

Slice cabbage finely, discarding core. Peel and slice apples and onions. Peel and chop garlic. Put cabbage, apples, onions and garlic into an ovenproof dish with bouquet garni, water, vinegar, sugar, orange peel, spices, salt and pepper. Mix well.

Cut ham into thick fingers and bury in cabbage mixture. Cover tightly and bake for 3-4 hours.

About 20 minutes before cabbage is ready, add sausage. It may be whole or cut into short lengths, as liked.

Discard bouquet garni and orange peel. Check seasoning. Serve with plain boiled potatoes.

Spinach roll

Overall timing 2 hours

Freezing Not suitable

To serve 4-6

3 cups	Flour
	Salt
2	Eggs
Filling	
1 lb	Fresh bulk spinach
¾ cup	Cottage cheese
1½ cups	Grated Parmesan cheese
2	Eggs
	Grated nutmeg

Sift the flour and 1 tsp of salt into a bowl. Make a well in the center and add the ggs. Mix together, adding enough lukewarm water to make a soft dough. Chill for 30 minutes.

Meanwhile, rinse the spinach and cook in the water that clings to the leaves until tender. Drain well, then sieve or purée in a blender or food processor with the cottage cheese. Beat in the Parmesan cheese, eggs, and salt and nutmeg to taste.

Roll out the dough to a thin rectangle and spread over the spinach mixture, leaving a border clear all the way round. Roll up like a jelly roll. Roll up in a clean dish towel and tie the ends with string.

Cook in simmering salted water for about 1 hour. Unwrap and place on a warm serving dish. Slice and serve with hot tomato sauce

Mexican-style corn

Overall timing 20 minutes

Freezing Not suitable

To serve 4-6

1 lb	Frozen whole kernel corn
4	Tomatoes
1	Sweet green pepper
1	Sweet red pepper
1	Hot chili pepper
3 tbsp	Oil
	Salt
	Cayenne pepper

Thaw and drain corn. Blanch, peel and finely chop tomatoes. Wash, seed and finely chop sweet and hot peppers.

Heat oil in a skillet. Cook tomatoes and peppers for 10 minutes. Season with salt and cayenne pepper, then add corn. Heat through, shaking the pan to prevent sticking. Serve hot.

Chickpea and spinach casserole

Overall timing 1 hour

Freezing Not suitable

To serve 3-4

1	Thick slice of bread
6 tbsp	Olive oil
1	Onion
3-4	Tomatoes
1 lb	Fresh bulk spinach
1 tbsp	Paprika
	Salt and pepper
3 cups	Cooked or canned chickpeas (garbanzo beans) with liquid
1	Garlic clove

Cut crusts from bread and fry till golden in 2 tbsp oil. Drain and set aside.

Peel and slice onion and tomatoes. Heat another 2 tbsp oil in skillet and fry onion until soft. Add tomatoes and cook for about 3 minutes. Drain and set aside.

Wash spinach, shake dry and chop coarsely. Heat remaining oil in skillet, add paprika and stir, then add spinach. Add salt to taste. Cook for 2-3 minutes.

Put spinach into a casserole and add onion, tomatoes and chickpeas with their liquid (from cooking or the cans). Mix well.

Peel garlic and pound in a mortar with a pestle. Add fried bread and pound to fine crumbs with garlic. Alternatively use a blender or food processor.

Add garlic mixture to casserole and stir well. Cover and simmer for 30 minutes. Taste for seasoning and serve hot.

Chickpea balls

Overall timing 20 minutes plus standing

Freezing Not suitable

Makes 20

2 cups	Cooked chickpeas (garbanzo beans)
1	Medium-size onion
2 tbsp	Soft bread crumbs
2 tbsp	Chopped parsley
1 tbsp	Ground cumin
1 tsp	Ground coriander
	Salt
	Cayenne pepper
	Oil for deep frying

Process the chickpeas in a blender or food processor. Peel and chop onion and add to the chickpeas with the bread crumbs, 2 tbsp water, the parsley, spices, salt and cayenne pepper. Blend or process again briefly, then put into a bowl and leave to stand for 1 hour.

Taste the mixture and adjust the seasoning. Roll into 1 inch balls between floured hands. Heat oil in a deep-fryer to 360° and fry the balls, a few at a time, for about 3 minutes until golden. Drain thoroughly on paper towels, then spike with toothpicks and serve with fingers of toasted pita bread and wedges or thinly cut slices of lemon.

Alsace onion mold

Overall timing 1 ½ hours

Freezing Not suitable

To serve 6

1 ½ lb	Onions
6 tbsp	Butter
2 tbsp	Flour
½ cup	Light cream
2	Eggs
¼ tsp	Grated nutmeg
	Salt and peper

Preheat the oven to 425°. Grease a 5 inch mold or cake pan and put in the oven for 10 minutes to heat up.

Peel and thinly slice the onions. Melt the butter in a saucepan and add the onions. Cook till transparent.

Add the flour and cook, stirring for 2 minutes. Gradually add the cream and bring to a boil, stirring constantly. Cook for 2 minutes till thick. Remove from the heat and beat in the eggs and nutmeg. Season to taste. Pour into the hot mold or pan.

Bake for about 45 minutes till lightly set and golden. Run a knife around the edge of the mold and turn out onto a warmed serving dish. Serve immediately, cut into wedges. Provide a pepper mill, so everyone can add as they wish.

Eggplant cheese bake

Overall timing 2¼ hours

Freezing Suitable: bake from frozen in 350° oven for 45 minutes

To serve 4

1¼ lb	Eggplants
	Salt and pepper
2 tbsp	Flour
	Oil
1	Small onion
16 oz	Can of tomatoes
½ tsp	Dried basil
½ lb	Mozzarella cheese
¾ cup	Grated Parmesan cheese

Remove stalks from eggplant and cut lengthwise in ½ inch thick slices. Sprinkle with salt. Leave for 1 hour, then rinse and pat dry. Coat with flour.

Preheat the oven to 350°. Heat oil in a large skillet and fry eggplant slices on both sides till golden. Drain on paper towels and keep warm.

Peel and finely chop onion. Fry till transparent, adding more oil to pan if necessary. Mash tomatoes and juice and add to pan with seasoning. Cook for 10 minutes. Stir in basil and simmer for a further 5 minutes.

Place a layer of eggplant in oiled ovenproof dish. Cover with slices of Mozzarella and spoon on a little tomato sauce. Sprinkle with Parmesan and a pinch of salt. Repeat layering, ending with Parmesan. Sprinkle a little oil over surface and bake for 15 minutes or until top begins to brown.

Eggplant boxes

Overall timing 1 ½ hours

Freezing Not suitable

To serve 4

4 small	Eggplants
	Salt and pepper
3	Anchovy fillets
2 oz	Mozzarella cheese
1 tsp	Dried basil
2 tsp	Capers
1	Large onion
2	Garlic cloves
2 tbsp	Oil
16 oz	Can of tomatoes
1 tbsp	Worcestershire sauce
4-5	Fresh tomatoes
	(optional)

Cook eggplants in boiling salted water for 5 minutes. Drain and leave to cool, then cut off stalks and make a lengthwise cut through the eggplants leaving the halves still attached at one side. Ease open and remove most of the flesh with a teaspoon. Finely chop or mash the flesh and put into a bowl.

Drain and chop anchovies. Dice Mozzarella. Mix together eggplant flesh, anchovies, basil, Mozzarella, capers and seasoning. Stuff the hollowed-out eggplant shells with mixture.

Preheat the oven to 350°.

Peel and chop onion. Peel and crush garlic. Heat oil in flameproof casserole and fry onion till brown. Stir in garlic, tomatoes, Worcestershire sauce and seasoning. Simmer gently for about 10 minutes or until the sauce has become quite pulpy.

Arrange the stuffed eggplants on top of sauce and bake for 45 minutes. You can add 4-5 fresh tomatoes about 15 minutes before the end of the cooking time — they add attractive colour as well as taste.

Cabbage parcels

Overall timing 1 ¼ hours

Freezing Not suitable

To serve 4

1	Head white cabbage
½ cup	Long grain rice
1	Small onion
6 tbsp	Oil
½ lb	Ground beef
	Salt and pepper
¼ tsp	Grated nutmeg
1 tsp	Dried oregano
1 cup	Beef broth
2 tbsp	Butter
1 tbsp	Flour
1	Egg
2	Egg yolks
6 tbsp	Lemon juice
2 cups	White sauce

Remove core from cabbage and cook in boiling water for 5 minutes. Drain and cool, then peel away 16-20 leaves. Add rice to same pan of boiling water and cook till tender.
Drain.

Peel and chop onion. Heat ¼ cup oil in a skillet and cook onion till transparent. Add beef, salt, pepper, nutmeg and oregano. Cook for 5-8 minutes. Cool, then mix in rice.

Place a little stuffing on each cabbage leaf. Fold in sides and roll into tight parcels. Heat rest of oil in flameproof casserole. Pack cabbage rolls tightly in casserole and pour in broth. Cut leftover cabbage heart in two and place on top. Cover and simmer gently for 40 minutes.

Transfer cabbage rolls to warmed serving dish. Pour cooking liquid into a measuring cup and make up to 1 cup with water if necessary.

Melt butter in saucepan, then stir in flour and cooking liquid and simmer until thickened. Beat egg and egg yolks with lemon juice till foamy. Add to pan off heat. Return to a gentle heat. Don't allow sauce to boil. Stir in white sauce and heat. Pour sauce over rolls.

Braised lettuce

Overall timing 40 minutes

Freezing Not suitable

To serve 4

4	Small heads Boston lettuce
	Salt and pepper
2	Onions
2	Carrots
¼ lb	Bacon slices
2 tbsp	Butter
1 ¼ cups	Chicken broth

Trim lettuces. Blanch in boiling salted water for 2 minutes, then drain thoroughly.

Peel and slice onions and carrots. Cut bacon into crosswise strips. Melt butter in saucepan, add onions, carrots and bacon and fry gently for 10 minutes, stirring occasionally. Pour in broth and add blanched lettuces and seasoning.

Cover and simmer for 20 minutes.

Transfer bacon and vegetables to warmed serving dish and keep hot. Boil cooking liquid rapidly to reduce by half. Taste and adjust seasoning. Pour over lettuce and serve immediately with roast meats.

Casseroled lettuce rolls

Overall timing 1 hour

Freezing Not suitable

To serve 4

1	Onion
2 tbsp	Oil
½ lb	Chicken livers
¼ cup	Long grain rice
1¼ cups	Chicken broth
	Bouquet garni
	Salt and pepper
½ lb	Bacon slices
10	Large lettuce leaves
2	Onions
2	Carrots
½ cup	Broth
2 tbsp	Lemon juice

To make the stuffing, peel and chop onion. Heat oil in pan and fry onion till golden. Chop chicken livers. Add to pan and brown on all sides.

Add rice, broth, bouquet garni and seasoning. Bring to a boil. Cover and simmer for 15 minutes, shaking pan frequently.

Meanwhile, halve bacon slices, then use them to line bottom and sides of ovenproof dish. Wash and dry lettuce leaves. Peel and slice onions into rings. Peel and thinly slice carrots. Blanch onions and carrots in boiling salted water for 3 minutes. Blanch lettuce for 30 seconds. Drain thoroughly.

Preheat the oven to 350°.

Spread out lettuce leaves. Taste stuffing and adjust seasoning. Divide between lettuce leaves. Fold in sides of leaves, then roll up tightly around stuffing. Arrange, join side down, in ovenproof dish. Add blanched onions and carrots. Mix broth, lemon juice and seasoning. Pour over lettuce. Cover tightly and bake for 25-30 minutes.

Sausage meat tomatoes

Overall timing 45 minutes

Freezing Not suitable

To serve 4

8	Large tomatoes
1	Large onion
¼ cup	Oil
¾ lb	Bulk pork sausage meat
1 cup	Soft bread crumbs
1 tbsp	Chopped parsley
	Salt and pepper
1	Egg

Preheat the oven to 350°.

Cut lids off the tomatoes and scoop out the flesh. Discard the seeds and chop the flesh. Peel and chop onion. Heat half the oil in a skillet and fry onion till transparent. Add sausage meat and fry until browned.

Remove from heat and stir in tomato flesh, bread crumbs, parsley and seasoning. Bind with egg. Press mixture into tomato shells and replace lids.

Arrange tomatoes in ovenproof dish and brush with remaining oil. Bake for 30 minutes. Serve hot.

Lamb-stuffed onions

Overall timing 1 ¼ hours

Freezing Not suitable

To serve 6

6	Large onions
	Salt and pepper
2 tbsp	Oil
1 ½ tsp	Apple pie spice
1 lb	Ground lamb
½ cup	Soft bread crumbs
½ cup	Cottage cheese
2 tbsp	Butter
2 tbsp	Flour
3 tbsp	Tomato paste
1 ¼ cups	Light broth

Peel onions and cook in boiling salted water for 15 minutes. Drain and cool. Remove slice from bottom of each onion. Cut slice from top and scoop out centers, leaving a ½ inch shell. Put shells in flameproof casserole. Chop onion centers.

Heat oil and fry chopped onion with spice for 3 minutes. Add lamb and fry for 5 minutes. Stir in bread crumbs, cheese and seasoning. Press into onion shells.

Melt butter, add flour and stir in tomato paste, broth and seasoning. Bring to a boil and pour over onions. Cover and simmer for 45 minutes till onions are tender.

Tomatoes stuffed with vegetables

Overall timing 30 minutes

Freezing Not suitable

To serve 4

3	Large waxy potatoes
3	Large carrots
¼ lb	Green beans
2	Stalks of celery
	Salt and pepper
1 cup	Frozen peas
6 tbsp	Mayonnaise
	Lemon juice
4	Large tomatoes
	Basil leaves
	Hard-cooked eggs

Peel the potatoes. Scrape the carrots. Trim the beans. Wash and trim the celery. Dice all the vegetables. Cook in boiling salted water for 5 minutes. Add the peas and cook for a further 5 minutes or until tender. Drain well and cool.

Add the mayonnaise to the vegetables with a few drops of lemon juice and seasoning and mix well.

Halve the tomatoes and scoop out the seeds and centers. Fill with the vegetable mixture and arrange on a serving plate. Serve garnished with basil leaves and sliced hard-cooked egg.

Endive bake

Overall timing 45 minutes

Freezing Not suitable

To serve 2

2	Heads of Belgian endive
	Salt and pepper
½ tsp	Sugar
2 tbsp	Butter
½ tsp	Lemon juice
2	Slices of Gruyère cheese
2	Tomatoes
	Lettuce leaves

Place endive in saucepan of boiling water. Add pinch of salt, sugar, a pat of butter and lemon juice. Cook for 30 minutes.

Preheat the oven to 425°.

Drain endive. Wrap each head in slice of cheese. Place seam-side down in greased ovenproof dish and surround with halved tomatoes. Season well, dot with the rest of the butter and bake for 15 minutes. Garnish with lettuce leaves and serve hot.

Corn shrimp salad

Overall timing 15 minutes plus 1 hour chilling

Freezing Not suitable

To serve 2

11½ oz	Can of whole kernel corn
3	Tomatoes
½ bl	Shelled shrimp
Dressing	
1	Onion
2 tbsp	Herb vinegar
3 tbsp	Oil
	Salt and pepper
1 tbsp	Chopped fresh sage
1 tbsp	Chopped parsley
1 tbsp	Chopped chives

Drain corn. Blanch and peel tomatoes and cut into strips.

Put corn, tomatoes and shrimp in a serving dish.

To make the dressing, peel and finely chop onion. Mix together vinegar, oil and sesoning, then add the onion, sage, parsley and chives.

Pour dressing over salad, mix in well, cover and chill for 1 hour before serving.

Endive rolls in cheese sauce

Overall timing 1 ¼ hours

Freezing Suitable: bake from frozen in cold oven set to 350° for 1 hour; increase to 450°for extra 10 minutes

To serve 4-6

½ cup	Butter
8	Large heads of Belgian endive
2 tbsp	Lemon juice
1 tsp	Sugar
	Salt and pepper
2 tbsp	Flour
1 ¼ cups	Milk
	Grated nutmeg
2	Egg yolks
½ cup	Grated Parmesan cheese
8	Thin slices of cooked ham

Melt half butter in a saucepan and add endive, lemon juice, sugar and seasoning. Cover and cook gently for about 30 minutes, turning the endive occasionally.

Meanwhile, make the sauce. Melt 2 tbsp of remaining butter in another saucepan and stir in the flour. Remove from heat and gradually add milk. Return to heat and bring to a boil, stirring until thickened. Remove from heat and stir in a pinch of nutmeg, egg yolks, cheese and seasoning.

Preheat the broiler.

Lift out endive with slotted spoon. Reserve cooking liquid. Wrap each endive head in a slice of ham and arrange in a greased ovenproof dish. Add reserved liquid to sauce, heat well, then pour over endive. Dot with the rest of the butter and broil for 5-10 minutes till golden on top. Serve immediately.

Asparagus milanese

Overall timing 30 minutes

Freezing Not suitable

To serve 4

1 lb	Asparagus
	Salt
½ cup	Grated Parmesan cheese
¼ cup	Butter

Cook asparagus in boiling salted water for 15-20 minutes till tender. Drain carefully on a dishtowel or paper towels, then place on a serving dish and cool slightly.

Sprinkle Parmesan over the asparagus.

Melt the butter in a small saucepan over a low heat. When golden brown, pour over the Parmesan. Serve immediately.

Alsace salad

Overall timing 15 minutes

Freezing Not suitable

To serve 6

2	Apples
3	Boiled potatoes
1	Small cooked beet
2	Frankfurters
1	Onion
1	Hard-cooked egg
2 tsp	Chopped parsley
	Sprigs of parsley
8	Walnuts
3 tbsp	Olive oil
1 tbsp	Wine vinegar
1 tsp	Powdered mustard
	Salt and pepper

Peel, core and chop apples. Peel and dice potatoes and beet. Slice frankfurters. Peel onion and cut into rings. Shell egg and cut into 6 wedges.

Arrange prepared ingredients in rows in a serving dish and sprinkle with parsley. Garnish with parsley sprigs and walnuts.

To make dressing, mix oil with vinegar, mustard and seasoning. Pour dressing over salad and serve immediately.

Chive and mushroom crêpes

Overall timing 1¼ hours

Freezing Suitable: bake filled crêpes with sauce in 350° oven for 20 minutes.

To serve 4-6

1 lb	Button mushrooms
2 tbsp	Butter
1 cup	Milk
	Salt and pepper
¼ tsp	Grated nutmeg
1½ tbsp	Lemon juice
1 cup	White sauce
Crêpes	
1¼ cups	Flour
¼ tsp	Salt
2	Eggs
2 tbsp	Chopped chives
	Oil for frying

Finely chop mushrooms. Melt butter in a saucepan and fry mushrooms for 3 minutes. Add milk, seasoning, nutmeg and lemon juice. Bring to a boil and simmer for 10 minutes. Strain, reserving the milk for the crêpes.

Make the crêpes. Mix flour and salt, beat in eggs, chives and reserved milk to make a smooth batter. Heat a little oil in a small skillet, add enough batter to coast base thinly. Flip over to cook other side. Slide out of pan and cook 11 more crêpes in the same way.

Preheat the oven to 350°.

Divide the mushroom filling between the crêpes and roll them to enclose it. Arrange in a greased ovenproof dish and pour the white sauce over. Bake for about 20 minutes. Serve immediately, garnished with extra fluted mushrooms, if liked.

Cottage bake potatoes

Overall timing 2 hours

Freezing Not suitable

To serve 6

6 x ½ lb	Potatoes
6 tbsp	Melted butter
	Salt and pepper
6 tbsp	Cottage or cream cheese
5 tbsp	Milk
1 tsp	Paprika

Preheat the oven to 400°.

Scrub and dry the potatoes and push a metal skewer lengthwise through each one. Brush potatoes with a little melted butter and place on a baking sheet. Bake for 1-1¼ hours till tender.

Take the potatoes out of the oven, remove skewers and cut a cross in the top of each. Lift the center of each cross and scoop out some of the flesh. Put the flesh into a bowl and mash with a fork. Add half the remaining melted butter and mix thoroughly. Season well.

Mix the cheese, milk and rest of the butter in a bowl and beat till creamy. Spoon into the potatoes and cover with the mashed potato mixture. Sprinkle with paprika and salt. Replace the potatoes on the baking sheet and bake for about 15 minutes till the topping is golden. Arrange on a serving dish and serve immediately.

Carrots in batter

Overall timing 1 hour

Freezing Not suitable

To serve 4

1 lb	Carrots
1 cup	Water
¼ tsp	Salt
	Oil for frying
	Flour for coating
Batter	
1 cup	Flour
⅔ cup	Milk
2	Eggs
¼ tsp	Salt
	Sprigs of parsley

Scrape carrots and halve crosswise. Heat water in a saucepan. When boiling, add carrots and salt, cover and cook for 20 minutes.

To make the batter, sift flour into a large bowl and mix in the milk, eggs and salt until well combined and smooth. Heat oil in deep fryer to 360°.

Drain carrots and dry well on paper towels. Dip carrot pieces first in extra flour, then coat in batter. Use a skewer to lower carrots (four or five at a time) into the oil. Cook for 3 minutes till golden. Remove with a slotted spoon, drain on paper towels and serve hot, garnished with parsley.

Country-style peas

Cheese and potato bake

Overall timing 45 minutes

Freezing Not suitable

Overall timing 1¼ hours

Freezing Not suitable

To serve 6

¼ lb	Pearl onions
2 lb	Fresh peas
3	Carrots
½ lb	New potatoes
1	Head Boston lettuce
1	Thick bacon slice
2 tbsp	Butter
	Sprig of thyme
	Sprig of tarragon
	Bay leaf
	Salt and pepper

To serve 6

2 lb	New potatoes
3	Onions
2 tbsp	Oil
1	Sweet red pepper
½ lb	Sliced cooked ham
16 oz	Can of tomatoes
¾ lb	Brick cheese
½ cup	Sour cream
2	Egg yolks
	Salt and pepper
¼ tsp	Grated nutmeg
1 tbsp	Butter

Blanch and peel onions. Shell peas; scrape and dice carrots. Scrub potatoes. Tear lettuce into pieces, cut bacon into strips.

Melt butter in a flameproof casserole and fry bacon and onions till bacon fat begins to run. Add remaining vegetables, herbs tied together, seasoning and ½ cup water. Cover and simmer for 25 minutes till vegetables are tender. Remove herbs before serving.

Preheat the oven to 400°.

Scrub potatoes. Cook in boiling water for 30 minutes. Peel and thinly slice onions. Fry in oil for 5 minutes. Seed and slice pepper, add to onion and fry for 5 minutes. Shred ham; add to pan with tomatoes. Season.

Drain potatoes and cool. Slice thickly. Slice cheese. Layer potatoes, cheese and tomato mixture in greased ovenproof dish. Mix sour cream, egg yolks, seasoning and nutmeg and pour over top. Dot with butter. Bake for 20 minutes.

Swiss-style potatoes

Overall timing 1 hour

Freezing Not suitable

To serve 4

2 lb	Potatoes
3 tbsp	Caraway seeds
1 tbsp	Sea-salt
¼ cup	Butter
1 cup	Cottage cheese
½ cup	Milk
1	Onion
2 tbsp	Chopped parsley
2 tbsp	Chopped garden cress
	Salt and pepper
Garnish	
	Parsley sprigs
	Garden cress

Preheat the oven to 350°.

Halve potatoes. Mix caraway seeds and sea-salt together in a bowl. Dip the cut sides of potatoes into mixture. Place potatoes in greased ovenproof dish with the caraway seeds facing up.

Melt the butter and pour a little over each potato half. Bake for 45 minutes.

Mix cheese with milk in a bowl. Peel and finely chop onion and add to bowl with parsley, cress and seasoning.

Divide cheese mixture between warmed serving plates and place the potatoes on top. Garnish with parsley and cress.

Tomatoes stuffed with smoked trout

Overall timing 40 minutes plus chilling

Freezing Not suitable

To serve 2

1	Smoked trout
1½ tbsp	Thick mayonnaise
2 tsp	Lemon juice
	Salt
1	Hard-cooked egg
1 tsp	Chopped parsley
1 tsp	Chopped chives
2	Large tomatoes
2	Slices of Pumpernickel bread
	Butter
	Lettuce leaves
	Parsley

Skin and bone the trout. Chop flesh finely and place in a bowl. Add mayonnaise, lemon juice and salt. Shell and dice the hard-cooked egg and add with herbs to trout mixture. Mix well.

Cut tops off tomatoes and remove the inside (this can be mixed into trout mixture if you like). Fill tomatoes with the trout mixture and replace tops. Chill for 30 minutes.

Just before serving, put each tomato onto a slice of buttered Pumpernickel which should be slightly bigger than the base of the tomato. Serve on a bed of lettuce and garnish with parsley.

Zucchini with Mozzarella

Overall timing 30 minutes plus chilling

Freezing Not suitable

To serve 2

1	Onion
1	Garlic clove
2 tbsp	Butter
3 tbsp	Oil
8oz	Can of tomatoes
¼ tsp	Dried basil
4	Zucchini
2 tbsp	Flour
	Salt and pepper
¼ lb	Mozzarella cheese

Peel and finely chop onion. Peel and crush garlic. Heat butter and 1 tbsp oil in a skillet and fry onion and garlic till transparent.

Drain tomatoes. Add to pan with basil and cook over a low heat for 20 minutes. Purée mixture in a blender or food processor.

Trim and slice zucchini. Coat slices with flour. Heat remaining oil in another skillet and fry zucchini till lightly golden and tender. Drain on paper towels and season with salt and pepper.

Thinly slice Mozzarella. Layer zucchini, Mozzarella and tomato sauce in serving dish. Chill for 2-3 hours. Serve with hot garlic bread or toast and butter curls.

Deep-fried endive

Overall timing 40 minutes

Freezing Not suitable

To serve 4

4	Heads of Belgian endive
	Salt and pepper
2 tbsp	Lemon juice
	Oil for deep frying
1	Egg
1 tbsp	Milk
⅔ cup	Dried bread crumbs

Blanch endive in boiling salted water, with the lemon juice, for 10 minutes. Drain and leave on a wire rack until cool enough to handle, then pat dry with paper towels. Heat oil in a deep-fryer to 350°.

Lightly beat egg in a large bowl with a pinch each of salt and pepper. If endive heads are very large, add milk to the egg mixture to ensure there is sufficient coating mixture. Dip the endive heads in the egg, then coat completely in the bread crumbs.

Deep-fry coated endive, two at a time, in the hot oil for 2-3 minutes or until golden brown. Drain on paper towels and keep warm while frying remaining endive heads. Serve with any hot or cold meat and accompanied by sea-salt and butter to be added as you would with baked potatoes — make a cross cut, add a pat of butter and freshly-ground sea-salt.

Deep-fried zucchini

Overall timing 2¼ hours including salting

Freezing Not suitable

To serve 4

1¼ lb	Zucchini
	Salt
3 tbsp	Flour
	Oil for frying

Trim zucchini and cut into thin strips. Sprinkle with salt and leave for 1½ hours.

Dry zucchini well on paper towels and coat in flour. Shake in a strainer to remove excess flour.

Heat oil in a deep-fryer

Fry zucchini till lightly golden, then drain well on paper towels. Serve hot with tartare sauce

Variation

Season the flour with a little paprika or ground coriander before coating zucchini.

Braised fennel

Overall timing 1 hour

Freezing Suitable

To serve 6

5	Bulbs of fennel
	Salt and pepper
¼ lb	Slab bacon
1	Onion
¼ cup	Butter
1 cup	Chicken broth
	Bouquet garni
	Sprigs of parsley

Trim fennel. Cut each bulb in half and blanch in boiling water for 10 minutes. Drain.

Finely chop bacon. Peel and chop onion. Melt butter in flameproof casserole and fry bacon for 5 minutes.

Arrange onion and fennel pieces on top of bacon. Cover with broth and add bouquet garni and seasoning. Cover and simmer for about 45 minutes till tender.

Remove bouquet garni. If liked, sprinkle fennel with grated Parmesan cheese. Garnish with parsley and serve with chicken or a baked ham.

Tunisian stuffed zucchini

Overall timing 1 ¼ hours

Freezing Suitable: bake from frozen, covered, in 350° oven for about 45 minutes

To serve 4

1 lb	Zucchini
1	Onion
½ lb	Ground lamb
1 tbsp	Chopped parsley
2	Eggs
	Cayenne
	Salt and pepper
¼ cup	Flour
¼ cup	Oil
8 oz	Can of tomatoes
	Parsley

Trim zucchini. Using a long thin knife or melon-baller, scoop out center of each whole zucchini, working from both ends if necessary and trying to keep the sides an even thickness. Reserve cut-out flesh.

Peel and finely chop onion and mix with chopped zucchini flesh, ground lamb, parsley, 1 egg, a pinch of cayenne and seasoning.

Fill zucchini with prepared mixture. Roll any leftover mixture into little meat balls. Beat remaining egg in a bowl and dip stuffed zucchini and meat balls in in. Coat lightly with flour.

Heat oil in a large skillet. Add zucchini and meat balls and cook for about 20 minutes, turning to brown all sides. Remove from pan and drain on paper towels.

Sieve tomatoes and their juice. Add to pan juices with seasoning and cook over a moderate heat for about 15 minutes.

Return zucchini and meat balls to pan and cook for a further 15 minutes. Serve hot sprinkled with chopped parsley.

Avocado and pepper omelettes

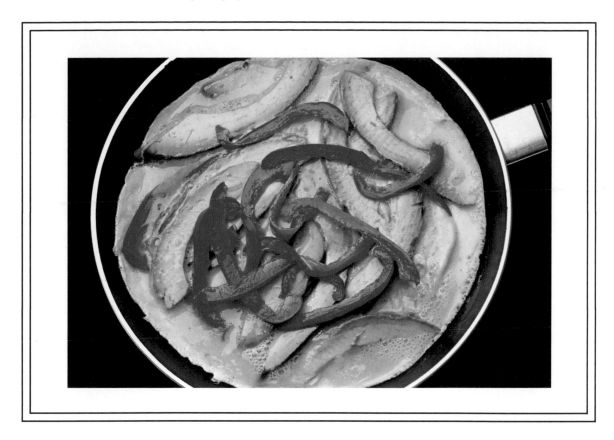

Overall timing 15 minutes

Freezing Not Suitable

To serve 4

1	Sweet red pepper
6 tbsp	Butter
2	Ripe avocados
1 tbsp	Lemon jice
12	Eggs
1 tbsp	Water
	Salt and pepper

Seed pepper and cut into long strips. Melt 2 tbsp of the butter in a omelette pan and fry pepper till just tender. Remove from pan and set aside.

Cut avocados in half lengthwise and lift out seeds. Peel, then cut avocado flesh into thick strips. Sprinkle with lemon juice to prevent discoloration.

Lightly beat together eggs, water and seasoning in a pitcher. Divide remaining butter into four pieces. Melt one piece in omelette pan.

Pour one-quarter of egg mixture into pan and cook till omelette starts to set. Run a spatula around the edge to loosen it and tilt the pan to the the uncooked egg run underneath. Continue to cook till the omelette is just soft and creamy.

Spread one-quarter of the pepper and avocado strips on top. Cook for 1 further minute, then fold over the omelette and slide it onto a warm serving plate. Serve immediately or keep it warm while you cook three more omelettes in the same way.

Avocado soufflé

Overall timing 45 minutes

Freezing Not suitable

To serve 4

2 tbsp	Butter
2 tbsp	Flour
½ cup	Milk
2	Ripe avocados
1 tsp	Lemon juice
	Pinch of grated nutmeg
	Salt and pepper
1 tsp	Grated lemon rind (optional)
3	Eggs

Preheat the oven to 400°.

Melt the butter in a saucepan, stir in the flour and cook for 1 minute. Gradually stir in the milk. Bring to a boil, stirring till thickened. Remove from the heat.

Cut the avocados in half lengthwise and lift out the seeds. Cut out four very thin slices, sprinkle with lemon juice and reserve for the garnish. Remove remaining flesh with a teaspoon, place it in a bowl and mash well. Add to the sauce and beat vigorously until well blended. Add nutmeg, seasoning and lemon rind, if used.

Separate the eggs. Add the yolks one by one to the saucepan, beating well after each addition. Beat egg whites with a pinch of salt till very stiff, then gently fold into the sauce.

Pour mixture into a greased 1 quart soufflé dish. Place on a baking sheet and bake for about 30 minutes till well risen. Garnish with reserved avocado slices and serve immediately.

Chicory ring

Overall timing 1 hour

Freezing Not suitable

To serve 4

2 lb	Chicory
	Salt and pepper
¼ cup	Butter
¼ cup	Flour
2 cups	Milk
	Grated nutmeg
3	Eggs

Trim the chicory and blanch in boiling salted water for 5 minutes. Plunge pan into cold water to cool quickly, then drain chicory well and chop.

Preheat the oven to 325°.

Melt butter in a saucepan, stir in flour and cook for 1 minute. Gradually stir in the milk. Bring to a boil, stirring, and simmer till thickened. Season with salt, pepper and nutmeg.

Remove pan from heat and stir in chicory. Allow to cool slightly, then beat eggs into mixture. Turn into greased ring mold. Place mold in roasting pan containing 1 inch water. Bake for 30 minutes. Unmold onto a warmed serving dish and serve hot.

French stuffed lettuce

Overall timing 40 minutes

Freezing Not suitable

To serve 4

4	Heads Romaine lettuces
2½ cups	Chicken broth
¼ cup	Butter
2 tbsp	Flour
1 cup	Milk
	Salt
	Grated nutmeg
¼ lb	Cooked ham
3 oz	Mozzarella cheese
2	Egg yolks

Preheat the oven to 350°.

Trim lettuces, discarding outer leaves if necessary. Bring broth to a boil in a large saucepan. Add lettuces, cover and cook for 2 minutes. Drain thoroughly, reserving cooking liquid. Allow lettuces to cool.

Melt 2 tbsp of the butter in another saucepan. Add flour and cook, stirring, for 2 minutes. Gradually stir in milk. Bring to a boil, stirring, and cook for 3 minutes. Season with salt and a pinch of grated nutmeg. Dice ham and Mozzarella and stir into sauce with egg yolks. Cook over a low heat for 2 minutes. Remove from heat and taste and adjust seasoning.

Cut cooled lettuces in half lengthwise. Arrange four lettuce halves in a greased ovenproof dish, cut sides uppermost. Spoon sauce into each half and top with remaining lettuce halves. Add ½ cup of the reserved cooking liquid and dot with remaining butter.

Cover with foil and bake for 15 minutes. Serve hot with French bread.

Baked sweet potatoes

Overall timing 1 hour

Freezing Not suitable

To serve 4

4 x ½ lb	Sweet potaotes
	Salt and pepper
¼ cup	Butter

Preheat the oven to 400°.

Wash the sweet potatoes gently to avoid breaking the skin. Arrange on a greased baking sheet and bake for about 45 minutes till tender when pierced with a skewer.

Arrange the sweet potatoes on a warmed serving dish and cut open along the top. Sprinkle a little salt and pepper into each and top with a pat of butter. Serve immediately.

Cauliflower ring

Overall timing 1 ¼ hours

Freezing Not suitable

To serve 4-6

1	Large cauliflower
	Salt and pepper
½ cup	Butter
¼ cup	Flour
2 cups	Milk
¼ tsp	Grated nutmeg
1 cup	Grated Gruyère or
	Cheddar cheese
3	Eggs
1 tbsp	Dried bread crumbs
	Sprigs of parsley

Preheat oven to 375°.

Trim cauliflower and divide into florets. Cook for 7-10 minutes in boiling salted water. Drain, chop and put in a bowl. To make sauce, melt ¼ cup of the butter in a pan, stir in flour and cook for 1 minute. Gradually stir in milk. Bring to a boil, stirring, and cook for 1 minute. Add seasoning and nutmeg. Stir ¾ cup of cheese into sauce.

Remove pan from heat. Pour about two-thirds of the sauce into a bowl and set aside. Stir eggs into sauce left in pan. Mix sauce thoroughly into cauliflower.

Grease a 9½ inch ring mold with half remaining butter. Sprinkle bread crumbs on bottom. Fill with cauliflower mixture, pressing down well, and bake for 30-35 minutes.

Remove from oven and immerse mold up to rim in cold water. Turn up oven to 450°. Run a knife blade around the sides of the mold, then carefully turn out on to ovenproof dish (if any of the mixture sticks to mould, quickly smooth it back into position with a knife and a little of remaining sauce).

Spread reserved sauce over cauliflower ring and sprinkle with remaining cheese. Melt remaining 2 tbsp butter and pour over. Return to oven and bake for about 15 minutes until golden brown. Serve hot.

Cauliflower bake

Overall timing 1 ½ hours

Freezing Not suitable

To serve 4

1	Cauliflower
	Salt and pepper
	Grated nutmeg
1	Soft bread roll
2½ cups	Milk
1	Onion
4	Tomatoes
½ lb	Ground beef
5	Eggs
½ tsp	Paprika
¼ cup	Butter

Remove any leaves and trim cauliflower stalk. Put whole cauliflower into a pan containing 1½ inches of boiling salted water. Add a pinch of grated nutmeg, cover and cook for 10 minutes.

Crumble the bread roll into a little of the milk in a large bowl. Peel and chop the onion. Chop three of the tomatoes. Add the bcef, onion, chopped tomatoes and 1 egg to the bowl. Season with salt and pepper and mix well.

Preheat oven to 400°.

Drain cauliflower; place in greased ovenproof dish. Spoon meat mixture around. Mix remaining eggs with the rest of the milk. Season with salt, pepper, a pinch of nutmeg and paprika. Pour over cauliflower and meat.

Cut the butter into pieces and put on top. Cut remaining tomato into quarters and place around cauliflower. Cover and bake for 1 hour.

Broccoli vinaigrette

Overall timing 20 minutes plus marination

Freezing Not suitable

To serve 6

1 lb	Broccoli
	Salt and pepper
10 tbsp	Oil
1 tsp	Powdered mustard
¼ cup	White wine vinegar
1 tsp	Brown sugar
1	Onion
2 tbsp	Chopped chives
2 tbsp	Chopped parsley
1 tbsp	Chopped fresh tarragon
5	Small gherkins
2	Hard-cooked eggs
2	Tomatoes
5	Radishes

Trim broccoli leaves and coarse stems, then cook in boiling salted water for about 10 minutes. Drain well, then chop and divide pieces between six serving dishes or place in salad bowl.

Beat together oil, mustard, vinegar, sugar and seasoning. Peel and finely chop the onion and add to dressing with herbs. Finely chop gherkins and eggs and stir into dressing.

Blanch, peel and finely chop tomatoes. Chop radishes and stir both into dressing. Pour over broccoli and mix well. Leave for 20 minutes until completely cold. Serve with buttered toast.

Celery in yogurt sauce

Overall timing 45 minutes

Freezing Not suitable

To serve 4-6

1 lb	Green celery
	Salt and pepper
1	Onion
2 tbsp	Bacon fat or pork drippings
¼ cup	Butter
2 cups	Chicken broth
Sauce	
1 tbsp	Butter
1 tbsp	Flour
½ cup	Sour cream
½ cup	Plain yogurt
	Grated nutmeg
	Salt and pepper

Trim celery and cut into short lengths. Blanch in boiling salted water for 5 minutes, then drain well.

Peel and chop onion. Heat bacon fat or drippings and butter in large skillet and fry onion till transparent. Add the celery and sprinkle with pepper. Add the broth, cover and cook over a low heat for 20 minutes.

Remove from heat and drain liquid into a measuring cup. There should be 1 cup — make up to this amount with a little extra broth if necessary. Keep celery warm in a serving dish.

To make sauce, melt butter in a saucepan. Stir in flour and cook for 1 minute. Gradually stir in reserved broth. Bring to a boil stirring. Add sour cream, yogurt, a pinch of nutmeg and seasoning. Stir till smooth and creamy. Pour sauce over celery and serve hot.

Turkish potato fritters

Overall timing 50 minutes plus rising

Freezing Not suitable

To serve 4-6

½ lb	Floury potatoes
	Salt
1 tsp	Baking soda
	Grated rind of ½ lemon
10oz	Package of white bread mix
	Oil for deep frying
Syrup	
1¾ cup	Sugar
2 tbsp	Lemon juice
1 tbsp	Rose-water or liqueur

Peel and quarter potatoes. Cook in boiling salted water for 20 minutes till tender. Drain and mash. Beat in soda and lemon rind.

Put bread mix into a bowl and mix in mashed potatoes. Gradually add sufficient warm water to make a thick smooth dough. Turn onto a floured board and knead till little bubbles appear on the surface. Place in a bowl, cover with oiled plastic wrap and leave to rise in a warm place for about 1 hour till doubled in size.

Meanwhile, to make the syrup, place sugar in a saucepan with 2 cups water, lemon juice and rose-water or liqueur and heat till sugar dissolves. Bring to a boil and boil gently for 15 minutes till syrupy. Remove from heat and keep warm.

Heat oil in a deep-fryer to 360°.

Break off lumps of dough with a spoon and lower into oil on a slotted spoon. Fry for 3-5 minutes, turning once, till golden all over. Remove, and drain on paper towels. Keep hot while you fry the rest. Put in a deep dish and pour warm syrup over.

Stuffed tomatoes au gratin

Overall timing 50 minutes

Freezing Not suitable

To serve 4

4	Large tomatoes
1½ lb	Fresh peas
1	Onion
2 tbsp	Oil
	Salt and pepper
¼ cup	Butter
2 tbsp	Flour
1 cup	Milk
1 cup	Grated cheese
1 tbsp	Soft bread crumbs

Preheat the oven to 400°.

Halve the tomatoes and scoop out the flesh. Discard the seeds and chop the flesh. Shell the peas. Peel and finely chop the onion.

Heat the oil in a skillet and fry the onion till transparent. Add the peas, cover and cook for 5 minutes. Stir in the chopped tomato flesh, season and continue cooking, covered, for 10 minutes.

Meanwhile, melt the butter in a saucepan. Stir in the flour and cook for 1 minute. Gradually stir in the milk and bring to a boil, stirring until thickened.

Mix three-quarters of the cheese into the sauce with the pea mixture. Use to fill the tomato halves and arrange in an ovenproof dish. Mix the remaining cheese with the bread crumbs and sprinkle over the tomatoes. Bake for 20 minutes and serve hot.

Vegetable croquettes

Overall timing 1 ¼ hours plus chilling

Freezing Suitable: deep fry after thawing

To serve 4

1 ½ lb	Floury potatoes
1	Large parsnip
	Salt and pepper
2	Large leeks
1	Stalk of celery
2	Large carrots
¼ cup	Butter
2 tbsp	Chopped parsley
¼ tsp	Grated nutmeg
2	Eggs
	Oil for deep frying
¼ cup	Flour
	Sprigs of parsley

Peel and chop the potatoes and parsnip. Cook in boiling salted water for 15-20 minutes till tender.

Meanwhile, trim and finely shred leeks and celery. Peel and grate carrots. Melt butter in a skillet, add leeks and celery and fry till golden.

Drain potatoes and parsnip, return to pan and shake over a low heat to dry thoroughly. Remove from heat and mash to a smooth purée. Stir in fried vegetables and any pan juices. Add carrots, parsley, nutmeg and seasoning. Beat in eggs. spread the mixture on a plate, cool, then chill for 2-3 hours till firm.

Heat oil in a deep-fryer to 340°. Shape vegetable mixture into 20 balls with floured hands. Fry, a few at a time, for 5-6 minutes, till crisp and golden. Drain on paper towels. Serve hot, garnished with parsley.

Chicory soufflé

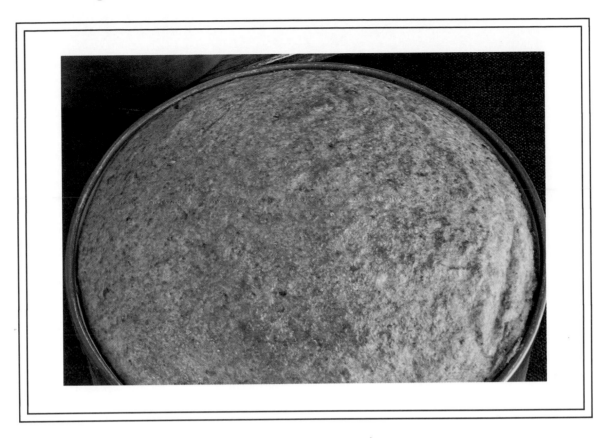

Overall timing 50 minutes

Freezing Not suitable

To serve 4

4 tbsp	Butter
2 tbsp	Finely chopped bacon
¼ cup	Diced cooked potato
2 tbsp	Finely chopped onion
2 tbsp	Flour
1 cup	Milk
½ lb	Chopped chicory
6	Eggs
	Salt and pepper

Preheat the oven to 375°.

Fry bacon in a skillet until fat runs. Add onion, fry till transparent. Drain mixture in a sieve. Add the diced potato and set aside. Melt the butter in the skillet, stir in the flour and cook for 1 minute. Gradually stir in the milk and bring to a boil, stirring. Simmer for 3 minutes, then remove from heat and add chicory. Cool slightly.

Separate the eggs. Beat yolks into the sauce, then fold in the potato and bacon mixture and seasoning. Beat the egg whites in a bowl till stiff. Stir 1 tbsp of the whites into the sauce to lighten it, then carefully fold in the remaining egg whites.

Turn the mixture into a greased 1 quart soufflé dish and bake for 25-30 minutes till the soufflé is well risen and golden in color. Serve immediately.

Cauliflower polonaise

Overall timing 35 minutes

Freezing Not suitable

To serve 4

1	Small cauliflower
	Salt
4	Hard-cooked eggs
½ cup	Butter
2 tbsp	Dried bread crumbs
1 tsp	Paprika

Trim the cauliflower and cook whole in boiling salted water for about 20 minutes till just tender.

Meanwhile, shell and finely chop eggs.

Drain cauliflower. Place in a warmed serving dish and sprinkle with the eggs. Keep warm.

Melt butter in skillet. Add breadcrumbs and paprika and stir-fry until crisp. Sprinkle over cauliflower and serve.

Cauliflower fritters

Overall timing 25 minutes

Freezing Not suitable

To serve 4

1	Large cauliflower
	Salt
1	Egg
1	Egg white
½ cup	Flour
1⅓ cup	Dried bread crumbs
	Oil for frying
	Grated Parmesan cheese
	Chopped parsley

Trim cauliflower and divide into 25-30 florets. Cook in boiling salted water for 7-10 minutes or till just tender.

Drain and allow to cool.

In a bowl, beat together egg, egg white and a pinch of salt till frothy. Dip each floret into flour, then into egg mixture, then roll in bread crumbs, till well coated.

Heat oil to 320°. Deep fry cauliflower till golden brown and crisp. Remove cauliflower from pan with a slotted spoon and drain on paper towels. Serve hot, sprinkled with salt and a little grated Parmesan and chopped parsley mixed together.

Brussels sprouts with chestnuts

Overall timing 1 hour

Freezing Not suitable

To serve 4-6

¾ lb	Chestnuts
2 cups	Hot beef broth
1½ lbs	Brussels sprouts
	Salt
	Grated nutmeg
¼ cup	Butter

Make a cut in each chestnut with a sharp knife, then place them in a saucepan. Cover with cold water, bring to a boil and cook for 10 minutes.

Drain chestnuts and peel off both outer and inner skins. Add to the broth and simmer gently for about 20 minutes till tender.

Meanwhile, trim the sprouts and cut a cross in the base of each one. Cook in boiling salted water for 10-12 minutes till tender. Drain and season with nutmeg.

Melt the butter in a pan, then add the drained chestnuts and sprouts. Gently shake the pan to coat the vegetables with butter. Turn into a warmed serving dish and serve.

Potato and onion bake

Overall timing 1 hour

Freezing Not suitable

To serve 4

1 ½ lb	Potatoes
¾ lb	Onions
6 tbsp	Butter
	Salt and pepper

Preheat the oven to 400°.

Peel the potatoes and slice very thinly (use a mandolin for best results). Put into a bowl of cold water to prevent discoloration. Peel and thinly slice the onions.

Drain the potatoes and dry with paper towels. Butter an ovenproof dish and cover the bottom with a layer of potato. Dot with butter, season and cover with a layer of onion. Dot with butter, season and repeat the layers till all ingredients have been used, finishing with potato. Dot the top with the remaining butter.

Bake for about 40 minutes till the potatoes are tender and golden. Serve immediately.

Potato cake

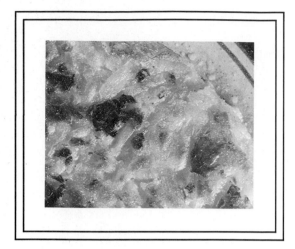

Overall timing 50 minutes

Freezing Not suitable

To serve 4

2 lb	Potatoes
1½ cups	Grated cheese
3	Eggs
1 cup	Milk
	Salt and pepper

Preheat the oven to 375°.

Peel potatoes and grate into bowl. Add cheese to potatoes. Beat in eggs, milk and seasoning. Pour into an ovenproof dish and bake for 40 minutes till top is golden. Serve hot.

Potato omelette

Overall timing 30 minutes

Freezing Not suitable

To serve 4

4x6 oz	Waxy potatoes
	Salt and pepper
1 cup	Butter
2	Sage leaves
12	Eggs

Peel and dice potatoes. Cook in boiling salted water for 4 minutes. Drain and pat dry.

Melt ¼ cup of the butter in a skillet, add the potatoes and sage and fry over a moderate heat for 5-10 minutes till the potatoes are tender and golden. Discard sage leaves, remove potatoes and keep hot.

Lightly beat three of the eggs in a bowl with salt and pepper. Heat omelette pan and add one-quarter of the remaining butter. Pour eggs into pan and cook omelette. When almost set, put one-quarter of the potatoes along the center and fold the sides in to cover them. Turn onto warm plate with the join down and keep hot while you cook the remaining three omelettes in the same way.

Just before serving, cut along the tops of the omelettes to expose the filling. Serve immediately with a mixed salad.

Vegetable moussaka

Overall timing 2 hours

Freezing Not suitable

To serve 4-6

2	Large onions
1	Garlic clove
1	Large eggplant
	Salt and pepper
¼ cup	Butter
½ cup	Brown lentils
2 tbsp	Tomato paste
2½ cups	Light broth
4	Small globe artichokes
1 tbsp	Lemon juice
	Bouquet garni
¼ cup	Oil
	Sprigs of parsley

Peel and finely chop onions; peel and crush garlic. Slice eggplant, sprinkle with salt and leave to drain for 15 minutes.

Melt the butter in a saucepan, add onion, and garlic and fry till golden. Add lentils, tomato paste and broth and simmer for about 1 hour till a thick purée.

Meanwhile, remove stem and coarse outer leaves from artichokes. Bring a pan of water to a boil, add lemon juice, bouquet garni and artichokes and simmer for 20-30 minutes till tender.

Rinse eggplant and dry on paper towels. Heat oil in a skillet, add eggplant and fry till crisp and golden.

Preheat oven to 350°.

Drain artichokes thoroughly, cut in half and remove chokes. Arrange cut sides up in greased ovenproof dish. Pour half lentil mixture over artichokes, then cover with half fried eggplant slices. Repeat the layers of lentil and eggplant and press down lightly. Bake for 30 minutes. Unmold and serve hot, garnished with parsley.

Venetian green beans

Overall timing 1 ¼ hours

Freezing Suitable

To serve 4-6

1 ¼ lb	Green beans
1 lb	Fresh tomatoes or
16 oz	Can of tomatoes
1	Medium-size onion
1	Garlic clove
¼ cup	Butter or
2 tbsp	Oil
	Bouquet garni
¼ tsp	Dried oregano or marjoram
	Salt and pepper

Trim beans and remove strings if necessary. If using fresh tomatoes, blanch, peel and chop them; drain and chop canned tomatoes. Peel and chop the onion. Peel and crush garlic.

Heat the butter or oil in a saucepan and fry the onion till browned. Add beans, tomatoes, garlic, bouquet garni, oregano or marjoram and seasoning. Cover and simmer over a very low heat for 1 hour. If necessary add a little boiling water during cooking to prevent sticking. Serve hot.

Potato gnocchi

Overall timing 1 ½ hours plus chilling

Freezing Not suitable

To serve 6

2 lb	Floury potatoes
	Salt and pepper
2 cups	Flour
1 tsp	Baking powder
2	Eggs
6 oz	Sliced cheese
¼ cup	Butter
3 tbsp	Grated Parmesan cheese
	Grated nutmeg

Scrub the potatoes and cook in boiling salted water for about 30 minutes till tender. Drain, peel and press through a ricer into a large bowl.

Sift the flour and baking powder together, add to the potatoes and mix in with a wooden spoon. Beat in the eggs and seasoning. Spread out on a plate and chill for 2-3 hours till firm.

Preheat the oven to 425°.

Bring a large pan of salted water to a boil, then reduce heat till simmering. Put teaspoonfuls of the potato mixture into the water and cook for about 4 minutes or till they rise to the surface. Remove with a slotted spoon and keep hot while you cook the rest.

Layer cooked dumplings in an ovenproof dish with slices of cheese and butter and sprinkle Parmesan on top. Brown in the oven for 5-10 minutes. Sprinkle nutmeg over.

Fried ham and spinach

Overall timing 30 minutes

Freezing Not suitable

To serve 4

2 lb	Bulk spinach
	Salt and pepper
6 oz	Slice of cooked ham
1	Garlic clove
3 tbsp	Oil
2	Hard-cooked eggs
2 tbsp	Pine nuts
	(optional)

Wash and pick over the spinach, discarding any withered leaves or coarse stalks. Drain thoroughly and blanch in lightly salted boiling water for 1 minute. Remove from heat, rinse under cold water and drain thoroughly. Chop coarsely.

Dice the ham and peel the garlic. Heat the oil in a large skillet, add ham and garlic and fry for 2-3 minutes. Stir in the spinach, add plenty of pepper and fry gently for 5 minutes, stirring occasionally.

Meanwhile, shell and finely chop the eggs. Add to the pan with the pine nuts, if used, and cook for 2 minutes.

Discard garlic clove. Adjust seasoning to taste and arrange on a warmed serving dish. Serve immediately with thick slices of crusty bread.

Carrot soufflé

Overall timing 1 hour

Freezing Not suitable

To serve 4

1 lb	Carrots
½ cup	Butter
	Salt and pepper
¼ cup	Flour
2½ cups	Milk
	Salt and pepper
3	Eggs

Peel and thinly slice the carrots, then cook in boiling water for 15 minutes. Drain and plunge into cold water to cool carrots quickly.

Melt half the butter in another pan, add drained carrots and mash with a fork. Season with salt and pepper.

Preheat the oven to 375°.

Melt remaining butter in a saucepan and stir in flour. Gradually add milk and bring to a boil, stirring until thickened. Season with salt and pepper and cool.

Separate the eggs. Mix the egg yolks and carrots into the sauce. Beat the whites in a bowl until very stiff, then carefully fold into the carrot mixture. Pour into a greased 1 quart soufflé dish. Bake for about 30 minutes until the soufflé is golden and well risen. Serve immediately.

Bubble and squeak

Overall timing 15 minutes

Freezing Not suitable

To serve 4-6

2 cups	Mashed potatoes
3 cups	Cooked shredded cabbage
¼ cup	Butter
	Salt and pepper
2 cups	Diced leftover cooked meat

Beat together mashed potatoes and cabbage with a wooden spoon, adding plenty of seasoning.

Melt the butter in a heavy skillet and add the potato and cabbage mixture, spreading it over the bottom of the pan. Mix in meat. Fry, turning the mixture occasionally, until crisp and golden brown. Serve immediately.

Boxty on the griddle

Overall timing 40 minutes

Freezing Suitable: reheat from frozen in 400° oven for 10 minutes

To serve 4

½ lb	Waxy potatoes
½ cup	Cooked mashed potatoes
1 cup	Flour
½ tsp	Baking soda
2 cups	Milk
	Salt and pepper
	Oil for frying

Peel the potatoes and grate into a large bowl. Add the mashed potatoes, sifted flour and baking soda and mix together well. Make a well in the center and gradually stir in enough milk to make a stiff batter. Season well.

Heat a lightly oiled griddle or heavy-based skillet. Drop the batter in large spoonfuls onto the griddle or skillet and cook over a moderate heat for 4 minutes on each side till crisp and golden.

Serve hot with fried blood sausage, bacon and eggs.

Potato pancakes

Overall timing 45 minutes

Freezing Not suitable

To serve 4

1 ¼ lb	Waxy potatoes
2	Eggs
1 tbsp	Flour
	Salt and pepper
¼ cup	Oil

Peel the potatoes and grate coarsely into a bowl of cold water. Drain and squeeze dry in a cloth, then put into a dry bowl. Add the eggs, flour and seasoning and mix well.

Heat a little of the oil in a skillet and add one-quarter of the potato mixture. Flatten into a pancake with the back of a spatula and fry over a moderate heat for about 5 minutes till the edges are golden. Turn carefully and brown the other side. Remove from the pan and keep hot while rest of mixture is cooked.

Serve hot with roast or broiled meats and a green vegetable.

Rumanian vegetable casserole

Overall timing 1 ¼ hours

Freezing Not suitable

To serve 6-8

2	Waxy potatoes
2	White turnips
2	Medium-size onions
2	Garlic cloves
2	Carrots
1	Medium-size eggplant
2	Zucchini
2	Small leeks
¼ lb	Green beans
3	Large tomatoes
2 tbsp	Butter
2 tbsp	Oil
1 cup	Shelled fresh peas
2 tbsp	Tomato paste
	Bouquet garni
	Salt and pepper

Peel the potatoes, turnips, onions, garlic and carrots. Cut the potatoes, turnips, carrots, eggplant and zucchini into ¾ inch chunks. Cut the leeks and beans into 1 inch lengths. Quarter the tomatoes; slice the onions.

Heat the butter and oil in a flameproof casserole and fry the onions, leeks and garlic till golden. Add the remaining vegetables, tomato paste, bouquet garni and 2½ cups water and mix well. Season and bring to a boil. Simmer gently for 45 minutes till the vegetables are tender.

Rutabaga purée

Overall timing 35 minutes

Freezing Not suitable

To serve 4-6

2 lb	Rutabaga
	Salt and pepper
6 tbsp	Butter

Peel the rutabaga thickly, wash and cut into 1 inch chunks. Put into a saucepan of lightly salted cold water and bring to a boil. Reduce the heat, cover and simmer for 15-20 minutes till tender.

Drain thoroughly, then mash well till smooth with two-thirds of the butter. Season to taste.

Arrange in a warmed serving dish, top with the remaining butter and grind a little pepper over. Serve immediately.

Variations

"Clapshot" is a traditional mixed rutabaga and potato dish from the Orkney Islands, off the north coast of Scotland. Cook equal quantities of rutabaga and floury potatoes in separate pans till tender. Drain well, then mash together with butter and seasoning and 1 small finely chopped onion or 2 tbsp chopped chives. Any leftovers can be fried in butter.

To turn clapshot into a tasty lunch or supper dish, spread the mashed rutabaga, potato and onion mixture in a shallow ovenproof dish. Make 4 hollows with the back of a spoon and break an egg into each one. Season and dot with butter, then bake in the oven, preheated to 425° for 8-10 minutes till the eggs are lightly set. Serve immediately with strips of crispy fried bacon.

German broad beans

Overall timing 45 minutes

Freezing Suitable

To serve 4

2 lb	Unshelled broad or fava beans
	Salt and pepper
1	Chicken bouillon cube
4	Bacon slices
2	Onions
3 tbsp	Flour
	Pinch of grated nutmeg
1 cup	Light cream
1 tbsp	Chopped parsley

Shell beans. Place in boiling, salted water and cook for 20 minutes or until tender. Drain cooking liquid into measuring cup and make up to 1 cup with water. Crumble in bouillon cube. Set beans and liquid in cup aside for the moment.

Dice bacon; peel and chop onions. Put bacon and onions into a saucepan and fry gently for about 10 minutes. Remove pan from heat and stir in the flour. Gradually stir in the liquid from the cup. Return pan to heat and cook gently for about 5 minutes, stirring constantly until sauce thickens. Remove from heat and season to taste with salt, pepper and nutmeg.

Stir in beans and cream and heat gently for a further 5 minutes, stirring. Transfer to warmed serving dish, garnish with parsley and serve.

Italian cauliflower omelette

Overall timing 20 minutes

Freezing Not suitable

To serve 2

¾ lb	Cauliflower
	Salt and pepper
1	Onion
¼ cup	Butter
6	Eggs
2 tbsp	Grated Parmesan cheese
½ tsp	Grated nutmeg

Preheat the broiler.

Cut cauliflower into tiny florets and cook in boiling salted water for 3-5 minutes till just tender.

Meanwhile, peel and finely chop onion. Melt butter in a skillet and fry onion till golden. Add the drained cauliflower and seasoning and cook for 2 minutes, spreading evenly in the pan.

Beat the eggs in a bowl with the Parmesan and nutmeg. Pour evenly over the cauliflower and cook over a moderate heat till the omelette is nearly set.

Put the skillet under the broiler and cook till the top of the omelette is golden. Slide the omelette onto a warmed serving plate and cut in two to serve.

Stuffed baked potatoes

Overall timing 1 ½ hours

Freezing Not suitable

To serve 8

8 x ½ lb	Waxy potatoes
1	Large onion
6 tbsp	Butter
½ lb	Cooked ham
6 tbsp	Dry white wine or hard cider
1 cup	Soft bread crumbs
2 tbsp	Chopped parsley
	Salt and pepper
½ cup	Chicken broth

Preheat the oven to 400°.

Peel the potatoes. Cut a slice from one end of each so they stand upright. Cut a slice from the other end of each and hollow out the centers with a sharp knife, leaving a thick shell. Finely chop the scooped out pieces and slices cut from the tops of the potatoes.

Peel and finely chop the onion. Melt 2 tbsp of the butter in a saucepan and fry the onion till transparent. Dice the ham and add to the pan with the wine or cider, chopped potatoes and bread crumbs. Cover and cook for 5 minutes, then stir in the parsley and seasoning.

Spoon the mixture into the potatoes, pressing it down firmly. Stand potatoes upright in a greased ovenproof dish. Melt remaining butter with the broth and pour into the dish.

Bake for 50 minutes to 1 hour, basting frequently, till the potatoes are tender. Serve hot with a green salad.

Stuffed cabbage

Breton beans

Overall timing 2 hours 10 minutes

Freezing Not suitable

To serve 6

½ lb	Slab bacon
2	Onions
1	Head green cabbage
2	Tomatoes
1	Garlic clove
1¾ lb	Bulk sausage meat
½ cup	Long grain rice
1 cup	Frozen peas
	Salt and pepper
1 quart	Hot beef broth

Chop bacon. Peel and finely chop onions. Heat a skillet, add bacon and cook till crisp. Add onions and cook gently for 10 minutes.

Remove all large outer leaves of cabbage. On a large piece of cheesecloth make two layers of leaves in a circular shape. Finely chop remaining cabbage.

Finely chop tomatoes. Peel and crush garlic. Add tomatoes and garlic to chopped cabbage with sausage meat, rice, peas, bacon and onion and seasoning. Mix well and form into a ball. Place in center of cabbage leaves, then remake cabbage shape so leaves enclose stuffing. Lift corners of cheesecloth and tie at top. Place cabbage in broth, cover and simmer for 1½ hours.

Overall timing 1 hours

Freezing Suitable: thaw overnight, reheat gently

To serve 4-6

1 cup	Dried navy beans
2	Onions
2	Cloves
1	Carrot
1	Garlic clove
¼ tsp	Dried mixed herbs
2	Bay leaves
	Salt and pepper
1 lb	Tomatoes
¼ cup	Butter

Place beans in a saucepan, cover with water and simmer for 15 minutes.

Peel one onion and spike with cloves; peel and slice carrot. Peel and crush garlic. Drain beans and return to pan. Add onion, carrot, garlic and herbs. Cover with boiling water and bring to a boil. Cover and cook for 50 minutes; add salt and cook for another 20.

Meanwhile, peel and chop remaining onion. Blanch, peel and quarter tomatoes. Melt butter in a saucepan and add onions, tomatoes and seasoning. Simmer for 20 minutes. Drain beans and mix into tomato sauce. Adjust seasoning and heat through before serving.

Italian fried vegetables

Overall timing 1 hour

Freezing Not suitable

To serve 6

1	Large eggplant
	Salt and pepper
½ lb	Zucchini
½	Cauliflower
½ lb	Large flat mushrooms
2	Large apples
4	Eggs
2 cups	Fine bread crumbs
¾ cup	Flour
	Oil for deep frying
	Sprigs of parsley

Cut the eggplant into ¼ inch thick slices. Sprinkle with salt and leave for 15 minutes.

Meanwhile, halve zucchini lengthwise, then cut into 2 inch lengths. Divide cauliflower into florets. Blanch in boiling salted water for 3 minutes, then drain and rinse under cold water.

Quarter mushrooms. Peel and core apples and cut into thick rings. Rinse eggplant and pat dry with paper towels.

Beat eggs in shallow dish and spread bread crumbs on a board. Coat vegetables in seasoned flour, then dip into egg and bread crumbs.

Heat oil in a deep-fryer to 340°. Fry eggplant slices for about 4 minutes, turning occasionally, till crisp and golden. Drain on paper towels and keep hot.

Fry zucchini and cauliflower florets for 5-6 minutes, and mushrooms and apples for 3-4 minutes. Drain on paper towels and keep hot.

Arrange all the fried vegetables on a warmed serving dish and garnish with parsley. Serve immediately with Tartare sauce and a green salad.

Stuffed cucumbers

Overall timing 1 hour

Freezing Not suitable

To serve 6

3	Large cucumbers
¼ cup	Diced cooked ham
¼ lb	Ground beef
2 tbsp	Soft bread crumbs
1 tbsp	Chopped parsley
3 tbsp	Milk
1	Egg
	Salt and pepper
Sauce	
1	Onion
1	Leek
¼ cup	Butter
2 tbsp	Flour
1 cup	Broth
1 tbsp	Chopped parsley
	Paprika
	Salt
1 tbsp	Vinegar
½ cup	Half-and-half

Peel cucumbers. Halve them lengthwise and scoop out seeds. Mix ham with beef, bread crumbs, parsley, milk, egg and seasoning. Stuff cucumbers with mixture.

To make sauce, peel and finely chop onion. Trim and finely chop leek. Melt butter in a saucepan and fry onion and leek till golden. Sprinkle flour into pan and cook for 1 minute, stirring. Gradually stir in broth, then add parsley, a pinch each of paprika and salt and the vinegar. Bring to a boil, stirring.

Arrange cucumbers on top of sauce and surround with any leftover stuffing. Cover and cook gently for 30 minutes. Turn cucumbers over halfway through cooking time.

Stir half-and-half into sauce and heat through uncovered for 2 minutes.

Stuffed celeriac

Overall timing 1 ½ hours

Freezing Not suitable

To serve 4

4 x ½ lb	Bulbs of celeriac
	Salt and pepper
1 tbsp	Lemon juice
¼ cup	Diced bacon
1	Large onion
½ lb	Ground beef
½ cup	Soft bread crumbs
1 oz	Grated Parmesan cheese

Peel celeriac, cook in boiling salted water with lemon juice for 20 minutes. Drain and allow to cool slightly, then cut off tops and reserve. Scoop out insides and reserve.

Preheat the oven to 400°. Cook bacon in a skillet for 3 minutes. Peel and finely chop onion, cutting a few large pieces for the garnish. Fry onions till golden. Remove large pieces and set aside. Add beef to pan and cook for 5 minutes. Chop inside of two celeriac bulbs and add to pan with bread crumbs, Parmesan and seasoning.

Fill celeriac with meat mixture. Replace tops, then place in greased ovenproof dish. Bake for 40 minutes, basting with pan juices halfway through. Garnish with onion.

Spanish stuffed peppers

Overall timing 1 hour

Freezing Suitable: bake for 1 hour

To serve 4

1 lb	Tomatoes
1	Onion
1	Garlic clove
½ cup	Olive oil
½ tsp	Dried oregano
	Salt and pepper
8	Firm green peppers
1 lb	Slab bacon
2 cups	Soft bread crumbs

Blanch, peel and chop tomatoes. Peel and chop onion. Peel and crush garlic. Heat 2 tbsp oil in saucepan, add tomatoes, onion, garlic, oregano and seasoning. Simmer till reduced by half.

Cut off stalk end of each pepper, then remove seeds. Blanch in boiling salted water for 5 minutes. Drain. Preheat oven to 400°.

To make stuffing, grind bacon. Mix with crumbs and seasoning.

Pour 1 tsp oil into each pepper, then fill with stuffing. Pour remaining oil into oven-proof dish. Place peppers in dish with tomato sauce between them. Cover with foil and bake for 45 minutes.

Romanian peppers

Overall timing 1 ¼ hours

Freezing Not suitable

To serve 6

1 lb	Lean boneless pork
2	Onions
¼ cup	Butter
¼ lb	Button mushrooms
½ lb	Tomatoes
1 cup	Water
	Salt and pepper
½ tsp	Paprika
6	Green peppers
2 tsp	Cornstarch
¼ cup	Half-and-half
	Hot pepper sauce

Dice the pork. Peel and finely chop onions. Melt the butter in saucepan. Fry onions and pork for 10 minutes.

Slice mushrooms. Blanch, peel and chop tomatoes. Add mushrooms and tomatoes to the saucepan. Pour in water and cook for 40 minutes over a low heat. Season with salt, pepper and paprika.

Cut tops off peppers. Remove seeds. Place peppers and their tops in a saucepan of boiling water and cook for 5 minutes or until just soft. Lift out and drain. Keep warm.

Blend cornstarch with half-and-half. Stir into pork mixture, then bring just to a boil to thicken. Season with a few drops of hot pepper sauce. Mix well, then use mixture to fill peppers. Place tops on peppers to serve.

Leeks with mustard sauce

Overall timing 30 minutes

Freezing Not suitable

To serve 4-6

2 lb	Leeks
	Salt and pepper
1	Small onion
1	Garlic clove
¼ cup	Butter
1 tbsp	Flour
2 cups	Milk
1 tbsp	Prepared mustard
1 cup	Grated cheese

Trim leeks. Cook in boiling salted water for 15-20 minutes till tender. Drain, saving ½ cup cooking liquid. Arrange leeks in warmed serving dish. Keep hot.

Peel and chop onion and garlic. Melt the butter in a saucepan and fry the onion and garlic till golden. Stir in the flour and cook for 1 minute. Gradually add reserved cooking liquid and milk. Bring to a boil, stirring, and cook for 3 minutes. Stir in mustard, cheese and seasoning and heat through gently without boiling. Pour over the leeks and serve immediately.

Leek and cheese soufflé

Overall timing 1 hour

Freezing Not suitable

To serve 4

¼ cup	Butter
¼ cup	Flour
1 cup	Warm milk
½ cup	Grated brick cheese
½ lb	Leeks
	Salt and pepper
3	Large eggs

Melt the butter in a pan, stir in the flour and cook for 1 minute. Gradually add warm milk and bring to a boil, stirring. Simmer for 2 minutes. Remove from heat and leave to cool.

Trim and finely chop leeks. Blanch in boiling water for 5 minutes and drain thoroughly. Stir the grated cheese and leeks into sauce and season. Separate eggs. Beat the yolks into the sauce.

Beat egg whites in a bowl till stiff but not dry. Stir 1 tbsp whites into sauce to lighten it, then carefully fold in the rest. Turn mixture into greased 1 quart soufflé dish, place on baking sheet and bake for 30-35 minutes till well risen and golden. Serve immediately.

Irish cabbage

Overall timing 40 minutes

Freezing Not suitable

To serve 4-6

1 lb	Potatoes
2	Small leeks
	Milk
1 lb	Head green cabbage
	Salt and pepper
	Pinch of mace
½ cup	Butter
	Sprigs of parsley

Cook unpeeled potatoes in lightly salted water till just tender. Meanwhile, trim the leeks, then roughly chop both white and green parts. Just cover with milk and cook gently till soft.

Roughly chop cabbage and cook in boiling, lightly salted water for 7 minutes. Drain and cut into smaller pieces.

Keep cabbage warm.

Drain potatoes; peel and put through a ricer or mash well. Mash in the leeks/milk mixture and season well with salt, pepper and mace. Place bowl over a pan of boiling water and gradually beat in the cabbage till light and fluffy.

Melt butter. Place vegetable mixture in warmed serving dish, make a well in the center and pour in the hot butter. Garnish with parsley sprigs and serve immediately.

Corn fritters

Overall timing 30 minutes

Freezing Not suitable

To serve 4

1 lb	Can of whole kernel corn
1	Egg
½ cup	Flour
	Salt
1 tbsp	Oil
½	Grated rind of lemon
	Oil for deep frying
	Grated Parmesan cheese

Drain corn. Separate egg. Sift flour and pinch of salt into a mixing bowl. Make a well in center, then put in egg yolk, oil and grated lemon rind. Stir until a smooth batter forms. Add a little water if necessary.

In another bowl, beat egg white until stiff. Fold into batter with corn.

Heat oil in deep-fryer to 340°.

Drop spoonfuls of batter into the hot oil — be careful because corn can burst — a few at a time, and fry for 5 minutes on each side or until golden. Remove with a spatula and drain on paper towels. Keep warm while frying the rest.

Sprinkle grated Parmesan over and serve hot.

Lemon-braised leeks

Overall timing 1 hour

Freezing Not suitable

To serve 4

2 lb	Leeks
	Salt and pepper
2	Carrots
1	Onion
6 tbsp	Butter
½ cup	Broth
2 tbsp	Flour
½	Lemon

Preheat the oven to 350°.

Trim leeks and blanch in boiling salted water for 5 minutes.

Drain.

Peel and slice carrots. Peel and slice onion. Melt 2 tbsp of the butter in a flameproof casserole and fry the carrots and onion till golden. Arrange leeks on top and add broth and seasoning.

Cream remaining butter with the flour to make a paste. Squeeze juice from lemon and work into the mixture with a fork. Spread over the leeks. Cover and cook for 30-35 minutes. Serve with side dish of grated cheese and chunks of brown bread.

Cheesy vegetables

Overall timing 10 minutes

Freezing Not suitable

To serve 6

½ lb (1 cup)	Cream cheese
½ cup	Light cream
4 cups	Hot cooked mixed vegetables (including beans, cauliflower, peas, carrots and mushrooms)
2 tbsp	Grated Parmesan cheese
	Salt and pepper

Beat the cream cheese and cream together in a bowl. Place the bowl over a pan of simmering water and heat through gently, stirring occasionally. Do not boil.

Arrange the vegetables in a warmed serving dish. Keep hot.

Beat the Parmesan into the cream cheese mixture and season to taste. Pour the hot sauce over the vegetables and serve immediately with roast or broiled meat, or as vegetarian lunch.

Greek pumpkin

Overall timing 1 hour

Freezing Not suitable

To serve 4-6

2 lb	Pumpkin
2	Medium-size onions
3 tbsp	Olive oil
16 oz	Can of tomatoes
¼ tsp	Ground cumin
2	Sprigs of flat-leafed parsley
	Salt and pepper
1 cup	Water

Scrape the seeds and fibrous center out of the pumpkin. Cut into chunks, leaving the skin on. Peel the onions and cut through the root into eight wedges.

Heat the oil in a saucepan, add onions and fry till transparent. Add the tomatoes and juice, cumin and pumpkin. Chop the parsley and add with seasoning and the water. Bring to a boil, then cover and simmer for 25-35 minutes till the pumpkin is tender.

Adjust the seasoning and pour into a warmed serving dish. Serve hot with roast or broiled meat.

Lentils with bacon

Overall timing 1 ½ hours

Freezing Suitable

To serve 4

1 cup	Brown lentils
1	Large onion
½ lb	Slab bacon
3 tbsp	Oil
1 tsp	Salt
3 tbsp	Tomato paste
1 quart	Broth

Wash and pick over the lentils. Peel and finely chop the onion. Dice the bacon. Heat oil in a saucepan and fry onion and bacon till golden. Add the lentils and salt and cook for 10 minutes, stirring frequently.

Stir in the tomato paste and the broth and simmer for about 1 hour until the lentils are tender. Taste and adjust seasoning. Serve on slices of fried bread with a mixed salad.

Lentils with zucchini and potatoes

Overall timing 1 ½ hours

Freezing Not suitable

To serve 6

1 cup	Brown lentils
	Salt and pepper
2	Bay leaves
1	Onion
2 tbsp	Oil
¾ lb	Zucchini
1	Garlic clove
2 tbsp	Lemon juice
5	Fennel leaves
	Basil leaves
	Sprig or rosemary
1 tsp	Cumin seeds
½ lb	Potatoes
2 tbsp	Butter
	Chopped parsley

Put lentils in a large saucepan. Add 1 quart water, seasoning and bay leaves. Bring to a boil and simmer for 5 minutes, then drain, reserving the liquid.

Peel and finely chop onion. Heat oil in a large saucepan and fry onion till transparent. Trim and thickly slice zucchini. Add to pan and stir-fry for 5 minutes. Peel and crush garlic and add to pan with lentils and lemon juice. Finely chop fennel leaves and add to pan with a few basil leaves, a sprig of rosemary, the cumin and reserved lentil liquid. Simmer for 45 minutes.

Meanwhile, peel potatoes and cut into large chunks. Add to pan and simmer for a further 20 minutes or till the lentils are cooked.

Add the butter, and taste and adjust seasoning. Sprinkle with chopped parsley and serve hot with grated cheese or slices of boiled ham.

Russian potatoes with cream

Overall timing 1 ¼ hours

Freezing Not suitable

To serve 4

1 ½ lb	Waxy potatoes
	Salt and pepper
½ cup	Button mushrooms
1	Small onion
¼ cup	Butter
½ cup	Sour cream
2 tbsp	Chopped parsley

Cook the potatoes in boiling salted water for about 30 minutes till tender. Drain and peel the potatoes, then cut into ¼ inch thick slices. Slice the mushrooms. Peel and thinly slice the onion.

Melt the butter in a skillet and fry the onion till transparent. Add the mushrooms and fry for 2-3 minutes, stirring. Add the sliced potatoes and fry for 5 minutes, turning once.

Pour the cream over and season well. Turn potatoes gently till coated and continue cooking over a low heat for about 10 minutes till the potatoes have absorbed most of the cream.

Stir in the parsley, adjust the seasoning and serve hot.

Lettuce and ham supper

Overall timing 40 minutes

Freezing Not suitable

To serve 4

4	Heads romaine lettuce
1	Onion
2 tbsp	Butter
1 cup	Chicken broth
	Salt and pepper
4	Thick slices of cooked ham
1 tsp	Cornstarch
2 tbsp	Water
½ cup	Sherry wine

Trim and wash lettuces. Drain well and cut in half lengthwise. Peel and chop the onion.

Melt the butter in a saucepan and fry onions till golden. Add lettuces and fry for 3 minutes. Add broth, salt and pepper. Tightly cover pan and simmer for 15-20 minutes.

Cut ham slices in half and add to pan. Heat through gently for 3 minutes.

Carefully lift out the lettuce halves and ham, draining thoroughly. Arrange on a warmed serving dish and keep hot.

Blend cornstarch with water, then stir into cooking liquid. Bring to a boil, stirring continuously. Remove from heat and stir in sherry. Taste and adjust seasoning. Pour over lettuce and ham and serve immediately with mashed potatoes and wholewheat bread.

Savory pumpkin

Overall timing 1 ¼ hours plus
30 minutes standing

Freezing Not suitable

To serve 4-6

2 lb	Pumpkin
	Salt and pepper
2 cups	Grated cheese
¼ teasp	Ground cumin
3	Eggs
1 cup	Soft bread crumbs
2 tbsp	Chopped parsley
2 tbsp	Butter

Scrape the seeds and fibrous center out of the pumpkin. Remove the skin and grate the flesh into a bowl. Sprinkle with salt, mix well and leave to stand for 30 minutes.

Preheat the oven to 350°.

Press the pumpkin with the back of a spoon to squeeze out as much liquid as possible. Add the cheese to the pumpkin with cumin, eggs, bread crumbs, parsley and seasoning and beat the mixture till smooth.

Pour into a greased ovenproof dish and smooth the top. Dot with butter and bake for about 45 minutes till set. Serve immediately with a tomato salad and fresh crusty bread and butter.

Penne with artichokes

Overall timing 35 minutes

Freezing Not suitable

To serve 2

2	Small globe artichokes
1 tsp	Lemon juice
1	Garlic clove
2 tbsp	Olive oil
1 tbsp	Chopped parsley
½ lb	Penne pasta
	Salt and pepper

Cut off stems, tough outer leaves and pointed tops of artichokes and snip off the tips of outside leaves. Cut artichokes into quarters, remove chokes and place in bowl with lemon juice. Cover with water and leave to soak for 10 minutes.

Peel and crush garlic. Heat the oil in saucepan. Drain artichokes and add to pan with garlic. Cook gently over low heat for about 10 minutes till tender, turning them several times. Add parsley and cook for a further 5 minutes, stirring occasionally.

Meanwhile, cook penne in boiling salted water till tender. Drain thoroughly and add to artichokes. Mix well to coat pasta with oil and parsley, adding lots of seasoning, then turn into warmed serving dish. Serve hot with grated Parmesan cheese.

Lyonnaise beans

Overall timing 1 hour plus soaking

Freezing Not suitable

To serve 6

1½ cups	Dried lima beans
	Salt and pepper
2	Medium-size onions
¼ cup	Butter
1 tbsp	Chopped parsley

Soak beans in water to cover overnight. Drain.

Place beans in saucepan and add 1 quart fresh water. Cover and cook for about 1 hour till tender. Add a little salt toward the end of cooking time.

Peel and finely chop onions. Melt the butter in a saucepan and add the onions, parsley and seasoning. Cook gently till onions are transparent.

Drain beans well, then toss them in the onion and parsley mixture. Transfer to a warmed dish and serve.

Sicilian broad beans

Overall timing 1 hour plus optional cooling

Freezing Not suitable

To serve 4

¾ lb	Fresh broad or fava beans
¾ lb	Fresh peas
1	Small onion
2 tbsp	Oil
¼ cup	Water or broth
	Pinch of grated nutmeg
	Salt and pepper
4	Canned artichoke hearts
6	Leaves of fresh mint
½ tsp	Sugar
2 tsp	Vinegar

Shell beans and peas. Peel and chop onion. Heat oil in a saucepan and fry onion till transparent. Add beans, peas, water or broth, nutmeg and seasoning. Cover the pan and simmer gently for 10 minutes.

Drain artichokes and cut into eighths. Add to pan and continue cooking for 10 minutes. Stir in mint (some whole leaves, some chopped) and cook for 5 minutes more. Leave to cool slightly before serving.

If you wish to serve the dish cold, add sugar and vinegar with the mint. Stir well, then transfer to a serving dish and leave till cold. Chill for 15 minutes before serving.

Scalloped Chinese cabbage

Overall timing 45 minutes

Freezing Not suitable

To serve 4

2lb	Chinese cabbage (bok choy)
1	Onion
2½ cups	Milk
	Salt and pepper
1	Egg
2 tbsp	Chopped parsley
2 tbsp	Butter
1 cup	Grated cheese

Preheat the oven to 375°.

Trim stalk end of Chinese cabbage. Remove any damaged outer leaves, then separate remaining leaves. Rinse and drain.

Peel and slice the onion and put into a large saucepan with the milk and a little salt. Bring just to a boil, then add the Chinese cabbage. Cover and simmer for 5 minutes.

Lift the Chinese cabbage out of the milk with a slotted spoon and arrange in a shallow ovenproof dish. Beat the egg in a bowl with the parsley and gradually add the milk, beating constantly. Add pepper and the butter and stir till melted. Pour over the Chinese cabbage. Sprinkle the cheese over the top. Bake for about 30 minutes till golden. Serve immediately with brown bread rolls.

Spicy stuffed peppers

Overall timing 1 ¼ hours

Freezing Not suitable

To serve 4

8	Sweet green or red peppers
	Salt and pepper
1	Onion
2 tbsp	Oil
1 lb	Ground beef
2½ cups	Beef broth
¾ cup	Long grain rice
1 tsp	Grated nutmeg
1 tbsp	Brown sugar
½ cup	Grated cheese

Cut stalk ends off peppers and remove seeds and membrane. Blanch in boiling salted water 5 minutes, then drain. Arrange in a greased ovenproof dish.

Peel and chop onion and pepper lids. Heat oil in a saucepan and fry onion and pepper lids till just golden. Add beef and brown well. Stir in broth and bring to a boil. Add rice, nutmeg, sugar and seasoning and simmer for 15-20 minutes till rice is tender and has absorbed the liquid.

Remove from heat. Stir cheese into stuffing. Use to fill the peppers. Cover the dish with foil and bake for 20 minutes. Remove foil, bake for a further 10 minutes.

Stuffed baked turnips

Overall timing 1 ¼ hours

Freezing Not suitable

To serve 4

4 x ½ lb	White turnips
	Salt and pepper
1	Onion
2 tbsp	Butter
1 cup	Soft bread crumbs
½ lb	Sliced cooked ham
1	Egg yolk
½ cup	Chicken broth
¾ cup	Grated cheese

Preheat the oven to 375°.

Peel turnips. Cut off top third of each to make a lid. Scoop flesh out of base, leaving a thick shell, and chop flesh. Cook shells and lids in boiling salted water for 5 minutes, then drain.

Peel and chop onion. Melt butter in a saucepan, add onion and chopped turnip and fry till golden. Stir in bread crumbs. Reserve four slices of ham, chop rest and add to stuffing with seasoning and egg yolk.

Press stuffing into turnips. Place a slice of ham on each and cover with lids. Put in ovenproof dish. Pour broth over, cover and bake for 20 minutes.

Uncover turnips, sprinkle over cheese and bake for a further 10-15 minutes.

Vegetable Marrow Ratatouille

Overall timing 40 minutes

Freezing Suitable: add olives and Parmesan after reheating

To serve 2

1 lb	Vegetable marrow
	Salt and pepper
1	Onion
1	Garlic clove
2	Tomatoes
2 tbsp	Butter
1 tbsp	Oil
1 tbsp	Tomato paste
5 tbsp	Chicken broth
1 tsp	Chopped fresh marjoram
1 tsp	Chopped fresh basil
½ tsp	Chopped fresh thyme
6	Olives
2 tbsp	Grated Parmesan cheese

Peel vegetable marrow, cut in half lengthwise and scoop out seeds. Cut flesh into thick slices. Blanch in boiling salted water for 5 minutes. Drain well.

Peel and slice onion. Peel and crush garlic. Blanch, peel and chop tomatoes.

Heat butter and oil in skillet, add onion and garlic and cook for 5 minutes till transparent. Add vegetable marrow, tomatoes, tomato paste, chicken broth, herbs and seasoning. Simmer for 10-15 minutes till the vegetable marrow is just tender.

Add olives and sprinkle with grated Parmesan cheese. Serve hot with french bread, or as an accompaniment to broiled meats.

Spinach dumplings

Overall timing 40 minutes plus setting

Freezing Suitable: cook from frozen for 12-15 minutes, then add melted butter and cheese

To serve 6

2 lb	Bulk spinach
½	Chicken bouillon cube
5 tbsp	Warm milk
3 cups	Flour
3	Eggs
	Salt and pepper
½ cup	Butter
4 cups	Soft bread crumbs
¼ tsp	Grated nutmeg
1 tbsp	Chopped parsley
1 tbsp	Chopped chives
1 cup	Grated Swiss cheese

Wash spinach and put into a saucepan with only water that clings to it. Cover and cook for 5 minutes.

Dissolve bouillon cube in milk. Sift flour into a bowl, add eggs, milk and seasoning and mix to a soft dough.

Drain spinach thoroughly and chop finely. Melt half the butter in a skillet, add bread crumbs and fry till crisp and golden. Add to dough with nutmeg, parsley and chives. Add spinach and mix to a stiff dough.

Roll dough between floured hands into long sausage-shapes about ½ inch in diameter. Leave to set.

Cut across dough into 1 inch lengths. Cook in boiling salted water for about 10 minutes till they float to the surface.

Lift out dumplings with a slotted spoon, drain thoroughly and arrange in a warmed serving dish. Melt remaining butter, pour over dumplings and sprinkle with grated cheese. Toss lightly before serving with casseroles.

Spinach omelette

Overall timing 15 minutes

Freezing Not suitable

To serve 2

¼ cup	Butter
2 cups	Shredded spinach
	Salt and pepper
6	Eggs
2 tbsp	Light cream

Melt 3 tbsp butter in a saucepan, add spinach and seasoning, cover and cook over a low heat for about 5 minutes till a purée.

Lightly beat the eggs in a bowl with seasoning. Melt the remaining butter in a heavy skillet, add the egg mixture and cook gently till the omelette is lightly set.

Spread the spinach purée over half the omelette and spoon the cream over. Slide omelette out of the skillet on to a warmed serving dish, tilting the skillet so the omelette folds in half. Serve immediately with french fries and a salad.

Marseilles squash

Overall timing 45 minutes

Freezing Not suitable

To serve 6

1½ lb	Summer squash
	Salt and pepper
¾ lb	Ripe tomatoes
2	Large onions
3 tbsp	Olive oil
½ cup	Long grain rice
2½ cups	Water
1 tbsp	Chopped parsley

Blanch whole squash in boiling salted water for 10 minutes. Drain thoroughly. Cut in half lengthwise, then cut across each half into 1 inch thick slices, removing the seeds.

Blanch, peel and halve the tomatoes. Peel and slice the onions. Heat the oil in a flameproof casserole and fry onions till pale golden.

Add the rice to the casserole and fry, stirring, for 2 minutes till the oil is absorbed. Add the water, tomatoes, squash and seasoning. Bring to a boil, then cover and simmer gently for 15-20 minutes till rice is tender and most of the water has been absorbed.

Taste and adjust the seasoning, sprinkle with parsley and serve hot.

Sweet potato soufflé

Overall timing 1 ¼ hours

Freezing Not suitable

To serve 2

½ lb	Yam or sweet potatoes
½ cup	Milk
	Salt
2 tbsp	Butter
1 ½ tsp	Flour
2	Eggs
	Pinch of cayenne
½ cup	Grated cheese

Preheat the oven to 375°.

Peel the yam or sweet potato and cut into ½ inch cubes. Put into a saucepan with the milk and a little salt and bring to a boil. Cover and simmer for about 20 minutes till tender. Drain the yam or sweet potato, reserving the cooking liquid, then return it to the pan and mash over a low heat to make a dry, fluffy purée.

Melt the butter in a saucepan, add the flour and cook for 1 minute. Make the reserved cooking liquid up to ½ cup with extra milk if necessary and gradually add to the pan.

Bring to a boil, stirring constantly, and simmer for 2 minutes. Remove from the heat and allow to cool slightly. Separate the eggs and beat the yolks into the sauce with the cayenne, grated cheese, a little salt and the yam or potato purée. Beat the egg whites till stiff and fold into the sauce with a metal spoon.

Pour the mixture into a greased soufflé dish and bake for 30-35 minutes till well risen and golden. Serve immediately.

Mixed vegetables in milk

Peas bonne femme

Overall timing 35 minutes

Freezing Not suitable

Overall timing 45 minutes

Freezing Not suitable

To serve 4

1	Large potato
1	Bulb of celeriac
2	Carrots
1	White turnip
1	Small cauliflower
½ lb	Green beans
2 cups	Milk
¼ cup	Butter
	Salt and pepper
1 tbsp	Flour
¼ cup	Light cream

Peel and dice potato, celeriac, carrots and turnip. Divide cauliflower into small florets. Trim the beans, remove strings and chop.

Heat milk with half the butter and salt. Add potato, celeriac, carrots and turnip and cook for 10 minutes. Add cauliflower and beans and cook for a further 5 minutes. Drain vegetables, reserving milk.

Melt remaining butter in pan, stir in flour and cook for 1 minute. Gradually stir in reserved milk and simmer till thickened. Add vegetables and heat through. Remove from heat and stir in cream and seasoning to taste.

To serve 4

2 lb	Fresh peas
6	Small onions
1	Head Bibb lettuce
1	Thick bacon slice
6 tbsp	Butter
1 tbsp	Chopped parsley
½ tsp	Sugar
½ cup	Water
	Salt and pepper
1 tsp	Flour

Shell peas. Blanch onions in boiling water for 5 minutes, then peel. Shred lettuce. Chop bacon.

Melt ¼ cup butter in a saucepan and fry peas, onions, lettuce, parsley and bacon for 3 minutes, stirring. Add sugar, water and seasoning. Bring to a boil, cover and simmer for 15-20 minutes till peas and onions are tender.

Mix flour with remaining butter to a paste and add in small pieces to the vegetable mixture, stirring constantly. Cook for 3 minutes. Taste and adjust the seasoning and serve hot.

Stir-fried celery

Overall timing 15 minutes

Freezing Not suitable

To serve 4

1	Large head of celery
2 tsp	Salt
3 tbsp	Oil
2 tbsp	Soy sauce
½ tsp	Sugar

Cut off leaves from celery, then chop into 2 inch pieces. Sprinkle with salt.

Heat oil in skillet or wok. When oil is very hot, add the celery and stir-fry for 5 minutes. Add soy sauce and sugar, mix well and serve immediately.

Mushrooms in batter

Overall timing 30 minutes

Freezing Not suitable

To serve 2-4

¾lb	Large open mushrooms
1 cup + 2 tbsp	Flour
1 tsp	Salt
1	Egg
1 tbsp	Oil
¾ cup	Milk or water
2	Egg whites
	Oil for frying
	Sprigs of parsley

Trim the mushrooms, then toss in 2 tbsp of the flour.

Sift the remaining flour and salt into a bowl and make a well in the center. Add the egg and oil and begin to mix with a wooden spoon, drawing the flour into the liquid. Gradually stir in the milk or water to make a thick smooth batter. Add more liquid if necessary. Beat the egg whites in a bowl till stiff but not dry and fold gently into the batter.

Heat oil in a deep-fryer to 340°.

Spear a mushroom on a long skewer and dip into the batter. Using a second skewer, carefully push the mushroom off the first skewer into the oil. Fry the mushrooms, a few at a time, for 3-4 minutes till crisp and golden. Remove from the pan with a slotted spoon and drain on paper towels. Pile onto a warmed serving plate and garnish with sprigs of parsley.

Mushroom casserole

Overall timing 2½ hours

Freezing Not suitable

To serve 6

2 lb	Flat mushrooms
2 tbsp	Butter
1	Onion
1	Garlic clove
½ lb	Cooked ham
½ lb	Lean boneless pork
¼ lb	Slab bacon
4	Sprigs of parsley
2	Eggs
1 tbsp	Soft bread crumbs
	Salt and pepper
1 tbsp	Drippings
1 tbsp	Oil
1 tsp	Wine or cider vinegar

Preheat the oven to 325°.

Separate the mushroom stalks from the caps. Halve or quarter caps if large and reserve. Chop the stalks. Melt the butter in a saucepan, add the chopped mushroom stalks and fry over a high heat until all the liquid has evaporated. Remove pan from heat.

Peel and finely chop the onion and garlic. Grind the ham, pork, bacon and parsley. Add all these ingredients to the saucepan with the eggs, bread crumbs and generous seasoning. Mix well.

Heat the drippings and oil in a flameproof casserole. When hot, remove from heat and put in a layer of the ground mixture (don't pack tightly) followed by a layer of mushroom caps. Repeat until all the ingredients have been used up. Cover and bake for about 2 hours. Sprinkle with vinegar just before serving with a mixed salad.

Sweet-sour red cabbage

Overall timing 1 hour 20 minutes

Freezing Suitable

To serve 4

2 lb	Head red cabbage
4	Bacon slices
1	Onion
1	Tart apple
6	Whole allspice
½ tsp	Salt
2 tsp	Honey
6 tbsp	Red wine or wine vinegar

Discard any damaged outer leaves from the cabbage. Quarter, cut away core and thick ribs and shred leaves.

Chop bacon. Peel and chop onion. Cook bacon in flameproof casserole over a low heat until fat starts to run. Add onion and cook for 5 minutes, stirring.

Peel, core and chop apple and add to casserole with cabbage. Crush allspice and add to casserole with salt, honey and wine or vinegar. Mix well, then cover and simmer for 1 hour.

If there's too much liquid at the end of the cooking time, remove the lid and continue simmering. Serve hot.

Neapolitan beans

Overall timing 1 ½ hours plus soaking

Freezing Not suitable

To serve 6

½ cup	Dried navy beans
1	Stalk of celery
1	Carrot
1	Garlic clove
2 tbsp	Oil
2 tbsp	Chopped parsley
16 oz	Can of tomatoes
1 tbsp	Chopped fresh savory
	Salt and pepper
2 cups	Strong chicken broth
½ lb	Short macaroni

Put beans in a large pan and cover with plenty of cold water. Bring to a boil and boil for 2 minutes. Remove from heat, cover and leave to soak for 2 hours.

Drain beans well, then cover with boiling water and cook for 1 hour.

Chop celery. Peel and chop carrot. Peel and crush garlic. Heat oil in a saucepan, add celery, carrot, garlic and parsley and fry for 5 minutes.

Sieve tomatoes and juice and add to vegetables with savory and seasoning. Drain beans and purée two-thirds of them in a food processor or blender. Add bean purée, whole beans and broth to vegetables. Bring to a boil.

Add the macaroni and stir well. Cook for 15-20 minutes, stirring occasionally. Taste and adjust seasoning before serving.

Norwegian cauliflower

Overall timing 25 minutes

Freezing Not suitable

To serve 4

1	Cauliflower
	Salt and pepper
2 tbsp	Butter
1 cup	Soft white bread crumbs
1 cup	Milk
	Pinch of sugar
¼ lb	Shelled shrimp
1 tbsp	Brandy (optional)
3 tbsp	Light cream
	Sprigs of parsley

Remove any leaves from the cauliflower and trim the stalk. Put cauliflower into a saucepan containing 1½ inches of boiling salted water, cover and cook for 20 minutes.

Meanwhile, melt the butter in another pan, add bread crumbs and milk and cook for a few minutes, stirring. Add salt, pepper and sugar. Set aside a few shelled shrimp for the garnish and add the rest to the pan. Cook for 5 minutes more, stirring.

Remove pan from heat and add brandy, if used, and cream. Return to a gentle heat for 1 minute.

Drain cauliflower, place on a warmed serving dish and pour over sauce. Garnish with reserved shrimp and parsley.

Mushroom loaf

Overall timing 1 hour

Freezing Not suitable

To serve 4

1½ lb	Button mushrooms
3 tbsp	Butter
1 cup	White sauce
	Salt and pepper
	Grated nutmeg
3	Eggs

Preheat the oven to 350°.

Trim the mushrooms. Reserve four for decoration and finely chop the rest. Melt 2 tbsp butter in a saucepan and cook the chopped mushrooms for 5 minutes. Stir in the white sauce, then season with salt, pepper and a little grated nutmeg to taste.

Remove pan from heat and allow to cool slightly, then beat in the eggs one at a time. Pour the mixture into a greased 6 inch soufflé dish and bake for about 45 minutes till set.

Meanwhile, flute one of the reserved mushrooms and thinly slice the other three. Melt remaining butter in a saucepan and fry mushrooms till golden.

Unmold mushroom loaf and serve hot, garnished with fried mushrooms, on a bed of lettuce leaves.

Moravian mushrooms

Overall timing 30 minutes

Freezing Not suitable

To serve 6

1 ¼ lb	Button mushrooms
2 tbsp	Butter
½ tsp	Salt
1 tsp	Cumin seeds
1 tbsp	Finely chopped parsley
1 tbsp	Flour
1 tsp	Vinegar or lemon juice
½ cup	Milk
2 tbsp	Heavy cream

Trim and quarter the mushrooms.

Melt the butter in a saucepan and add the mushrooms, salt, cumin seeds and chopped parsley. Stir-fry over a high heat for 5 minutes, then stir in flour.

Gradually add vinegar or lemon juice and milk, stirring constantly. Lower the heat and simmer for 10 minutes, stirring frequently. Stir in cream and serve.

Bean cake

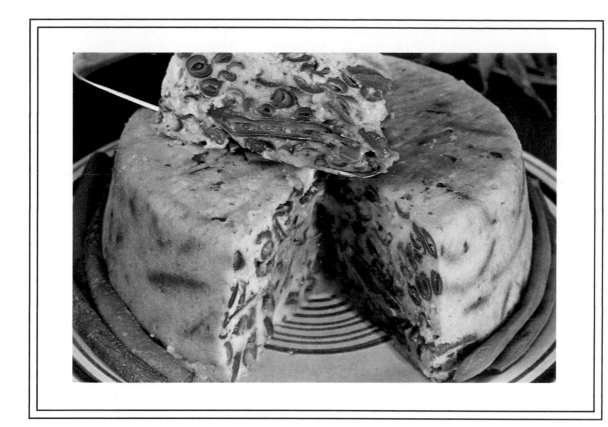

Overall timing 1 1/4-1 1/2 hours

Freezing Suitable: reheat after thawing in 300° oven for 30 minutes

To serve 4

1 lb	Green beans
	Salt and pepper
1	Celery stalk
6 tbsp	Butter
2 tbsp	Oil
1 tbsp	Chopped onion
1 tbsp	Chopped parsley
2 tbsp	Flour
1 cup	Milk
1 cup	Grated sharp cheese
2 tbsp	Crisp bread crumbs
3	Eggs

Preheat the oven to 425°.

Trim the beans. Blanch for 5 minutes in boiling salted water. Drain.

Chop celery. Melt 1/4 cup of the butter with the oil in a skillet and brown the onion, celery and chopped parsley. Add beans, cover and cook very gently for 10 minutes.

Meanwhile, melt the remaining butter in a saucepan. Stir in flour and cook for 2 minutes, then gradually stir in milk. Simmer until thick. Add cheese to sauce with seasoning.

Grease ovenproof dish and coat bottom and sides with bread crumbs. Drain bean mixture and mix it into sauce until well combined, then mix in lightly beaten eggs. Spoon mixture into dish. Place dish in roasting pan of water and bake for 25 minutes. Reduce heat to 400° and bake for 10 more minutes.

Remove dish from oven, leave to stand for 5 minutes, then invert onto a serving plate. Serve hot or cold.

Bean gratin

Overall timing 40 minutes

Freezing Not suitable

To serve 6

4 slices	Bread
	Milk
1	Garlic clove
1 tbsp	Chopped parsley
1 cup	Chopped leftover cooked lamb or beef
	Salt and pepper
2x16 oz	Cans of green beans
	or
1 lb	Cooked frozen beans
	or
1 ¼ lb	Cooked fresh beans
2 tbsp	Butter
2 tbsp	Flour
2 cups	Milk
¾ cup	Grated cheese
1	Egg

Preheat oven to 450°.

Soak the bread in a little milk. Squeeze out, then put through a grinder or food processor with the peeled garlic, parsley and meat. Season with salt and pepper.

If using canned beans, drain them. Fill a well-greased gratin dish with alternate layers of beans and meat mixture, finishing with a bean layer.

Melt butter in a saucepan. Stir in flour and cook for 1 minute, then gradually add milk. Bring to a boil, stirring until thickened. Add cheese to sauce. Cool slightly, then mix in beaten egg and seasoning.

Cover bean mixture in gratin dish with the sauce. Bake for about 10 minutes until the sauce is lightly browned.

Beans with egg sauce

Overall timing 25 minutes

Freezing Not suitable

To serve 6

1½ lb	Fresh green beans
	or
2x16 oz	Cans of whole or cut green beans
	Salt
6 tbsp	Butter
¼ cup	Soft bread crumbs
2 tbsp	Flour
	Nutmeg
1 tsp	Lemon juice
¼ tsp	Dried mixed herbs
3 tbsp	White wine or hard cider
2	Hard-cooked eggs
1 tsp	Chopped chives

If using fresh beans wash, trim them and remove strings. Break or cut into short lengths. Cook for 10-15 minutes in boiling salted water until tender. Drain, saving 1 cup of the cooking liquid, and put beans into a warmed serving dish. Heat canned beans in their liquid and use this, made up to required amount with water, for sauce.

Melt ¼ cup of the butter in a saucepan, add the bread crumbs and lightly brown. Sprinkle over beans and keep warm.

To make the sauce, melt the remaining butter in the saucepan then stir in the flour. Remove pan from heat and blend in the reserved cooking liquid. Stir sauce over a medium heat until it comes to a boil and thickens, then add pinches of salt and nutmeg, the lemon juice and mixed herbs.

Remove pan from heat and stir in wine or cider, chopped hard-cooked eggs and chives. Pour sauce over beans. Serve with lamb steaks and potato croquettes.

Boston baked beans

Baked stuffed onions

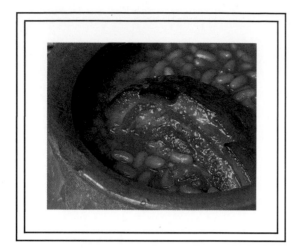

Overall timing 8 hours

Freezing Not suitable

Overall timing 1 ½ hours

Freezing Not suitable

To serve 6

1 lb	Dried white beans
2 tbsp	Molasses
⅓ cup	Brown sugar
2 tsp	Dijon-style mustard
½ tsp	White pepper
1 lb	Piece of salt pork

Soak the beans for 2 hours.

Preheat oven to 350°.

Drain the beans and cover them with fresh cold water. Bring to a boil and simmer for about 1½ hours. Drain and reserve 1 cup of the cooking liquid.

Add the molasses, sugar, mustard, pepper and reserved cooking liquid to the beans.

Cut two or three slices from the salt pork, and place these in the bottom of a heavy-based casserole. Pour in the bean mixture and top with the rest of the salt pork. Cover tightly and bake for 4½-5 hours or till the beans are tender and deep brown.

Use two forks, one in each hand, to shred the pork and mix it in with the beans. Serve hot.

To serve 6

6	Large white onions
⅓ cup	Long grain rice
	Salt and pepper
3 tbsp	Chopped parsley
2 tbsp	Butter

Peel the onions, then blanch in boiling water for 10 minutes. Drain and cool.

Meanwhile, cook the rice in boiling salted water for 20 minutes or until tender. Drain if necessary, then mix with the parsley, butter and seasoning.

Cut a thin slice from the tops of the onions, then hollow out the centers with a spoon. Fill with the rice mixture. Arrange the onions around a roast for the last 30-45 minutes of the cooking time, till tender.

Celeriac with onions

Overall timing 50 minutes

Freezing Not suitable

To serve 4-6

1½lb	Celeriac
	Salt and pepper
1 tbsp	Lemon juice
2	Medium-size onions
¼ cup	Butter
2 tbsp	Pork drippings or oil
2 tbsp	Flour
2 cups	Chicken broth

Peel celeriac and cut into ⅛ inch slices. Blanch in boiling salted water with the lemon juice for 5 minutes, then drain.

Peel and finely chop onions. Heat half the butter and all the drippings or oil in a large skillet. Add onions and celeriac and cook till onions are transparent, turning the celeriac over once with tongs — take care not to break up the fragile slices.

Tilt the pan, sprinkle the flour over the fat and stir. Add the broth and seasoning. Move the pan to distribute the liquids evenly, then cover and cook over a very low heat for 30 minutes.

Transfer celeriac to a warmed serving dish. Strain the cooking juices, stir in remaining butter and seasoning to taste and pour over the celeriac.

Sunshine salad

Overall timing 15 minutes plus chilling

Freezing Not suitable

To serve 2

½ lb	Poached smoked haddock (finnan haddie)
1	Orange
1	Grapefruit
1	Green pepper
1	Onion
1 tbsp	Chopped parsley
3 tbsp	Olive oil
1 tbsp	Lemon juice
	Salt and pepper
½ cup	Ripe olives

Cut the haddock into small strips. Peel orange and grapefruit and slice or chop the flesh. Seed and slice pepper. Peel onion and cut into thin rings.

Put prepared ingredients into salad bowl with the parsley. Add oil, lemon juice and seasoning. Toss salad well and chill. Garnish with olives just before serving.

Italian chickpea salad

Overall timing 15 minutes plus chilling time

Freezing Not suitable

To serve 4

2	Small onions
½ lb	Mozzarella cheese
2 cups	Cooked chickpeas (garbanzo beans)
1 tsp	Mustard
2 tbsp	Vinegar
	Salt and pepper
1 tbsp	Lemon juice
¼ cup	Oil
2	Hard-cooked eggs

Peel onions and cut into rings. Dice the Mozzarella. Put into a salad bowl with the cooked chickpeas, mustard, vinegar and seasoning. Sprinkle with the lemon juice and oil and mix well together.

Chill salad for 30 minutes, then serve garnished with hard-cooked eggs, cut into quarters or eighths.

Jamaican salad

Overall timing 30 minutes plus chilling

Freezing Not suitable

To serve 6

1	Garlic clove
1 tbsp	Vinegar
6 tbsp	Olive oil
1	Head of romaine lettuce
2	Bananas
1 tbsp	Lemon juice
3	Large tomatoes
1	Sweet green or yellow pepper
1	Fresh hot red chili pepper
¼ cup	Pitted green olives
	Salt and pepper
2	Hard-cooked eggs
¼ cup	Chopped almonds

Peel the garlic clove and cut in half. Put into a bowl with the vinegar and oil and leave to marinate for 30 minutes.

Divide the lettuce into leaves and wash and dry thorougly. Tear the leaves into bite-size pieces. Peel the bananas and cut into chunks, then toss in the lemon juice. Wash and slice the tomatoes. Wash, seed and slice the sweet pepper. Wash, seed and finely chop the chili pepper. Roughly chop the olives.

Remove the garlic from the vinegar and oil and rub around the inside of salad bowl. Discard garlic, then put prepared vegetables and bananas in bowl. Season the dressing, mix with a fork and pour over the salad. Toss lightly and chill for 30 minutes.

Shell and slice the eggs and arrange on top of the salad with the almonds just before serving.

Pepper salad

Overall timing 20 minutes

Freezing Not suitable

To serve 6

2	Large sweet red peppers
2	Large sweet green peppers
1	Small onion
¼ cup	Oil
2	Garlic cloves
	Salt
1 tsp	Ground cumin
2 tbsp	Lemon juice

Preheat the broiler.

Halve the peppers and seed them, then broil, cut sides down, until the skins are blackened. Rub off the charred skin, and cut peppers into thick strips or chunks. Peel and finely chop onion.

Heat the oil in a skillet, add the onion and the peeled and crushed garlic and cook till golden. Add peppers and fry gently for 10 minutes. Stir in the salt, cumin and lemon juice and cook for a further 5 minutes.

Serve hot as a vegetable or cold as a salad (chill for 30 minutes before serving).

French beet salad

Overall timing 30 minutes plus chilling

Freezing Not suitable

To serve 4

2	Cooked beets
3	Anchovy fillets
1	Garlic clove
1 tbsp	Chopped parsley
¼ cup	Olive oil
2 tbsp	Wine vinegar
	Pinch of salt
1	Small onion

Peel beets. Slice or cut into cubes and place in a salad bowl. Refrigerate for 15 minutes.

To make the dressing, chop anchovies and peel and crush garlic. Put them into a bowl with the parsley, oil, vinegar and salt. Mix together to combine the flavors.

Pour dressing over beets, mix well, and return bowl to refrigerator for 10 minutes. Garnish with onion rings.

Endive salad

Overall timing 15 minutes

Freezing Not suitable

To serve 4

3	Heads of Belgian endive
½ lb	Cheese
1 tbsp	Drained capers
1 tbsp	Dijon-style mustard
3 tbsp	Oil
1 tbsp	Lemon juice
	Salt and pepper

Trim the endive, removing any damaged outer leaves, cut off the base and remove the bitter core. Divide into leaves, wash and drain well. Shred lengthwise with a stainless steel knife and put into a bowl.

Dice the cheese. Add to the bowl with the capers. Mix the mustard, oil and lemon juice together with plenty of seasoning. Pour over the salad and toss lightly.

Variations

A more colorful salad with a very similar texture and flavor can be made by using shredded radicchio or red-leaved lettuce. Endive can be cut across the heads into rings instead of lengthwise for a different effect. Diced or shredded cooked meat will also add a touch of color, and extra protein if you want to serve this salad as a light lunch with bread.

Or, make an alternative dressing by mixing mayonnaise or plain yogurt with a little tomato paste and seasoning to taste with powdered mustard, sugar, salt and pepper.

Cucumber and pepper salad

Overall timing 25 minutes plus chilling

Freezing Not suitable

To serve 4

1	Cucumber
1	Sweet red pepper
1	Sweet green pepper
½ lb	Ripe tomatoes
2	Medium-size onions
1	Garlic clove
¼ cup	Oil
2 tbsp	Wine vinegar
½ tsp	Sugar
½ tsp	Paprika
	Salt and pepper
1 tbsp	Chopped parsley

Peel the cucumber, slice finely and put into a bowl. Wash, halve, seed and thinly slice the peppers and add to the bowl. Wash and slice the tomatoes; peel and thinly slice the onions into rings. Add to the cucumber and pepper.

Peel and crush the garlic into a bowl. Add the oil, vinegar, sugar, paprika and seasoning and mix well with a fork. Pour over the vegetables and chill for 30 minutes.

Arrange some of the cucumber slices around the edge of a shallow serving dish. Pile the salad in the center and sprinkle with parsley. Serve with broiled meat and boiled new potatoes or with a platter of cold cuts.

Coleslaw

Overall timing 20 minutes plus chilling and soaking

Freezing Not suitable

To serve 4

	White cabbage
	Brown sugar
	Grated carrot
	Grated apple
	Golden raisins
	Plain yogurt
	Mayonnaise
	Salt and pepper

Quarter the cabbage and core it, then soak in iced, lightly sugared water for 30 minutes.

Drain the cabbage well and shred it. Place in a bowl with the carrot, apple and golden raisins and mix together.

Make a dressing of equal parts of yogurt and mayonnaise and season to taste. Add to the cabbage mixture and fold together gently. Cover and chill for 30 minutes before serving.

Celery and cheese salad

Overall timing 10 minutes

Freezing Not suitable

To serve 4

2	Small celery hearts
¼ cup	Walnuts
Cheese dressing	
2 oz	Blue cheese
3 tbsp	Oil
1 tbsp	White wine vinegar
	Salt and pepper

Wash celery and leaves and drain well. Cut celery into matchsticks and put into a salad bowl. Reserve the leaves.

To make the dressing, crumble the cheese into another bowl and mix in the oil, vinegar and pepper. Taste and add a pinch of salt if necessary.

Pour dressing over celery and toss. Garnish with celery leaves and walnuts.

Camembert and pickle salad

Overall timing 15 minutes plus chilling

Freezing Not suitable

To serve 4

5 oz	Camembert cheese
1	Small onion
9 oz	Jar of mixed pickled vegetables
½	Sweet red pepper
	Sprigs of parsley
Dressing	
1 tbsp	Lemon juice
¼ tsp	Sugar
¼ tsp	Salt
	Hot pepper sauce
¼ cup	Oil

Cut Camembert into small cubes. Peel onion and cut into rings. Drain pickled vegetables, reserving 1 tbsp of the vinegar. Chop any large pieces of pickled vegetable. Seed and chop pepper. Mix all together in salad bowl.

To make dressing, beat together the reserved vinegar, lemon juice, sugar, salt, a few drops of chili sauce and the oil. Taste and adjust seasoning. Pour over salad and lightly mix in. Chill for 30 minutes. Serve garnished with parsley.

Artichoke and asparagus salad

Overall timing 15 minutes

Freezing Not suitable

To serve 4-6

8 oz	Can of artichoke hearts
8 oz	Can of asparagus (or use freshly cooked if available)
½ lb	Mushrooms
	Lettuce leaves
Dressing	
¼ cup	Oil
2 tbsp	Lemon juice
	Salt and pepper

Drain and slice the artichoke hearts. Drain and chop the asparagus. Wipe and thinly slice the mushrooms. Line a serving dish with lettuce leaves and arrange the artichokes hearts, asparagus and mushrooms on top, in separate piles.

Beat together the dressing ingredients and serve separately.

Sweet and sour corn salad

Overall timing 45 minutes including chilling

Freezing Not suitable

To serve 6

8 oz	Can of whole kernel corn
2 tbsp	Wine vinegar
3 tbsp	Oil
	Salt and pepper
1 lb	Cold boiled potatoes
½ lb	Tomatoes
8 oz	Can of pineapple chunks
2	Bananas
5 tbsp	Lemon juice
1	Small head lettuce
Dressing	
1 tbsp	Dijon-style mustard
½ cup	Sour cream or plain yogurt
2 tbsp	Milk
	Salt and pepper
1 tsp	Paprika

Drain corn and place in a bowl. Mix together vinegar, oil and seasoning and add to bowl. Mix well. Cover and chill.

Peel and dice potatoes. Slice tomatoes. Drain pineapple, reserving 2 tbsp of the juice. Peel and slice bananas. Put all these in a bowl and pour lemon juice over.

Mix together dressing ingredients with reserved pineapple juice. Add to potato mixture. Chill for 30 minutes.

Line serving dish with lettuce leaves and spoon potato mixture in a ring around the edge. Pile corn in the middle and serve.

Bacon and potato salad

Overall timing 55 minutes

Freezing Not suitable

To serve 6-8

2 lb	Medium-size waxy potatoes
	Salt and pepper
½ lb	Bacon slices
1	Large onion
¼ cup	White wine vinegar
¼ cup	Water
1 tsp	Powdered mustard
1 tbsp	Chopped chives

Scrub the potatoes, cover with cold salted water and bring to a boil. Cook for about 30 minutes till tender.

Meanwhile, dice the bacon and fry over a moderate heat till crisp and brown. Lift out of the pan with a slotted spoon and put into a warmed serving dish. Cover with foil to keep hot.

Drain the potatoes and cut into ½ inch thick slices. Add to the bacon and cover again.

Peel and roughly chop the onion, add to the bacon fat in the pan and fry over a moderate heat till golden. Add the vinegar, water, salt, pepper and mustard and bring to a boil.

Pour over the potatoes and bacon, turning them carefully till coated. Sprinkle with chives and serve immediately with fresh crusty bread.

Swiss salad

Overall timing 35 minutes

Freezing Not suitable

To serve 4

¾ lb	Boiled new potatoes
1	Apple
2 tbsp	White wine vinegar
1 tsp	Prepared mustard
¼ cup	Oil
	Salt and pepper
½	Head Bibb lettuce
6 oz	Gruyère cheese
4	Hard-cooked eggs
2 tsp	Chopped chives
1 tsp	Paprika

Peel and slice the potatoes into a bowl. Peel, core and slice the apple and toss it in the vinegar. Add to the potatoes.

Mix the mustard, oil and seasoning together in a bowl and pour over the potatoes and apple. Toss lightly.

Wash and dry the lettuce leaves and use to line salad bowl. Arrange the potato mixture on the lettuce.

Cut the cheese into matchsticks. Scatter the cheese around the edge, and in the center of the salad. Shell and slice the eggs and arrange on the salad. Sprinkle with the chives and paprika and serve immediately with crusty or whole wheat bread or rolls and butter.

Tropical salad

Overall timing 25 minutes plus cooling

Freezing Not suitable

To serve 2

½ cup	Long grain rice
1	Leek
½ lb	Cooked chicken meat
1	Small onion
¼ lb	Shelled shrimp
Dressing	
2 tbsp	Mango chutney
2 tbsp	Oil
2 tbsp	Lemon juice
1 tsp	Vinegar
½ tsp	Worcestershire sauce
½ tsp	Curry powder
	Salt and pepper
Garnish	
	Lettuce leaves
1	Banana

Put rice in a pan of boiling salted water and cook for 10 minutes.

Wash, trim and finely slice the leek. Add to the pan and cook for a further 5 minutes or until rice is cooked. Drain and leave to cool.

Slice cooked chicken into thin strips. Peel and finely slice the onion. Add both to the rice with the shrimp and mix.

To make the dressing, finely chop the mango chutney and put into a bowl with the oil, lemon juice, vinegar, Worcestershire sauce, curry powder and salt and pepper. Mix well.

Arrange rice mixture on top of lettuce leaves in a serving dish. Garnish with slices of banana and pour dresssing over.

Tuna salad

Overall timing 15 minutes

Freezing Not suitable

To serve 4

1	Bulb of fennel
	Salt and pepper
4	Tomatoes
7 oz	Can of tuna
3 tbsp	Oil
1 tbsp	Wine vinegar
	Chopped parsley
¼ cup	Ripe olives

Trim and slice the fennel. Blanch in boiling salted water for 5 minutes. Drain. Slice tomatoes. Drain tuna.

Place tuna in center of serving dish and arrange fennel and tomato slices around it.

In a bowl, mix together oil, vinegar and seasoning. Pour dressing over salad and sprinkle with chopped parsley. Garnish with ripe olives and fennel leaves, if available.

Apple and salami salad

Overall timing 40 minutes

Freezing Not suitable

To serve 4

3	Small onions
3	Apples
½ lb	Salami
2	Large gherkins
1 tbsp	Vinegar
1 tbsp	Lemon juice
3 tbsp	Oil
	Salt and pepper
	Pinch of sugar
¼ tsp	Celery or mustard seeds

Peel onions and cut into thin rings. Peel, core and chop apples. Dice salami and gherkins. Put them all in a salad bowl and mix well together.

Combine all remaining ingredients to make the dressing and pour over salad, mixing it in well. Leave for 20 minutes to blend the flavors before serving with crusty bread and butter.

Spinach and avocado salad

Overall timing 20 minutes plus cooling

Freezing Not suitable

To serve 6

½ lb	Bulk spinach
½	Head lettuce
1	Avocado
1 tbsp	Oil
1 tbsp	Lemon juice
	Salt and pepper
¼ cup	Thick mayonnaise
1	Hard-cooked egg

Trim spinach and wash thoroughly. Put into a pan with no extra water, cover and cook for 8-10 minutes till tender. Turn into a colander and press with wooden spoon to remove excess liquid. Leave to cool.

Wash, trim and dry lettuce. Reserve six medium-size leaves and finely shred the rest. Cut avocado in half and remove seed. Scoop out flesh and chop finely. Place in bowl with cooled spinach, shredded lettuce, oil and lemon juice. Mix together well and season to taste.

Arrange reserved lettuce leaves on serving plate and divide spinach mixture between them. Pipe or spoon mayonnaise on top. Cut hard-cooked egg into wedges and use to garnish.

Avocado and pine nut salad

Overall timing 15 minutes plus chilling

Freezing Not suitable

To serve 2

1	Large ripe avocado
1½ tsp	Lemon juice
2	Gherkins
1 tbsp	Pine nuts
1½ tbsp	Olive oil
	Salt and pepper
1	Garlic clove
4	Fresh mint leaves
2 tbsp	Plain yogurt

Cut the avocado in half and remove the seed. Peel away the skin, dice the flesh and put into a bowl. Sprinkle with lemon juice and toss lightly till the avocado is coated.

Slice the gherkins thinly and add to the avocado with the pine nuts. Sprinkle with oil, season and toss.

Peel and crush the garlic into a small bowl. Wash the mint leaves and shred finely. Add to the garlic with the yogurt and mix well. Pour over the avocado and toss lightly. Chill for 1 hour.

Divide salad between two individual dishes and serve immediately with crusty rolls.

Asparagus and potato salad

Overall timing 25 minutes plus chilling

Freezing Not suitable

To serve 4

1 lb	New potatoes
	Salt and pepper
1	Small onion
1 tbsp	Lemon juice
½ cup	Thick mayonnaise
12 oz	Can of asparagus spears or tips
1	Hard-cooked egg
4	Anchovy fillets
2 tsp	Drained capers

Scrape the potatoes and cut into even-sized chunks. Cook in boiling salted water for about 5 minutes till tender. Drain and place in a large bowl.

Peel the onion and chop finely. Stir gently into the potatoes with the lemon juice and plenty of seasoning. Add the mayonnaise and mix well.

Drain the asparagus (if using spears, cut into 2 inch lengths), and fold gently into the salad. Arrange in a serving dish.

Shell the hard-cooked egg and cut into quarters lengthwise. Arrange around the dish. Arrange anchovy fillets in a cross on the salad. Garnish with capers and chill for 30 minutes before serving with whole wheat or black bread.

Esau's salad

Overall timing 1 hour plus cooling

Freezing Not suitable

To serve 6

2 cups	Brown lentils
2 oz	Slab bacon
¼ cup	Oil
2	Frankfurters
1 tbsp	Vinegar
1 tsp	Prepared mustard
	Salt and pepper
1	Onion
1	Green pepper
2	Tomatoes
2	Hard-cooked eggs
1 tbsp	Chopped parsley or chives

Put lentils into a saucepan and add enough water just to cover. Bring to a boil, cover and simmer for about 1 hour till tender. Drain and leave to cool.

Cut bacon into strips. Heat 1 tbsp of the oil in a skillet, add bacon and cook until golden. Remove from pan and allow to cool.

Put frankfurters in a pan, cover with water and bring to a boil. Drain and leave to cool.

Meanwhile, beat together the rest of the oil, the vinegar, mustard and seasoning in a serving dish.

Peel and slice onion. Slice pepper. Put cooled lentils, bacon, onion and pepper into the dish with the dressing and mix well.

Cut tomatoes into wedges. Shell eggs and cut into wedges. Slice frankfurters. Arrange on top of lentil salad and sprinkle with parsley or chives. Serve with black bread.

Fennel and tomato salad

Overall timing 30 minutes

Freezing Not suitable

To serve 4

1	Large bulb of fennel
	Salt and pepper
1	Onion
4	Tomatoes
3 tbsp	Oil
1 tbsp	Wine vinegar or lemon juice

Trim fennel. Cut into thin slices and blanch in boiling salted water for 5 minutes. Drain. Peel onion and cut into rings. Slice tomatoes. Arrange fennel, onion and tomatoes in layers in salad bowl.

In another bowl, mix together oil, vinegar or lemon juice and seasoning. Pour over salad. Chill for 15 minutes before serving.

Fish and potato salad

Overall timing 25 minutes

Freezing Not suitable

To serve 4

1	Onion
1	Carrot
1	Stalk of celery
1 quart	Cold water
1	Slice of lemon
1 lb	Boneless white fish
1½ lb	Waxy potatoes
1 tbsp	Wine vinegar
½ tsp	Powdered mustard
¼ cup	Oil
2 tbsp	Chopped parsley
	Salt and pepper

Peel and halve the onion; scrape and halve the carrot. Wash, trim and halve the celery. Put into a saucepan with the water and slice of lemon and bring slowly to a boil.

Meanwhile, cut the fish into 2 inch pieces. Peel the potatoes and cut into ¼ inch thick slices. Add the fish and potatoes to the boiling court bouillon and bring almost back to the boiling point. Skim off any scum, reduce the heat, cover and poach for 8-10 minutes till the potatoes and fish are tender.

Drain the fish and potatoes carefully in a colander, discarding the other vegetables and lemon.

Put the wine vinegar, mustard and oil into a serving dish with the parsley and mix well. Add the fish and potatoes and toss lightly till coated. Taste and add seasoning if necessary. Serve while still warm with a crisp green salad.

Florida salad

Overall timing 20 minutes plus chilling

Freezing Not suitable

To serve 4

1	Fresh red chili pepper
3 tbsp	Olive oil
2 tsp	Vinegar
	Salt and pepper
4	Slices of fresh pineapple
	or
8 oz	Can of pineapple slices in natural juice
1	Sweet red pepper
1	Sweet yellow or green pepper
3	Medium-size bananas
1	Large avocado

Seed and finely chop the chili. Put into a bowl with the oil, vinegar and seasoning and mix well with a fork.

Peel and chop the fresh pineapple, or drain and chop the canned pineapple, and add to the bowl. Seed and chop the peppers and add to the bowl. Peel and slice the bananas. Halve the avocado, discard the seed, peel and cut into chunks. Add to the bowl with the bananas.

Toss the salad lightly and put into a serving dish. Chill for 30 minutes before serving with chicken or seafood.

Vegetable and herb salad

Overall timing 30 minutes

Freezing Not suitable

To serve 6

1 lb	Potatoes
	Salt and pepper
½ lb	Cauliflower
¼ lb	Green beans
1 cup	Frozen peas
¼ cup	Oil
2 tbsp	Vinegar
2 tbsp	Chopped fresh mixed herbs

Scrub the potatoes and cut into small chunks. Place in a saucepan, cover with water, add salt and bring to a boil. Boil gently for 2 minutes.

Divide cauliflower into florets. Add to the pan. Bring back to the boil. Cut beans into 1 inch lengths and add to pan with the peas. Simmer gently for 5 minutes or until the potatoes are tender.

Meanwhile, beat together the oil, vinegar, herbs and seasoning.

Drain the vegetables well and place in salad bowl. While still hot, pour dressing over the vegetables and toss well. Allow to cool before serving.

Egg and parsley mayonnaise

Overall timing 15 minutes plus chilling

Freezing Not suitable

To serve 4

8	Hard-cooked eggs
2	Scallions
3 tbsp	Chopped parsley
½ cup	Thick mayonnaise
½ cup	Sour cream
	Salt and pepper

Shell and slice the hard-cooked eggs. Trim the scallions and slice thinly. Arrange half the eggs in a shallow dish and sprinkle the scallions and 2 tbsp of the parsley over.

Mix together the mayonnaise and sour cream and add seasoning to taste. Spoon three-quarters of the mayonnaise mixture over the eggs. Arrange the remaining egg slices decoratively on top and spoon the rest of the mayonnaise between them.

Chill for 1 hour before serving. Sprinkle with the reserved parsley and serve with slices of crusty brown bread.

Walnut cabbage salad

Overall timing 30 minutes plus
maceration

Freezing Not suitable

To serve 4

½	Head red cabbage
¼ cup	Walnut or olive oil
2 tbsp	Lemon juice
2	Large oranges
1	Large apple
1	Banana
½ cup	Walnut halves
3 tbsp	Raisins

Shred the cabbage and toss with the oil and
lemon juice. Leave to macerate in the
refrigerator for 1 hour.

Peel the oranges and separate into sections.
Peel, core and chop the apple. Peel and
thickly slice the banana. Add the fruit to the
cabbage with the walnuts and raisins. Toss
together well, then serve.

Asparagus and ham salad

Overall timing 20 minutes plus chilling

Freezing Not suitable

To serve 4

12 oz	Can of asparagus spears
¼ lb	Cooked ham
4	Pineapple rings
	Lettuce leaves
½ cup	Mayonnaise
½ tsp	Brandy (optional)
2 tbsp	Lemon juice
	Pinch of cayenne
Garnish	
2	Tomatoes
2	Hard-cooked eggs
	Chopped parsley

Drain and chop asparagus and place in a mixing bowl. Dice ham. Chop the pineapple rings. Add both to asparagus and mix together well.

Place lettuce in the bottom of individual glasses. Divide asparagus mixture evenly between them.

Mix mayonnaise with brandy, if using, lemon juice and cayenne. Divide dressing equally between glasses. Garnish with sliced tomato, sliced hard-cooked egg and chopped parsley. Chill for 10 minutes before serving.

Caesar salad

Overall timing 15 minutes plus chilling

Freezing Not suitable

To serve 4

6 tbsp	Oil
2 tbsp	Vinegar
2	Garlic cloves
	Salt and pepper
½	Head romaine lettuce
4	Eggs
2	Slices of bread
½ cup	Crumbled Roquefort or grated Parmesan cheese
4	Anchovy fillets

Beat together ¼ cup of the oil, the vinegar, 1 peeled and crushed garlic clove and seasoning in a bowl. Cover and chill for 30 minutes.

Wash and dry lettuce. Tear leaves into pieces, put in a bowl and leave in the refrigerator to crisp.

Put eggs in a pan of cold water, bring to a boil and cook for 4-5 minutes. Drain and place in a bowl of cold water. Shell.

Rub bread slices all over with remaining halved garlic clove, then cut into 1 inch cubes. Fry in rest of oil till golden. Drain croûtons on paper towels.

Divide lettuce and croûtons between serving plates. Arrange eggs on top of lettuce, sprinkle over crumbled or grated cheese, then spoon dressing over. Garnish with rolled anchovy fillets and serve with crusty bread.

Carrot and cabbage slaw

Overall timing 15 minutes plus chilling

Freezing Not suitable

To serve 4

½ lb	Carrots
½ lb	Head white cabbage
¼ cup	Wine vinegar
¼ cup	Oil
½ tsp	Caraway seeds
¼ tsp	Sugar
	Salt and pepper
2 oz	Slab bacon
1	Large onion

Peel and grate carrots. Shred cabbage. In a salad bowl, mix together vinegar, 4 tbsp of the oil, caraway seeds, sugar and seasoning. Add carrots and cabbage and mix well. Cover the bowl and chill for 30 minutes.

Chop the bacon. Heat remaining oil in frying pan and fry bacon for 3 minutes till crisp. Peel and finely chop onion, saving a few rings for garnish. Add chopped onion to pan and fry for a few minutes.

Remove salad from refrigerator. Put the hot bacon and onion mixture on top and garnish with onion rings. Serve with roasts or cold meat.

Cauliflower mayonnaise

Overall timing 30 minutes plus chilling

Freezing Not suitable

To serve 4

1	Large cauliflower
	Salt and pepper
6 tbsp	Oil
2 tbsp	Lemon juice
3	Tomatoes
8	Lettuce leaves
½ cup	Thick mayonnaise

Divide cauliflower into large florets. Cook in boiling salted water for 5-10 minutes till just tender.

Meanwhile, put the oil, lemon juice and seasoning into a bowl and mix together with a fork.

Drain the cauliflower thoroughly and add to the dressing while still hot. Toss lightly, then chill for 1 hour.

Meanwhile, slice two of the tomatoes; cut the other in half in a zigzag pattern.

Arrange six lettuce leaves on a serving dish and pile the cauliflower on top. Shred the remaining lettuce and scatter over the cauliflower. Put a tomato half on top and arrange the tomato slices around the edge.

Pipe or spoon the mayonnaise into the tomato half and between florets. Serve immediately with cold cuts or smoked fish.

Chef's salad

Overall timing 20 minutes

Freezing Not suitable

To serve 4-6

1	Head Boston lettuce
2	Heads of radicchio
	or
¼	Head red cabbage
¼ lb	Cooked ham
3 oz	Gruyère or
	Swiss cheese
1	Small onion
2	Tomatoes
Dressing	
2 tbsp	Oil
1 tbsp	Wine vinegar
1 tsp	Dijon-style mustard or
	prepared English
	mustard
	Salt and pepper

Wash and dry lettuce. Line salad bowl with crisp whole leaves. Tear the rest into bite-size pieces and arrange on top.

Wash and dry radicchio and tear into pieces, or shred cabbage. Cut ham into ½ inch dice. Slice cheese, then cut into small strips. Peel and slice onion and separate into individual rings. Cut tomatoes into wedges. Arrange all the prepared ingredients on top of the lettuce.

Mix together the dressing ingredients and pour over the salad. Toss thoroughly but gently.

Tunisian tuna salad

Overall timing 25 minutes plus chilling

Freezing Not suitable

To serve 6

2	Green peppers
1	Small onion
2x7 oz	Cans of tuna in oil
	Olive oil
2 tsp	Red wine vinegar
1 tsp	Lemon juice
	Salt and pepper
1	Garlic clove
¼ lb	Gruyère or Cheddar cheese
¾ cup	Pitted green olives
1 lb	Large firm tomatoes

Seed the peppers and cut into thin strips. Peel the onion and slice thinly into rings.

Drain the oil from the tuna and put into a small bowl with enough olive oil to make it up to ¼ cup. Add the vinegar, lemon juice, seasoning and peeled and crushed garlic.

Flake the tuna; slice the cheese thickly, then cut into thin strips. Put into a large bowl with the onion, pepper and olives. Pour the dressing over and toss lightly till ingredients are evenly coated.

Wash and thinly slice the tomatoes and use to line the salad bowl. Arrange the tuna mixture on top, cover and chill for 30 minutes before serving.

Waldorf salad

Overall timing 15 minutes plus chilling

Freezing Not suitable

To serve 4

4	Stalks of celery
½ lb	Apples
1 tbsp	Lemon juice
	Salt and pepper
6 tbsp	Thick mayonnaise
½ cup	Chopped nuts

Chop celery. Peel, core and dice apples. Place in salad bowl with celery, lemon juice and a little salt. Chill for about 1 hour.

Remove from refrigerator and stir in mayonnaise, chopped nuts and seasoning to taste.

If serving this salad on a special occasion, divide mixture between hollowed-out apples that have been sprinkled with lemon juice. For a simpler, yet still effective presentation, serve on lettuce (shredded or leaves) in individual glass dishes and garnish with fine lemon slices.

Bean and herring salad

Overall timing 20 minutes plus chilling

Freezing Not suitable

To serve 2

½ lb	Green beans
	Salt and pepper
1 tbsp	Butter
2	Matjes herring fillets
2	Cooked potatoes
1	Onion
2 tbsp	Mayonnaise
2 tbsp	Plain yogurt
1 tsp	Lemon juice
	Sugar
	Chopped parsley

Trim the beans and remove strings. Cut into short lengths. Put the beans into a saucepan of boiling salted water, add butter and cook for 5 minutes till just tender.

Drain and leave to cool.

Slice the herrings and potatoes. Peel and finely chop the onion. Place in salad bowl and add herrings and potatoes. Lightly mix in beans.

Make the dressing by combining mayonnaise, yogurt, lemon juice and pepper and sugar to taste. Pour over the salad and chill for 1 hour. Serve garnished with chopped parsley.

Beet and apple salad

Overall timing 1 hour 40 minutes plus cooling

Freezing Not suitable

To serve 4-6

1¾ lb	Fresh beets
	Salt
¼ cup	Oil
2 tbsp	Wine vinegar or lemon juice
1 tsp	Sugar
½ lb	Apples
1	Onion

Wash beets, then cut off green tops. Take care not to pierce the skin when you are preparing beets or the color will boil out, leaving them a rather washed out pink. Place prepared beets in saucepan and cover with water. Add a little salt, cover and simmer for 1¼ hours over a low heat. Leave to cool.

Drain beets, cut off root and pull off skin. Slice with a mandolin or fluted grater. Dry slices and put them in layers in a salad bowl.

Mix together oil, wine vinegar or lemon juice and sugar and pour over beets. Chill for 2 hours.

Peel, core and chop apples. Peel and finely chop onion. Mix into beets and serve before the beets color the apple and onion.

Smoked trout and potato salad

Overall timing 30 minutes

Freezing Not suitable

To serve 4-6

3	Smoked trout
½ lb	Cold boiled potatoes
½ lb	Red apples
¼ cup	Olive oil
3 tbsp	Lemon juice
	Salt and pepper
2	Tomatoes
2	Hard-cooked eggs
	Sprig of dill or fennel

Slice trout along backbone. Skin and fillet. Break fish into large pieces and place in serving bowl.

Cut the potatoes into cubes and add to bowl. Core and dice apples. Add to fish and potatoes.

Mix the olive oil, lemon juice and seasoning together to make a dressing. Pour over the fish mixture. Toss carefully and leave for 15 minutes for the flavors to develop.

Wash tomatoes and cut into eighths. Shell and slice eggs and arrange with the tomatoes and herbs around the salad. Serve with hot, crusty bread.

Salade Béatrice

Overall timing 10 minutes plus chilling

Freezing Not suitable

To serve 4

1 lb	Cooked green beans
	Salt and pepper
3 tbsp	Oil
1 tbsp	White wine vinegar
2	Tomatoes
1	Bunch of watercress
1	Hard-cooked egg yolk

Break or cut the beans into short lengths and put into a salad bowl. Season, add oil and vinegar and mix together well. Chill for 15 minutes.

Cut tomatoes into quarters and arrange around the edge of the salad bowl with the watercress.

Just before serving, garnish with sieved or finely chopped egg yolk. Toss salad at the table.

Salade niçoise

Overall timing 25 minutes

Freezing Not suitable

To serve 4

1 lb	Waxy potatoes
	Salt and pepper
½ lb	Green beans
¾ cup	Large ripe olives
2 tbsp	Drained capers
1	Garlic clove
¼ cup	Olive oil
1 tbsp	Tarragon vinegar
1 tsp	Lemon juice
1 tbsp	Chopped parsley
1	Large firm tomato
6	Anchovy fillets

Peel and dice the potatoes. Cook in boiling salted water for about 5 minutes till just tender. Trim the beans and cut into 1 inch lengths. Cook in another pan of boiling salted water for 5 minutes till tender.

Drain the vegetables and rinse under cold water. Drain thoroughly and put into a salad bowl. Add half the olives and the capers.

Peel and crush the garlic clove into a bowl. Add the oil, vinegar, lemon juice, parsley and pepper to taste and mix well, then pour over vegetables. Toss lightly till evenly coated.

Cut the tomato into thin wedges. Arrange on the salad with the remaining olives. Cut the anchovies into strips and arrange in a lattice on top of the salad. Serve immediately with French bread.

Raw mushroom salad

Overall timing 20 minutes plus chilling

Freezing Not suitable

To serve 4

¾ lb	Button mushrooms
1 tsp	Lemon juice
1 tsp	Prepared mustard
2 tbsp	Light cream
2 tbsp	Oil
1½ tsp	White wine vinegar
	Salt and pepper
	Chopped parsley

Thinly slice the mushrooms. Put into a salad bowl and sprinkle with the lemon juice.

Mix together the mustard, cream, oil, vinegar and seasoning. Pour this dressing over the mushrooms and toss carefully. Sprinkle chopped parsley on top. Chill for 30 minutes before serving.

Spanish salad

Overall timing 45 minutes plus 1 hour refrigeration

Freezing Not suitable

To serve 4

½	Cucumber
	Salt and pepper
¾ lb	Potatoes
12 oz	Can of asparagus spears
1 cup	Mayonnaise
1 tbsp	Dijon-style mustard
½ tsp	Dried tarragon
½	Sweet red pepper

Peel and slice cucumber. Sprinkle with salt and chill for 1 hour.

Peel and dice potatoes, then cook in boiling salted water for 10 minutes. Drain and leave to cool.

Drain asparagus and dry spears on paper towels.

Mix together potatoes, mayonnaise, mustard, tarragon and seasoning and put into a shallow dish. Arrange asparagus on top like the spokes of a wheel. Drain cucumber slices and put one between each asparagus spear and one in the center. Seed and dice pepper and place on top of cucumber to add color.

Sausage and potato salad

Overall timing 25 minutes

Freezing Not suitable

To serve 2

¾ lb	Medium-size new potatoes
	Salt and pepper
1 tbsp	Dry white wine
4-6 oz	Cooked German spicy sausage
1½ tsp	Chopped parsley
½ tsp	Prepared mustard
2 tbsp	Oil
1½ tsp	Vinegar
	Sprigs of parsley

Scrub the potatoes, put into a saucepan, cover with cold salted water and bring to a boil. Simmer for about 15 minutes till tender. Drain and peel, then slice thickly and put into a serving dish. Sprinkle with the white wine.

Remove outer covering from the sausage and slice thickly. Add to the potatoes with the chopped parsley.

Mix the mustard, oil, pepper and vinegar together and pour over the salad. Toss gently. Garnish with sprigs of parsley and serve warm or cold.

Rice salad with anchovy dressing

Overall timing 40 minutes plus chilling

Freezing Not suitable

To serve 4

1 cup	Long grain rice
	Salt and pepper
1	Can of anchovy fillets
2	Large hard-cooked eggs
1 tsp	Powdered mustard
5 tbsp	Olive oil
1	Carrot
1	Small onion
1	Green chili pepper
1	Sweet red pepper
1	Small bulb of fennel
½ cup	Pitted ripe olives
1 tsp	Chopped chives

Cook rice in boiling salted water for 15 minutes till tender. Drain and rinse under cold water to cool.

Drain anchovies and reserve half for garnish. Put the rest into a mortar and pound to a paste with the pestle. Shell and finely chop eggs. Add to mortar with mustard and pound together, gradually adding oil a few drops at a time. Season.

Peel carrot and cut shallow grooves at intervals along its length. Slice thinly and place in large bowl with rice.

Peel and finely chop onion; thinly slice chili pepper; seed and slice pepper. Add these to the rice. Thinly slice fennel; chop fennel tops and add to salad. Toss lightly. Chill salad and dressing for 30 minutes.

Put salad into a serving dish and arrange reserved anchovies on top with olives and chives. Serve with dressing.

Greek salad

Overall timing 40 minutes including chilling

Freezing Not suitable

To serve 2

2	Large tomatoes
¼	Cucumber
1	Small onion
¼ cup	Ripe olives
8	Anchovy fillets
¼ lb	Feta cheese
Dressing	
3 tbsp	Olive oil
1 tbsp	Lemon juice
	Salt and pepper
	Pinch of dried marjoram

Quarter tomatoes. Slice cucumber. Peel onion and cut into rings. Pit olives (optional). Roll up anchovy fillets. Cut cheese into chunks. Place all these ingredients in a serving bowl or divide them between two serving dishes.

To make the dressing, mix the oil and lemon juice with a pinch of salt, pepper to taste and marjoram. Pour over salad, mix well and chill for another 30 minutes before serving.

Other cheeses may be used instead of feta, but the important thing is to use a crumbly white cheese with a slightly sour taste. As in the authentic Greek version, it will absorb all the flavour of the oil dressing.

Kipper salad

Overall timing 20 minutes

Freezing Not suitable

To serve 4

4	Kipper fillets
4	Cold boiled potatoes
1	Cooked beet
1 tbsp	Chopped onion
½ cup	Mayonnaise
	Sprigs of parsley

Place kippers upright in a jug, fill with boiling water and leave for 5 minutes. Drain, pat dry with paper towels, then chop into pieces. Cube potatoes and beet.

Put kippers, potatoes, beet and onion in a salad bowl. Mix well. Spoon mayonnaise over and garnish with parsley sprigs.

Israeli sweet-sour salad

Overall timing 20 minutes plus chilling

Freezing Not suitable

To serve 4

2 tbsp	Golden raisins
1 lb	Carrots
4	Oranges
2	Avocados
2 tbsp	Lemon juice
3 tbsp	Oil
1 tbsp	Wine or cider vinegar
	Salt and pepper
	Ground ginger

Put the raisins into a bowl, cover with warm water and leave to soak.

Peel carrots and grate into serving dish. Add the juice of two of the oranges and mix well. Peel remaining oranges and separate into sections.

Peel avocados and remove seeds. Cut flesh into chunks and sprinkle with lemon juice.

Drain raisins and add to serving dish with oranges and avocados.

In a small bowl, beat the oil and vinegar with a pinch each of salt, pepper and ground ginger. Pour over salad and toss. Chill for 15 minutes before serving.

Fruity celeriac salad

Tangy avocado salad

Overall timing 15 minutes plus chilling

Freezing Not suitable

Overall timing 15 minutes plus chilling

Freezing Not suitable

To serve 4

½ lb	Celeriac
2	Apples
1	Orange
2 tbsp	Lemon juice
2 oz	Cooked tongue
3 tbsp	Light cream
5 tbsp	Plain yogurt
½ tsp	Prepared strong mustard
	Pinch of sugar
	Salt and pepper

To serve 4-6

2	Avocados
2	Dill pickles
½ cup	Pine nuts
1	Small onion
2 tbsp	Oil
1 tbsp	Lemon juice
	Salt and pepper
2	Garlic cloves
1 tbsp	Chopped fresh mint
1 cup	Plain yogurt

Peel celeriac. Peel and core apples. Peel orange and roughly chop flesh. Grate celeriac and apples into a bowl, add orange and sprinkle with lemon juice. Cut tongue into thin strips and add to salad.

To make the dressing, mix together the cream, yogurt, mustard, sugar and seasoning. Add to salad, toss well and chill for 30 minutes before serving.

Halve avocados and remove seeds. Scoop out flesh and dice. Grate or chop pickles. Roughly chop pine nuts.

Peel and finely chop onion.

Put prepared ingredients into serving dish and stir in oil, lemon juice and seasoning.

Peel and crush garlic and put into a bowl with mint and yogurt. Beat lightly with a fork. Pour over salad and mix in well. Chill for 1 hour.

Russian salad

Overall timing 30 minutes

Freezing Not suitable

To serve 4

3	Medium-size potatoes
2	Carrots
¼ lb	Green beans
2	Stalks of celery
	Salt and pepper
1 cup	Frozen peas
2 tbsp	Capers
	Juice of ½ lemon
1 cup	Heavy cream
2	Hard-cooked eggs

Peel and dice potatoes and carrots. Trim beans and remove strings. Cut beans into small pieces. Trim and finely dice celery.

Place potatoes in boiling salted water and cook for 5 minutes. Remove with slotted spoon, place in colander and rinse under cold water. Add carrots to pan and cook for 5 minutes. Remove and rinse. Add beans, peas and celery to pan and cook for 4 minutes. Remove and rinse.

Drain cooled vegetables and place in bowl with capers. Add lemon juice and salt and pepper. Pour cream over and mix carefully. Pile salad onto a serving plate.

Shell and quarter eggs and arrange around the edge of the plate.

Tunisian mixed salad

Overall timing 25 minutes plus chilling

Freezing Not suitable

To serve 4

1½ lb	Cooked waxy potatoes
½ lb	Cooked carrots
3	Canned artichoke hearts
1½ cups	Cooked peas
2 tbsp	Drained capers
12	Pitted ripe olives
12	Pitted green olives
¼ cup	Olive oil
2 tbsp	Lemon juice
1 tbsp	Chopped parsley
¼ tsp	Ground coriander
	Salt and pepper

Dice the potatoes and carrots. Drain the artichokes and cut into quarters. Put all the vegetables into a serving dish with the capers and olives.

Beat the oil and lemon juice together with the parsley, coriander and plenty of seasoning. Pour the dressing over the salad and toss lightly. Chill for 30 minutes before serving with crusty bread.

Goat's cheese salad

Overall timing 15 minutes plus 1 hour chilling

Freezing Not suitable

To serve 4

¾ lb	Goat's cheese
	Salt and pepper
¼ cup	Olive oil
2 tbsp	Wine vinegar
4	Stalks of celery
⅔ cup	Walnut halves
	Fennel seed (optional)

Slice cheese and put into serving bowl. Grind black pepper over it. Beat 2 tbsp oil and 1 tbsp vinegar together and pour over cheese.

Chop celery. Add celery and nuts to bowl. Toss lightly.

Beat together the rest of the oil and vinegar and pour over. Sprinkle with salt and crushed fennel seed, if used, and chill for 1 hour. Serve with crusty French bread.

Gouda salad

Overall timing 15 minutes

Freezing Not suitable

To serve 4-6

Salad	
1	Head iceberg lettuce
2 oz	Corn salad or watercress
1	Head of Belgian endive
4	Tomatoes
1	Hard-cooked egg
1	Onion
½ cup	Ripe olives
¼ lb	Gouda cheese
Dressing	
2 tbsp	Oil
1 tbsp	Wine vinegar
1 tbsp	Chopped fresh mixed herbs
	or
1 tsp	Dried mixed herbs
	Salt and pepper

Trim and wash lettuce and corn salad or watercress. Dry thoroughly. Trim, wash and shred endive. Arrange lettuce leaves in salad bowl, scatter the endive over and arrange corn salad or watercress in the center.

Wipe and slice tomatoes. Shell and quarter hard-cooked egg. Peel and finely slice onion. Arrange on top of lettuce with the olives.

Cut cheese into thin matchstick strips. Sprinkle over top of salad.

To make dressing, put the oil, vinegar, herbs, salt and pepper into a bowl and mix well together. Pour over salad just before serving and toss.

Mimosa salad

Overall timing 15 minutes

Freezing Not suitable

To serve 4

3 tbsp	Light cream
1 tbsp	Lemon juice
	Salt and pepper
1	Head Bibb lettuce
1	Orange
¼ lb	Purple and green grapes
1	Banana
1	Hard-cooked egg yolk

In a salad bowl, mix together the cream, lemon juice and seasoning.

Wash and dry lettuce leaves. Peel the orange and cut into thin slices. Wash grapes. Peel and slice banana. Place the lettuce, orange, grapes and banana in salad bowl on top of dressing. Toss just before serving and garnish with sieved egg yolk.

Normandy salad

Overall timing 10 minutes plus chilling

Freezing Not suitable

To serve 4

1	Head Boston lettuce
2	Apples
½	Lemon
3 tbsp	Light cream
1 tbsp	Cider vinegar
	Grated nutmeg
	Salt and pepper
⅔ cup	Walnut halves

Wash and dry lettuce. Peel and core apples. Cut into thin rings. Rub cut surface of the lemon half over both sides of the apple rings to prevent browning. Place lettuce leaves and apple in a salad bowl and chill for 15 minutes.

Mix together the cream, cider vinegar, a pinch of grated nutmeg and seasoning in a small bowl. Just before serving, pour dressing over salad and toss. Garnish with walnut halves.

Pepper and cheese salad

Overall timing 30 minutes including cooling

Freezing Not suitable

To serve 4

4	Large sweet red and yellow peppers
½ cup	Olive oil
¼ cup	Grated Parmesan or sharp Cheddar cheese
1 tbsp	Dried bread crumbs
2 tbsp	Capers
	Pinch of dried marjoram or mint
	Sea-salt
1 tbsp	Vinegar

Preheat the broiler.

Halve peppers and place, rounded side up, under broiler. Cook for a few minutes till skins are charred, then peel. Cut in half again and remove seeds.

Heat oil in skillet and fry peppers gently for 7 minutes on each side. Arrange peppers in serving dish, alternating colors to achieve a spoked effect.

Sprinkle cheese over peppers with breadcrumbs, capers, marjoram or mint and sea-salt. Leave to cool slightly, then pour vinegar over. Serve immediately or cool and serve chilled.

Shrimp and endive salad

Overall timing 30 minutes plus chilling

Freezing Not suitable

To serve 4

2	Small heads of Belgian endive
3 tbsp	Lemon juice
4	Tomatoes
1	Fresh green chili pepper
½ lb	Shelled shrimp
1 tbsp	White wine vinegar
	Salt and pepper
½ cup	Cream cheese
3 tbsp	Plain yogurt
1	Garlic clove
¼ tsp	Powdered mustard
2 tbsp	Oil

Remove any wilted outside leaves from the endive, cut off the bases and scoop out the cores. Cut across into ½ inch thick slices. Put into a bowl, add 2 tbsp of the lemon juice and toss.

Blanch, peel and quarter the tomatoes. Seed and thinly slice the chili. Put into a salad bowl with the tomatoes, shrimp, vinegar and seasoning. Add the endive and toss together lightly.

Put the cheese and yogurt into a bowl and beat till smooth. Add the peeled and crushed garlic, mustard, oil and remaining lemon juice. Season to taste and trickle over the salad. Chill for 15 minutes.

Just before serving, toss salad lightly till ingredients are evenly coated.

Shrimp and egg salad

Overall timing 35 minutes

Freezing Not suitable

To serve 4-6

1	Lemon
¾ lb	Shelled shrimp
¼ teasp	Hot pepper sauce
	Salt and pepper
4-6	Hard-cooked eggs
½ cup	Thick mayonnaise
1 tsp	Tomato paste
½ tsp	Anchovy paste
	Lettuce leaves
½ cup	Ripe olives
¼ lb	Shrimp in shell

Cut lemon in half across the sections; reserve one half. Finely grate rind of the other and reserve. Squeeze juice into a bowl.

Add shelled shrimp to lemon juice with pepper sauce and seasoning. Leave to marinate for 15 minutes.

Meanwhile, shell eggs and cut in half lengthwise. Divide the mayonnaise between two bowls. Add tomato paste and anchovy paste to one and grated lemon rind to the other.

Put the yellow mayonnaise mixture into a pastry bag fitted with a star tube and pipe onto half the eggs. Pipe the pink mixture on to the remaining eggs.

Line a serving dish with lettuce leaves. Arrange the marinated shrimp in a circle in the center. Place eggs around the edge, alternating the colors, and garnish with the ripe olives.

Cut the remaining lemon half into a basket shape and place in center of the dish. Hang the whole unshelled shrimp on the lemon and serve immediately.

Endive and anchovy salad

Overall timing 15 minutes

Freezing Not suitable

To serve 4

4	Heads of Belgian endive
4	Anchovy fillets
2 tbsp	Lemon juice
½ tsp	Salt
2 tbsp	Chopped parsley
2	Hard-cooked egg yolks
Dressing	
1 tbsp	Wine or cider vinegar
1 tsp	Dijon-style mustard
	Salt and pepper
3 tbsp	Oil

Trim and chop endive. Drain and chop anchovy fillets. Place both in salad bowl. Add lemon juice and salt.

To make the dressing, mix together vinegar, mustard and seasoning in a small bowl. Gradually beat in oil until the dressing thickens.

Pour dressing over salad and toss. Sprinkle with chopped parsley and sieved or crumbled egg yolks.

Clam salad

Overall timing 1 hour 20 minutes

Freezing Not suitable

To serve 4

2 lb	Fresh clams
	Coarse salt
1	Small onion
½ cup	Dry white wine
1	Head lettuce
1 tbsp	Prepared strong mustard
3 tbsp	Oil
1 tbsp	Vinegar
1 tbsp	Chopped parsley or chives
	Salt and pepper

Scrub clams well under running cold water.

Add as much coarse salt to a bowl of water as will dissolve and place the clams in the water so that they open and release any sand or grit.

Remove clams from bowl, then rinse under cold running water and drain.

Peel and chop onion. Put into saucepan with wine and boil till wine begins to evaporate. Add clams and cook, stirring, for about 3 minutes till the shells open. Discard any that do not open. Strain the juice and reserve.

Line salad bowl with lettuce leaves. Remove clams from shells and pile them on the lettuce. Mix together the reserved strained juice, mustard, oil, vinegar, parsley or chives and seasoning. Pour over clams just before serving.

Crispy lettuce and cheese salad

Overall timing 15 minutes plus chilling

Freezing Not suitable

To serve 4-6

1	Large bulb of fennel
	Salt and pepper
1	Head Romaine lettuce
1	Onion
¼ cup	Oil
1 tbsp	Lemon juice
¾ cup	Grated Parmesan cheese
1 tbsp	Chopped parsley

Trim fennel. Cut into small pieces and blanch in boiling salted water for 2 minutes. Drain.

Wash and dry lettuce. Shred finely. Peel and thinly slice onion. Put into a salad bowl with blanched fennel and lettuce and mix well together. Chill for 15 minutes to crisp.

Meanwhile, beat the oil and lemon juice together in a small bowl. Add salt and lots of freshly-ground black pepper.

Add Parmesan and chopped parsley to salad bowl and pour dressing over. Toss and serve immediately.

This salad makes a good accompaniment to many Italian-style dishes incorporating pasta and tomato sauce.

Cucumber and cider salad

Overall timing 10 minutes plus 1 hour chilling

Freezing Not suitable

To serve 4

2	Cucumbers
½ cup	Hard cider
3 tbsp	Chopped parsley
1 tsp	Sugar
	Salt and pepper

Peel cucumbers. Cut them in half lengthwise and scoop out the seeds with a spoon. Thinly slice cucumbers and put into a bowl.

Mix together the cider, parsley, sugar and seasoning. Pour over the cucumber and chill for at least 1 hour. Toss gently before serving.

Cucumber and fruit salad

Overall timing 15 minutes

Freezing Not suitable

To serve 2

½	Cucumber
1	Orange
¼	Honeydew melon
½ cup	Purple grapes
	Sprigs of dill
Dressing	
3 tbsp	Sour cream
1½ tsp	Lemon juice
1 tbsp	Sugar
1 tbsp	Chopped fresh dill
	Salt and pepper

Thinly slice cucumber. Put into a bowl. Peel orange, remove seeds and cut flesh into pieces. Peel melon, remove seeds and cut flesh into thin slices. Add orange and melon to cucumber with grapes. Chill for 20 minutes.

To make the dressing, beat sour cream, lemon juice, sugar, dill and seasoning in a bowl.

Divide salad between two serving glasses and spoon a little of the dressing over each. Garnish with dill sprigs and keep in refrigerator till ready to serve.

Pears in chocolate sauce

Overall timing 40 minutes plus chilling

Freezing Not suitable

To serve 6

6	Firm pears
2 cups	Water
1 tbsp	Lemon juice
½ cup	Sugar
1	Vanilla bean
4 x 1 oz	Squares semisweet chocolate
1 tbsp	Butter
	Vanilla ice cream
	Crystallized violets (optional)

Peel the pears and remove the stalks. Put the water, lemon juice, sugar and vanilla bean into a saucepan and heat gently till the sugar dissolves. Bring the syrup to a boil, add the pears and simmer for about 15 minutes till just tender. Leave pears to cool in the syrup, then lift them out with a slotted spoon and chill for several hours. Reserve the syrup.

Break the chocolate into small pieces and put into the top of a double boiler with the butter. Place over simmering water and stir till melted. Remove from the heat and beat in 2 tbsp of the pear syrup.

Arrange the pears in a serving dish and place scoops of ice cream between them. Decorate with crystallized violets, if liked. Spoon the chocolate sauce over the pears and serve.

Spicy fruit purée

Overall timing 1 ½ hours plus
overnight maceration and cooling
Freezing Suitable

To serve 2

½ lb	Mixed dried fruit (figs, apricots, peaches, pears, prunes)
2½ cups	Water
6 tbsp	Sugar
1	Apple
1 tsp	Ground cinnamon
1 tbsp	Cornstarch

Put the dried fruit in a large bowl with three-quarters of the water and the sugar and leave to soak overnight.

Pit the prunes. Transfer fruit to a saucepan, add remaining water and bring to a boil. Cook over a low heat for about 15 minutes.

Peel, core and slice the apple and add with cinnamon to the pan. Cook for a further 45 minutes.

Drain fruit and return liquid to the pan. Process or blend to a purée, then return to the pan.

Mix cornstarch with 1 tbsp cold water in a bowl, then stir into fruit mixture. Bring to a boil and boil for 5 minutes, stirring, until thick. Remove from heat and allow to cool. Pour into two serving glasses and chill for 2 hours before serving.

Pears in red wine

Overall timing 1 ¼ hours plus chilling

Freezing Not suitable

To serve 8

1	Orange
1 cup	Sugar
1 cup	Red wine
1 cup	Water
2 inch	Cinnamon stick
8	Ripe pears

Preheat the oven to 350°.

Wash the orange and thinly pare away the rind with a potato peeler. Shred the rind finely and put into a deep, flameproof casserole. Add the sugar, wine and water and heat gently, stirring till the sugar dissolves. Add the cinnamon stick and boil for 2 minutes. Remove from the heat.

Peel the pears, leaving the stalks on, and stand them in the red wine syrup. Cover the dish with a large piece of foil, pushing the stalks through the foil to hold the pears upright.

Bake in the center of the oven for about 25 minutes, till the pears are tender. Remove from the syrup and arrange in a serving dish.

Boil the syrup rapidly till reduced by half. Remove the cinnamon stick and spoon the sauce over the pears. Leave to cool, then chill for 2-3 hours, basting the syrup over the pears occasionally.

Serve with whipped cream and ladyfingers.

Pineapple boat

Overall timing 40 minutes plus marination

Freezing Not suitable

To serve 4

1	Large ripe pineapple
¼ cup	Kirsch
¾ cup	Confectioners' sugar
3 cups	Strawberries
1	Orange
¼ cup	Heavy cream
1 tsp	Granulated sugar
	Vanilla
	Candied fruit peel

Halve the pineapple lengthwise. Cut out the pulp, keeping the shells intact with leaves. Discard the hard core and dice the pulp. Mix with the kirsch and confectioners' sugar and leave to marinate for 45 minutes.

Wash, dry and hull the strawberries. Marinate in the juice of the orange.

Whip the cream with the granulated sugar and a few drops of vanilla until stiff.

Mix most of the strawberries with the pineapple and pile into the pineapple shells. Pipe the whipped cream on top and decorate with the remaining strawberries and strips of candied fruit peel.

Oranges in caramel

Overall timing 30 minutes plus marination

Freezing Not suitable

To serve 4

4	Large onions
1 cup	Sugar
2	Cloves
1½ cups	Water
3 tbsp	Cointreau
4	Candied violets

Pare the rind from two oranges with a potato peeler. Shred rind into fine long strands and blanch in boiling water for 5 minutes. Drain and rinse in cold water, then dry on paper towels.

Put the sugar into a saucepan with the cloves and water and heat, stirring, till dissolved. Bring to a boil and boil rapidly, without stirring, till a golden caramel color.

Meanwhile, peel the remaining oranges, collecting any juice. Place all oranges in a flat-bottomed dish with shredded rind.

Remove caramel from the heat. Carefully add the Cointreau and any orange juice, and stir over a low heat to dissolve the caramel. Pour over the oranges and leave to marinate for 3 hours, turning the oranges in the caramel occasionally.

Arrange the oranges on individual serving plates and spoon the caramel over them. Pile the shredded rind onto the oranges and decorate each with candied violet, and an orange leaf, if desired. Serve with cream.

Liqueur fruit salad

Overall timing 15 minutes plus chilling

Freezing Suitable

To serve 4

2 lb	Mixed fresh fruit
1	Lemon
1	Orange
¼ cup	Sugar
3 tbsp	Orange liqueur

Wash and prepare fruit, cutting into small chunks as necessary, and put into a bowl.

Pare away a small strip of lemon and add to bowl. Squeeze juice from lemon and orange and add to fruit with the sugar and liqueur. Mix carefully without damaging the fruit. Cover and chill for 2-3 hours.

Remove lemon rind and serve with whipped cream and crisp cookies.

Rum and raisin cheesecake

Overall timing 1 hour 55 minutes plus chilling and cooling

Freezing Suitable

To serve 10-12

Base

1 cup	Flour
2	Egg yolks
¼ cup	Sugar
¼ tsp	Vanilla
	Pinch of salt
¼ cup	Softened butter

Filling

½ cup	Large raisins
½ cup	Rum
2 cups	Small curd cottage cheese
½ cup	Softened butter
½ cup	Sugar
½ cup	Grated rind of 1 lemon
4	Eggs

Preheat the oven to 400°. To make cheesecake base, put flour into a large bowl. Make a well in the center and add the egg yolks, sugar, vanilla and salt. Add the butter in pieces and quickly knead mixture together to make a dough. Wrap and chill for 30 minutes.

Roll out dough an use to line the bottom and sides of an 8-inch springform or loose-bottomed cake pan. Prick with a fork, then bake in center of the oven for 20 minutes.

Meanwhile, place raisins in pan with the rum. Bring to boiling point, remove from heat, cover and set aside to cool.

Push cheese through a sieve into a bowl. Add softened butter, sugar and lemon rind and beat till well combined. Add eggs and beat till creamy. Stir in cooled raisin mixture.

Remove base from oven. Reduce temperature to 350°. Pour cheese mixture into pan, smooth top and bake for 1 hour and 10 minutes. Cool in pan. Run lightly oiled knife around edges before releasing the spring. Serve chilled.

Lemon and grape cheesecake

Overall timing 45 minutes plus chilling

Freezing Suitable: open freeze cake and decorate after thawing

To serve 6

½ cup	Butter
2 tbsp	Light corn syrup
2 cups	Crushed graham crackers
Filling	
1 envelope	Unflavored gelatin
2 tbsp	Water
¾ cup	Cream cheese
¼ cup	Sugar
2	Eggs
1	Lemon
¾ cup	Plain yogurt
½ cup	Heavy cream
¼ lb	Seedless black and green grapes

Melt the butter and syrup in a pan, add the crushed graham crackers and stir until combined. Press into the bottom of a 7-inch loose-bottomed cake pan. Leave to cool.

Dissolve the gelatin in the water. Put the cream cheese and sugar in a bowl and beat till soft and creamy. Separate the eggs and add yolks to creamed mixture. Grate rind from lemon and squeeze out juice. Add both to bowl and beat well together. Trickle gelatin into bowl, stirring well. Mix in yogurt.

Whip cream until thick. In another bowl, beat egg whites till stiff but not dry. Fold cream and egg whites into cream cheese mixture. Spread mixture over graham cracker base and smooth surface. Chill in refrigerator till firm.

Remove cheesecake from pan and place on serving dish. Before serving decorate with rings of green and black grapes.

Kiwi and orange salad

Overall timing 15 minutes plus marination

Freezing Not suitable

To serve 4

4	Kiwi fruit
4	Large oranges
¼ cup	Orange juice
¼ cup	Sugar
1-2 tbsp	Orange liqueur (optional)

Peel and thinly slice the kiwis. Peel oranges, then remove pith and cut into segments. Put kiwis and orange in a bowl.

Mix together the orange juice, sugar and orange liqueur. Pour over fruit and leave for at least 1 hour in the refrigerator. Serve in chilled glass dishes with whipped cream and crisp cookies.

Baked alaska

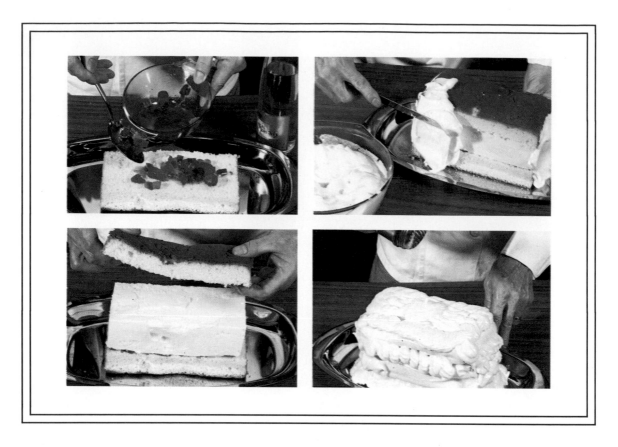

Overall timing 30 minutes plus 1 hour

Freezing Not suitable

To serve 6

½ cup	Chopped candied fruit
¼ cup	Kirsch or other liqueur
6	Egg whites
3 cups	Confectioners' sugar
	Pinch of cream of tartar
	Pinch of salt
1 tbsp	Lemon juice
1	Flat sponge or pound cake
1 pint	Block of vanilla ice cream

Put candied fruit and liqueur in a bowl and chill for 1 hour.

Preheat the oven to 475°.

Put egg whites, sifted confectioners' sugar, cream of tartar, salt and lemon juice in the top of a double boiler. Beat over a very gentle heat till meringue is stiff and dry.

Cut sponge cake into two layers. Place 1 layer on baking sheet. Spoon fruit and liqueur over, then put ice cream on top. Cover with the other sponge layer.

Working quickly, pipe or spread meringue all over cake, making sure all the ice cream is covered.

Dust with a little confectioners' sugar and bake for 5 minutes or until meringue is golden. Serve immediately.

Cold orange soufflé

Overall timing 50 minutes plus chilling

Freezing Not suitable

To serve 8-10

8	Eggs
1 cup	Sugar
2 tbsp	Grated orange rind
1 tbsp	Grated lemon rind
1 cup	Orange juice
	Pinch of salt
2 envelopes	Unflavored gelatin
¼ cup	Lemon juice
2½ cups	Heavy cream
	Orange segments
	Cherries

Separate the eggs. Place the yolks in a bowl with ¼ cup of the sugar, the rinds, orange juice and salt. Beat until the mixture is fluffy. Dissolve the gelatin in the lemon juice.

Place the egg yolk mixture over a pan of hot water and stir until it thickens enough to coat the back of the spoon. Stir in the gelatin, then allow to cool until beginning to thicken.

Whip the cream until thick. Beat the egg whites with the remaining sugar until stiff. Fold the cream and egg whites into the orange custard. Spoon into a large soufflé dish fitted with a paper collar. Chill until set.

Carefully remove the paper collar and decorate the top of the soufflé with orange segments and cherries.

Chocolate hearts

Overall timing 1 ½ hours

Freezing Not suitable

Makes 40

4 oz	Unsweetened or bittersweet chocolate
3	Egg whites
1 ½ cups	Sugar
3 cups	Ground almonds
½ tsp	Ground ginger
10 oz	Semisweet chocolate
1 tbsp	Coconut oil
5	Pieces of candied ginger

Preheat the oven to 300°. Grease baking sheets.

Finely grate unsweetened chocolate.

Beat egg whites in a bowl till stiff. Stir in sugar, ground almonds, grated chocolate and ground ginger.

Mix well, then knead with your hands. Sprinkle a cutting board with sugar and roll out the dough to about ¼ inch thickness. Cut out heart shapes. Knead trimmings, roll and cut out.

Place the hearts on baking sheets and bake in the center of the oven for 30 minutes. Remove from oven. Lift off baking sheets and place on wire rack to cool.

Break the semisweet chocolate into the top of a double boiler and melt over gently boiling water. Stir in the coconut oil. Remove from heat and allow to cool slightly but not set.

Put foil beneath wire rack (this way you can scrape up leftovers and add to bowl). Spoon a little chocolate onto flat side of each heart. Allow to cool (refrigerate if necessary), then turn hearts over and coat rounded side. If some are uneven, reheat chocolate and apply a second coat. Sprinkle hearts with chopped candied ginger.

Chilled peaches with raspberries

Overall timing 45 minutes plus chilling

Freezing Not suitable

To serve 6

6	Large peaches
1 cup	Sugar
2½ cups	Water
	Juice of 1 orange
3 cups	Raspberries
1 tbsp	Brandy (optional)

Plunge the peaches into boiling water, drain and remove the skins. Halve the peaches and remove the pits.

Put the sugar, water and orange juice into a large pan and stir over a gentle heat till sugar dissolves. Bring to a boil, add the peaches and poach for 5-10 minutes till tender. Lift out with a slotted spoon and place, hollow side down, in a serving dish. Leave to cool. Boil the poaching syrup steadily till reduced by half.

Meanwhile, hull the raspberries, reserving 1 cup for decoration. Remove syrup from heat and add remaining raspberries, squashing them gently with the back of a spoon. Stir in the brandy, if used, and leave to cool. Spoon over the peaches and chill for 2-3 hours in the refrigerator.

Decorate with the whole raspberries and serve with crisp cookies.

Cherry compote

Overall timing 2½ hours plus chilling

Freezing suitable

To serve 2

3 cups	Ripe cherries
¼ cup	Sugar
1	Small cinnamon stick
	Strip of lemon rind
5 tbsp	Red wine

Remove the pits from the cherries. Place cherries in a saucepan with the sugar. Stir gently and leave to marinate for 2 hours.

Add the cinnamon stick, lemon rind and wine and bring to a boil. Simmer for about 15 minutes, till cherries are just tender but not broken. Remove from the heat and allow to cool.

Discard the cinnamon stick and lemon rind and spoon the fruit and syrup into two dishes. Chill for 2 hours before serving.

Spicy pumpkin dessert

Overall timing 45 minutes plus chilling

Freezing Not suitable

To serve 6

14 oz	Can of pumpkin purée
¼ cup	Butter
1 cup	Milk
5 tbsp	Sugar
3	Eggs
½ tsp	Ground cinnamon
¼ tsp	Ground ginger
¼ tsp	Grated nutmeg
	Salt
½ cup	Whipping cream
	Glacé cherries
	Candied angelica

Preheat the oven to 350°.

Put the pumpkin purée into a bowl and beat in the melted butter, milk, sugar, eggs, spices and a pinch of salt. In a separate bowl, whip the cream till it forms soft peaks, and fold into the mixture.

Pour the mixture into a greased 1 quart mold and bake for about 30 minutes. Remove from the oven and leave to cool completely, then chill for 3-4 hours till firm.

Unmold the dessert onto a serving dish and decorate with glacé cherries and angelica. Serve with pouring cream.

Raspberries jubilee

Overall timing 10 minutes plus 2 hours maceration

Freezing Not suitable

To serve 6

¾ lb (3 cups)	Fresh or frozen raspberries
¼-½ cup	Sugar
3 tbsp	Lemon juice
	Vanilla ice cream
3 tbsp	Kirsch or brandy

Put raspberries, sugar (add according to taste) and lemon juice in a bowl and macerate for 2 hours in the refrigerator. Chill serving plate.

Transfer raspberries and soaking juices to a saucepan and heat through gently.

Remove ice cream from freezer and place on serving plate. Spoon raspberries and syrup over. Warm Kirsch or brandy in ladle. Set alight and pour over ice cream. Serve immediately.

Marbled ice cream with chocolate sauce

Overall timing 20 minutes

Freezing Not suitable

To serve 4-6

2 tsp	Cornstarch
1¼ cups	Cold milk
2x1 oz	Squares semi-sweet chocolate
2 tbsp	Sugar
½ tsp	Vanilla
	Chocolate and vanilla ice cream
4-6	Lady fingers

Blend the cornstarch in a bowl with a little milk. Put rest of milk in saucepan with the broken up chocolate. Heat slowly until the chocolate melts, then stir in cornstarch. Cook, stirring constantly, until the sauce comes to a boil and thickens. Stir in sugar and vanilla and cook, stirring, for 3 minutes more.

Unmold ice cream onto chilled serving plate and press lady fingers into the top. Pour some of the sauce over. Serve immediately with the remaining sauce.

Rum and almond pastry cake

Overall timing 2¼ hours

Freezing Suitable: refresh from frozen at 350° for 30 minutes

Serve 6-8

¾ lb	Frozen puff pastry
6 tbsp	Butter
6 tbsp	Sugar
2	Eggs
1 cup	Ground almonds
2 tbsp	Rum
1 tbsp	Confectioners' sugar

Thaw pastry. To make filling, cream butter with sugar till light and fluffy. Beat in one whole egg and one egg yolk, reserving white. Fold in the ground almonds and rum. Cover and chill for 40 minutes.

Roll out dough to ¼ inch thickness. Cut out two rounds, one 8 inch and the other 9 inch. Place smaller one on a dampened baking sheet. Place almond filling in a ball in center of dough round, leaving at least a 2 inch border all around. Brush edges with water.

Place second dough round on top and press edges together to seal. Using a knife, trim, then push up edges and crimp. Chill for 15 minutes.

Preheat the oven to 450°.

Brush pie with reserved beaten egg white. Leave for 1 minute, then brush again. Using the tip of a sharp knife, score top of pie to make a swirl pattern. Bake for 20 minutes, then reduce temperature to 400° and bake for a further 25 minutes, or until well risen and golden brown.

Remove from oven and increase heat to 475°. Sift icing sugar over pie and return to oven to bake for 4-5 minutes to glaze. Remove from baking sheet with a spatula and place on serving plate.

Strawberries and cream

Overall timing 15 minutes plus chilling

Freezing Not suitable

To serve 4

1 lb (3-4 cups)	Strawberries
1 cup	Heavy cream
¼ tsp	Vanilla
	Confectioners' sugar

Hull and wipe the strawberries. Divide between individual serving dishes and chill for 1 hour.

Whip the cream till stiff peaks form, then fold in the vanilla and sugar to taste. Pipe the cream on top of the strawberries and serve immediately.

Variation

Sprinkle the strawberries with fresh orange juice, or an orange liqueur such as Cointreau, before chilling.

Honey and lemon cheesecake

Overall timing 1 ¼ hours plus cooling

Freezing Suitable

To serve 12

½ lb	Rich pie pastry
2	Eggs
1 lb	Cottage cheese
6 tbsp	Thick honey
2	Lemons
⅔ cup	Golden raisins

Preheat the oven to 400°.

Roll out dough and use to line 8½ inch loose-bottomed cake pan, reserving any trimmings. Prick bottom. Bake blind for 10 minutes, then remove from oven and reduce temperature to 350°.

Separate the eggs. Put the yolks into a bowl with the cheese, honey and the grated rind of one of the lemons. Squeeze juice from both lemons and add to the bowl with the raisins. Mix well.

In another bowl, beat the egg whites to soft peaks and fold into the cheese mixture with a metal spoon. Pour into pastry case and smooth the surface.

Roll out dough trimmings and cut into thin strips with a pastry wheel. Arrange in a lattice pattern over the filling. Bake for 50-55 minutes till set. Cool in pan, then unmold and serve cold.

Strawberries Melba

Overall timing 15 minutes plus maceration

Freezing Not suitable

To serve 4-6

1 lb (3-4 cups)	Strawberries
1 cup	Raspberries
¼ cup	Sugar
2 tsp	Lemon juice
¼ cup	Slivered almonds

Hull the strawberries and pile in a serving dish.

Sieve the raspberries, then stir in the sugar and lemon juice until the sugar has dissolved. Pour over the strawberries and toss gently to coat. Leave to macerate for 1 hour.

Scatter the almonds over the top and serve.

Rum and apricot pudding cake

Overall timing 55 minutes

Freezing Not suitable

To serve 6

2½ cups	Milk
½ tsp	Vanilla
4	Eggs
4 tbsp	Sugar
2 cups	Crumbled sponge cake
2 tbsp	Rum
⅔ cup	Chopped candied fruits
2 tbsp	Butter
¾ cup	Apricot jam

Preheat the oven to 375°.

Put the milk and vanilla into a saucepan and bring to a boil. Meanwhile, separate the eggs. Add the sugar to the yolks and beat together with a fork. Pour the hot milk over the yolks, stirring constantly.

Put the sponge cake into a bowl. Strain the custard over the cake and mix in half the rum, the candied fruits and butter. Leave to cool.

Beat the egg whites till stiff. Fold into the crumb mixture with a metal spoon. Pour the mixture into a greased and lined 1 quart soufflé dish and smooth the top. Bake for about 35-40 minutes till well risen and golden.

Put the apricot jam into a saucepan with remaining rum and heat gently till melted.

Serve the cake hot from the dish, with the apricot sauce separately in a sauceboat. Or, leave the cake to cool completely and unmold onto a serving dish. Pour the hot apricot sauce on top and serve immediately.

Sherry trifle

Overall timing 1 ½ hours including chilling time

Freezing Not suitable

To serve 6-8

2½ cups	Milk
3 tbsp	Imported custard powder
2 tbsp	Sugar
6 slices	Sponge cake
2 tbsp	Raspberry jam
1 lb 13 oz	Can of sliced peaches
6 tbsp	Sherry
½ cup	Heavy or whipping cream
¼ cup	Toasted split almonds

Blend 6 tbsp of the milk with the custard powder and sugar. Bring remaining milk to a boil, then pour onto powder and stir well. Return to pan and bring back to a boil, stirring continuously until thickened. Put to one side to cool, covering surface with wet wax paper to prevent a skin forming.

Cut sponge into small pieces and spread with jam. Arrange around the bottom and sides of serving dish.

Drain peaches. Mix 3 tbsp of syrup from can with the sherry and sprinkle over the sponge. Reserve a few peaches for decoration and arrange the rest on top of sponge.

Remove wax paper and beat cooled custard well. Pour over fruit and chill for 1 hour.

Whip cream until stiff, then pipe onto trifle. Decorate with reserved peaches and sprinkle with toasted almonds.

Lemon sherbet

Overall timing 20 minutes plus freezing

Freezing See method

To serve 6

1 cup	Sugar
2½ cups	Water
½ cup	Fresh lemon juice
1	Egg white

Put the sugar and water in a pan and heat slowly, stirring until sugar dissolves. Bring to a boil and simmer for 10 minutes without stirring — do not let the syrup color. Remove from heat and leave to cool.

Add lemon juice to syrup, then strain into freezer tray and freeze until mushy.

Remove mixture from freezer, turn into a bowl and beat well to break down crystals. Beat egg white till soft peaks form. Fold into frozen mixture. Return to freezer tray and freeze till firm.

Plum crumb pudding

Overall timing 1 ½ hours plus chilling

Freezing Not suitable

To serve 8

2 cups	Crumbled sponge cake
3	Eggs
¼ cup	Sugar
2½ cups	Milk
2 tbsp	Butter
	Grated rind of 1 lemon
½ tsp	Ground cinnamon
1 lb	Red plums

Preheat oven to 350°. Grease and base-line a 9 inch springform pan.

Put the cake into a bowl. Separate two of the eggs, putting the yolks and remaining whole egg into a bowl with the sugar. Put the milk and butter into a saucepan and bring almost to a boil.

Beat the yolks and sugar together and pour the milk onto them, stirring constantly. Strain over the cake crumbs. Add the lemon rind and cinnamon, mix well and leave to stand for 15 minutes.

Meanwhile, wash and halve the plums, discarding the pits. Dry thoroughly on paper towels.

Beat the 2 egg whites in a large bowl till stiff but not dry and fold into the crumb mixture with a metal spoon. Pour the mixture into the pan.

Arrange the plums cut sides down on the mixture and bake for about 50 minutes till set.

Remove from the oven and leave to cool in the pan, then chill for 3-4 hours. Remove pudding from pan and place on a serving dish. Serve cut into slices, with pouring cream.

Loganberry gelatin ring

Overall timing 25 minutes plus chilling

Freezing Suitable

To serve 6

16 oz	Can of loganberries
1	Package raspberry-flavored gelatin
½ cup	Whipping cream
	Langue de chat cookies

Drain loganberries, reserving syrup, and press through a sieve. Make up gelatin, using loganberry syrup as part of the required amount of liquid. Stir in sieved fruit and leave to cool and set slightly.

Whip cream and fold into berry mixture, then pour into dampened 3 cup ring mold. Chill till firm (2-4 hours). Chill serving plate at the same time.

Dip the mold in hot water to loosen, turn out onto chilled serving plate and arrange cookies in center of ring just before serving.

Chocolate mousse

Overall timing 15 minutes plus 3 hours chilling

Freezing Not suitable

To serve 4

1	Orange
4 x 1 oz	Squares semisweet chocolate
2 tbsp	Butter
4	Eggs
	Pinch of salt

Grate the orange rind finely, being careful not to remove any pith. Break the chocolate into pieces and melt in the top of a double boiler over gently simmering water. Immediately the chocolate has melted pour into a heavy-based pan and add the butter and orange rind.

Separate the eggs. Add the yolks to the chocolate, stirring vigorously with a wooden spoon to prevent the mixture from boiling. Remove from heat. Cool.

Add pinch of salt to egg whites and beat till stiff peaks form. Fold one or two spoonfuls into the chocolate mixture, to make it more liquid, then gently fold in the rest of the whites with a spatula or metal spoon. Take care not to let the mixture become flat and heavy.

Pour into a serving bowl and chill for 3 hours before serving.

Black currant sorbet

Overall timing 4½ hours including refrigeration

Freezing See method

To serve 8

2 lbs (4 pints)	Black currants or blueberries
	Black currant cordial or liqueur
1 cup	Sugar
2	Egg whites

Reserve a handful of black currants, and put the rest through a food mill or sieve to make a purée. Measure the purée — you should have about 2½ cups. Top up with blackcurrant cordial or liqueur and/or water if necessary.

Add the sugar to the purée and mix well to dissolve sugar. Pour into a freezer tray and freeze for about 2 hours till mushy.

Beat the egg whites till stiff. Turn black currant mixture into a bowl, mash lightly with a fork, then fold in the beaten egg whites, stirring to distribute evenly through purée. Turn into lightly oiled or dampened shallow container or 1 quart mold. Freeze for 2 hours till firmly set.

Immerse mold in hot water up to the rim, then quickly unmold sorbet onto a serving dish. Decorate sorbet with remaining black currants, and allow to soften at room temperature for 20 minutes before serving.

Candied fruit bombe

Overall timing 15 minutes plus maceration and freezing

Freezing See method

To serve 6-8

⅔ cup	Chopped candied fruit
¼ cup	Apricot brandy or sweet sherry wine
1 quart	Vanilla ice cream
¾ cup	Apricot jam

Put a 9 x 5 x 3 inch loaf pan in the freezer. Place fruit in a bowl, add apricot brandy or sherry and leave to macerate for 30 minutes.

Put softened ice cream into a bowl, add fruit and liqueur and quickly mix well with a wooden spoon.

Remove pan from freezer and coat bottom and sides with a thick layer of the ice cream mixture. Spoon jam into the center of the pan, then cover with remaining ice cream. Smooth surface with a dampened knife.

Freeze for at least 2 hours. Unmold and cut into slices to serve.

Coffee charlotte

Overall timing 50 minutes plus chilling

Freezing Suitable

To serve 8

2 tbsp	Brandy
30	Ladyfingers
10 tbsp	Sugar
½ cup	Strong black coffee
2 tsp	Unflavored gelatin
4	Egg yolks
2 tbsp	Vanilla sugar
1 cup	Heavy cream
16	Sugar coffee beans

Mix brandy with ½ cup water in a shallow dish. Dip ladyfingers quickly in mixture to moisten them, then use them to line sides of greased 10 inch springform pan. Place cookies upright, sugared sides against pan, and trim ends to height of pan. Press lightly into place.

Put sugar and 3 tbsp water in heavy-based saucepan. Stir to dissolve sugar, then heat until golden brown. Stir in coffee and simmer for 2 minutes till caramel dissolves. Cool.

Dissolve gelatin in 2 tbsp cold water.

Put egg yolks and vanilla sugar in a bowl over a pan of hot water and beat together till light and foamy. Stir coffee caramel into egg mixture and beat till it starts to thicken. Stir in gelatin, then leave to cool until just on the point of setting.

Whip two-thirds of the cream until it holds soft peaks. Using a metal spoon, fold lightly into coffee mixture. Pour into center of ladyfinger-lined pan and chill till set.

Unclip pan and carefully transfer charlotte to a serving plate. Whip remaining cream until it holds stiff peaks. Pipe 16 rosettes around edge of charlotte. Place a coffee bean on top of each one. Pipe smaller rosettes around base.

Strawberry vacherin

Overall timing 2¼ hours plus cooling

Freezing Not suitable

To serve 8

6	Egg whites
1½ cups	Sugar
1 lb (3-4 cups)	Strawberries
Crème Chantilly	
1 cup	Heavy cream
1 tbsp	Cold milk
1	Ice cube
1 tbsp	Sugar
¼ tsp	Vanilla

Preheat the oven to 300°.

Line two baking sheets with non-stick paper. Draw a 10 inch square on one, and a 6 inch square on the other.

Beat egg whites till stiff and dry. Sprinkle over 2 tbsp of the sugar and beat in, then gradually beat in remaining sugar to make a stiff, glossy meringue.

Using the marked squares as a guide, put large spoonfuls of meringue onto paper to make two squares with scalloped edges. Swirl into peaks. Place large square in center of oven with small square below. Bake for about 1¼ hours till slightly browned and crisp. Cool.

Meanwhile, hull strawberries. To make the Crème Chantilly, whip cream with milk, ice cube, sugar and vanilla till it forms soft peaks. Chill till required.

Just before serving, carefully peel the paper from the meringue squares and place the large one on a flat board or serving dish. Spread or pipe two-thirds of the Crème Chantilly over and arrange two-thirds of the strawberries on top. Place the small meringue square on top and spread with the remaining crème. Decorate with remaining strawberries and serve immediately.

Champagne sorbet

Overall timing 20 minutes plus freezing

Freezing See method

To serve 6

1 cup	Sugar
2½ cups	Water
½ cup	Champagne or dry hard cider
1 tbsp	Lemon juice
2	Egg whites

Put the sugar and water in a pan and heat gently, stirring until sugar dissolves. Bring to a boil and simmer for 10 minutes without stirring. Do not let the mixture color. Remove from the heat and cool.

Add the champagne or cider and lemon juice to the syrup, then pour into a 1 quart freezer tray. Freeze till mushy. Remove mixture from freezer, turn into a bowl and beat well to break down any ice crystals. Beat the egg whites until stiff and fold into the mixture. Return to the freezer tray and freeze till firm.

Strawberry milk ring

Overall timing 30 minutes plus setting

Freezing Not suitable

To serve 6

1	Lemon
5 tsp	Unflavored gelatin
5 tbsp	Sugar
1	Large can of evaporated milk
1 cup	Buttermilk
	Pink food coloring
1	Egg white
½ cup	Heavy cream
1 lb (3-4 cups)	Fresh strawberries

Grate the rind from the lemon and reserve. Squeeze out the juice and place in a small bowl. Sprinkle the gelatin over and dissolve. Stir in the sugar. Allow to cool slightly.

Pour the well-chilled evaporated milk into a large bowl and beat till very thick and foamy. Beat in the buttermilk, gelatin mixture, reserved lemon rind and a few drops of food coloring. Pour into a dampened 1-quart ring mold and chill for 3-4 hours till set.

Dip the mold up to the rim in hot water for a few seconds and unmold onto a serving plate.

Beat the egg white till stiff. Whip the cream till stiff and fold into the beaten egg white. Hull the strawberries and pile half in the center of the ring. Pipe the cream mixture on top and around the base of the ring. Decorate with the remaining strawberries and serve immediately.

Crème caramel

Overall timing 45 minutes

Freezing Not suitable

To serve 6

2½ cups	Milk
½	Vanilla bean
1	Piece lemon rind
4	Eggs
½ cup	Sugar

Preheat the oven to 350°.

Put the milk, vanilla bean and lemon rind in a saucepan and bring to a boil. Remove from heat and lift out the vanilla bean and lemon rind.

In a bowl, beat eggs with half the sugar and gradually pour in the hot milk, stirring constantly.

Melt the remaining sugar in a saucepan over a moderate heat till golden brown. Divide between six small molds and turn them so the caramel coats the bottoms and sides.

Strain the custard mixture into the molds and place them in a roasting pan half-filled with hot water. Bake for 45 minutes till set. Allow to cool in molds and chill before unmolding.

Blackberry special

Overall timing 4 hours including chilling but not cooling

Freezing Not suitable

To serve 6-8

1½ cups	Flour
2	Egg yolks
6 tbsp	Sugar
6 tbsp	Butter
¼ tsp	Salt
Filling	
1 lb	Blackberries
⅓ cup	Chopped mixed candied peel
3	Egg whites
¾ cup	Sugar
1½ cups	Ground almonds
1 tsp	Grated lemon rind
¼ tsp	Ground cinnamon
½ cup	Flaked almonds

Sift flour into a mixing bowl. Add egg yolks, sugar, small flakes of butter and salt. Mix to a pliable dough. Add a little water if necessary. Chill for 2 hours.

Preheat the oven to 375°.

Roll out dough and use to line 9 inch tart ring on a baking sheet. Bake blind for 15 minutes.

Remove pastry case from oven and reduce heat to 300°. Add blackberries to pastry case and sprinkle with peel.

Beat egg whites until very stiff. Fold in sugar followed by ground almonds, lemon rind and cinnamon. Put a quarter of the mixture in a pastry bag fitting with a large rose tube. Spread the remainder over blackberries. Sprinkle edges of tart with flaked almonds and decorate the top with swirls of piped egg white mixture.

Bake for 1 hour 10 minutes. Remove from oven and cut flan into wedges before it cools. When cold, remove tart ring and serve.

Caramel cornmeal mold

Overall timing 1 hour

Freezing Not suitable

To serve 6-8

2 cups	Milk
	Pinch of salt
½ cup	Sugar
1	Bay leaf
18	Sugar cubes
½ cup	Warm water
1 tbsp	Lemon juice
5	Eggs
⅔ cup	Fine cornmeal

Preheat the oven to 400°.

Put the milk in a saucepan with the salt, sugar and bay leaf. Bring to a boil. Remove from the heat, cover and leave to infuse for 10 minutes.

Put the sugar cubes, water and lemon juice into a small saucepan and heat gently, stirring, till sugar dissolves. Bring to a boil and boil without stirring till a deep golden caramel color. Watch pan carefully to see that caramel does not burn. Pour into an 8 inch round deep cake pan, turning it so that the bottom and sides are coated with the caramel.

Separate the eggs. Put the egg yolks and cornmeal into a bowl and mix together with a wooden spoon. Remove bay leaf from the milk. Gradually pour the hot milk onto the egg yolks, stirring continuously. Beat the egg whites till stiff and fold into the mixture.

Pour the mixture into the prepared pan and place in a roasting pan containing 1 inch hot water. Bake for 35-40 minutes. While still warm, run knife around edge of pan and unmold onto serving plate. Serve warm or cold, with pouring cream.

Cider and grape ring

Overall timing 15 minutes plus setting

Freezing Not suitable

To serve 4-6

2½ cups	Medium-sweet hard cider
1 tbsp	Unflavored gelatin
1 tbsp	Lemon juice
½ lb	Green grapes
½ lb	Purple grapes
2 tbsp	Sugar

Put 6 tbsp of the cider in a bowl, sprinkle over the gelatin and dissolve over a pan of hot water.

Stir in the remaining cider and lemon juice. Remove bowl from the heat. Spoon enough of the cider gelatin into a dampened 1-quart ring mold just to cover it. Leave it to set in the refrigerator.

Reserve half of each kind of grape. Wash and cut remainder in half and remove seeds. Arrange halves over the set gelatin, then cover with more liquid gelatin and leave to set.

Continue layers, ending with gelatin, then chill in refrigerator till set. Wash remaining grapes and remove most of the moisture. Toss in sugar.

Dip the mold quickly in and out of hot water and invert over a serving plate so gelatin slides out. Fill center with sugared grapes. Serve with whipped cream and gingersnaps.

Fruit salad with prunes

Overall timing 15 minutes plus maceration and chilling

Freezing Not suitable

To serve 6

½ lb (1½ cups)	Plump prunes
2 cups	Hot strong tea
3	Oranges
1	Grapefruit
2	Bananas
1 tbsp	Lemon juice
8 oz	Can of pineapple slices
2 tbsp	Brandy or sherry

Put pitted prunes in a bowl and cover with strained tea. Soak for 30 minutes.

Cut the rind and pith away from the oranges and grapefruit with a serrated knife. Cut into slices across the sections, cutting large slices in halves or quarters. Place in glass serving bowl.

Peel and cut the bananas into thick slices and sprinkle with lemon juice to prevent discoloration. Add to bowl with drained prunes, lemon juice and pineapple slices with their syrup. Stir in the brandy or sherry and chill for at least 1 hour before serving.

Rum trifle

Overall timing 35 minutes plus chilling

Freezing Not suitable

To serve 4-6

2 tbsp	Cocoa powder
½ cup	Sugar
3½ cups	Milk
4	Egg yolks
¼ cup	Flour
¼ cup	Rum
¼ cup	Water
8	Sponge cake slices

Mix the cocoa with 2 tbsp of the sugar. Heat the milk in a saucepan and add ½ cup of it to the cocoa mixture. Stir till well blended.

In another bowl, beat the egg yolks with remaining sugar and flour. Gradually add the remaining hot milk. Return to the saucepan and bring to a boil, stirring. Cook for 2 minutes till custard thickens. Pour half of the custard back into bowl and stir in cocoa mixture.

Line base of a glass bowl with wax paper. Put rum and water on a plate. Split the cake slices in half, then halve each half. Dip cake in rum mixture just to moisten. Line bottom and sides of bowl with half the cake.

Pour in the plain custard and cover with a layer of cake. Pour the chocolate custard into the bowl and cover with remaining cake. Cover with foil or plastic wrap and chill for at least 3 hours but preferably overnight.

Unmold trifle onto a plate, carefully remove wax paper and decorate with whipped cream, if liked.

Banana split

Overall timing 30 minutes

Freezing Not suitable

To serve 2

1 cup	Strawberries
½ cup	Grapes
1	Small orange
1	Kiwi fruit
1 tsp	Arrowroot
2 tbsp	Fruit syrup
5 tbsp	Heavy cream
2	Bananas
	Vanilla ice cream
4	Small meringues or macaroons

Hull strawberries and cut them in half. Halve the grapes and remove seeds. Peel orange (be careful to remove pith) and divide into segments. Peel and slice kiwi. Place all the fruits in a bowl, and chill for 15 minutes.

Mix the arrowroot with a little hot water and blend into fruit syrup to thicken it. Whip cream to piping consistency.

Peel bananas. "Split" in half lengthwise and place halves down each side of two serving dishes. Arrange fruit between bananas and place scoops of ice cream on top. Pour over a little syrup, pipe on cream swirls and top with meringues. Serve immediately.

Cherry bread pudding

Overall timing 1 hour

Freezing Not suitable

To serve 4-6

7	Slices of bread
16 oz	Can of cherries
4	Eggs
½ cup	Sugar
2 cups	Milk
	Grated rind of
	½ lemon
1 tbsp	Confectioners' sugar

Preheat the oven to 350°.

Cut the slices of bread into quarters diagonally. Arrange eight of the bread triangles over the bottom of an ovenproof dish.

Drain the cherries; halve and remove pits. Spread half the cherries over bread and cover with eight more triangles. Sprinkle over the remaining cherries and cover with the remaining bread, arranged in overlapping rows.

Beat the eggs with the sugar and add the milk. Sprinkle lemon rind over the bread and strain the egg mixture over. Sprinkle the surface with confectioners' sugar and bake for 35 minutes. Serve hot.

Spotted dick

Overall timing 2¼ hours

Freezing Suitable: boil for a further 2 hours

To serve 8

1¼ cups	Self-rising flour
½ tsp	Salt
2½ cups	Fresh bread crumbs
⅔ cup	Shredded suet
6 tbsp	Sugar
1 cup	Currants
¾ cup	Milk

Mix together the flour, salt, bread crumbs, suet, sugar and currants in a large bowl. Make a well in the center. Gradually add enough milk to make a soft but not sticky dough, using a knife to mix the dry ingredients into the liquid.

Form the dough into a roll on a floured surface. Wrap in greased parchment paper with a pleat in the top to allow room for the dough to rise. Wrap the roll loosely in foil, allowing room for expansion, and seal the joins tightly to keep water out.

Place in a large pan of boiling water, cover and simmer for 2 hours.

Remove from heat, unwrap carefully and roll the pudding off the paper onto a warmed serving plate. Serve hot in slices with custard sauce.

Apricot dumplings

Overall timing 1 ¼ hours including refrigeration

Freezing Not suitable

Makes 16

¼ cup	Butter
1 cup	Cottage cheese
2	Eggs
1¼ cups	Flour
16	Small apricots
16	Sugar cubes
¾ cup	Butter
2 tbsp	Sugar
8 tbsp	Dried bread crumbs
1 tsp	Ground cinnamon
	Confectioners' sugar

Beat together butter, sieved cheese, eggs and flour. Chill 30 minutes.

Make a small slit in each apricot. Remove pit and replace with a sugar cube.

Roll dough on a floured board. Cut into 16x2 inch squares. Put an apricot onto each square and draw dough around to form a dumpling. Drop dumplings into simmering water, and cook for 10 minutes. Turn over halfway through cooking.

Melt butter in pan. Stir in sugar, bread crumbs and cinnamon. Drain dumplings and toss in butter mixture. Dredge with confectioners' sugar and serve hot.

Black currant crêpe tower

Overall timing 45 minutes

Freezing Suitable: assemble tower and make sauce after reheating crêpes

To serve 4-6

1½ lb	Black currants
10 tbsp	Sugar
Crêpes	
6	Eggs
	Pinch of salt
½ cup	Milk
1 cup	Flour
2 tbsp	Sugar
6 tbsp	Oil

Put black currants into a bowl and sprinkle with sugar.

To make crêpes, separate eggs. Beat yolks with salt and milk, then gradually beat in flour.

In another bowl, beat egg whites till frothy. Add sugar and beat until stiff. Fold whites into yolk mixture.

Heat 1 tbsp of the oil in an 8 inch skillet. Add one-sixth of the batter and cook till crêpe is golden brown underneath. Turn and cook other side. Place on serving dish and top with some of the fruit. Cook five more crepes in the same way, placing each one on the "tower" as it is cooked with a layer of fruit.

Serve hot with custard sauce.

Almond apricot desserts

Overall timing 1 ¼ hours

Freezing Not suitable

To serve 6

2 tbsp	Butter
2 tbsp	Sugar
⅔ cup	Apricot jam
3 tbsp	Lemon juice
3	Eggs
½ cup	Ground almonds

Preheat the oven to 300°.

Melt the butter in a saucepan and use to grease six small ovenproof dishes. Coat the inside of each dish with sugar.

Put the apricot jam and lemon juice into a saucepan and heat gently, stirring. Put pan into water to cool mixture slightly.

Separate the eggs. Stir the yolks and almonds into the jam mixture. Beat the egg whites in a mixing bowl until very stiff. Gently fold in the jam mixture.

Fill each dish to the top with the mixture. Place on a baking sheet and bake for about 45 minutes.

Serve in the dishes with custard sauce, whipped cream or ice cream.

Raisin and macaroon pudding

Overall timing 1 hour 20 minutes

Freezing Suitable: serve cold

To serve 6

2½ cups	Milk
2 cups	Soft bread crumbs
6 tbsp	Butter
3	Eggs
¼ cup	Sugar
1 cup	Golden raisins
½ lb	Macaroons
Rum cream	
4	Eggs
6 tbsp	Sugar
¼ cup	Rum
	Juice of ½ lemon

Preheat the oven to 400°.

Put the milk into a saucepan and bring to a boil. Add the bread crumbs and cook gently — just simmering — for 10 minutes.

Meanwhile, cream butter in a bowl till softened. Separate the eggs. Beat the yolks with the sugar till light and fluffy, then gradually beat into the butter. Add the milk and bread crumbs and the raisins and mix well. Beat the egg whites till stiff and fold into the mixture.

Arrange the raisin mixture and the macaroons in layers in a greased 8 inch brioche or kugelhopf mold, beginning and ending with the raisin mixture. Bake for 1 hour.

To make the rum cream, mix the eggs, sugar, rum, lemon juice and 6 tbsp water in the top of a double boiler. Place over simmering water and cook, stirring constantly, till the mixture is thick enough to coat the back of a spoon. Strain into a warmed sauceboat or serving dish.

Unmold the pudding onto a warmed serving plate and serve hot, cut into thick wedges with the rum cream.

Grapefruit soufflés

Overall timing 45 minutes

Freezing Not suitable

To serve 6

6	Grapefruit
6 tbsp	Butter
¼ cup	Flour
	Finely grated rind of 1 orange
2-4 tbsp	Sugar
3	Eggs

Preheat the oven to 375°.

Slice tops off grapefruit. Scoop out flesh and membranes with grapefruit knife. Press to obtain 1 cup of juice. Discard pulp. Retain shells.

Melt the butter in a saucepan, stir in the flour and cook for 2 minutes. Gradually stir in the grapefruit juice. Bring to a boil and cook, stirring, for 2 minutes until the sauce thickens. Add orange rind and sugar and stir until sugar dissolves. Remove from heat and leave to cool slightly.

Separate the eggs and beat the yolks into the sauce. Beat the egg whites in a bowl till stiff, then carefully fold into the sauce mixture.

Place empty grapefruit shells in foil-lined cup cake pans and fill with the mixture. Bake for 15-20 minutes till well risen and golden. Serve immediately.

Sussex pond pudding

Overall timing 4 hours

Freezing Not suitable

To serve 6-8

2 cups	Self-rising flour
½ cup	Shredded suet
¾ cup	Milk
½ cup	Butter
⅔ cup	Brown sugar
1	Large thin-skinned lemon

Mix the flour and suet in a large bowl. Add the milk a little at a time to give a soft, but not sticky, dough. Knead the dough lightly. Roll out three-quarters of the dough and use to line a well-greased 1½ quart pudding basin.

Cream the butter and sugar together until fluffy and spread half the mixture over the bottom and sides of the pastry.

Pierce the lemon all over with a fine skewer (to help the juices run out during cooking). Stand the lemon upright in center of the basin, then add the remaining creamed mixture.

Roll out remaining dough and cover the filling, sealing pastry edges well. Cover the basin with a piece of greased parchment paper which has a large pleat to allow for expansion. Cover with pleated foil and tie with string, making a handle to aid removal from saucepan.

Place basin in saucepan containing 3 inches boiling water. Cover and leave to boil for 3½ hours, replenishing with extra boiling water as it evaporates.

Lift basin from saucepan. Remove foil and paper and run a knife around the sides of the basin to release the pudding. Invert onto a warmed serving plate and serve hot with custard sauce or cream.

Tapioca and caramel mold

Overall timing 1 1/4 hours

Freezing Not suitable

To serve 6

2/3 cup	Seed pearl tapioca
3 1/2 cups	Milk
3/4 cup	Sugar
	Grated rind of 1 lemon
2 tbsp	Butter
3	Eggs

Preheat the oven to 400°.

Put the tapioca, milk, 1/4 cup sugar and lemon rind into a saucepan and bring to a boil, stirring. Simmer for 15 minutes, stirring occasionally with a wooden spoon to prevent the mixture sticking to the pan.

Meanwhile, put the remaining sugar into a saucepan with 2 tbsp water and stir over a low heat till the sugar dissolves. Stop stirring and boil steadily till golden brown. Pour into a 7 inch round deep cake pan, turning so the bottom and sides are coated.

Remove the tapioca from the heat and beat in the butter. Separate the eggs, putting the whites into a large bowl. Beat the yolks into the tapioca, then leave to cool, stirring occasionally.

Beat the egg whites till stiff but not dry and fold gently into the tapioca with a metal spoon. Pour the mixture into the caramel-lined pan and bake for about 35 minutes till well risen and golden.

Run a knife around the edge of the pan and unmold onto a serving dish. Serve hot or cold with pouring cream.

Viennese sweet semolina

Overall timing 50 minutes

Freezing Not suitable

To serve 4-6

⅓ cup	Golden raisins
2½ cups	Milk
3 tbsp	Butter
½ cup	Semolina
¼ cup	Sugar

Preheat the oven to 350°.

Soak the raisins in warm water. Put the milk into a saucepan with butter. Heat till warm, then pour in the semolina and bring to a boil, stirring constantly. Simmer for 5 minutes, then stir in all but 1 tbsp of the sugar.

Drain raisins and mix into semolina. Turn into a greased ovenproof dish and smooth top. Bake for 30 minutes.

Remove dish from oven and increase heat to 400°. Mix the semolina with a fork to break it up. Return dish to oven for 5 minutes till mixture is dry and crisp. Unmold onto a warmed serving dish, sprinkle with the reserved sugar and serve hot.

Coconut and cherry surprise

Overall timing 1 hour

Freezing Suitable: reheat in 375° oven for 10 minutes.

To serve 8-10

½ lb	Pie pastry
10 tbsp	Ground almonds
16 oz	Can of cherry pie filling
⅓ cup	Shredded coconut
Filling	
6 tbsp	Butter
6 tbsp	Sugar
2	Eggs
¼ tsp	Almond extract
2 tbsp	Milk
½ cup	Self-rising flour
⅔ cup	Shredded coconut
10 tbsp	Ground almonds

Topping	
3 tbsp	Shredded cocnut
1	Egg yolk
1 tsp	Milk

Roll out dough and use to line a greased 10 inch springform pan. Sprinkle ground almonds over. Spread pie filling to within 1 inch of edge, then cover with coconut.

Preheat the oven to 400°.

Make filling by creaming butter with sugar till pale and fluffy. Add eggs, almond extract and 1 tbsp milk and beat well. Fold in flour, followed by remaining milk, coconut and almonds.

Place mixture in blobs over pie filling and smooth evenly so no fruit is visible. Sprinkle with coconut and bake for 30 minutes.

Mix egg yolk and milk together. Brush over tart and bake for a further 10 minutes. Serve hot.

Flamed fruit salad

Overall timing 30 minutes

Freezing Not suitable

To serve 4

	Selection of any firm fresh fruit: apple, banana, cherries, orange, clementine, pear, peach, strawberries and grapes
1	Lemon
2 tbsp	Butter
3 tbsp	Sugar
½ cup	Flaked almonds
3 tbsp	Rum

Prepare the fruit and chop it into pieces. Mix these together in a bowl. Grate lemon and squeeze out juice. Add juice to fruit.

Put the butter and sugar into a saucepan. Heat without stirring, until the sugar caramelizes and becomes light brown. This will take about 5 minutes. Add the grated lemon rind and almonds. Cook for about 5 minutes, stirring occasionally, until the caramel and nuts are golden brown.

Remove pan from the heat. Add juices from mixed fruits and stir until caramel becomes a smooth syrup. Add the fruit and heat through for about 5 minutes, turning the mixture over frequently to distribute the syrup. Remove from heat.

Warm rum in a metal ladle, then set alight and pour over fruit. Serve immediately with whipped cream or ice cream.

Fruit brochettes

Overall timing 20 minutes

Freezing Not suitable

To serve 6

3	Bananas
2	Oranges
1	Lemon
8 oz	Can of pineapple chunks
2 tbsp	Rum
½ cup	Sugar
2 tbsp	Butter
3	Thick slices of bread

Peel the fruit. Cut bananas into 1 inch pieces; divide oranges and lemon into sections; drain pineapple chunks. Place fruit in a bowl, pour rum over and sprinkle with 2 tbsp of the sugar.

Preheat the broiler or a charcoal grill.

Butter the bread on both sides, cut into small cubes and roll in sugar to coat. Thread fruit and bread cubes onto skewers.

Broil or grill for 10 minutes, turning brochettes over from time to time and sprinkling them with any remaining sugar. Serve immediately with whipped cream or vanilla ice cream.

Apricot crêpes

Overall timing 45 minutes

Freezing Suitable: fill crêpes after thawing and reheating

To serve 4

2	Eggs
¾ cup	Milk
¼ cup	Water
¾ cup	Flour
2 tbsp	Sugar
	Vanilla
	Pinch of salt
7 tbsp	Butter
½ cup	Apricot jam
	Confectioners' sugar
¼ cup	Ground hazelnuts

Put eggs, milk and water into a bowl. Add the flour, sugar, a few drops of vanilla and salt. Beat well together until creamy and smooth.

Melt a pat of butter in a small crêpe pan. Pour in a little of the batter and spread in a thin layer over the pan. When underside is cooked, flip the crêpe over to brown the other side.

As soon as each crêpe is ready, spread with apricot jam and roll up. Put onto a dish and keep warm in the oven while you cook the other crêpes, adding more butter to the pan as necessary.

Before serving, dredge with confectioners' sugar and sprinkle with ground hazelnuts or chopped nuts of your choice.

Blackberry crêpes

Overall timing 30 minutes

Freezing Not suitable

To serve 2

6 tbsp	Flour
2 tsp	Sugar
	Pinch of salt
1	Egg
½ cup	Milk
	Oil for frying
Topping	
1 cup	Canned blackberries
3 tbsp	Honey
1 ½ tbsp	Brandy
	Vanilla ice cream
¼ cup	Chopped walnuts

Sift flour, sugar and salt into a bowl. Make a well in the center and add egg and milk. Beat till smooth. Pour into a pitcher and leave to stand for 5 minutes.

Lightly oil an 8 inch crêpe pan and heat. Make four thin crêpes. Fold into quarters, arrange on a warmed serving plate and keep hot.

Place drained blackberries in a sieve. Drain on paper towels.

Gently heat honey with brandy in a saucepan. Remove from heat before it boils.

To assemble crêpes, put a cube of ice cream on top of each and scatter with blackberries. Pour over hot honey mixture and sprinkle with chopped walnuts. Serve immediately.

Baked bananas

Overall timing 15 minutes

Freezing Not suitable

To serve 4

4	Large ripe bananas
¼ cup	Butter
2 tsp	Sugar
2 tbsp	Water
	Ground cinnamon

Preheat oven to 425°.

Peel the bananas three-quarters of the way down. Fold back the skin to give a petal effect. Place in a greased ovenproof dish and dot each banana with butter. Sprinkle with sugar, water and a little ground cinnamon.

Bake for 10 minutes. Serve immediately with custard sauce or vanilla ice cream.

Baked noodle pudding

Overall timing 1 hour

Freezing Not suitable

To serve 4

1 cup	Milk
2½ cups	Water
½ lb	Noodles
¼ cup	Butter
2	Eggs
2	Large apples
½ cup	Walnut pieces
6 tbsp	Sugar
2 tsp	Poppy seeds

Preheat the oven to 325°.

Put the milk and water into a saucepan and bring to a boil. Add the noodles, bring back to a boil and simmer till tender. Drain noodles and put into a large bowl. Stir in the melted butter and beaten eggs till lightly coated.

Spread one-third of the noodles over the bottom of a greased ovenproof dish. Core and thinly slice the apples. Arrange half the slices over the noodles with half the walnuts. Sprinkle with one-third of the sugar and poppy seeds.

Repeat the layers, finishing with a layer of noodles arranged in a lattice pattern. Sprinkle with the remaining sugar and poppy seeds.

Bake for about 35 minutes till the apples are tender. Remove from the oven and cool completely before serving.

Bananas flambé

Overall timing 15 minutes

Freezing Not suitable

To serve 4

½ cup	Water
6 tbsp	Sugar
4	Bananas
5 tbsp	Rum
1	Small block of vanilla ice cream
½ cup	Flaked almonds

Put the water and sugar into a saucepan, stir until sugar dissolves. Bring to a boil and cook until it starts to turn golden.

Peel the bananas. Leave whole or cut in half crosswise. Add to the pan. Cook, uncovered, for 7 minutes, spooning syrup over occasionally. Remove from heat, stir in ¼ cup of the rum and keep warm.

Place scoops of ice cream on a chilled serving dish. Cover with the bananas and spoon the syrup over.

Warm the remaining rum in a metal spoon or ladle. Set alight and pour over the bananas. Decorate with flaked almonds and serve immediately, while flaming.

Plum pudding

Overall timing 5 hours plus maceration

Freezing Suitable: boil from frozen for about 2 hours

To serve 8-10

1 lb	Mixed golden raisins and currants
¾ lb	Prunes
1 cup	Chopped mixed candied peel
¼ cup	Rum
½ cup	Beer
3	Eggs
2 cups	Flaked almonds
1	Apple
2 tsp	Apple pie spice
2 tsp	Salt
2 cups	Brown sugar
2	Oranges
2	Lemons
1 cup	Shredded suet
1½ cups	Flour
2½ cups	Soft bread crumbs

Put dried fruits and candied peel in a large bowl, add 3 tbsp rum and the beer and leave to macerate overnight.

Drain fruit, reserving liquid. Pit prunes, then add eggs, almonds, grated apple, spice, salt, sugar and the juice and grated rind of oranges and lemons. Mix well.

Put suet in a bowl and work in flour and bread crumbs. Mix in any liquid from macerated fruit and add a little more beer if mixture is too dry. Knead to a dough and mix in all remaining ingredients. Tip mixture onto a clean, floured dishtowel and tie the corners together. Suspend from a long wooden spoon in a large saucepan half filled with boiling water. Boil for 5 hours.

Drain pudding for 5 minutes before removing dishtowel. Warm remaining rum, set alight and pour over pudding. Serve hot with custard sauce.

Fruity crêpes

Overall timing 1 hour

Freezing Not suitable

To serve 2

6 tbsp	Flour
2 tsp	Sugar
	Pinch of salt
1	Egg
½ cup	Milk
2 tbsp	Hard cider or white wine
	Grated rind of ½ orange
	Vanilla
3	Sugar cubes
1	Orange
½ tsp	Ground cinnamon
2	Apples
	Oil for frying

Sift flour, sugar and salt into a bowl. Make a well in the center and add egg, milk, cider or wine, orange rind and a few drops of vanilla. Beat till smooth. Pour batter into a pitcher.

Rub sugar cubes over surface of orange to absorb zest. Crush them and add cinnamon.

Peel orange, then chop flesh roughly. Place in a bowl. Peel, core and cube apples, then mix well with orange.

Preheat the broiler.

Lightly oil an 8 inch crêpe pan and heat. Pour in one-quarter of the batter and cook for 1-2 minutes till base bubbles and is firm. Spoon over one-quarter of the fruit and crushed sugar and cinnamon mixtures. Place under broiler and cook for a few minutes till bubbling. Fold crêpe and lift out onto a warmed serving dish. Cover and keep hot while you cook three more crêpes in the same way.

Serve whipped cream flavored with orange juice separately, or serve with vanilla ice cream.

Honey-baked bananas

Overall timing 40 minutes

Freezing Not suitable

To serve 4

4	Bananas
¼ cup	Lemon juice
3 tbsp	Honey
½ cup	Blanched almonds
3 tbsp	Soft bread crumbs
¼ cup	Butter
½ cup	Sour cream
3 tbsp	Orange juice

Preheat the oven to 400°.

Peel bananas. Arrange side by side in a greased ovenproof dish. Pour over lemon juice and honey. Mix the chopped almonds with the bread crumbs and sprinkle over bananas. Cut butter into small pieces and scatter over bananas.

Bake for 30 minutes. Serve with sour cream mixed with orange juice.

Plum soufflé

Overall timing 1 hour

Freezing Not suitable

To serve 6

1 ½ lb	Ripe plums
¼ cup	Sugar
6 tbsp	Water
5 tbsp	Butter
1 tbsp	Dried bread crumbs
½ cup	Flour
1 ½ cups	Warm milk
3	Large eggs
	Grated rind of
	1 orange

Preheat oven to 375°.

Pit the plums and cut into quarters. Put into a saucepan with the sugar and water. Bring to a boil, cover and simmer for 10 minutes. Grease a 2 quart soufflé dish with 1 tbsp butter and coat with the bread crumbs. Put two thirds of the plums in the dish with any juice.

Melt the remaining butter in a large saucepan, stir in the flour and cook for 1 minute. Gradually add the warm milk and bring to a boil, stirring constantly. Simmer for 2 minutes, then remove from heat. Cool slightly.

Separate the eggs. Beat the yolks into the sauce with the orange rind and remaining plums. Beat the egg whites till stiff but not dry. Stir one spoonful into sauce and fold in remainder. Pour mixture over the plums in the dish.

Stand dish in a roasting pan containing 1 inch hot water. Bake for 30-35 minutes till well risen and golden. Serve immediately.

Baked apricots

Overall timing 1 hour

Freezing Suitable: reheat from frozen in 400° oven for 15 minutes, then add syrup

To serve 6-8

12	Large apricots
1 cup	Milk
2 tbsp	Imported custard powder
1 tbsp	Sugar
1 cup	Blanched almonds
1½ cups	Crumbled macaroons
¼ cup	Candied orange peel
	Pinch of ground cinnamon
6 tbsp	Currant jelly
¼ cup	Water

Preheat the oven to 400°.

Halve apricots and remove pits. Arrange, cut sides up, in a greased ovenproof dish.

Prepare the custard according to package instructions, using the milk, custard powder and sugar. Cool quickly by standing the pan in cold water. Stir the custard frequently to prevent a skin forming.

Chop almonds, and candied peel finely and stir into the custard with the macaroons and cinnamon. Fill apricot halves with custard mixture. Bake for 30 minutes.

Meanwhile, mix together the currant jelly and water in a small pan over a low heat. Spoon syrup carefully over the apricots and bake for a further 10 minutes.

Serve hot with whipped cream, or leave to cool, then chill and serve with ice cream or whipped cream.

Apricots flambé

Overall timing 20 minutes

Freezing Not suitable

To serve 4

½ cup	Sugar
1	Vanilla bean
½ cup	Water
8	Fresh apricots
2 tbsp	Arrowroot or cornstarch
2 tbsp	Sliced almonds
¼ cup	Orange liqueur or brandy

To make the syrup, put the sugar, vanilla bean and water into a saucepan. Stir until sugar dissolves, then bring to a boil and cook over low heat, uncovered, for about 10 minutes without stirring.

Wash, dry and halve the apricots. Remove the pits and put the halves into the boiling syrup. Leave for 2-3 minutes to soften. Remove from heat. Lift out vanilla bean and discard it. Lift out apricots and arrange them in a flameproof serving dish.

Blend arrowroot or cornstarch with a little water, then mix it into the syrup. Cook for 3-4 minutes over low heat, stirring continuously. Pour hot syrup over apricots and sprinkle with almonds.

Warm the liqueur in a ladle. Set it alight and pour it over the apricots. Serve immediately.

Apple and marmalade charlotte

Overall timing 1 hour

Freezing Suitable: reheat in 400° oven for 10 minutes

To serve 8

2½ lb	Tart apples
¼ cup	Water
2 tbsp	Sugar
⅓ cup	Marmalade
1	Large stale loaf sliced bread
6 tbsp	Butter

Preheat the oven to 400°.

To make the filling, peel apples, core and slice into a large saucepan. Add water, cover and bring to a boil. Cook over medium heat for 12 minutes without removing the lid during cooking. Remove from heat and beat in sugar and marmalade with a wooden spoon.

Remove crusts and butter bread. Cut a third of slices into triangles and the rest into wide fingers.

Grease a 1 quart charlotte mold and line the bottom with some of the bread triangles, buttered-side out. Overlap the slices as the bread tends to shrink during cooking. Line sides of mold with overlapping bread fingers, butter-side out.

Pour in apple mixture and top with remaining bread triangles, butter-side up. Bake for 30-40 minutes till golden brown.

Remove from oven. Leave to cool slightly in the mold. Run a knife around the edge and unmold onto a warmed serving plate. Serve hot with custard sauce or cream.

Fruity rice pudding

Overall timing 1 ¼ hours

Freezing Suitable: reheat in 300° oven for 30 minutes

To serve 6-8

3 cups	Milk
	Salt
4	Strips of lemon rind
⅔ cup	Round grain rice
1 ½ lb	Apples
2	Bananas
2 tbsp	Butter
½ cup	Sugar
1 tsp	Ground cinnamon
4 oz	Bottle of Maraschino cherries
½ cup	Chopped walnuts
3	Eggs

Preheat oven to 350°.

Put the milk, pinch of salt and strips of lemon rind into a saucepan and bring to a boil. Add the rice. Cover and cook for 40 minutes on a low heat, stirring occasionally.

Meanwhile, peel and slice the apples and bananas. Melt the butter and ¼ cup of the sugar in a saucepan until golden brown. Add the apples and cook for 5 minutes, then add the bananas and cook for 2-3 minutes more. Sprinkle on the cinnamon, then stir in drained cherries and chopped walnuts.

Remove from heat, put mixture into a greased ovenproof dish and smooth over. Work quickly to prevent caramel setting.

Separate the eggs. Cream together the yolks and 2 tbsp sugar in one bowl. In another, beat the whites and remaining sugar together until mixture is very stiff. Fold both mixtures into the cooked rice (take out the lemon rind first) then pour over the fruit. Bake for 30 minutes. Serve hot with cream.

Jam omelettes

Overall timing 10 minutes

Freezing Not suitable

To serve 2

3	Eggs
	Pinch of salt
2 tbsp	Butter
3 tbsp	Jam
1 tbsp	Sugar

Beat eggs with salt in a bowl. Melt half butter in omelette pan. Add half the egg mixture and cook until set. Slip omelette out of pan onto plate, cooked side down.

Repeat with remaining butter and egg mixture to make another omelette. Spoon jam into the middle of each omelette. Roll them up like crêpes and sprinkle with sugar.

To make the caramelized stripes, heat a skewer or toasting fork over a naked flame, then press lightly on top of the omelettes at intervals. Serve at once.

Nutty apple pudding

Overall timing 50 minutes

Freezing Not suitable

To serve 4-6

1½ lb	Tart apples
½ cup	Water
½ cup	Flaked almonds
⅓ cup	Golden raisins
7 slices	Wholewheat bread
⅔ cup	Light brown sugar
¼ cup	Butter

Preheat the oven to 425°.

Peel and core apples and slice into a saucepan. Add water, almonds and raisins. Cover and cook over a gentle heat for 10 minutes. Remove from heat.

Crumble the bread into a bowl and mix in half the sugar. Grease an ovenproof dish with some of the butter and spread half the bread mixture over the bottom. Cover with apple mixture, then top with remaining bread. Sprinkle on rest of sugar and dot with remaining butter. Bake for about 20 minutes.

Peach meringue pudding

Overall timing 50 minutes

Freezing Not suitable

To serve 6

2½ cups	Milk
¼ cup	Semolina
2	Eggs
6 tbsp	Sugar
4	Ripe peaches
3 tbsp	Peach or raspberry jam
¼ cup	Toasted flaked almonds

Preheat the oven to 350°.

Heat the milk in a saucepan and sprinkle in the semolina, stirring constantly. Bring to a boil and cook, stirring, for 3 minutes till thickened. Remove from the heat.

Separate the eggs. Beat the yolks into the semolina with 2 tbsp of the sugar. Pour mixture into a 7 inch soufflé dish and smooth surface.

Peel and halve the peaches. Remove pits. Place a little jam in each peach half. Arrange in soufflé dish, some with the cut sides pressing against the sides of the dish and the rest jam-side down on the semolina.

Beat the egg whites till stiff, then beat in half the remaining sugar. Fold in the finely chopped almonds and the rest of the sugar. Pipe or spoon the meringue over the peaches.

Bake for 20 minutes till the meringue is lightly browned. Serve hot or leave to cool completely and chill before serving.

Pear brown betty

Overall timing 1 hour

Freezing Not suitable

To serve 6-8

2 lb	Ripe pears
3 cups	Stale bread crumbs
½ cup	Sugar
¼ cup	Butter

Preheat the oven to 375°.

Peel and halve the pears. Remove the cores and cut flesh into ¼ inch slices.

Cover the bottom of a greased 8 inch springform pan with a quarter of the bread crumbs. Arrange one-third of the pears on top and sprinkle with a little sugar. Repeat the layers till all the ingredients have been used.

Dot with the butter and bake for about 45 minutes till the pears are tender and the top is crisp and golden. Remove from the pan and serve hot or cold with pouring cream or custard sauce.

Pear dumplings

Overall timing 1 ¼ hours plus chilling

Freezing Not suitable

To serve 4

3 cups	Flour
¼ tsp	Salt
¾ cup	Butter
	Grated rind of 1 orange
2 tbsp	Sugar
1	Egg yolk
Filling	
4	Ripe pears
¼ cup	Butter
2 tbsp	Brown sugar
½ tsp	Ground cinnamon

Sift flour and salt into a bowl and rub in butter. Stir in the grated orange rind and sugar and add enough water to bind to a dough. Knead till smooth. Chill for 30 minutes. Preheat the oven to 400°.

Roll out dough and cut into four 8 inch squares.

Peel and halve pears and remove cores. Cream butter with brown sugar and cinnamon till pale and fluffy. Use to fill center of pears. Press halves together and place one on each dough square.

Brush edges of dough squares with water. Bring the four corners of each square together at top of pears, sealing edges well. Roll out dough trimmings and cut into leaves. Lightly beat egg yolk with 1 tbsp water and brush over dough. Dip leaves in egg and press in place on top.

Place on a greased baking sheet and bake for about 30 minutes till crisp and golden. Serve hot with whipped cream or vanilla ice cream.

French toast

Overall timing 25 minutes

Freezing Not suitable

To serve 4-6

10	Thin slices of bread
1½-2 cups	Milk
2-3	Eggs
¼ cup	Butter
¼ cup	Sugar
1 tsp	Ground cinnamon (optional)

Place bread on a baking sheet or jelly roll pan and pour over the milk. The more stale the bread, the more milk you will need to make the bread spongy. Soak for 10 minutes.

Beat the eggs in a shallow dish till creamy. Lightly press bread with a fork to remove excess milk.

Melt butter in skillet (reserve some if you cannot cook all slices at once). Dip bread in egg to coat, add to pan and fry for 3-4 minutes on each side. Sprinkle with sugar and cinnamon, if used, and serve immediately, with jam or maple syrup.

Pineapple fritters

Overall timing 25 minutes

Freezing Not suitable

To serve 6

16 oz	Can of pineapple rings
1 cup	Flour
1½ tsp	Sugar
1	Whole egg
1 tbsp	Oil
½ cup	Milk or water
2	Egg whites
	Oil for frying
3 tbsp	Confectioners' sugar

Drain the pineapple rings and dry on paper towels.

Sift flour and sugar into bowl. Beat in egg, oil and liquid till smooth. Beat egg whites till stiff and fold into batter. Heat oil in a deep-fryer to 340°. Spear the pineapple rings on a fork, dip into the batter and carefully lower into the oil. Fry three at a time for 2-3 minutes till crisp and golden. Remove from the pan, drain on paper towels and keep hot while remaining fritters are cooked.

Arrange on a warmed serving plate, sift the confectioners' sugar over and serve immediately with whipped cream.

Apple strudel

Overall timing 1¾ hours

Freezing Not suitable

To serve 8

2½ cups	Flour
1	Large egg
½ cup	Butter
	Pinch of salt
2½ lb	Tart apples
6 tbsp	Sugar
2 tsp	Ground cinnamon
⅔ cup	Raisins
1 tbsp	Grated lemon rind
1 cup	Ground almonds
1 cup	Soft bread crumbs

Sift flour onto a work surface. Add egg. Melt half butter in a pan, then add 6 tbsp water and salt. Add mixture to flour and mix to a soft, sticky dough. Knead till smooth. Leave in a warm place for 20 minutes.

Meanwhile, peel and core apples, then slice half very thinly. Coarsely grate rest into a bowl and mix in sugar, cinnamon, raisins, lemon rind, almonds and half bread crumbs.

Place a large patterned dishtowel on a flat surface and sprinkle it with flour. Roll out dough on top till it is same shape as towel. Slide your hands between dough and dishtowel. Lift and stretch dough till thin enough to see pattern of dishtowel through. The rectangle should eventually measure about 20 x 16 inches.

Preheat the oven to 400°.

Brush dough with half remaining melted butter. Sprinkle with remaining bread crumbs, leaving a 1 inch border all around. Spread almond mixture evenly over dough. Arrange apple slices on top. Fold border over filling, then roll up. Place on greased baking sheet, curving to fit.

Brush with remaining butter and bake for 10 minutes. Reduce heat to 375° and bake for a further 30 minutes. Sprinkle with confectioners' sugar and serve warm.

Apple soufflé omelette

Overall timing 50 minutes

Freezing Not suitable

To serve 2

Filling

¾ lb	Tart apples
1 tbsp	Water
1 tbsp	Butter
3 tbsp	Sugar
	Vanilla

Omelette

2	Eggs
2 tbsp	Sugar
¼ cup	Milk
¼ tsp	Vanilla
2 tbsp	Butter
	Confectioners' sugar
2 tbsp	Brandy

To make the filling, peel, core and roughly chop apples. Place in saucepan with water and butter, cover and cook for 15 minutes. Remove from heat and add sugar and a few drops of vanilla. Mix well, then cool.

To make omelette, separate one egg. Put the yolk in a bowl with the whole egg and the sugar and beat till light and frothy. Stir in milk and vanilla.

In another bowl, beat the egg white till very stiff. Stir 1 tbsp into yolk mixture to lighten it, then carefully fold in the rest with a metal spoon.

Preheat the broiler.

Melt the butter in an omelette pan. When it begins to turn a light brown, pour in the egg mixture. Cook over a low heat for 5-7 minutes. Place under the broiler until the top has set. Spread over the filling and fold over in half. Slide onto a warmed serving dish. Dredge with confectioners' sugar. Warm the brandy, pour over the omelette and set alight. Serve flaming.

Individual coconut soufflés

Overall timing 45 minutes

Freezing Not suitable

To serve 8

1 cup	Milk
5 tbsp	Sugar
2 tbsp	Flour
¼ cup	Butter
4	Eggs
1 ⅓ cups	Shredded coconut
1 tbsp	Confectioners' sugar

Beat ¼ cup of the milk with 3 tbsp of the sugar and the flour. Bring the remaining milk to a boil in a saucepan. Add 2 tbsp of the boiling milk to the sugar mixture and beat in well, then add to the milk in the pan, beating vigorously all the time. Simmer gently till thickened, then cover, remove from heat and leave to cool for 15 minutes.

Preheat the oven to 375°. Grease eight ovenproof molds or ramekins with the butter and sprinkle with 1 tbsp of the sugar.

Separate the eggs. Add the yolks to the sauce with the coconut, beating all the time. In a large bowl, beat the egg whites till they hold stiff peaks, gradually adding the remaining sugar. Fold into the egg yolk mixture.

Three-quarters fill the molds or ramekins with the mixture and sprinkle with confectioners' sugar. Place on baking sheet and bake for 20 minutes. Serve hot.

Banana pudding with rum sauce

Overall timing 1 1/4 hours

Freezing Suitable: reheat in 350° oven

To serve 6

2 lb	Bananas
7 tbsp	Sugar
1/4 cup	Softened butter
1/4 cup	Flour
	Grated nutmeg
2	Eggs
2 tbsp	Confectioners' sugar
1 tbsp	Rum or rum flavoring
1/2 cup	Light cream

Preheat the oven to 350°.

Reserve half a large or 1 medium-sized banana for decoration. Peel the rest. Mash them with a fork in a bowl with sugar, butter, flour and a pinch of nutmeg.

Separate the eggs. Add yolks to banana mixture and beat well with a wooden spoon until smooth and creamy. Beat the egg whites till very stiff, then gently fold into the banana mixture.

Lightly grease and flour a pudding basin or ovenproof mold. Fill with the banana mixture and bake for 1 hour.

Remove from oven. Leave to cool slightly then unmold onto a warmed serving plate. Sprinkle with confectioners' sugar and decorate with the reserved banana, sliced. Mix rum or few drops rum flavoring into cream and serve separately.

Banana soufflés

Overall timing 25 minutes

Freezing Not suitable

To serve 2

4	Ripe bananas
2 tbsp	Butter
6 tbsp	Sugar
	Vanilla
2 tbsp	Rum
2	Large eggs
2 tbsp	Confectioners' sugar

Preheat the oven to 425°.

Make two lengthwise slits with a sharp knife at the top of each banana, leaving the skin joined at the stalk end. Roll back skin. Remove banana pulp with a teaspoon and place in a bowl. Mash well to a purée.

Put the banana purée into a saucepan with the butter, sugar, a few drops of vanilla and the rum. Cook for about 3 minutes over a low heat, stirring constantly. Remove from heat.

Separate eggs. Stir yolks into the banana mixture. Place pan in cold water to cool mixture quickly. Beat egg whites till firm, then lightly fold into cold banana mixture with a metal spoon.

Fill banana skins with mixture. Place on a baking sheet and bake for about 10 minutes. Sprinkle with confectioners' sugar and serve immediately with pouring cream.

Blackberry and pear meringue

Overall timing 50 minutes

Freezing Not suitable

To serve 6-8

3 cups	Ripe blackberries
¼ cup	Sugar
3 tbsp	Ground almonds
4	Large ripe pears
3	Egg whites
1¾ cups	Confectioners' sugar

Preheat the oven to 350°.

Hull the berries and arrange over the bottom of a shallow ovenproof dish. Mix the sugar and 2 tbsp of the almonds together and sprinkle over the berries.

Peel and halve the pears lengthwise. Remove the cores. Arrange cut sides down in a single layer on the berries. Bake for 20 minutes.

Put the egg whites and sifted confectioners' sugar into a large heatproof bowl over a pan of simmering water. Beat till the meringue is stiff and glossy. Spoon or pipe the meringue over the pears and sprinkle with the reserved almonds.

Return to the oven and bake for a further 10 minutes till lightly browned. Serve immediately.

Baked apple toasts

Overall timing 40 minutes

Freezing Not suitable

To serve 4

6 tbsp	Butter
4	Thick slices of crusty bread
4	Apples
6 tbsp	Light brown sugar

Preheat the oven to 425°.

Butter the bread thickly on one side and arrange on a baking sheet, buttered side up.

Peel, core and thinly slice the apples. Arrange half the slices on the bread so they overlap slightly and cover the bread. Sprinkle with a little of the sugar and place remaining apples on top.

Sprinkle apples with the remaining sugar and bake for about 25 minutes till the sugar melts and caramelizes. Serve hot.

Berry-stuffed apples

Overall timing 30 minutes

Freezing Suitable: reheat from frozen in 375° oven for 20 minutes

To serve 4

16 oz	Can of loganberries
4	Large apples
¼ cup	Butter
¼ cup	Brown sugar

Preheat the oven to 375°.

Drain loganberries, reserving syrup. Core apples. Place in a greased ovenproof dish and fill centers with loganberries. Surround with remaining berries and reserved syrup. Place a pat of butter on each apple and sprinkle with 1 tbsp sugar.

Bake for 25 minutes, basting occasionally with the juices in the dish, till tender. Serve apples hot with pouring cream.

Cherry pudding with jam sauce

Overall timing 1¾ hours

Freezing Not suitable

To serve 4-6

½ cup	Butter
½ cup	Sugar
2	Eggs
1½ cups	Self-rising flour
⅔ cup	Glacé cherries
6 tbsp	Milk
½ tsp	Almond extract
Sauce	
¼ cup	Red jam
½ cup	Water
1 tsp	Arrowroot
1 tbsp	Lemon juice

Cream butter with sugar till pale and fluffy. Gradually beat in the eggs one at a time. Fold in the sifted flour and cherries, adding milk and almond extract to give a soft dropping consistency. Place in greased pudding basin or steaming mold and cover with greased foil.

Put basin into a pan and fill up to rim of basin with boiling water. Cover and steam for 1½ hours.

To make the sauce, melt the jam with the water in a small pan, then sieve. Blend arrowroot with lemon juice and stir into sauce. Bring to a boil, stirring.

Unmold pudding and serve immediately with the hot jam sauce.

Irish lemon pudding

Overall timing 1 hour

Freezing Not suitable

To serve 4-6

½ cup	Butter
¾ cup	Sugar
4	Eggs
1	Lemon
2 tbsp	Flour
1½ cups	Milk
1·tbsp	Confectioners' sugar

Preheat the oven to 400°.

Cream the butter and sugar in a bowl till light and fluffy. Separate the eggs and add the yolks to the creamed mixture. Beat well. Grate rind from lemon and squeeze out juice. Beat into the creamed mixture. Gradually stir in the flour, then the milk.

Beat egg whites till stiff, then carefully fold into mixture. Turn into a greased 7 inch soufflé dish and sift confectioners' sugar over. Place dish in roasting pan containing 1 inch hot water. Bake for 40-50 minutes till the pudding has risen and the top is golden. Serve hot or cold.

Caribbean crêpes

Overall timing 40 minutes

Freezing Not suitable

To serve 6

10 tbsp	Flour
	Pinch of salt
¼ tsp	Ground ginger
1	Egg
1 cup	Milk
¼ cup	Butter
Filling	
16oz	Can of pineapple rings
16oz	Can of creamed rice
¼ cup	Rum
6	Glacé cherries

Sift the flour, salt and ginger into a bowl. Add the egg and milk and beat till smooth. Melt butter and add one-quarter to batter.

Brush a little butter over an 8 inch pan and heat. Pour one-sixth of the batter into the pan, tilting it so that the bottom is covered. Cook till crêpe is golden brown underneath, then flip over and cook other side. Make five more crêpes in this way.

Preheat the oven to 375°.

Drain the pineapple rings, and reserve three. Finely chop the rest and put into a bowl. Add creamed rice and mix well. Divide the mixture between the crêpes. Roll up the crepes loosely and arrange in an ovenproof dish. Heat through in the oven for 10 minutes.

Meanwhile, cut the reserved pineapple rings in half. Warm the rum in a small saucepan. Remove crêpes from oven and decorate with the halved pineapple rings and cherries. Pour warm rum over, set alight and serve flaming, with scoops of vanilla ice cream.

Walnut pear pie

Overall timing 1 hour plus chilling

Freezing Suitable: decorate with cream after thawing

To serve 6-8

1 ½ cups	Flour
½ cup	Butter
¼ cup	Sugar
½ cup	Finely chopped walnuts
2 tsp	Ground cinnamon
1	Egg
Filling	
4	Ripe pears
3 tbsp	Sugar
½ cup	Whipping cream

Sift flour into a large bowl and rub in butter. Stir in sugar, finely chopped walnuts and cinnamon. Add egg with enough water to bind to a firm dough. Chill for 1 hour.

Preheat the oven to 375°.

Roll out two-thirds of dough and use to line an 8 inch fluted quiche pan. Peel, core and quarter pears. Arrange over pastry in a circle, core-side downwards and with the stem ends pointing towards the center but not joining up. Sprinkle with 2 tbsp sugar.

Roll out remaining dough and place over pears. Trim edges and pinch together to seal. Using a 3 inch pastry cutter, cut a circle out of the centre of the pastry lid. Brush pastry with egg white (from egg shell) and dredge with remaining sugar. Bake for 15 minutes, then reduce oven temperature to 350° and bake for a further 25 minutes. Cool in pan.

Whip cream and spoon or pipe into center of pie before serving.

English apple pie

Overall timing 1 hour

Freezing Not suitable

To serve 4-6

2 cups	Flour
	Pinch of salt
½ cup	Butter
1½ lb	Tart apples
¼ cup	Brown sugar
½ tsp	Ground cinnamon
¼ tsp	Grated nutmeg
¼ tsp	Ground cloves
⅓ cup	Golden raisins
	Milk
1 tbsp	Sugar

Preheat oven to 400°.

Sift flour and salt together into a bowl and rub in butter. Add enough water to mix to a firm dough.

Peel, core and slice apples into a bowl. Add brown sugar, spices and raisins. Put mixture in a buttered deep 1 quart pie dish. Sprinkle over 2 tbsp of water.

Roll out dough and cover pie. Decorate with dough trimmings. Brush with milk and sprinkle with sugar.

Bake for 20 minutes. Reduce heat to 350° and bake for a further 20 minutes.

Swedish cranberry tart

Overall timing 1 hour 50 minutes

Freezing Suitable

To serve 12

2 cups	Flour
	Pinch of salt
½ cup	Confectioners' sugar
½ cup	Butter
2 tbsp	Sour cream
1 tbsp	Rum or water
1 lb	Fresh cranberries
1 cup	Granulated sugar
1	Egg white
½ cup	Heavy cream

Sift flour, salt and confectioners' sugar into a bowl. Rub in the butter till mixture resembles fine bread crumbs. Add sour cream and rum or water and mix to a smooth dough. Cover and chill for 30 minutes.

Meanwhile, remove stalks from cranberries, wash and drain. Put them into a bowl and mix in the granulated sugar. Preheat the oven to 400°.

Roll out three-quarters of dough on a lightly floured board and use to line a 10½-inch loose-bottomed pie pan. Spread the cranberry and sugar mixture evenly over the dough. Roll out remaining dough, cut into thin strips and make a lattice pattern over the cranberries.

Lightly beat the egg white in a cup and brush over the top of the tart. Bake for 45 minutes. Remove tart from pan and leave to cool.

Whip cream till stiff peaks form. Spoon into a pastry bag fitted with a star nozzle and pipe small rosettes around the edge of the tart.

West Indian peanut pie

Overall timing 1 ¼ hours

Freezing Not suitable

To serve 6-8

Pastry	
1 cup	Self-rising flour
½ tsp	Salt
2 tbsp	Sugar
¼ cup	Softened butter
1	Egg yolk
2 tbsp	Milk
Filling	
1 cup	Roasted unsalted peanuts
1	Egg
6 tbsp	Sugar
⅓ cup	Light corn syrup
½ tsp	Vanilla

Preheat the oven to 350°.

To make pastry, sift flour, salt and sugar into a bowl. Rub in the butter. Add egg yolk and gradually mix in enough milk to bind to a soft dough. Roll out dough and use to line an 8 inch fluted quiche pan.

To make filling, preheat the broiler. Place nuts on a baking sheet and broil them for 2 minutes, shaking the sheet so they brown lightly all over. Remove and allow to cool.

Beat the egg and sugar in a bowl till light and frothy. Add syrup and continue to beat till thick. Stir in the peanuts and vanilla.

Pour the peanut mixture into the pastry case and bake for 30 minutes. Cover with foil and bake for a further 5-10 minutes. Lift off the foil, leave the pie till almost cool, then remove from pan.

Apple and mincemeat tart

Overall timing 1 hour

Freezing Suitable reheat in 350° oven for 40 minutes

To serve 6

½ lb	Pie pastry
1 lb	Jar of mincemeat
1 lb	Tart apples
6 tbsp	Sugar
½ tsp	Ground allspice
½ cup	Butter
1 tbsp	Flour

Preheat the oven to 425°. Roll out the dough and line a 9½ inch French flan ring placed on a baking sheet. Spread mincemeat evenly over pastry.

Peel, core and finely slice the apples. Mix with ¼ cup of sugar and the allspice. Arrange in circles on mincemeat. In a bowl, cut and fold the butter with remaining 2 tbsp sugar and flour until the mixture resembles fine bread crumbs. Sprinkle evenly over the apples.

Bake in oven for 15 minutes, then reduce temperature to 375° and bake for a further 30 minutes. Remove from oven and allow to cool.

Lift tart from flan ring and place on serving plate. Spoon any topping from baking sheet onto tart. Serve warm or cold, with whipped cream or vanilla ice cream.

Blueberry boats

Overall timing 1 hour 20 minutes

Freezing Not suitable

Makes 8

¾ cup	Flour
3 tbsp	Sugar
1	Egg
	Vanilla
3 tbsp	Butter
Filling	
3 cups	Blueberries
¼ cup	Sugar
¼ cup	Flaked almonds
½ cup	Heavy cream
1 tbsp	Confectioners' sugar

Preheat the oven to 425°.

Sift flour into a bowl, make a well in the center and add sugar, egg and a few drops of vanilla. Add the butter, cut into pieces, and knead to a dough. Add a little water if necessary. Chill for 30 minutes.

Roll out dough to ¼ inch thick and use to line eight boat-shaped tartlet molds. Prick and bake blind for 15-20 minutes till cooked and golden brown. Cool.

Rinse blueberries and place in bowl. Sprinkle over the sugar and leave for 1 hour.

Preheat the broiler. Spread flaked almonds on broiler pan and toast. Whip cream till stiff with confectioners' sugar. Spoon into pastry bag.

Drain blueberries and divide between pastry boats. Pipe on cream and decorate with toasted almonds.

Canadian cherry pie

Overall timing 1 ¼ hours

Freezing Not suitable

To serve 6

½ lb	Pie pastry
2 lb	Fresh cherries *or*
2 x 16 oz	Cans of cherries
⅓ cup	Ground rice
¼ cup	Sugar
1	Lemon
1	Egg white
	Sugar for sprinkling

Preheat the oven to 450°.

Roll out two-thirds of dough and use to line a 7½ inch fluted pie pan.

Pit cherries (drain first if canned) and put into saucepan with rice and sugar. Grate rind from lemon and squeeze out juice. Add both to pan and bring to boil, stirring. Simmer for 2 minutes. Cool.

Spread cherry mixture in pastry case. Roll out remaining dough and lay over filling. Moisten edges and press together to seal. Brush with lightly beaten egg white and dredge with sugar.

Bake for 10 minutes, then reduce heat to 350°. Bake for a further 40-45 minutes till top is golden.

Custard tart

Overall timing 1 ½ hours plus cooling

Freezing Not suitable

To serve 4-6

2 cups	Flour
¼ cup	Shortening
¼ cup	Butter
4-6 tbsp	Water
Filling	
2½ cups	Milk
1	Vanilla bean
	Strip of lemon rind
4	Eggs
¼ cup	Sugar
	Grated nutmeg

Preheat the oven to 400°.

Put the flour into a bowl and rub in the fats till the mixture resembles fine bread crumbs. Gradually add the water and mix to a smooth dough.

Roll out the dough on a lightly floured surface and use to line a 9 inch pie pan. Bake blind for 10 minutes. Remove from oven and reduce temperature to 350°.

Put milk, vanilla bean and lemon rind into a pan and bring almost to a boil. Remove from heat and leave to infuse for 10 minutes. Remove vanilla bean and lemon rind.

Beat eggs and sugar in bowl. Pour in milk, stirring. Strain into pastry case and sprinkle with nutmeg. Bake for 35 minutes or till just set. Cool.

Marmalade and ginger tart

Overall timing 1 ¼ hours

Freezing Not suitable

To serve 6-8

2 cups	Flour
1 tsp	Ground ginger
½ cup	Butter
2 tbsp	Sugar
1	Egg yolk
½ cup	Marmalade

Sift the flour and ginger into a bowl. Rub in the butter till the mixture resembles fine bread crumbs. Add sugar and mix to a dough with the egg yolk and a little water. Knead lightly till smooth, then chill for 30 minutes.

Preheat the oven to 375°.

Roll out about three-quarters of the dough on a floured surface and use to line a 9 inch pie pan. Crimp the edges and prick base.

Spread a thick layer of marmalade over the tart base. Roll out the remaining dough and cut into strips with a pastry wheel. Make a lattice over the marmalade filling, pressing the joins to seal. Bake for about 40 minutes, till golden. Remove from pan and serve hot or cold with custard sauce or ice cream.

Nectarine almond tart

Overall timing 50 minutes plus chilling

Freezing Suitable

To serve 4

2 cups	Flour
	Pinch of salt
½ cup	Butter
¼ cup	Sugar
1	Egg
Filling	
1 tbsp	Semolina
1 tbsp	Ground almonds
½ cup	Sugar
1¾ lb	Nectarines
1 tbsp	Split almonds

Sift the flour and salt into a bowl. Add butter, cut into flakes, sugar and egg and work into a dough. Add a little water if necessary. Chill for 30 minutes.

Preheat the oven to 425°.

Roll out dough on a floured surface and use to line a 9 inch fluted quiche pan. Mix together the semolina, ground almonds and half the sugar. Sprinkle over the pastry.

Halve the nectarines and remove the pits. Arrange the fruit in the pastry case, cut sides down, and sprinkle with the remaining sugar and split almonds. Bake for 35-40 minutes.

Allow to cool slightly, then serve warm or cold with pouring cream.

Orange lasagne tart

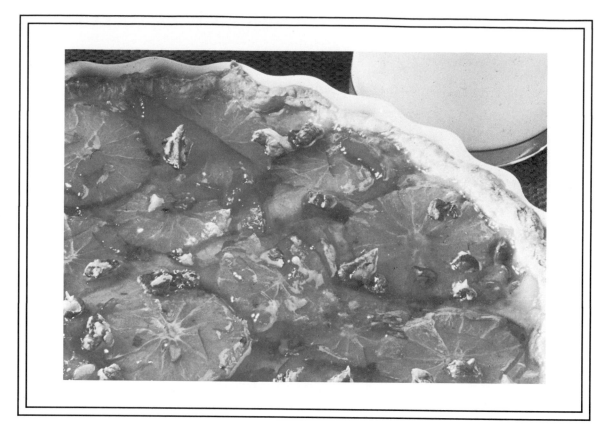

Overall timing 1½ hours

Freezing Suitable: reheat in 350° oven for 30 minutes

To serve 8

¼ lb	Lasagne
½ lb	Frozen puff pastry
3	Thin-skinned oranges
2 tbsp	Rum (optional)
5 tbsp	Thin-cut marmalade
1 tbsp	Chopped walnuts
Confectioners' custard	
2½ cups	Milk
1	Vanilla bean
	Strip of lemon rind
½ cup	Sugar
4	Medium eggs
¼ cup	Flour

Cook lasagne in boiling salted water till tender. Drain and cool.

Meanwhile, thaw pastry and make confectioners' custard. Put milk, vanilla and rind into pan and bring to a boil. Remove from heat and infuse for 10 minutes. Beat sugar, eggs and flour till smooth. Strain in milk, stirring. Return to pan and cook gently, stirring, till thick. Grate rind of one orange and stir into custard with rum, if used.

Preheat the oven to 375°.

Roll out dough and use to line 9 inch fluted quiche pan. Spread with 2 tbsp marmalade. Cover with half custard, then the lasagne and remaining custard.

Peel and thinly slice remaining oranges. Arrange slices over filling to cover completely. Bake for 45 minutes.

Melt remaining marmalade and spoon over oranges to glaze. Sprinkle with walnuts and serve warm with pouring cream.

Iced strawberry tartlets

Overall timing 40 minutes

Freezing Not suitable

Makes 4

6 oz	Rich pie pastry
⅓ cup	Gooseberry jam
2 tbsp	Sherry wine
2-3 cups	Strawberries
1 pint	Vanilla ice cream
	or lemon sherbet

Preheat the oven to 375°. Put baking sheet in oven to heat.

Divide dough into four. Put one-quarter into each of four 3 inch tartlet molds and press into shape. Prick bottoms with a fork and place on heated baking sheet. Bake for about 25 minutes till crisp and golden. Remove from oven and leave to cool completely.

Meanwhile, put the jam and sherry into a saucepan and heat gently till melted. Sieve into a sauceboat and leave to cool. Hull the strawberries. Cut a quarter of them in half lengthwise and put the rest into a serving dish.

Arrange the tartlets on a serving dish. Put a scoop of ice cream or sherbet into each and decorate with halved strawberries. Serve immediately with remaining strawberries and gooseberry sauce.

Lime tart

Overall timing 50 minutes plus chilling

Freezing Suitable

To serve 8

6 oz	Pie pastry
4 tsp	Unflavored gelatin
¼ cup	Water
4	Eggs
½ cup	Sugar
3	Limes
¾ cup	Heavy cream

Preheat the oven to 400°.

Roll out dough on a lightly floured surface and use to line an 8 inch straight-sided pie pan. Bake blind for 20 minutes till golden. Allow to cool, then carefully remove from the pan.

To make the filling, dissolve the gelatin in the water. Separate eggs. Beat the yolks and sugar together till pale and creamy. Grate rind from limes and squeeze out the juice. Stir two-thirds of the rind and all the juice into the egg mixture. Stir in the gelatin.

Whip cream till stiff. In another bowl, beat the egg whites till stiff peaks form. Carefully fold cream, then beaten whites into lime mixture. Spoon into pastry case and fluff up the surface.

Sprinkle with the remaining grated lime rind and chill for at least 3 hours or overnight before serving.

Hot apple tart

Overall timing 1 hour

Freezing Not suitable

To serve 6

1¾ cup	Flour
	Pinch of salt
1 tbsp	Confectioners' sugar
7 tbsp	Butter
Filling	
1½ lb	Tart apples
2 oz	Butter
1 cup + 2 tbsp	Confectioners' sugar
3 tbsp	Calvados or applejack

Preheat the oven to 400°.

To make pastry, sift flour, salt and sugar into a bowl. Add butter and rub in until mixture resembles fine bread crumbs. Add enough water to mix to a firm dough. Knead lightly. Roll out dough and use to line an 8 inch quiche pan. Bake blind for 20-25 minutes.

Meanwhile, make filling. Peel and core apples. Cut into quarters or eighths, depending on size. Melt butter in a saucepan, add apples and cook over a high heat for a few minutes till light brown. Add 1 cup confectioners' sugar and 1 tbsp Calvados or applejack. Cover and cook gently till apples are just tender.

Spoon apples and a little of the juice into the warm pastry case. Sift over remaining confectioners' sugar. Keep in a warm oven till needed.

Warm remaining Calvados or applejack in a ladle, then pour over apples. Light immediately and take tart to table while still flaming.

French cherry tart

Overall timing 1 hour plus chilling

Freezing Not suitable

To serve 8

2 cups	Flour
	Pinch of salt
¾ cup	Confectioners' sugar
½ cup	Butter
1	Lemon
1	Egg
Filling	
4 tsp	Dried bread crumbs
16 oz	Jar of cherry pie filling
3	Eggs
6 tbsp	Sugar
1 tbsp	Cornstarch
	Ground cinnamon
2 tbsp	Cream cheese

Put the flour, salt and confectioners' sugar into a bowl. Rub in butter. Grate rind and squeeze juice from lemon. Add rind to bowl with egg and mix to a dough. Chill for 30 minutes.

Preheat the oven to 425°.

Roll out dough and use to line 10 inch French flan ring placed on baking sheet. Bake blind for about 15 minutes. Remove pastry case from oven and reduce heat to 375°. Sprinkle bread crumbs over bottom of pastry case. Spread cherry pie filling on top.

Separate eggs. Beat egg yolks with 2 tbsp lemon juice, the sugar and cornstarch until creamy. Beat in cinnamon and cream cheese until smooth.

Beat egg whites until soft peaks form. Fold into yolk mixture. Pour over cherries. Bake for 30-40 minutes. Carefully remove tart from ring and place on serving dish. Dredge with more confectioners' sugar and serve warm with cream or ice cream.

Linzertorte

Overall timing 50 minutes

Freezing Suitable

To serve 12

2 cups	Flour
½ tsp	Ground cinnamon
10 tbsp	Butter
¾ cup	Ground almonds
6 tbsp	Sugar
½	Lemon
2	Egg yolks
⅔ cup	Raspberry jam

Sift flour and cinnamon into a large bowl. Rub in butter. Stir in almonds and sugar. Grate rind from lemon and squeeze out juice. Add both to bowl with egg yolks and mix to a soft dough. Add a little water if necessary. Knead lightly, then chill for 1 hour.

Preheat the oven to 375°.

Roll out two-thirds of the dough on a floured surface and use to line an 8 inch pie pan. Don't trim away excess dough.

Spread jam over the pastry case. Roll out remaining dough and cut into strips. Arrange in a lattice pattern across the jam. Fold dough edges in, crimping to make a decorative border.

Bake for 30-35 minutes. Leave to cool in pan. Serve with pouring cream.

Rhubarb and apple pie

Overall timing 2¼ hours plus cooling

Freezing Suitable

To serve 8

3 cups	Flour
½ tsp	Salt
¼ cup	Sugar
½ cup	Butter
1 cup	Water
1	Egg
Filling	
2 lb	Rhubarb
1 lb	Tart apples
1 cup	Sugar
1 tsp	Ground ginger
6 tbsp	Water

Preheat the oven to 375°.

Cut rhubarb into 1 inch lengths. Peel, core and slice apples. Put fruit into a saucepan with sugar, ginger and water and bring to a boil. Cover and simmer for 15 minutes till pulpy. Purée in a blender or food processor and leave to cool.

Sift flour and salt into a bowl and stir in sugar. Put butter and water into a pan and heat gently till butter melts. Bring to a boil, then pour into flour mixture and mix to a soft dough.

Quickly roll out two-thirds of dough and use to line a 7 inch springform cake pan. Pour fruit purée into pastry case. Roll out remaining dough and use to cover pie. Seal edges and crimp. Make a neat hole in center. Decorate top with remaining dough trimmings. Beat egg and brush over pie.

Bake for 1 hour till pastry is golden. Cool in the pan. Serve with pouring cream or ice cream.

Spicy rhubarb pie

Overall timing 1¾ hours

Freezing Not suitable

To serve 6-8

2¼ cups	Flour
	Pinch of salt
¼ tsp	
	Apple pie spice
½ tsp	
	Ground cinnamon
10 tbsp	
	Butter
¾ cup + 2 tbsp	
	Sugar
2 lb	
	Rhubarb
1	
	Egg yolk

Sift flour, pinch of salt and spices into a bowl. Rub in the butter till the mixture resembles fine bread crumbs. Stir in 2 tbsp sugar and enough water to make a soft but not sticky dough. Add a little water if necessary. Knead lightly till smooth, then chill for 30 minutes.

Meanwhile, trim the rhubarb and cut into 1 inch lengths. Put into a bowl with all but 1 tbsp of the remaining sugar and mix well.

Preheat the oven to 400°. Place a baking sheet in the oven. Roll out half the dough on a floured surface and use to line a 9 inch pie pan. Brush the edge with water. Pile the rhubarb into the pie in a dome shape. Roll out remaining dough and cover the pie, sealing and crimping the edges.

Beat the egg yolk and brush over top of pie. Place pie on hot baking sheet and bake for 20 minutes. Reduce the temperature to 350° and bake for a further 25 minutes till crisp and golden.

Remove from the oven, sprinkle remaining sugar over and serve immediately with cream or custard sauce.

Banana tart

Overall timing 1 hour 50 minutes

Freezing Not suitable

To serve 8

1¾ cups	Flour
½ tsp	Baking powder
½ tsp	Salt
3 tbsp	Sugar
7 tbsp	Butter
1	Medium-size egg
Filling	
½ cup	Raisins or
	pitted dates
2 tbsp	Rum
4	Ripe bananas
2	Eggs
6 tbsp	Sugar
½ cup	Heavy cream
½ cup	Split almonds

Sift flour, baking powder, salt and sugar into a bowl. Rub in butter. Add egg with a little water if necessary to bind to a dough. Chill for 1 hour.

Put raisins, or chopped dates, to steep in rum.

Preheat the oven to 400°.

Roll out dough and use to line a 9 inch fluted French flan ring set on a baking sheet. Prick and bake blind for 15 minutes. Remove from oven.

Drain dried fruit, reserving rum. Peel bananas and cut in diagonal slices. Cover bottom of pastry case with the banana and most of the dried fruit.

Beat eggs and sugar together till pale and thick. Whip cream with reserved rum. Blend both mixtures together and pour over the fruit in pastry case. Scatter over almonds and reserved dried fruit.

Bake for 25 minutes until puffed, golden brown and set. Serve hot with cream.

Sunburst peach tart

Overall timing 1 hour

Freezing Not suitable

To serve 6

6 tbsp	Butter
½ cup	Sugar
3	Eggs
1¼ cups	Flour
	Grated rind of 1 lemon
16 oz	Can of sliced peaches
½ cup	Hazelnuts

Preheat the oven to 350°.

Cream the butter and sugar together till pale and fluffy. Beat in the eggs one at a time, beating well between each addition. Fold in the sifted flour and lemon rind with a metal spoon. Pour the mixture into a greased and lined 8 inch springform pan and smooth the surface.

Drain the peaches thoroughly and arrange the slices in circles on the cake mixture. Sprinkle the finely chopped hazelnuts over. Bake for 45 minutes.

Remove from the pan, place on a warmed serving dish and serve immediately with custard sauce or cream.

Plum tart

Overall timing 1¾ hours

Freezing Not suitable

To serve 6-8

Filling	
2½ cups	Milk
1 tsp	Vanilla
1½ lb	Ripe yellow plums
4	Egg yolks
¾ cup	Sugar
6 tbsp	Flour
Pastry	
3 cups	Self-rising four
1 cup	Butter
3 tbsp	Sugar
1	Egg
	Milk to mix

To make filling, put milk and vanilla into a saucepan and bring to a boil. Remove from heat, cover and leave to infuse for 10 minutes.

Meanwhile halve and pit plums. Beat egg yolks with sugar till pale and thick. Beat in sifted flour, then gradually stir in milk. Pour back into saucepan and cook gently, stirring, till thick. Leave to cool.

Preheat the oven to 400°.

Sift flour into a bowl and rub in ¾ cup of the butter. Stir in sugar, and add egg and enough milk to give a soft dough. Roll out and use to line a greased 8 inch square deep cake pan, molding it into the corners. Rest in refrigerator for 15 minutes.

Pour filling into pastry-lined tin and arrange plums on top, pressing them in lightly. Bake for 30 minutes.

Meanwhile, melt remaining butter in a saucepan. Remove tart from pan and place on a baking sheet. Brush sides and top edge of pastry with butter and bake for a further 10 minutes till pastry is crisp and golden. Serve hot or cold.

Tarte Tatin

Overall timing 1 ¼ hours

Freezing Not suitable

To serve 8-10

½ lb	Frozen puff pastry
6 tbsp	Unsalted butter
6 tbsp	Sugar
7	Large apples

Thaw the pastry. Preheat the oven to 425°.

Cut butter into pieces and put into a 9 inch round cake pan with the sugar. Peel and core the apples; cut six of them in half. Arrange the apple halves on end around the side of the pan and place the whole apple in the center.

Place the pan over a low heat and heat till the butter melts. Increase the heat and cook, shaking the pan occasionally, till the sugar caramelizes and is golden. Remove from the heat. Brush a little water around the edge of the pan.

Roll out dough on a floured surface to a 9 inch round and place over the apples. Press down lightly.

Bake for 25-30 minutes till the pastry is well risen and golden brown. Leave to cool in the pan for 5 minutes.

Run a knife around the edge of the tart and unmold onto a serving dish so that the caramelized apples are on top. Serve hot or cold with whipped cream or scoops of vanilla ice cream.

Almond marmalade tart

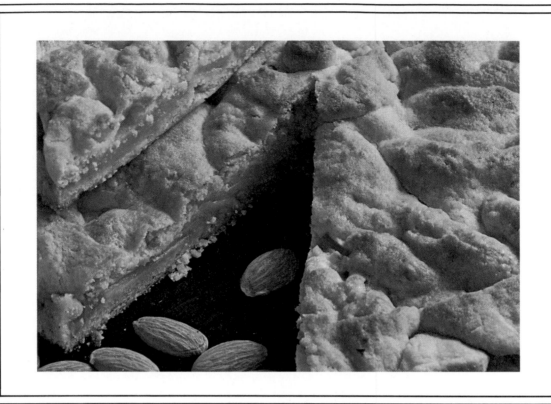

Overall timing 1 ¼ hours

Freezing Suitable

To serve 6-8

7 tbsp	Butter
7 tbsp	Sugar
1	Egg
1 cup	Ground almonds
1 ¼ cups	Self-rising flour
¼ tsp	Salt
Filling	
¾ lb	Tart apples
	Juice of ½ lemon
2 tbsp	Sugar
6 tbsp	Fine-cut marmalade
1 tbsp	Dried bread crumbs

Put butter, sugar and egg into a bowl and beat until light and fluffy. Add almonds, sifted flour and salt and mix to a soft, but not sticky dough. Add a little water if necessary. Chill for 30 minutes.

Meanwhile, peel and core apples. Slice thinly into a bowl and sprinkle with lemon juice. Stir in the sugar and marmalade and leave to stand till pastry is ready.

Preheat the oven to 400°.

Put half the dough into a greased 8 inch layer cake pan and spread out to cover the bottom. Prick and sprinkle bread crumbs over. Spread the apple mixture over and cover with small spoonfuls of remaining pastry.

Bake for about 35 minutes till golden. Remove from pan and serve hot or cold, cut into slices, with cream or custard sauce.

Honey snail

Overall timing 1 ¼ hours

Freezing Suitable

To serve 6-8

2½ cups	Flour
	Pinch of salt
1 tbsp	Baking powder
⅔ cup	Sugar
1 tsp	Vanilla
¾ cup	Milk
2	Eggs
1 tsp	Grated lemon rind
¼ cup	Softened butter

Topping	
¼ cup	Softened butter
2 tbsp	Sugar
3 tbsp	Honey
1	Egg white
½ cup	Mixed nuts

Preheat the oven to 350°.

Sift the flour, salt, baking powder and sugar into a bowl. Make a well in the center and add the vanilla, milk, eggs and lemon rind. Mix to a smooth dough. Put dough onto a floured board and spread out to an oblong. Smear with the butter and work it in with floured hands.

Form the dough into a long roll about 1½ inches in diameter. Arrange, in a spiral starting from the center, in a buttered 12 inch cake pan.

For the topping, beat the butter with the sugar, honey and egg white. Spread over the spiralled dough. Chop the nuts and sprinkle on top. Bake for 30 minutes or until risen and golden. Cool, then remove from the pan.

Apricot tart

Overall timing 1 ½ hours

Freezing Suitable: open freeze; thaw then refresh in oven at 400° for about 10 minutes.

To serve 4

1 ¾ cups	Flour
	Pinch of salt
½ cup + 1 tbsp	Sugar
7 tbsp	Butter
1 lb	Fresh apricots
2 tbsp	Apricot jam
2 tbsp	Kirsch
1 tbsp	Sliced almonds

Put flour, salt and 1 tbsp sugar into bowl, making a well in the center. Cut the softened butter into small pieces and put into the well. Rub in with fingertips till mixture resembles fine bread crumbs. Bind with cold water and knead lightly. Wrap in foil and chill for at least 30 minutes.

Preheat oven to 425°. Wash, dry and halve apricots. Remove pits.

Roll out pastry fairly thickly on a floured surface and use to line 9 inch pie pan. Sprinkle 2 tbsp of the sugar over the pastry. Arrange apricots on top, hollow side up, so that the juice doesn't run out during cooking. Sprinkle on the rest of the sugar. Bake for about 45 minutes until apricots begin to caramelize.

Put apricot jam and kirsch into a saucepan. Stir together over a low heat. Remove tart from oven and immediately pour on the syrup. Sprinkle on the almonds.

Almond and apple tart

Overall timing 1 hour plus chilling

Freezing Not suitable

Cuts into 8

1¾ cups	Flour
	Pinch of salt
⅔ cup	Butter
2 tbsp	Sugar
6-8 tbsp	Cold water
16 oz	Jar of applesauce
1 lb	Apples
¼ cup	Apricot jam
3 tbsp	Apricot brandy of Curaçao
½ cup	Almond pieces

Sift the flour and salt into a bowl. Rub in the butter till the mixture resembles fine bread crumbs. Stir in the sugar. Add the water, stirring, and knead into a smooth ball.

Roll out the pastry on a floured surface and use to line a greased 8-inch springform pan. Chill in the refrigerator for 30 minutes.

Preheat the oven to 425°. Place baking sheet in oven to heat.

Spread applesauce over bottom of tart. Peel, core and thickly slice the apples. Arrange the slices in overlapping circles on top of the filling. Warm the jam and brandy together till smooth and brush over the apple slices. Sprinkle the almonds around the edge and over the center.

Place the pan on the baking sheet in the center of the oven for 30 minutes. Remove from the oven and leave to cool completely. Remove from the springform pan, place on a serving dish and serve with whipped cream.

Wholewheat bread

Overall timing 3 hours minimum

Freezing Suitable

Makes 2-4 loaves

1 tbsp	Brown sugar
3¾ cups	Lukewarm water
3 pkg	Active dry yeast
12 cups	Wholewheat flour
1 tbsp	Salt
2 tbsp	Lard

Dissolve 1 tsp of the sugar in 1 cup of the warm water in a bowl. Sprinkle the dried yeast on top. Leave for about 10 minutes till frothy.

Mix flour, salt and the remaining sugar in a bowl. Rub in the lard, then add the yeast liquid and the rest of the water. Mix to a dough. Knead the dough thoroughly till it feels firm and elastic and no longer sticky. This should take 5-10 minutes. Shape the dough into a ball and place in an oiled plastic bag. Leave to rise till doubled in size.

Turn the dough onto a board and knead again till firm. Divide into two or four and flatten each piece firmly with the knuckles to knock out air. Shape and place in loaf pans.

Brush the tops with a little salted water and put each pan into an oiled plastic bag. Leave to rise till the dough comes to just over the top of the pan and springs back when pressed with a floured finger — about 1 hour at room temperature.

Preheat the oven to 450°. Bake the loaves for 30-40 minutes. Unmold to cool on a wire rack.

Brioche

Overall timing 1 ¼ hours plus rising

Freezing Suitable: shape dough and bake after thawing

Makes 1 large or 12 small

2 tsp	sugar
⅓ cup	Lukewarm water
2 tsp	Active dry yeast
2 cups	Flour
	Salt
¼ cup	Butter
2	Eggs
	Milk for glazing

Dissolve ½ tsp sugar in water and sprinkle yeast on top. Leave till frothy.

Sift flour, a pinch of salt and remaining sugar into a large bowl. Add yeast mixture, melted butter and eggs and mix to a soft dough. Knead till smooth and glossy. Leave to rise in a warm place till doubled in size.

Punch down dough and knead for 3-4 minutes till smooth. To make one large brioche, cut off one-quarter of the dough and shape both pieces into balls. Place large one in lightly greased 8 inch brioche mold and push a finger down through center to base. Place smaller ball in indentation and press down lightly.

To make 12 small brioches, divide dough into 12 pieces and remove one-quarter from each. Shape all pieces into balls. Place each large ball in a 3 inch brioche mold, push a finger down through center, then top with small balls, pressing down lightly. Leave to rise till doubled in size.

Preheat the oven to 450°. Brush each brioche with milk and bake for 8-10 minutes (small) or 15-20 minutes (large) till well risen and golden. Serve warm.

Italian fruit bread

Overall timing 1 ½ hours plus rising

Freezing Suitable: reheat in 350° oven for 10 minutes

To serve 6

3 cups	Flour
4 tsp	Active dry yeast
¼ cup	Sugar
1 cup	Lukewarm milk
¼ tsp	Salt
½ cup	Pine nuts
⅓ cup	Chopped candied peel
⅓ cup	Raisins
¼ cup	Butter
1	Egg
1 tbsp	Marsala

Mix together 1 cup flour, the yeast, 1 tsp sugar and the milk to a smooth batter. Leave till frothy.

Sift remaining flour and the salt into a large bowl. Add remaining sugar, the pine nuts, candied peel and raisins. Stir melted butter, beaten egg and Marsala into frothy batter, then add to fruit mixture. Mix to a soft dough. Turn onto a lightly floured surface and knead till smooth and glossy. Cover with oiled plastic wrap and leave to rise till doubled in size.

Punch down dough and knead till smooth. Shape into a smooth ball and place on greased baking sheet. Leave to rise till doubled in size.

Preheat the oven to 400°. Score a cross on top of the ball and bake for 10 minutes. Reduce the heat to 350° and bake for a further 25 minutes. Cool on a wire rack.

Caraway seed bread

Overall timing 1½ hours plus rising

Freezing Suitable: refresh in hot oven for 10 minutes

Makes 2 small or 1 large loaf

4 cups	Flour
3 tbsp	Sugar
2 tsp	Active dry yeast
5 tbsp	Lukewarm water
¾ cup	Lukewarm milk
1 tsp	Salt
2 tbsp	Caraway seeds
½ cup	Softened butter
2	Eggs
1 tbsp	Milk

Mix together 1 cup flour, 1 tsp sugar, the yeast, water and milk in a large bowl. Cover and leave in a warm place for about 20 minutes till frothy.

Mix remaining flour with salt, remaining sugar and caraway seeds. Add to yeast mixture with butter and beaten eggs. Mix well to a soft dough. Turn onto a lightly floured surface and knead till smooth and elastic. Cover and leave to rise until doubled in size.

Turn dough onto a lightly floured surface and knead till dough is firm again. Shape into two rolls about 6 inches long. Place on greased and floured baking sheet. Make three cuts across top of each loaf. Brush with milk. Cover with oiled plastic wrap and leave to rise until loaves double in size.

Preheat the oven to 400°. Bake the loaves for 30-35 minutes. Cool on a wire rack.

Currant buns

Overall timing 2¼ hours

Freezing Suitable

Makes 12

4 cups	Flour
6 tbsp	Sugar
1 pkg	Active dry yeast
1¾ cups	Lukewarm milk
½ tsp	Salt
1 tsp	Apple pie spice
⅔ cup	Currants
¼ cup	Butter
1	Egg

Mix together ½ cup flour, 1 tsp sugar, the yeast and milk to a batter. Leave till frothy.

Sift remaining flour, salt and spice into a mixing bowl. Add currants, ¼ cup sugar, the yeast mixture, melted butter and egg. Mix to a soft dough. Knead till smooth and elastic. Leave to rise till doubled in size.

Punch down dough, then divide into 12 pieces. Knead each piece into a smooth bun. Place on baking sheets, cover and leave to rise till doubled in size.

Preheat the oven to 375°.

To make glaze, dissolve remaining sugar in rest of milk and brush lightly over the buns. Bake for 15-20 minutes. While still hot, brush with remaining glaze.

Jam doughnuts

Overall timing 3-3½ hours including rising

Freezing Suitable: reheat from frozen in 400° oven for 8 minutes

Makes 12

2 cups	Flour
2 tsp	Active dry yeast
5 tbsp	Sugar
⅔ cup	Lukewarm milk
¼ tsp	Salt
3 tbsp	Butter
1	Egg
	Oil for frying
	Jam

Mix together ½ cup flour, the yeast, 2 tsp sugar and the milk to a batter. Leave till frothy.

Sift remaining flour and salt into bowl. Add yeast mixture, melted butter and beaten egg. Mix to a soft dough. Knead till smooth and elastic. Leave to rise till doubled in size.

Punch down dough, divide into 12 and shape into balls. Leave to rise.

Heat the oil in a deep-fryer to 360°. Press a deep hole in each dough ball and fill with about 1 tsp jam. Seal jam in well by pinching dough together. Deep fry for about 10 minutes. Drain on paper towels and roll in remaining sugar while still hot.

Lemon buns

Overall timing 1 hour plus cooling

Freezing Suitable: refresh in 400° oven for 10 minutes

Makes 12

¼ cup	Sugar
5 tbsp	Lukewarm milk
2 tsp	Active dry yeast
2 cups	Flour
	Salt
	Grated rind of 2 lemons
1	Egg
1	Egg yolk
¼ cup	Butter

Dissolve ½ tsp of the sugar in the milk and sprinkle the yeast on top. Leave in a warm place for 15 minutes till frothy.

Sift the flour and a pinch of salt into a bowl and stir in the remaining sugar and lemon rind. Add the yeast mixture, beaten egg and yolk and melted butter and mix to a stiff dough. Divide between greased 12-hole bun sheet. Cover with oiled plastic wrap and leave to rise in a warm place till doubled in size.

Preheat the oven to 375°. Bake the buns for about 25 minutes till well risen. Cool on a wire rack.

Cherry and lemon loaf

Overall timing 1 ½ hours

Freezing Suitable

To serve 16

2 cups	Self-rising flour
	Pinch of salt
½ cup	Butter
½ cup	Sugar
	Grated rind of
	1 lemon
1	Egg
¾ cup	Milk
⅔ cup	Glacé cherries

Preheat the oven to 350°.

Sift all but 1 tbsp of flour and the salt into a bowl. Rub in butter until mixture resembles fine bread crumbs. Stir in sugar and lemon rind. Make a well in center and break in egg. Mix together, adding enough milk to give a soft consistency that won't drop unless flicked from the spoon. Coat cherries into reserved flour and fold into mixture.

Pour into greased and lined 9 x 5 x 3 inch loaf pan and smooth surface. Bake for 45 minutes. Cover with parchment paper and bake for further 30 minutes. Cool on a wire rack.

Coffee ring cake

Overall timing 1½ hours

Freezing Suitable

To serve 16

10 tbsp	Butter
10 tbsp	Sugar
	Salt
2	Large eggs
1	Orange
1 tbsp	Instant coffee powder
1¼ cups	Self-rising flour
¼ tsp	Ground cinnamon
2 x 1 oz	Squares semisweet chocolate
Icing	
1½ cups	Confectioners' sugar
2 tsp	Instant coffee powder
1 tsp	Cocoa
2 tbsp	Hot water
	Vanilla

Preheat the oven to 325°.

Cream butter with sugar and a pinch of salt till light and fluffy. Add eggs one at a time and beat well. Grate orange and add rind to bowl. Squeeze orange and mix ¼ cup juice with the instant coffee. Sift flour and cinnamon and mix into the creamed mixture alternately with the orange/coffee mixture. Grate chocolate and fold in. Add more orange juice or water if necessary.

Spoon mixture into a greased 8½ inch ring mold. Bake for 40-50 minutes. Cool on a wire rack.

To make the icing, sift confectioners' sugar into bowl. Dissolve coffee and cocoa in hot water, then add to confectioners' sugar with a few drops of vanilla and mix well. Pour over cooled cake and smooth surface with a knife.

Sand cake

Overall timing 1 ¼ hours

Freezing Suitable: thaw at room
temperature for 2 hours

To serve 12

1 cup	Softened butter
1 cup	Sugar
5	Eggs
	Grated rind of
	1 lemon
	Pinch of salt
1 ¼ cups	Potato starch
¾ cup	Flour
	Confectioners' sugar

Grease and line cake pan. Preheat the oven to 375°.

Put the butter and sugar in a bowl and beat till pale and creamy. Separate the eggs. Add the yolks, lemon rind and salt to the bowl and beat in. Add potato starch and flour a little at a time, beating to a smooth, creamy mixture.

In another bowl, beat egg whites till stiff but not dry, then carefully fold into creamed mixture.

Pour batter into prepared pan and bake for about 45 minutes. Cool in pan, then unmold and dust top with confectioners' sugar. If you prefer, you can cut the finished cake into two layers and fill with jam and whipped cream.

Cream sponge cake

Overall timing 25-30 minutes plus cooling

Freezing Suitable: without filling and topping

Cuts into 8 slices

4	Large eggs
¾ cup	Sugar
2 tbsp	Warm water
1 cup	Flour
1 tsp	Baking powder
¼ cup	Milk
¼ cup	Butter
¼ cup	Apricot jam
½ cup	Heavy cream
2 tbsp	Strawberry jam
½ cup	Sliced almonds

Grease and flour 2 round 8-inch layer cake pans. Preheat oven to 375°.

Separate eggs. Place yolks in mixing bowl and beat till light and fluffy, then add sugar with warm water and beat well. Sift flour and baking powder and mix in a little at a time, alternating with milk. Melt butter and add.

Beat egg whites till stiff. Use a spatula or metal spoon to fold them carefully into egg/flour mixture. Divide batter between cake pans and bake on center shelf of oven for 15-20 minutes. When cooked, the cakes will pull away from the sides of the pans. Turn out onto wire rack and leave to cool.

When cold, spread top of one cake layer with apricot jam. Place second layer on top. Whip cream and fold in strawberry jam. Spread whipped cream over top of cake, then sprinkle almonds over it.

Parkin

Overall timing 1½ hours

Freezing Suitable

To serve 16

¼ cup	Butter
¼ cup	Lard or shortening
⅔ cup	Molasses
⅓ cup	Light syrup
2 cups	Flour
2 tsp	Baking powder
2 tsp	Ground ginger
1⅓ cups	Coarse oatmeal
⅔ cup	Dark brown sugar
1-1¼ cups	Milk

Preheat the oven to 350°.

Put the butter and lard in a small pan and melt over a gentle heat. Add the molasses and corn syrup and heat till runny. Sift the flour, baking powder and ginger into a large bowl. Stir in the oatmeal and brown sugar. Make a well in the center. Pour in the fat and molasses mixture and half the milk. Mix to a soft pouring consistency, adding more milk as necessary.

Pour into a greased and bottom-lined 8-inch square cake pan. Bake for about 1 hour or until firm to the touch. Leave to cool in the pan.

To serve, cut into squares.

Fruity nut loaf

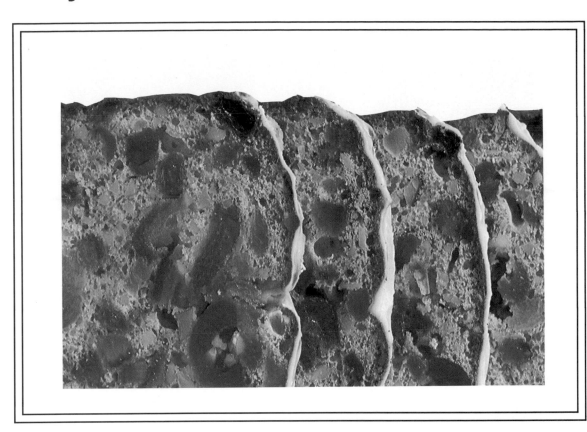

Overall timing 2 hours plus cooling time

Freezing Not suitable

Cuts into 20 slices

1 cup	Shelled Brazil nuts
⅔ cup	Dates
⅔	Dried apricots
⅔ cup	Golden raisins
⅓ cup	Chopped candied fruit peel
⅓ cup	Glacé cherries
4	Large eggs
⅔ cup	Sugar
	Vanilla
4 tsp	Rum
2¼ cups	Flour
2 tsp	Baking powder
¾ cup	Confectioners' sugar
2 tsp	Hot water
1 tsp	Lemon juice

Preheat oven to 350°. Line a 9x5 inch loaf pan with greased waxed paper.

Chop nuts. Pit dates and chop. Cut apricots into strips. Mix raisins with candied fruit peel in a bowl. Halve the cherries and add.

Lightly beat the eggs in another bowl. Mix in the sugar and beat till pale cream and foamy. Stir in a few drops of vanilla and 3 tsp rum, then sift in the flour and baking powder. Beat the mixture till smooth.

Add the fruit and nuts and stir well. Spoon mixture into prepared pan and bake in the middle of the oven for about 1-1½ hours till well risen and golden. Remove cake from oven. Cool for 30 minutes in pan, then unmold cake onto a wire rack and peel off the paper. Allow to cool.

To make the glacé icing, sift the confectioners' sugar into a bowl. Quickly mix in the hot water, lemon juice and remaining rum, then pour icing over the cold cake.

Dijon spice loaf

Overall timing 1 ½ hours

Freezing Suitable

To serve 12

3 cups	Flour
1 tbsp	Baking powder
	Pinch of salt
1 tsp	Powdered aniseed
	Pinch of cinnamon
½ cup	Butter or margarine
¾ cup	Milk
½ cup	Thick honey
3 tbsp	Rum
2 tbsp	Water
2	Small eggs
½ cup	Blanched almonds

Preheat oven to 350°. Grease and bottom-line loaf pan.

Sift the flour, baking powder, salt, powdered aniseed and cinnamon into a mixing bow. Add butter or margarine and rub it in lightly until the mixture resembles fine bread crumbs.

In a saucepan, heat milk to lukewarm. Remove from heat and add honey. Stir until well blended. Mix in the rum and water. Add to the flour mixture with beaten eggs and beat well.

Pour mixture into prepared pan and arrange almonds on the top. Bake for 1¼ hours.

Remove loaf from oven and unmold onto a wire rack to cool.

Banana cake

Overall timing 2¼ hours plus cooling. This cake tastes even better if kept for 24 hours.

Freezing Suitable

Cuts into 8 slices

2 lb	Bananas
4	Eggs
¾ cup	Butter
1½ cups	Sugar
2½ cups	Self-rising flour
1 tsp	Salt
½ tsp	Baking soda
1½ cups	Chopped walnuts
Frosting	
¼ cup	Butter
1 tbsp	Cocoa
3 cups	Confectioners' sugar
	Vanilla

Grease and flour a deep 8-inch cake pan. Preheat oven to 350°.

Put 1 banana aside for the frosting and mash the rest to a smooth purée. Beat the eggs. In a large bowl, cream the butter, adding sugar slowly till pale and fluffy. Beat in the eggs, then the bananas. Beat well till smooth.

Sift the flour with the salt and soda. Stir into the banana mixture. Add nuts and quickly pour the batter into prepared pan. Bake in center of the oven for 1½-2 hours or until a skewer inserted comes out clean. Unmold onto a cake rack and leave to cool.

To make frosting, mash reserved banana to a purée. Place butter and cocoa in a pan and heat till butter melts. Pour into banana purée. Beat well. Gradually add sifted confectioners' sugar to make a good consistency. Add a few drops of vanilla. Leave for a few minutes, then spread on cake.

Fatless sponge cake

Overall timing 1½ hours

Freezing Not suitable

To serve 8-10

4	Eggs
10 tbsp	Sugar
½ tsp	Vanilla
½ cup	Flour
½ cup	Potato flour
1	Egg white

Preheat the oven to 350°.

Separate eggs. Beat the yolks with the sugar and vanilla till mixture leaves a trail lasting 20 seconds when the beaters are lifted. Add the sifted flours and fold in with a wooden spatula or metal spoon.

Beat egg whites till stiff. Add about one-quarter of the whites to the yolk mixture and stir in, then fold mixture into the remaining egg white with a metal spoon.

Turn mixture into greased and floured 9 inch fluted cake pan. Bake for 50 minutes to 1 hour or until top springs back when lightly pressed.

Tunisian fruit and nut cake

Overall timing 1¾ hours

Freezing Suitable

To serve 8

¼ cup	Toasted hazelnuts
½ cup	Toasted pistachios
1	Orange
5	Eggs
1 cup	Sugar
1⅓ cups	Dried bread crumbs
½ cup	Flour
1 tsp	Baking powder
½ tsp	Baking soda
½ tsp	Ground cinnamon
⅔ cup	Golden raisins

Preheat the oven to 350°.

Chop the nuts finely. Finely grate rind from orange. Separate the eggs. Beat the yolks with the sugar in a bowl over a pan of hot water till pale and thick. Remove from the heat.

Add orange rind, bread crumbs, sifted flour, baking powder, baking soda, cinnamon and nuts and fold in with metal spoon. Squeeze the orange and add ¼ cup of the juice to the mixture with the raisins. Beat the egg whites till stiff but not dry and fold in carefully.

Pour mixture into greased and lined 9 inch springform pan. Bake for about 1 hour till firm and springy to the touch. Cool on a wire rack.

Whiskey cake

Overall timing 2 hours plus cooling

Freezing Suitable

To serve 12

⅔ cup	Raisins
¼ cup	Whiskey
⅔ cup	Chopped candied peel
	Grated rind of 1 orange
¾ cup	Butter
¾ cup	Sugar
3	Eggs
1 cup	Flour
1 cup	Self-rising flour
¼ tsp	Ground cinnamon

Preheat the oven to 350°.

Soak the raisins in the whiskey. Add the candied peel to the raisins with the orange rind. Mix well and leave to soak for 10 minutes.

Cream the butter with the sugar till pale and fluffy. Beat the eggs and add, a little at a time, to the creamed mixture, beating well between each addition. Sift the flours and cinnamon over, add the fruit and soaking liquid and fold into the mixture with a metal spoon.

Spread the mixture in a greased and lined 8 inch round deep cake pan, smooth the surface and make a slight hollow in the center. Bake for 1¼ – 1½ hours till a skewer inserted in the cake comes out clean. Allow to cool slightly in the pan, then transfer to a wire rack and leave to cool completely.

Moist date and ginger cake

Overall timing 1 ¼ hours

Freezing Suitable

To serve 12

½ lb (1 ½ cups)	Pitted dates
1 tsp	Baking soda
¾ cup	Boiling water
½ cup	Butter
⅔ cup	Dark brown sugar
2 tbsp	Molasses
1 tbsp	Light corn syrup
2	Eggs
2 cups	Self-rising flour
2 tsp	Ground ginger
2 tbsp	Confectioners' sugar

Preheat the oven to 350°.

Chop the dates and place in a small bowl. Sprinkle with baking soda, then pour on the boiling water. Leave to cool.

Cream the butter with the sugar till light and fluffy. Beat in the molasses and corn syrup, then the eggs, one at a time, beating well. Sift in the flour and ginger, and add the dates and soaking liquid. Stir till well blended.

Pour into a greased and lined 9 inch round cake pan. Bake for 50-60 minutes till the center of the cake springs back when lightly pressed. Cool on a wire rack. Dredge with confectioners' sugar before serving.

Raisin loaf cake

Overall timing 1 ½ hours

Freezing Suitable

To serve 16

2 cups	Self-rising flour
	Salt
1 tsp	Ground ginger
½ cup	Butter
¼ cup	Sugar
1 cup	Golden raisins
2 tbsp	Clear honey
1	Egg
½ cup	Milk

Preheat the oven to 350°.

Sift the flour, a pinch of salt and the ginger into a large bowl. Rub in butter till the mixture resembles fine bread crumbs. Stir in the sugar and raisins. Make a well in the center and add the honey, egg and half the milk. Mix together, adding more milk if necessary to give a soft dropping consistency.

Spread the mixture in a greased and lined 9x5x3 inch loaf pan and smooth the surface. Bake for 45 minutes. Cover the top lightly with foil and bake for a further 30 minutes till the loaf is springy when lightly pressed. Cool on a wire rack.

Marble ring cake

Overall timing 1 ½ hours

Freezing Suitable

To serve 10

½ cup	Butter
10 tbsp	Sugar
3	Eggs
1¾ cups	Self-rising flour
½ cup	Milk
¼ cup	Cocoa powder

Preheat the oven to 350°.

Cream the butter with the sugar till mixture is pale and fluffy. Beat in the eggs, one at a time. Divide the mixture into two. Sift 1 cup of the flour into one-half and fold in with half of the milk. Sift the rest of the flour and the cocoa into the other half of the mixture and fold in with the remaining milk. Add more milk to both mixtures if necessary.

Spread a little of the plain mixture over the bottom and sides of a greased and floured 7½ inch ring mold. Carefully spread a thin layer of the chocolate mixture over the layer. Repeat the careful layering until both mixtures are used up.

Bake for 1 hour till well risen and firm to the touch. Cool cake slightly in the mold before unmolding onto a wire rack to cool completely.

Jelly roll

Overall timing 30 minutes plus cooling

Freezing Suitable: fill after thawing

To serve 8

3	Large eggs
6 tbsp	Sugar
¼ tsp	Vanilla
¾ cup	Flour
	Pinch of salt
3 tbsp	Warm water
¼ cup	Jam

Preheat the oven to 400°.

Separate the eggs. Beat yolks with the sugar and vanilla till mixture forms trails when beaters are lifted. Sift flour and fold into mixture.

Beat the whites with salt till mixture forms soft peaks that curl downwards. Fold into yolk mixture with metal spoon, then fold in warm water. Place mixture in greased and lined jelly roll pan, spreading to sides. Bake for 12-15 minutes till sides of sponge shrink a little.

Unmold sponge onto sheet of wax paper sprinkled with sugar. Carefully peel away paper from sponge. Trim edges of sponge with a sharp knife.

Working quickly, spread jam over sponge. With the help of the paper, roll up sponge away from you. Place seam-side down on wire rack to cool.

Caramel ring cake

Overall timing 1¼ hours

Freezing Suitable: ice cake after thawing

To serve 12

½ cup	Butter
1 cup	Brown sugar
1 tbsp	Light corn syrup
2	Eggs
1½ cups	Self-rising flour
1 tsp	Ground cinnamon
	Pinch of salt
¼ tsp	Baking soda
½ cup	Milk
	Vanilla
Icing	
2 tbsp	Butter
2 tbsp	Light corn syrup
1 tbsp	Milk
1 tsp	Vanilla
2 cups	Confectioners' sugar
1 tsp	Ground cinnamon

Preheat oven to 350°.

Cream butter with sugar; beat in eggs and corn syrup. Sift in flour, cinnamon and salt and beat well. Mix soda with milk and a few drops of vanilla and add to mixture. Place in a greased and floured 9½ inch ring mold and bake for 45-50 minutes. Cool on wire rack.

For the icing heat butter and corn syrup in saucepan. Stir in milk and vanilla and remove from heat. Sift half of confectioners' sugar and the cinnamon into saucepan and stir well. Stir in rest of sifted sugar.

Pour icing over cake and smooth with spatula dipped in hot water.

Chocolate ring cake

Overall timing 1 ½ hours plus cooling

Freezing Suitable: ice and decorate after thawing

To serve 12

½ cup	Butter
10 tbsp	Sugar
	Pinch of salt
	Grated rind of 1 lemon
4	Eggs
1 tbsp	Rum
1 ¼ cups	Flour
½ cup	Cornstarch
1 tsp	Baking powder
Chocolate filling	
¾ cup	Unsalted butter
½ cup	Confectioners' sugar
2 tbsp	Cocoa powder

Icing and decoration	
8x1 oz	Squares semisweet chocolate
¼ cup	Chopped nuts
12	Glacé cherries

Preheat the oven to 350°.

Cream butter with sugar, then beat in salt, grated rind, eggs and rum. Sift flour, cornstarch and baking powder together and fold into creamed mixture. Spoon into greased 9 inch ring mold and bake for 55 minutes. Cool on a wire rack.

To make the filling, cream butter with sugar and cocoa powder. Cut cake into three or four thin layers and put back together with filling, saving some to decorate the top.

Melt chocolate and spread over cake. Toast chopped nuts till golden. Sprinkle around the bottom edge of the chocolate. Pipe remaining chocolate filling in swirls on cake. Add cherry to each.

Cocoa Madeira cake

Overall timing 1 hour 20 minutes

Freezing Suitable

To serve 10

¾ cup	Butter
¾ cup	Sugar
3	Eggs
1 cup	Self-rising flour
½ cup	Cocoa powder
	Pinch of salt
3 tbsp	Madeira
¼ cup	Milk
½ cup	Chopped walnuts

Preheat the oven to 350°.

Cream the butter with the sugar till light and fluffy. Beat the eggs and add to creamed mixture a little at a time, beating well after each addition. Sift together the flour, cocoa and salt. Add to creamed mixture a little at a time, alternating with the Madeira and milk. When the mixture is smooth and will flick easily from the spoon, fold in half the chopped walnuts.

Put mixture into greased and lined 7 inch round deep cake pan and smooth top. Bake for 45 minutes. Sprinkle with remaining walnuts and bake for further 15-20 minutes till skewer inserted into cake comes out clean. Cool on a wire rack.

Honey spice loaf

Overall timing 1 hour 20 minutes

Freezing Suitable

To serve 16

½ cup	Sugar
5 tbsp	Water
⅔ cup	Honey
2 cups	Rye flour
	Salt
1½ tsp	Baking soda
¼ tsp	Ground cloves
½ tsp	Ground cinnamon
¼ tsp	Ground mace
2 tsp	Ground aniseed
¼ cup	Ground almonds
½ tsp	Almond extract
1 cup	Glacé fruits

Preheat the oven to 325°.

Put the sugar and water into a saucepan and heat gently till sugar is dissolved. Pour into a large bowl, add the honey and beat for 2 minutes. Sift the flour, a pinch of salt, the baking soda and spices into the mixture. Add the almonds and extract and beat for 4-5 minutes.

Cut the glacé fruits into pieces and stir into the mixture. Spread in a greased and lined 9x5x3 inch loaf pan and smooth the top. Bake for about 55 minutes till a skewer inserted in the center comes out clean. Cool in the pan for 10 minutes, then unmold onto a wire rack and leave to cool completely. Cut into slices to serve.

Lemon and cardamom cake

Overall timing 1 ½ hours

Freezing Suitable

To serve 8

2 cups	Self-rising flour
1 tsp	Ground cardamom
½ cup	Butter
½ cup	Sugar
1	Lemon
1	Egg
¼ cup	Milk
¼ cup	Flaked almonds
½ tsp	Ground cinnamon

Preheat the oven to 350°.

Sift flour and cardamom into a large bowl. Rub in the butter till mixture resembles fine bread crumbs. Stir in all but 1 tsp of the sugar. Grate the lemon rind and squeeze out the juice. Add both to bowl with the egg. Gradually mix ingredients, adding enough milk to give a soft consistency that won't drop unless flicked from the spoon.

Put mixture into a greased and lined 7 inch round deep cake pan and smooth the surface. Mix together almonds, cinnamon and reserved sugar and sprinkle over cake. Bake for 1¼ – 1½ hours till cake comes away from the sides. Cool in pan for a few minutes, then unmold onto a wire rack and cool completely.

Lemon shortcake

Overall timing 1 hour

Freezing Suitable

To serve 8

1	Lemon
2 cups	Flour
	Salt
6 tbsp	Sugar
6 tbsp	Butter
1	Egg

Preheat the oven to 375°.

Grate the rind of the lemon and squeeze out the juice. Sift the flour and a pinch of salt into a mixing bowl and stir in the sugar. Add the melted butter, egg, grated lemon rind and 2 tbsp lemon juice. Mix well and knead lightly until mixture is smooth.

Roll out on a floured surface to fit a greased 8 inch layer cake pan or French flan ring placed on a baking sheet. Bake for 20 minutes till golden. Cool in the pan.

Yogurt cake

Overall timing 2 hours

Freezing Suitable

To serve 10

¾ cup	Plain yogurt
1¼ cups	Sugar
2½ cups	Flour
1 tbsp	Baking powder
	Salt
2	Eggs
5 tbsp	Corn oil
2 tbsp	Rum
1 tbsp	Confectioners' sugar

Preheat the oven to 350°.

Pour the yogurt into a large bowl and beat in the sugar. Sift the flour and baking powder with a pinch of salt. Beat together the eggs, oil and rum and add to the yogurt alternately with the flour mixture, beating till smooth.

Pour the mixture into a greased and lined 7 inch round deep cake pan. Bake for 1¾ hours, covering the top lightly with foil after 45 minutes, till a skewer inserted in the center comes out clean. Cool on a wire rack.

Sift the confectioners' sugar over the cake and mark the top into 10 slices. Serve with cherry jam.

Gingerbread

Overall timing 1 ¼ hours

Freezing Suitable

To serve 9

2 cups	Flour
1 tsp	Baking soda
1 ½ tsp	Ground ginger
3 tbsp	Molasses
⅓ cup	Light corn syrup
6 tbsp	Butter
⅓ cup	Brown sugar
2	Eggs
¼ cup	Milk

Preheat the oven to 325°.

Sift flour, soda and ginger into a bowl. Place molasses and corn syrup in a saucepan with butter and brown sugar. Heat till melted.

Beat eggs and milk. Add with melted ingredients to dry ingredients. Mix to a thick batter. Pour into a greased and lined 7 inch square cake pan. Bake for 1 hour.

Golden fruit cake

Overall timing 2 hours

Freezing Suitable

To serve 8-10

½ cup	Butter
½ cup	Sugar
2	Eggs
2 cups	Self-rising flour
	Pinch of salt
⅓ cup	Glacé cherries
½ cup	Golden raisins
⅓ cup	Candied peel
3-4 tbsp	Water

Preheat the oven to 400°.

Cream butter with sugar till light and fluffy. Add the eggs, one at a time, beating between each addition. Stir in the flour, salt, fruit and peel. Mix well, then add enough water to make a soft, but not sticky, dough.

Pour mixture into greased and lined 7x4x3 inch loaf pan. Bake for 30 minutes, then lower oven temperature to 350° and bake for a further 1 hour. Cover with a piece of foil if the top begins to turn brown too quickly. Cool on a wire rack.

Hazelnut and honey cake

Overall timing 1 ¼ hours

Freezing Suitable

To serve 8

¾ cup	Butter
⅔ cup	Light brown sugar
¼ cup	Clear honey
2	Whole eggs
2	Egg yolks
2 cups	Wholewheat self-rising flour
	Pinch of salt
1 cup	Toasted hazelnuts
½ cup	Milk

Preheat the oven to 350°.

Cream the butter with the sugar and honey, then beat in the whole eggs and yolks. Fold in flour, salt and chopped hazelnuts alternately with the milk.

Put mixture into a greased and lined 7 inch round deep cake pan. Bake for 1 hour until springy to the touch. Cool on wire rack. Coat with a fudgy frosting if a more elaborate cake is desired.

Nutty honey cake

Overall timing 1 hour

Freezing Not suitable

To serve 8-10

¾ cup	Butter
¼ cup	Clear honey
1¼ cups	Flour
1¼ cups	Whole wheat flour
Filling	
1 cup	Chopped mixed nuts
⅓ cup	Golden raisins
1 tsp	Ground cinnamon
	Clear honey

Preheat the oven to 350°.

Cream butter with honey till light and fluffy. Mix in sifted flours to make a dough. Roll out half dough on a floured surface and press into greased and lined 7 inch round cake pan.

Mix nuts with raisins and cinnamon. Bind with honey. Spread filling over dough in pan.

Roll out remaining dough and cover filling. Press edges to seal. Bake for 30-40 minutes till golden. Cool in the pan.

Orange and almond sponge

Overall timing 1 hour plus cooling

Freezing Suitable: ice after thawing

To serve 10

1	Large orange
5	Eggs
10 tbsp	Sugar
¾ cup + 2 tbsp	Self-rising flour
	Pinch of salt
¼ tsp	Ground ginger
½ tsp	Ground cinnamon
1¼ cups	Ground almonds
	Almond extract
1¼ cups	Confectioners' sugar
1 tbsp	Curaçao

Preheat the oven to 400°.

Grate the rind from the orange and squeeze out the juice. Separate the eggs. Beat egg yolks with the sugar till the mixture is pale and thick. Sift the flour, salt and spices over the mixture and add the ground almonds, three drops of extract, orange rind and 3 tbsp of the orange juice. Add more orange juice if necessary. Fold in gently.

Beat the egg whites till stiff and fold into the mixture with a metal spoon. Carefully pour mixture into a greased and lined 9 inch cake pan and smooth the surface. Bake for about 35 minutes till springy to the touch. Cool on a wire rack.

Sift the confectioners' sugar into a bowl and add the Curaçao and 1 tbsp of the remaining orange juice to make an icing that will coat the back of the spoon. Pour the icing onto the top of the cake. Lift the wire rack and tap it several times on the working surface so that the icing flows over the cake and trickles down the sides. Leave to set.

Praline-topped lemon cake

Overall timing 1 ½ hours

Freezing Suitable

To serve 8

½ cup	Butter
10 tbsp	Sugar
4	Eggs
1 ¼ cups	Flour
¾ cup	Cornstarch
2 tsp	Baking powder
2 tbsp	Grated lemon rind
½ cup	Chopped almonds
Buttercream	
10 tbsp	Butter
1 ¼ cups	Confectioners' sugar
1	Egg yolk
2 tbsp	Lemon juice

Preheat the oven to 350°.

Cream butter with ½ cup sugar till light and fluffy. Separate eggs and beat egg yolks into creamed mixture. Sift flour, cornstarch and baking powder together and fold into creamed mixture with lemon rind. Beat egg whites till stiff and fold in.

Pour into greased and lined 8 inch round deep cake pan and smooth surface. Bake for 50-60 minutes till top springs back when lightly pressed. Cool on wire rack.

Melt remaining sugar with 1 tsp water in a heavy-based saucepan. Boil until caramelized to a pale golden color. Add chopped almonds and mix well. Spread onto a greased baking sheet. Allow to cool and set hard, then break praline into tiny pieces with a rolling pin.

To make buttercream, cream butter with sifted confectioners' sugar till soft, then beat in egg yolk and lemon juice.

Cut cake into three layers and put back together with most of buttercream. Spread remainder on top and lightly press in praline.

Fresh cherry cake

Overall timing 1 ½ hours

Freezing Suitable

To serve 8

6	Graham crackers
2 lb	Fresh cherries
¾ lb	Ground almonds
1 cup + 2 tbsp	Sugar
½ tsp	Ground cinnamon
5	Eggs
2 tbsp	Kirsch
1	Lemon
1 cup	Flour

Preheat the oven to 350°.

Crush the crackers and sprinkle over the bottom and sides of an oiled 10 inch cake pan.

Pit cherries. Arrange over the bottom of the coated cake pan.

Mix together the almonds, ¼ cup of the sugar and the cinnamon. Separate the eggs. Beat together the egg yolks, remaining sugar, Kirsch and grated rind and juice of the lemon. Stir in the almond mixture, then fold in the flour lightly. Beat the egg whites till stiff and fold into the cake mixture using a metal spoon.

Spread the cake mixture over the cherries. Bake for 1 hour 10 minutes. Cool on a wire rack. Dredge with confectioners' sugar before serving.

Spicy slab cake

Overall timing 1 ¼ hours

Freezing Suitable

To serve 12

1 ¼ cups	Butter
1 ¼ cups	Sugar
5	Eggs
2 ½ cups	Self-rising flour
1 tsp	Ground ginger
1 tsp	Ground cinnamon
1 tsp	Ground nutmeg
¼ tsp	Ground cloves
½ lb	Pitted dates
1 cup	Chopped walnuts
6-8 tbsp	Milk

Preheat the oven to 350°.

Cream the butter with the sugar till pale and fluffy. Beat the eggs lightly with a fork, then gradually beat into the creamed mixture. Sift the flour and spices into the bowl, add the chopped dates and walnuts and fold in with a metal spoon, adding the milk to give a soft dropping consistency. Spread the mixture in a greased and lined 12x9 inch baking pan and smooth the top. Bake for about 45 minutes till firm and a skewer inserted in center comes out clean. Cool on a wire rack. Cut into squares to serve.

Queen of Sheba cake

Overall timing 2 hours plus cooling

Freezing Suitable

To serve 8

9 x 1 oz	Squares semisweet chocolate
6	Eggs
1 cup	Butter
⅔ cup	Honey
1¼ cups	Flour
1 tbsp	Oil
1 cup	Hazelnuts
1 cup	Split almonds
1 tbsp	Chocolate hundreds-and-thousands
3 tbsp	Confectioners' sugar

Preheat the oven to 350°.

Gently melt 8 squares of the chocolate. Separate the eggs. Cream the butter with the honey, then beat in the chocolate and egg yolks. Add sifted flour, oil and chopped nuts and beat well. Beat the egg whites till stiff and fold into the mixture.

Turn into a greased and lined 9 inch round deep cake pan. Bake for 1½ hours.

Meanwhile, make curls from remaining chocolate; melt chocolate in saucepan and pour onto oiled marble slab or hard, cold surface. When chocolate has almost set but is not hard, scrape off thin slivers or curls with a knife. Chill.

Cool cake on a wire rack.

Sprinkle chocolate hundreds-and-thousands over cake, then sift confectioners' sugar around edge. Arrange the chocolate curls in the center.

Sachertorte

Overall timing 1 ½ hours plus cooling

Freezing Not suitable

To serve 8

4 x 1 oz	Squares semisweet chocolate
½ cup	Unsalted butter
¾ cup	Sugar
5	Eggs
¾ cup	Ground almonds
¼ cup	Self-rising flour
1 cup	Heavy or whipping cream
	Hazelnuts
Icing	
8 x 1 oz	Squares semisweet chocolate
4 oz	Butter

Preheat the oven to 400°.

Melt chocolate with butter till smooth. Beat in the sugar. Separate eggs and gradually add yolks to chocolate mixture, beating well. Beat egg whites till stiff. Gently fold whites into chocolate mixture, followed by ground almonds and flour. Divide mixture between two greased 8 inch layer cake pans and smooth top. Bake for 20-25 minutes. Cool on a wire rack.

Whip half cream till thick and use to sandwich together the cooled cakes.

To make icing, melt chocolate with butter in the top of a double boiler over hot water. Leave to cool for 20-30 minutes until of a coating consistency, then spread over top and sides of cake. Whip remaining cream and pipe large swirls around the edge of the cake. Decorate each swirl with a hazelnut.

Special honey sponge

Overall timing 35 minutes plus cooling

Freezing Suitable: fill and decorate after thawing

To serve 8

1¾ cups	Self-rising flour
¼ cup	Cornstarch
½ tsp	Baking powder
¾ cup	Confectioners' sugar
½ cup	Butter
½ cup	Sugar
1 tbsp	Clear honey
2	Large eggs
⅔ cup	Milk
¾ cup	Chopped nuts
Filling and decoration	
¼ cup	Butter
1 cup	Confectioners' sugar
1 tbsp	Clear honey
1 tbsp	Warm water
½ cup	Chopped almonds and walnuts
½ cup	Heavy cream

Preheat the oven to 350°.

Sift flour, cornstarch, baking powder and confectioners' sugar together. Cream butter with sugar and honey. Beat in eggs, then fold in flour mixture alternately with milk. Stir in chopped nuts. Divide between two greased 7 inch layer cake pans. Bake for 20 minutes. Cool on wire rack.

To make the filling, cream butter with confectioners' sugar, honey and water. Spread on one cake, sprinkle with most of the chopped nuts, then place second cake on top. Whip cream until stiff. Spoon into pastry bag fitted with large star tube and pipe decorative swirls around top of cake. Decorate with rest of nuts.

Italian nut and honey cake

Overall timing 1 hour

Freezing Not suitable

To serve 10

1½ cups	Almonds
1 cup	Walnuts
1⅓ cups	Chopped mixed candied peel
¼ tsp	Ground allspice
½ tsp	Ground cinnamon
1 tsp	Ground coriander
1¼ cups	Flour
1 cup	Confectioners' sugar
1 tbsp	Water
½ cup	Clear honey

Preheat the oven to 425°.

Spread the nuts on a baking sheet and toast in the oven till golden. Remove from oven and roughly chop. Reduce oven temperature to 375°.

Add chopped mixed peel, spices and flour to nuts and mix well together. Reserve 1 tbsp of the confectioners' sugar and put the rest in a heavy-based pan with the water and honey. Stir constantly over a low heat until bubbles appear on the surface. Remove from heat immediately. Gradually stir nut and fruit mixture into the syrup.

Turn into 8 inch loose-bottomed cake pan lined with rice paper and smooth surface with a wet knife blade. Sprinkle with reserved confectioners' sugar. Bake for about 30 minutes. Mark into 10 portions and leave to cool in pan before cutting.

Mocha cake

Overall timing 1 ¼ hours

Freezing Suitable

To serve 12

2 tsp	Instant coffee powder
4	Large eggs
½ cup	Sugar
1 cup	Flour
¼ cup	Butter
Filling and topping	
1 tbsp	Cornstarch
½ cup	Milk
3 tbsp	Sugar
1 tbsp	Instant coffee powder
1	Egg yolk
¾ cup	Butter
¾ cup	Confectioners' sugar
	Chocolate shavings
	Candy coffee beans

Preheat the oven to 375°.

Dissolve coffee in 1 tbsp water in large bowl over pan of hot water. Add eggs, sugar and pinch of salt and beat till very thick. Remove bowl from pan. Sift flour and fold in alternately with melted butter. Pour into greased and lined 8 inch round deep cake pan. Bake for 40 minutes. Cool on wire rack.

To make filling, place cornstarch in small saucepan and blend in milk. Add sugar and coffee and bring to a boil, stirring. Simmer for 2-3 minutes, stirring constantly. Remove from heat and cool slightly, then add egg yolk and beat well. Cook over gentle heat for 2 minutes, then remove from heat and leave to cool.

Beat butter with sifted confectioners' sugar. Add cooled custard and beat to a smooth creamy consistency.

Cut cake into two layers and put back back together with one-third of filling. Coat and decorate cake with remainder and top with chocolate shavings and candy coffee beans.

Pear refrigerator cake

Overall timing 45 minutes plus 4 hours
chilling

Freezing Not suitable

To serve 6

2½ cups	Water
2 tbsp	Lemon juice
6 tbsp	Sugar
1	Vanilla bean
4	Large firm pears
½ cup	Softened butter
¾ cup	Confectioners' sugar
½ cup	Ground almonds
2 cups	Crushed plain cookies
2 tbsp	Kirsch
2x1 oz	Squares semisweet chocolate
2 tbsp	Light cream

Put water, lemon juice, granulated sugar and
vanilla bean into a saucepan and heat gently,
stirring till sugar dissolves. Bring to a boil.
Peel, core and quarter pears and add to the
syrup.

Simmer gently for 10 minutes till
transparent. Remove from the heat and leave
to cool in the syrup. Cream butter with sifted
confectioners' sugar and ground almonds.
Add cookies to mixture with the Kirsch.

Lift pears out of syrup and drain on paper
towels. Reserve syrup. Thinly slice pears and
fold into creamed mixture. Spoon into a 9x5x3
inch loaf pan lined with foil. Smooth top, fold
foil in over cake and put a weight on top.

Chill for at least 4 hours.

Melt chocolate in the top of a double boiler
over hot water. Remove from the heat and stir
in 2 tbsp pear syrup and the cream.

Remove cake from pan and place on a
serving dish. Spread warm chocolate icing
over and leave to set.

Refrigerator coffee cake

Overall timing 1 ½ hours

Freezing Suitable

To serve 12

¾ cup	Butter
¾ cup	Caster sugar
1 tsp	Vanilla essence
3	Eggs
½ lb	Self-raising flour
	Pinch of salt
4 tbsp	Milk
12	Sugar coffee beans
1 tbsp	Flaked almonds
Coffee cream	
4	Eggs
1 ¼ cups	Granulated sugar
1 ½ cups	Butter
2 tbsp	Coffee essence

Preheat the oven to 350°.

Cream butter with sugar till light and fluffy. Beat in vanilla essence and eggs. Sift flour and salt and add to mixture alternately with milk. Pour into greased and lined 2 lb loaf tin. Bake for 35 minutes. Cool on a wire rack.

Lightly beat eggs in a saucepan. Add sugar and heat very gently till sugar has dissolved. Remove from heat and allow to cool, stirring occasionally. Cream butter, then gradually beat in cold egg mixture and coffee essence.

Cut the sponge cake into three layers and sandwich back together with some of the cream. Place cake on a piece of foil on a plate and coat top and sides with cream, saving a little for decoration. Chill for at least 1 hour till cream is firm.

Slide cake off foil onto plate. Mark with ridges, using a fork. Decorate with remaining cream, coffee beans and almonds.

Battenberg cake

Overall timing 1 ½ hours plus cooling

Freezing Suitable: add marzipan after thawing

To serve 10

1 cup	Butter
1 cup	Sugar
4	Eggs
2 cups	Self-rising flour
½ cup	Milk
	Red food coloring
3 tbsp	Apricot jam
½ lb	Marzipan

Preheat the oven to 375°. Grease and line jelly roll pan, making pleat in paper down center to divide in half lengthwise.

Cream butter with sugar. Beat in eggs. Sift flour and fold into creamed mixture with milk. Spread half mixture into one side of pan. Add a few drops of food coloring to remaining mixture and spread into other half of pan. Bake for about 45 minutes.

Cut each cake in half lengthwise. Warm jam and use to stick cake pieces together in checkerboard patterns. Spread jam over cake. Sprinkle sugar over working surface, roll out marzipan and wrap around cake. Crimp edges and make diamond pattern on top using a sharp knife.

Coffee cream torte

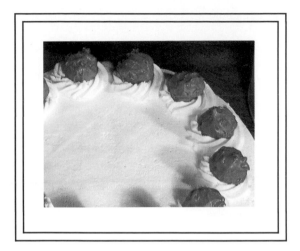

Overall timing 1 ½ hours plus chilling

Freezing Suitable: add cream after thawing

To serve 12

2 tsp	Instant coffee powder
4	Large eggs
10 tbsp	Sugar
1 cup	Flour
¼ cup	Butter
¾ cup	Strong black coffee
2 tbsp	Rum or Tia Maria
1 cup	Heavy cream
¼ cup	Confectioners' sugar
12	Chocolate truffles

Preheat the oven to 375°. Dissolve coffee in 1 tbsp water in a bowl placed over a pan of hot water. Add eggs, ½ cup sugar. Beat till thick. Remove bowl from pan. Sift flour, fold in alternately with melted butter. Pour into greased and lined 8 inch round deep cake pan. Bake for 40 minutes.

Dissolve remaining sugar in black coffee and stir in rum or Tia Maria. Spoon over cake, cool and chill. Whip cream with sugar till stiff. Unmold cake onto plate. Spread over half cream. Decorate with cream and truffles.

Banana and walnut layer cake

Overall timing 1 hour plus cooling

Freezing Not suitable

To serve 8-10

4	Large eggs
¾ cup	Sugar
2 tbsp	Warm water
1 cup	Flour
1 tsp	Baking powder
⅓ cup	Milk
¼ cup	Butter
1 cup	Heavy cream
5	Large bananas
	Chopped walnuts
	Walnut halves

Preheat the oven to 375°.

Separate eggs. Beat yolks with sugar and water till light and fluffy. Sift flour with baking powder and add to yolk mixture alternately with milk. Melt butter and add.

Beat egg whites till stiff and fold into mixture. Spoon into a greased and lined 8 inch round deep cake pan. Bake for 30-35 minutes. Cool on a wire rack.

Whip the cream till thick. Peel and slice the bananas.

Cut the cake into three layers. Put back together with most of the cream and banana slices and the chopped walnuts. Decorate the top with the rest of the cream and bananas and walnut halves. Serve immediately.

Chocolate log

Overall timing 40 minutes plus chilling

Freezing Not suitable

To serve 10-12

2	Eggs
3 tbsp	Sugar
¼ cup	Flour
¼ cup	Cornstarch
¼ cup	Chopped pistachio nuts or candied angelica
Filling and icing	
7 tbsp	Softened butter
1¾ cups	Confectioners' sugar
7 x 1 oz	Squares semisweet chocolate
2 tbsp	Rum or brandy (optional)

Preheat the oven to 400°.

Separate the eggs. Beat whites in a bowl with sugar till stiff peaks form. Beat yolks till pale, then fold into whites. Sift flour and cornstarch into mixture and fold in gently. Spread mixture evenly in greased and lined 13½ x 9½ inch jelly roll pan and bake for 10 minutes till lightly golden. Unmold cake onto dish-towel. Carefully peel off paper and roll up cake enclosing towel. Cool.

Cream butter with sugar. Melt chocolate and beat into creamed mixture with rum or brandy, if using.

Unroll cake and spread with half chocolate mixture. Roll up and place on a serving plate, seam underneath. Cover cake with remaining chocolate mixture. Make marks in chocolate icing with a fork so that it looks like bark. Sprinkle log with chopped pistachio nuts or angelica and chill before serving.

Christening cake

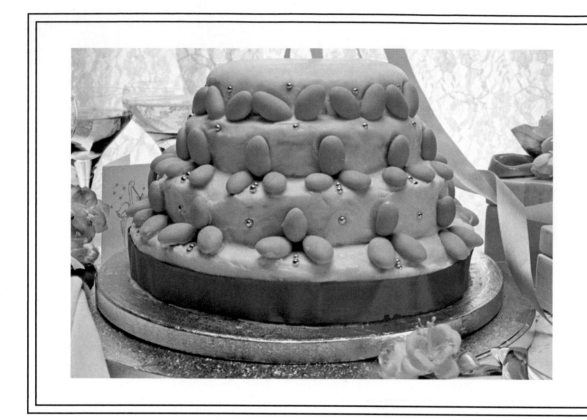

Overall timing 3 hours plus overnight chilling

Freezing Suitable: fill and ice after thawing

To serve 30

12	Eggs
1½ cups	Sugar
3½ cups	Flour
¼ cup	Butter
1 cup	Ground almonds
1 lb	Sugared almonds
	Silver balls
Filling	
5	Egg yolks
1 cup	Sugar
5 tbsp	Water
1½ cups	Unsalted butter
Icing	
4 cups	Confectioners' sugar
2	Egg whites

Preheat the oven to 375°.

Make cake mixture in two batches. Beat half eggs and sugar till thick and pale. Sift half flour and fold into egg mixture with half melted butter and almonds. Pour into greased and lined layer cake pans, one 6 inch and one 10 inch. Bake for 15-20 minutes for small cake and 30 minutes for large cake. Cool on a wire rack. Make second batch and bake in 7 inch pan and 9 inch pan, allowing 30-35 minutes.

To make filling, put egg yolks into a bowl and beat well. Dissolve sugar in water in a saucepan. Boil for 2-3 minutes, without allowing it to color. Pour hot syrup onto egg yolks, beating continuously. Cool, then gradually work in softened butter. Use to put cake layers together and to secure cakes on top of each other, largest on bottom. Chill overnight.

To make icing, sift confectioners' sugar into a large bowl, add egg whites and beat well. Add 1-2 tbsp hot water to give a coating consistency. Coat the entire cake with icing. Decorate with almonds and silver balls.

Christmas fruit cake

Overall timing Cake: 2-2½ hours.
Icing: 30 minutes plus 24 hours standing

Freezing Not suitable

3½ cups	Mixed dried fruit
⅓ cup	Chopped candied peel
1 cup	Dark brown sugar
3 tbsp	Light corn syrup
½ cup	Butter
1½ cups	Self-rising flour
1½ cups	All-purpose flour
2 tsp	Baking soda
2 tsp	Apple pie spice
2	Large eggs
3 tbsp	Apricot jam
¾ lb	Marzipan
2	Egg whites
4 cups	Confectioners' sugar
2 tsp	Lemon juice
1 tsp	Glycerine

Put fruit in saucepan with peel, sugar, syrup, butter and 1 cup water. Bring to a boil, then simmer for 3 minutes. Turn into a bowl and cool.

Preheat the oven to 325°.

Sift flours, soda and spice three times, then add to fruit mixture. Beat in eggs. Place in greased and lined 8 inch round deep cake pan, making a slight depression in center. Bake for about 1½-2 hours or till skewer inserted in center comes out clean. Cool in pan.

To decorate cake, brush top and sides with warmed apricot jam. Roll out marzipan and use to cover top and sides. Smooth all seams.

Beat egg whites to a fairly stiff foam. Gradually beat in sifted confectioners' sugar and lemon juice. When icing forms little peaks when lifted up with a knife blade, mix in glycerine. Cover bowl and leave for 24 hours.

Beat icing gently. Spread over cake, flicking up into peaks with a knife blade. Add decorations. Leave to set for a week before cutting.

Frosted walnut cake

Overall timing 1 ¼ hours plus cooling

Freezing Suitable: fill and ice after thawing

To serve 10

¾ cup	Shortening
1 ½ cups	Sugar
½ tsp	Vanilla
2 cups	Flour
1 tbsp	Baking powder
1 cup	Milk
4	Egg whites
Frosting	
1 lb	Cube sugar
¼ tsp	Cream of tartar
2	Egg whites
½ tsp	Vanilla
½ cup	Chopped walnuts
10	Walnut halves

Preheat the oven to 350°.

Cream shortening with sugar and vanilla till fluffy. Sift flour, baking powder and a pinch of salt together and fold into creamed mixture alternately with milk. Beat egg whites till stiff and fold in. Divide between three greased and lined 8 inch layer cake pans. Bake for 30-35 minutes. Cool on a wire rack.

To make frosting, put sugar, cream of tartar and ¾ cup water in a saucepan and stir over a low heat till sugar dissolves. Stop stirring and bring to a boil. Boil to a temperature of 240°.

Meanwhile, beat egg whites till stiff. Pour syrup in a thin stream onto whites, beating constantly till frosting stands in soft peaks. Beat in vanilla. Fold chopped walnuts into one-quarter of frosting and use to put cakes together. Spread remaining frosting over cake and decorate with walnut halves.

Pistachio cake

Overall timing 1 hour plus chilling

Freezing Not suitable

To serve 10

3 cups	Flour
	Pinch of salt
1 cup	Butter
10 tbsp	Sugar
2	Egg yolks
Filling	
1 cup	Shelled pistachios
4	Egg whites
1 cup	Sugar
1 cup	Ground almonds
	Grated rind of ½ lemon
1 tbsp	Rum
2 x 1 oz	Squares sweet chocolate

Sift the flour and salt into a bowl and rub in the fat till the mixture resembles fine bread crumbs. Stir in the sugar and egg yolks and mix to a soft dough. Chill for 30 minutes.

Preheat the oven to 400°.

Divide the dough in half. Roll out and use to line two 9 inch layer cake pans. Prick bottoms and bake blind for 15 minutes. Cool on a wire rack.

Reserve a few pistachios for decoration; finely chop the rest. Beat the egg whites till soft peaks form. Gradually beat in the sugar till the mixture is stiff and glossy. Fold the chopped nuts into the meringue with the ground almonds, grated lemon rind and rum. Spoon into the pastry cases. Place one pastry case on a baking sheet and invert the other on top. Return to the oven and bake for a further 15 minutes. Cool on a wire rack.

Melt the chocolate in the top of a double boiler over hot water. Spread over the top of the cake with a palette knife. Cut the reserved pistachios in half and arrange in a circle around the edge of the cake.

Brownies

Overall timing 45 minutes plus cooling

Freezing Suitable

Makes 30

4 x 1 oz	Squares semisweet chocolate
½ cup	Unsalted butter
1 tsp	Vanilla
4	Eggs
½ tsp	Salt
1¾ cups	Sugar
1 cup	Flour
1 cup	Chopped walnuts

Preheat the oven to 350°.

Put chocolate into the top of a double boiler with the butter and vanilla and place over simmering water. Stir till melted, then remove bowl from heat and cool.

Beat eggs and salt till pale and fluffy. Sprinkle the sugar on top and continue beating till evenly mixed. Fold in the chocolate mixture with a metal spoon, then fold in the sifted flour and coarsely chopped nuts.

Pour into a greased and lined 9 x 13 inch pan and smooth the top. Bake for about 25 minutes till firm. Cool in the pan, then cut into squares.

Iced marzipan cookies

Overall timing 1 ½ hours plus cooling

Freezing Not suitable

Makes 30

3½ cups	Flour
1 cup	Sugar
	Pinch of salt
1	Large egg
1 cup	Butter
Filling and icing	
½ lb	Marzipan
1¼ cups	Confectioners' sugar
1 tbsp	Rum
	Lemon or almond extract
⅓ cup	Apricot jam
2 tbsp	Water

Sift flour, sugar and salt into a bowl. Add egg and butter, cut into small pieces. Quickly knead together to form a smooth dough. Add a little water if necessary. Chill for 30 minutes.

Preheat the oven to 350°.

Roll out dough to ¼ inch thickness. Cut out small shapes with a cookie cutter and place on a greased baking sheet. Bake for 15 minutes.

Meanwhile, knead marzipan, ½ cup confectioners' sugar, rum and a few drops of extract together. Roll out to ⅛ inch thickness on a board dusted with confectioners' sugar. Cut out shapes using the same cutter as for the pastry.

Remove pastry shapes from oven and immediately spread thickly with jam. Sandwich a piece of marzipan between two hot cookies. Work quickly — the hot cookies and jam need to adhere to the marzipan. Lift off baking sheets and place on wire rack.

To make icing, mix together remaining confectioners' sugar, a little almond extract and water and use to coat the warm cookies. Leave to dry and cool.

Duchesses

Overall timing 2 hours

Freezing Not suitable

Makes 12

2	Egg whites
½ cup	Sugar
½ cup	Ground hazelnuts
¼ cup	Toasted hazelnuts
2 x 1 oz	Squares semisweet chocolate

Preheat the oven to 250°.

Beat the egg whites with half the sugar till stiff. Carefully fold in the ground nuts, then the remaining sugar. Spoon the mixture into a pastry bag fitted with a plain wide tube. Pipe 1 inch wide fingers about 3 inches long onto a baking sheet lined with rice paper. Sprinkle with chopped toasted hazelnuts and bake for 1½ hours.

Cut paper around fingers with a sharp knife, then remove from baking sheet.

Melt the chocolate. Spread rice-papered sides of half the fingers with chocolate and join to remaining fingers. Leave to set.

Honey galettes

Overall timing 40 minutes plus chilling

Freezing Suitable: refresh in 375° oven for 5 minutes

Makes 8

1 ½ cups	Self-rising flour
½ cup	Butter
3 tbsp	Thick honey
1 tbsp	Sugar
1	Lemon
1	Egg
	Sugar for sprinkling

Preheat the oven to 375°.

Sift the flour into a mixing bowl. Make a well in the center and add the softened butter, honey and sugar. Grate the rind from the lemon and add to the bowl with 1 tbsp of the juice. Separate the egg and add the yolk to the bowl. Mix well together with a wooden spoon until the mixture forms a ball and leaves the sides of the bowl clean. Add a little water if necessary. Chill for 30 minutes.

Divide mixture into eight and roll out each piece on a lightly floured surface to a round about ½ inch thick. Place on baking sheets.

Beat egg white lightly and brush over cookies. Sprinkle each cookie with 1-2 tsp sugar. Bake for about 15 minutes, then remove from sheets and cool on wire rack.

Crunchy nut cookies

Overall timing 1 ¼ hours

Freezing Not suitable

Makes about 24

½ lb	Shelled hazelnuts
¾ cup	Sugar
¼ tsp	Ground cinnamon
4	Egg whites
	Pinch of cream of tartar
¼ tsp	Vanilla

Preheat the broiler. Preheat oven to 300°. Grease and flour baking sheets.

Spread shelled nuts on broiler pan and toast on all sides till golden brown. Roughly chop nuts and put in a bowl with sugar and cinnamon.

In another bowl, beat egg whites with cream of tartar and vanilla till very stiff. Gently fold in nut mixture. Scrape the egg/nut mixture into a greased heavy-based skillet and cook over a very low heat for about 15 minutes, turning mixture constantly with a wooden spoon, until it is pale brown.

Put spoonfuls of the mixture on prepared baking sheets, about 1 inch apart. Bake for about 30 minutes, then reduce temperature to 250° and bake for a further 10 minutes until the cookies are crisp.

Coconut macaroons

Overall timing 1¼ hours

Freezing Not suitable

Makes 15

1⅓ cups	Shredded coconut
1 tsp	Vanilla
	Salt
¼	Can of condensed milk
2	Egg whites
½ tsp	Cream of tartar

Preheat the oven to 300°.

Place coconut, vanilla and a good pinch of salt in mixing bowl. Add condensed milk and mix to firm paste. Beat egg whites and cream of tartar till stiff, then fold into paste.

Heap small spoonfuls of mixture onto baking sheet lined with rice paper, leaving spreading space. Bake for 45 minutes. Turn off oven and leave inside for 15 minutes.

Choc-topped cookies

Overall timing 1 hour

Freezing Not suitable

Makes 55-60

½ cup	Pitted dates
½ cup	Raisins
1¼ cups	Ground hazelnuts
3 oz	Sweet chocolate
¾ cup	Cornstarch
3	Egg whites
	Salt
1 cup	Sugar
4x1 oz	Squares semisweet chocolate

Preheat the oven to 350°.

Coarsely chop dates and mix with raisins, hazelnuts, grated milk chocolate and cornstarch. Beat egg whites with pinch of salt till stiff, then gradually beat in sugar. Fold in chocolate mixture.

With a teaspoon, place small portions on baking sheets lined with rice paper, leaving spreading space. Bake for 35 minutes. Cool, then cut paper around cookies.

Melt semisweet chocolate and brush over top and sides of cookies. Leave to set before serving.

Lemon refrigerator cookies

Overall timing 20 minutes plus
overnight chilling

Freezing Suitable: bake after thawing

Makes 48

2 cups	Flour
1 tsp	Baking powder
½ cup	Butter
6 tbsp	Sugar
	Grated rind of
	2 lemons
½ tsp	Ground cinnamon
1	Egg

Sift flour and baking powder into a bowl. Rub in butter till mixture resembles fine bread crumbs. Add sugar, lemon rind and cinnamon, then beat the egg and mix well into the dough.

Shape the mixture into one or two sausage shapes about 1½ inches in diameter. Wrap in foil, twisting the ends to seal. Chill overnight.

Preheat the oven to 375°.

Remove dough from foil wrapper and thinly slice. Place slices on greased baking sheets. Bake for 10-12 minutes, till golden. Cool on wire rack.

Lemon spice squares

Overall timing 1 ½ hours

Freezing Suitable

Makes 9

½ cup	Butter
½ cup	Sugar
	Grated rind of 1 lemon
2	Eggs
⅓ cup	Chopped candied lemon peel
1 cup	Flour
½ tsp	Ground cinnamon
½ tsp	Ground cloves
1 ½ tsp	Baking powder
½ cup	Ground almonds
2 tbsp	Lemon juice

Preheat the oven to 325°.

Cream butter with sugar till light and fluffy. Add lemon rind and beat in the eggs. Stir in the candied lemon peel. Sift together the flour, spices and baking powder and fold into mixture, followed by the almonds and lemon juice.

Turn the mixture into a greased and lined 7 inch square cake pan and smooth the surface. Bake for 1 hour till top springs back when lightly pressed. Cool on a wire rack. Cut into squares to serve.

Shortbread fingers

Overall timing 1 ½ hours plus cooling

Freezing Not suitable

Makes 6

1 ½ cups	Butter
½ cup	Sugar
2 cups	All-purpose flour
2 cups	Self-rising flour
¼ tsp	Salt

Preheat the oven to 275°.

Cream the butter with the sugar till pale and fluffy. Sift the two flours and salt together and work into the creamed mixture to make a dough. Add a little water if necessary.

Turn dough onto a floured surface and press out to a thick rectangle. Make decorative notches down the long sides by pinching with the fingers. Place on a baking sheet and prick all over with a fork. Mark lines for the fingers.

Bake for 1 hour. Cool, then break into fingers on the marked lines. Dredge with extra sugar.

Scones

Overall timing 20 minutes

Freezing Not suitable

Makes 8

2 cups	Flour
1 tbsp	Baking powder
	Pinch of salt
¼ cup	Butter
2 tbsp	Sugar
¾ cup	Milk
	Milk or egg for glazing

Preheat the oven to 450°.

Sift flour, baking powder and salt into a mixing bowl. Rub in butter. Add sugar and milk and mix to a soft dough. Add more milk if necessary.

Roll out quickly to ½ inch thickness on a lightly floured board. Lightly flour a round cutter and cut out scones. Place on lightly floured baking sheet and glaze tops with milk or lightly beaten egg. Bake for 10 minutes. Wrap in dish-towel till ready to serve.

Variation

Peel, core and grate 1 apple and scatter over rolled-out dough. Fold in half and press firmly together. Cut and bake as above.

Madeleines with cinnamon

Overall timing 50 minutes plus chilling

Freezing Suitable: bake after thawing

Makes 16

1½ cups	Flour
6 tbsp	Butter
1 tbsp	Sugar
1	Egg yolk
Filling	
½ cup	Butter
½ cup	Sugar
2	Eggs
½ cup	Ground almonds
¼ tsp	Almond extract
1 cup	Self-rising flour
1 tsp	Ground cinnamon
	Milk to mix
	Apricot jam
1 tbsp	Confectioners' sugar

Sift flour into a bowl and rub in butter. Stir in sugar, egg yolk and enough water to bind to a soft dough. Roll out to ¼ inch thickness and use to line two madeleine sheets. Trim the edges and chill for 30 minutes.

Preheat the oven to 375°.

To make filling, cream butter with all but 1 tbsp sugar. Gradually beat in eggs, then mix in almonds and almond extract. Sift in flour and cinnamon and fold in with enough milk to give a soft dropping consistency.

Put ½ tsp jam into each pastry case, then spoon filling into each case. Bake for 15-20 minutes till the filling is golden and springs back when lightly pressed. Cool on a wire rack.

Mix confectioners' sugar and remaining sugar together and sift over tartlets before serving.

Spicy raisin biscuits

Overall timing 1 hour plus chilling

Freezing Not suitable

Makes 40

1 cup	Butter
1 cup	Sugar
1	Egg
2 tbsp	Rum
1 ⅓ cups	Raisins
3 cups	Self-rising flour
	Salt
½ tsp	Ground cloves
1 tsp	Ground ginger
1	Egg white

Cream butter with all but 1 tbsp sugar till pale and fluffy. Gradually beat in egg and rum. Stit in raisins. Sift flour, pinch of salt and spices into mixture and mix to a soft dough. Chill for 30 minutes.

Preheat the oven to 350°.

Roll out dough on a floured surface till ¼ inch thick. Stamp out rounds with cookie cutter. Arrange on greased baking sheets.

Beat egg white and remaining sugar together till frothy and brush over cookies. Bake for about 15 minutes till pale golden. Cool on the sheets for 3-4 minutes till firm, then transfer to a wire rack and leave to cool completely.

Lady fingers

Overall timing 30 minutes

Freezing Suitable

Makes 16

4	Eggs
½ cup	Sugar
¼ cup	Cornstarch
¾ cup	Flour
	Confectioners' sugar

Preheat the oven to 375°.

Separate the eggs. Beat whites in a bowl with 2 tbsp of the sugar till soft peaks form. In another bowl, beat egg yolks with remaining sugar. Fold yolks into whites carefully, then gradually fold in the sifted flours.

Put mixture into a pastry bag fitted with a wide tube and pipe fingers 3-4 inches long onto greased and floured baking sheets, spacing them well apart. Dust lightly with sifted confectioners' sugar and bake for 12 minutes. Cool on wire rack.

Golden arcs

Overall timing 30 minutes

Freezing Not suitable

Makes 30

1⅔ cups	Fine cornmeal
1½ cups	Flour
2 tsp	Ground cardamom
½ tsp	Ground coriander
½ cup	Sugar
¼ tsp	Vanilla
1 cup	Butter
4	Egg yolks

Preheat the oven to 400°.

Sift the cornmeal, flour and spices into a bowl and stir in the sugar. Add the vanilla, butter and egg yolks and mix to a soft dough.

Put the mixture into a pastry bag fitted with a star tube and pipe in 3 inch lengths onto a greased and floured baking sheet. Bake for about 15 minutes till golden. Remove from the oven and allow to cool for 5 minutes. Transfer to a wire rack and leave to cool completely.

Sweet and spicy fritters

Overall timing 45 minutes

Freezing Not suitable

Makes 20

2¼ cups	Flour
½ tsp	Ground ginger
½ tsp	Ground allspice
½ tsp	Ground mace
	Salt
1 cup	Confectioners' sugar
3	Egg yolks
1 tbsp	Orange-flower water
½ cup	Butter
1	Grated rind of lemon
	Oil for deep frying

Sift flour, spices, pinch of salt and ¾ cup confectioners' sugar into a bowl. Mix egg yolks and flower water with 2 tbsp cold water. Add to bowl with butter and rind. Mix to a soft dough.

Roll out dough till ¼ inch thick. Cut out fancy shapes with cookie cutters.

Heat oil in a deep-fryer to 340°. Fry cookies, a few at a time, for about 5 minutes till golden. Drain on paper towels. Sift the remaining confectioners' sugar over.

Orange liqueur cookies

Overall timing 45 minutes plus chilling

Freezing Suitable: cut out and bake after thawing

Makes 36

2	Hard-cooked egg yolks
2 cups	Flour
½ cup	Sugar
	Salt
	Ground cinnamon
½ cup	Butter
2 tbsp	Orange liqueur

Push egg yolks through a sieve into a mixing bowl. Sift in the flour and mix well. Make a well in center and add sugar and a pinch each of salt and cinnamon.

Cut the butter into pieces and work into the mixture, a little at a time. Work in the liqueur and roll paste into a ball. Add a little more liqueur or water if necessary. Lightly dust with flour and leave in a cool place (not the refrigerator) for at least 1 hour.

Preheat the oven to 375°.

Roll out the paste thinly and stamp out shapes with fancy cookie cutters. Place cookies on a greased and lined baking sheet and bake for 10-15 minutes, till light golden. Remove cookies carefully from paper and cool on a wire rack.

Rhine cookies

Overall timing 45 minutes plus chilling

Freezing Not suitable

Makes 30

2¼ cups	Flour
1 tsp	Ground cinnamon
½ tsp	Ground cloves
¾ cup	Butter
½ cup	Sugar
	Grated rind of
	1 lemon
1	Egg
½ cup	Milk

Sift the flour and spices into a bowl. Add the butter and rub in till the mixture resembles fine bread crumbs. Stir in the sugar and lemon rind. Add the egg and enough milk to make a stiff dough. Knead lightly and chill for 1 hour.

Preheat the oven to 350°.

Roll out the dough on a floured board till ¼ inch thick, then cut out shapes with a cookie cutter. Arrange on a greased and floured baking sheet. Bake for 15-20 minutes till golden. Remove from the oven and leave to cool for 3 minutes. Transfer to a wire rack and leave to cool completely.

Almond crescents

Overall timing 30 minutes plus cooling

Freezing Suitable; bake from frozen, allowing 20-25 minutes

Makes 20

1½ cups	Ground almonds
¼ cup	Sugar
	A few drops of vanilla
1	Egg white
¼ cup	Flour
1	Egg
¼ cup	Flaked almonds
2 tbsp	Milk sweetened with confectioners' sugar

Preheat the oven to 400°.

Mix ground almonds with sugar and vanilla. Moisten with egg white until evenly combined. Add flour and gather mixture together with fingertips. Divide into "nut-sized" pieces. With lightly floured hands, roll into small cigar shapes with pointed ends. Brush each one with beaten egg and sprinkle with flaked almonds. Bend into a crescent shape.

Place on a greased baking sheet and brush lightly with any remaining egg. Bake for about 10-15 minutes till evenly colored. Remove from oven and brush immediately with sweetened milk. Using a palette knife or spatula, carefully loosen crescents and transfer to wire rack to cool.

Macaroons

Overall timing 2½ hours

Freezing Not suitable

Makes 55

4	Egg whites
1½ cups	Sugar
2¾ cups	Ground almonds
	Grated rind of 1 orange
	Grated rind of 1 lemon
	Pinch of salt
1 tsp	Ground cinnamon
½ tsp	Ground cardamom

Preheat the oven to 275°.

Beat the egg whites till stiff. Gradually beat in the sugar, a spoonful at a time. Fold in the almonds, orange and lemon rind, salt and spices.

Place heaped teaspoonfuls of mixture on baking sheets lined with rice paper. Put on the middle and lower shelves of the oven and leave to dry for 1½-2 hours. Halfway through, swap sheets around.

Cool on baking sheets. Break paper from around each macaroon.

Pastry horns

Overall timing 4½ hours

Freezing Suitable: shape and bake after thawing

Makes 6

2¼ cups	Flour
	Pinch of salt
1 cup	Butter
1 cup	Cold water
1	Egg
	Sugar
	Whipped cream
	Jam

Sift flour and salt into a bowl. Rub in half the butter, then add water and mix to a dough. Chill for 1 hour. Chill remaining butter.

Place chilled butter between two sheets of wax paper and roll out to a 5 x 3 inch rectangle.

Roll out dough on floured surface to 10 x 8 inch rectangle. Put butter in center. Fold down top third over butter, then fold up bottom third. Turn so that folds are to the side. Roll out to 5 x 14 inch rectangle and fold again as before. Chill for 15 minutes.

Repeat the rolling, turning and folding four more times, chilling between each process.

Preheat the oven to 425°.

Roll out dough to ⅛ inch thick. Trim to a 15 x 6 inch wide rectangle, then cut lengthwise into six 1 wide inch strips. Glaze the strips with beaten egg, then wrap them, glazed side out, around six pastry horn molds, starting at the point and overlapping the dough slightly.

Place on a baking sheet and dredge with sugar. Bake for 10 minutes till crisp and golden. Slide off the molds and cool.

Fill the horns with cream and jam.

Sour cream pastries

Overall timing 50 minutes plus chilling

Freezing Not suitable

Makes 20

3 cups	Flour
¾ cup	Butter
1	Egg yolk
¾ cup	Sour cream
Filling	
½ lb	Cream cheese
¼ cup	Sugar
⅓ cup	Golden raisins

Sift the flour into a bowl and rub in the butter till the mixture resembles fine bread crumbs. Add the egg yolk and sour cream and mix with a palette knife to make a soft dough. Chill for 1 hour.

Mix together the cream cheese, sugar and raisins.

Preheat the oven to 400°.

Roll out the dough and cut out 40 rounds with a fluted 2 inch cutter. Put a spoonful of the filling onto half the rounds, then cover with the remaining rounds and press the edges together to seal. Arrange on a baking sheet and bake for 25 minutes till golden brown.

Mille feuilles

Overall timing 40 minutes plus cooling

Freezing Not suitable

Makes 6

½ lb	Frozen puff pastry
2½ cups	Milk
	Pinch of salt
1	Vanilla bean
	Strip of lemon rind
½ cup	Sugar
4	Medium eggs
¼ cup	Flour
2 tbsp	Rum
	Confectioners' sugar

Thaw pastry. Preheat the oven to 425°.

Put the milk, salt, vanilla bean and lemon rind into a saucepan and bring to a boil. Remove from the heat and infuse for 10 minutes.

Beat together the sugar, eggs and flour in a bowl till smooth. Gradually strain the milk into the bowl, stirring, then pour the mixture back into the saucepan. Bring to a boil, stirring, and simmer till thick. Stir in the rum. Remove from the heat. Cover with damp wax paper and cool.

Divide dough and roll out into three rectangles, 12 x 4 inches. Trim edges. Place on dampened baking sheets. Mark one rectangle into six 2 inch slices with a sharp pointed knife. Bake for about 10 minutes till well risen and golden. Allow to cool.

Place unmarked pastry rectangles on a board and spread with rum custard. Layer with marked pastry rectangle on top and dredge well with confectioners' sugar. Cut into slices along marked lines. Eat same day.

Baklava

Overall timing 1 ½ hours

Freezing Suitable

Makes 8

½ cup	Unsalted butter
1 lb	Ready-made phyllo pastry
2 cups	Chopped walnuts, almonds or pistachios
2 tbsp	Sugar
½ tsp	Ground cinnamon
Syrup	
⅓ cup	Clear honey
½ cup	Water
2 tbsp	Lemon juice

Preheat the oven to 425°.

Melt the butter in a small saucepan and brush a little over the bottom and sides of a 10 x 8 inch roasting pan.

Layer half the pastry sheets in the pan, brushing liberally with butter between each sheet, and folding in the edges so that the sheets fit the pan. Keep rest of the pastry covered to prevent it drying out.

Mix together the chopped nuts, sugar and cinnamon and spread over pastry. Cover with remaining pastry layers, brushing each with butter. Brush the top layer well with any remaining butter.

Cut through the top two layers of pastry with a sharp knife to divide into two lengthwise and four widthwise, then cut each square in half diagonally to make triangles. Bake for 15 minutes, then reduce heat to 350° and bake for a further 25-30 minutes till well risen and golden.

Meanwhile, make the syrup. Melt the honey in the water and add to the lemon juice. Allow to cool.

Remove baklava from oven, pour cold syrup over and leave to cool in pan. Cut along the marked lines to serve.

Irish apple turnovers

Overall timing 2 hours including refrigeration

Freezing Suitable: refresh in 350° oven for 10-15 minutes

Makes 20 small or 12 large

2¼ cups	Flour
2 tsp	Baking powder
10 tbsp	Sugar
10 tbsp	Butter
⅓ cup	Cold water
1 lb	Apples
1 tbsp	Apricot jam
2 tbsp	Mixed dried fruit
	Confectioners' sugar

Sift flour, baking powder and sugar into a bowl and make a well in the center. Cut the softened butter into small pieces and put around the edge. Add water and knead to make a smooth dough. Chill for 1 hour.

Preheat the oven to 350°.

Core apples. Place them on a baking sheet and bake for 20 minutes till tender. Peel them, then mash and mix with the apricot jam and dried fruit.

Increase the oven temperature to 400°.

Roll out dough on a lightly floured board to ⅛ inch thickness. Cut out rounds or squares. Spoon a little apple mixture into the center of each dough shape. Moisten edges with water, fold the dough over to form a half moon, triangle or rectangle, and press edges well together. Place on a greased baking sheet.

Bake for 15-20 minutes. Dredge with confectioners' sugar and serve warm with whipped cream or vanilla ice cream.

Jam puffs

Overall timing 20 minutes plus thawing

Freezing Not suitable

Makes 12

½ lb	Frozen puff pastry
1	Egg
5 tbsp	Jam

Thaw pastry. Preheat the oven to 425°.

Roll out dough to ¼ inch thickness. Cut into 2 inch rounds with cookie cutter. Mark the centers with a small cutter or a bottle lid. Do not cut through.

Place on a dampened baking sheet and brush with beaten egg. Bake for about 10 minutes till well risen and golden. Cool on a wire rack.

Remove centers and put a large teaspoonful of jam in each. Use centers of pastry as lids, if liked. Serve warm.

Palmiers

Overall timing 1 ½ hours plus chilling

Freezing Suitable: shape and bake after thawing

Makes 12-16

2 cups	Flour
½ tsp	Salt
¾ cup	Butter
2 tsp	Lemon juice
¾ cup	Cold water
	Sugar

Sift flour and salt into a bowl and rub in 3 tbsp butter. Mix in lemon juice and enough water to make a soft but not sticky dough. Knead till smooth.

Roll out dough on floured surface to 15 x 5 inch rectangle. Divide remaining butter into three and cut into small pieces. Dot one-third of butter over top two-thirds of dough. Fold up bottom third, then fold top third over it. Press edges to seal and turn dough so folds are to the side.

Repeat rolling out, adding another third of butter and folding, then chill for 15 minutes.

Repeat process again, using rest of butter, and chill for 15 minutes.

Preheat the oven to 425°.

Roll out dough to ¼ inch thick. Sprinkle with sugar. Fold the long sides in to meet at the center and sprinkle again with sugar. Fold the long sides in again to make four layers. Cut across folds into ½ inch slices.

Arrange slices on dampened baking sheet and flatten slightly. Bake for 6 minutes on each side. Serve warm.

Almond tartlets

Overall timing 1 hour plus cooling

Freezing Suitable: ice and decorate after thawing

Makes 12

¾ lb	Pie pastry
4	Eggs
½ cup	Sugar
1 cup	Ground almonds
Decoration	
1 cup	Confectioners' sugar
2-3 tbsp	Milk
2-3 tbsp	Lemon juice
12	Glacé cherries
	Candied angelica leaves

Preheat the oven to 400°.

Roll out the dough and use to line 12 tartlet pans. Bake blind for 10 minutes, then remove from oven.

Separate the eggs. Add sugar to yolks and beat together till pale and thick. Fold in ground almonds. In another bowl, beat egg whites till stiff, then fold into almond mixture.

Fill pastry cases with almond mixture. Bake for 15-20 minutes, till center is firm and springy. Leave to cool.

Sift the confectioners' sugar into a bowl and beat in milk and lemon juice till smooth. Spread over tartlets. Decorate with whole glacé cherries and angelica leaves and leave till set.

Mince pies

Overall timing 30 minutes

Freezing Suitable: bake from frozen in 425° oven for 20-30 minutes

Makes 15-20

½ lb	Pie pastry
1 cups	Mincemeat
3 tbsp	Brandy
6 tbsp	Milk
2 tbsp	Sugar

Preheat the oven to 400°.

Roll out the dough on a floured surface. Stamp out 20 rounds with a 2½ inch cutter, then 20 rounds with a 2 inch cutter. Press the larger rounds into a greased 20-hole muffin tin.

Mix the mincemeat and brandy in a small bowl and divide between the pastry cases. Dip small dough rounds in the milk, then place one on each pie. Using a fork, press the edges together firmly to seal.

Sprinkle the sugar over the top. Bake for about 20 minutes till golden. Serve hot or cold.

Eclairs

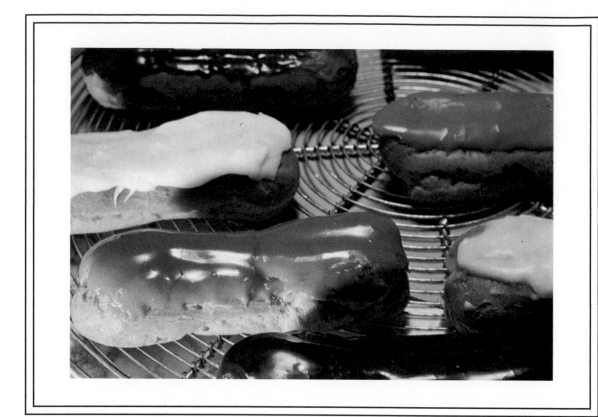

Overall timing 1 ½ hours

Freezing Suitable: bake from frozen

Makes 16

¼ lb	Choux paste
1 cup	Whipping cream
2 tbsp	Sugar
1 cup	Confectioners' sugar
2 tsp	Hot chocolate powder
1-2 tbsp	Hot water

Preheat the oven to 425°.

Spoon paste into pastry bag fitted with ½ inch plain tube and pipe fingers about 3 inches long, on greased baking sheets. Leave plenty of space between fingers so they have room to expand during baking. Bake for about 30 minutes till golden and crisp. Transfer to a wire rack. Make a slit down side of each éclair to allow steam to escape and leave to cool.

Whip cream with sugar until just thick and holding soft peaks. Spoon cream into cooled éclairs and return to wire rack placed over wax paper.

Mix confectioners' sugar with chocolate powder and hot water. The glacé icing should be thick enough to coat the back of a spoon. If too thick, add a little more water; if too runny, add more confectioners' sugar. Dip top of one éclair at a time into icing. Leave on wire rack till icing is set. Eat the same day.

Chocolate profiteroles

Overall timing 1 ½ hours

Freezing Suitable: filling and sauce

To serve 4-6

1 cup	Flour
1 ¼ cups	Water
6 tbsp	Sweet butter
¼ tsp	Salt
3	Large eggs
2 ½ cups	Whipping cream
Chocolate sauce	
6 oz	Semisweet chocolate
2 tbsp	Butter

Preheat the oven to 425°.

Sift flour. Put water, butter and salt into saucepan and bring to a boil, stirring to melt butter. Remove from heat and beat in flour all at once. Return to heat and beat till dough pulls away from sides of pan. Gradually beat in eggs to make a soft, glossy dough.

Using a spoon, drop paste in balls onto greased baking sheets, easing them off with a second spoon. Bake for 20-25 minutes till golden and crisp. Transfer to a wire rack. Make a slit in each bun to release steam. Cool.

Whip cream and use to fill buns. Pile on a serving dish.

To make sauce, melt chocolate with butter and 2 tbsp water in a double boiler. Cool slightly, the pour over choux buns.

Index